Books by Charles Walters Jr.

•

HOLDING ACTION

•

(humor)

OLD AIRMEN NEVER FLY

HALCYON HOUSE

NEW YORK ● KANSAS CITY

HOLDING

ACTION

BY

CHARLES WALTERS JR.

HOLDING ACTION

Library of Congress catalog card number: 68-26115

*Dedicated to the American
farmer, who has lived and
relived this book.*

CONTENTS

JUST FOR THE RECORD

THIS BOOK deals with 15 of the most electric days of our times—the two weeks in early 1967 when farmers in 25 states, in a coordinated effort, dumped their milk. The story does not begin or end there. But its focal point remains two weeks, the single "moment" in time when the Hydra that is the farm problem came to a single head. From the instant that National Farmers Organization President Oren Lee Staley signaled the start of the milk holding action, March 15, 1967, things were foreordained never to be the same again.

The NFO holding action was much more than a bid for higher milk prices and contracts. It was an indictment that no social criticism had ever symbolized before. A society had so organized itself that it no longer paid its board bill, and those who were producing the food were falling into abject poverty and being fed into city slums. Farmers, having been warned about being failures themselves, now warned the society of its own failure, one that cancelled out its showy successes.

It was during the second week of that holding action that I decided to write this book.

When Thomas Carlyle called economics "the dismal science," he must have had something on the order of American agriculture in mind. His quite accurate statement went forth at a time when abstractions concerning the science of production, distribution and use of wealth were the private property of professors and officials on half rations—"dignified poverty." Things have changed. The best economic literature today is being written by story tellers, not by academically trained social scientists or economists. I am not sure it has not always been that way.

Certainly one can best understand the industrial revolution by reading the novels of Charles Dickens, just as one can best understand the real meaning of war by reading novels like Tolstoi's *War and Peace*. No social scientist or economist will ever describe the heartbreak and torment that must surely go with every fall of the hammer at auctions in the corn belt these days, but surely some competent novelist will one day plumb the depth of that strange apparition in the farm country.

All the economic theory in the world cannot convey half as well as did John Steinbeck the bent of procedures in Oklahoma and California during the 1930s. *The Grapes of Wrath* did more to explain the dismal science than a thousand texts on mathematical models, *supply and demand* equilibrium, and surplus disposal. Then as now, there were the "great owners" who "bought a cannery," and cut the price of fruit below the cost of production at the farm. "And as a cannery owner he paid himself a low price for the fruit and kept the price of canned goods up and took his profit." The little farmers lost their farms to the banks, and the banks remanded them to the "great owners." Steinbeck's lines are still poignant. "The little farmers moved into town for a while and exhausted their credit, exhausted their friends, their relatives. And then they too went on the highway."

I can still remember, as a youngster, seeing the vintage cars roll across the red country of Oklahoma, out of Kansas, out to California, just as I can remember being part of such a family caravan in the dust bowl days. My father was a farmer. He knew what was being done to the people, and why. What he didn't know was *how* it was being done. At some point before WWII, I decided to find out *how*. I have concerned myself with economics ever since.

There always have been clues. Writers have hammered at the farmer, and politicians have betrayed him. Earlier, much earlier, Abraham Lincoln prevented the giants from getting "all" of the vast virgin wilderness that was western America, and so when Europe's misfits arrived they developed the country, farmed it, and built a civilization—in Walter Bowers' words—"with little white churches and little red school houses."

When I was a youngster in the early 1930s, the American farmer had been brought to ruin. The pseudo-sophisticated, i.e., those who dealt with abstractions and remained unsoiled by experience, had no reason to listen to a farmer, because in their hearts they felt they knew all the answers. A prime example can be gleaned from *The American Mercury* of January 1931.

"Getting rid of farmers," wrote H. L. Mencken, *"would not only reduce the cost of living by at least a half; it would also improve the politics of the country, and have a good effect upon religion. As things stand, the farmer is always on the verge of bankruptcy, and so he hates everyone who is having a better time. Prohibition is almost wholly a metaphysic of farmers; so is Methodism. Turn the hind into a wage slave, and he will respond quickly to the better security. The city proletariat, though it is made up largely of fugitives from the farms, is devoid of moral passion. It not only likes to have a good time itself; it is willing to see its betters have an even better time . . . Thus I look forward to their ruin with agreeable sentiments. It will make living cheaper in the United States, and very much pleasanter. The country has been run from the farms long enough; the business becomes an indecorum, verging almost upon the obscene. We'll all be better off when the men who raise wheat and hogs punch timeclocks . . ."*

Only a very learned man could have been as hopelessly and articulately wrong as that, both on economics and sociology. Yet it was such prime examples of frustration sociology and frustration economics that came to hold sway over the minds of those in power. Prevailing theories caused government to hitch its wagon to the sanctity of *supply and demand.*

Even to a high school student, the record of the 1930s came clear on one point. The effect of man-made scarcity was not an improved economy, but one stabilized at a very low level. The institutional arrangements of business made it impossible for farmers to achieve fair prices simply because farm production continued to move into markets on a distress sale basis. Except for sporadic local attempts at organization, farmers continued to sell as rugged individualists. The opening sentence in every sale was probably, "What'll you give me?"

Businessmen cannot be blamed too much for doing what businessmen must do. They bought cheap and sold as dear as the competition would permit. Farmers went broke, or continued to consume their capital until World War II. And, in the main, the people of the United States did not eat well. Paul V. McNutt, who was Federal Security Administrator under Franklin D. Roosevelt, estimated that 75% of the American people in the year 1940 needed better diets, and he documented this fact in a motion picture called *Hidden Hunger.*

Then as now, the reason for hidden hunger lay not in the inability of America to feed its people, but in the inability of the economic planners to solve the problem of low income. Then as now, low income for a sizeable section of the economy started on the farm before it churned its way through the entire economy.

It takes a lot of tongue biting nowadays to endure a *supply and demand* lecture in Washington one day ["... farmers are producing too much, hence low farm prices ..."] and then attend a conference in New York a day or two later and hear eminent sociologists tell of 40 million in poverty, many of them not eating properly.

I first met up with NFO in a rather oblique way. In 1958 I asked Earl F. Crouse of Doane Agriculture Service to write a farm article for *Veterinary Medicine,* a publication over which I commanded the editorial pencil in such matters. "Livestock production," wrote Crouse, "and marketing procedures are undergoing a dramatic metamorphosis —a change as far reaching in its impact upon the American economy as that brought about by the industrial revolution. Indeed, we are in the midst of an industrial revolution in agriculture. Farming as we have always known it was organized after the fashion of the craft shops. Today it is being recast as an integral part of the streamlined production and marketing system which reaches all the way from the farmer to the consumer."

Crouse wrote in bright, optimistic homilies, reflecting essentially the philosophy of Dr. John H. Davis of Harvard, who coined the term *agribusiness* to accompany other terms, such as *vertical integration, contract farming* and *specification buying,* concepts many economists believed to be remaking agriculture to better effect. Implied, but never stated, was the observation that agriculture had to be remade through "operation freeze-out" of family farm units.

It all sounded so clear-cut, so "economic." But there were the NFO members in the halls of the Kansas City Livestock Exchange Building a little later on, and there was the test holding action. These men were not abstractions. Like my dad, they knew what was being done to them, and *why,* but they didn't really understand *how.* Indeed, the cause was most elusive. The immediate cause was price, but what caused the price to be too low? The stock answers were available, of course—*supply and demand,* inefficiency, etc. But what caused the cause? The continuity and consecutiveness of causes was precisely what made the term lose much of its common sense significance for the farmers. As a red headed comedian would have said, *"This just don't sound right!"*

Lots of things weren't sounding right in the 1950s.

For one thing, there was no clear cut economic mandate for big farms, any more than there was a mandate for oligopoly auto manufacturing firms that were already bigger than the size of the optimum plant. New forces were intervening. A single case report should illustrate the point.

A couple of decades ago, the Bureau of Agricultural Economics wrote a classic study entitled, *A Tale of Two Cities*. The cities were Arvin and Dinuba, both located in the San Joaquin Valley in California. The study was the last of its kind, the last to deal with agriculture in terms of land, the people who work it and the society they erect.

Arvin was essentially a corporation farm town. Dinuba sat squarely in the middle of modest family farm plots. Those who farmed in the Arvin area had gone down the drain during the great depression. Dinuba-centered farms had survived, but were under economic assault. Yet production on the family farms near Dinuba rated with production on the corporation holdings at Arvin in economic efficiency.

On the Arvin side of the valley, where migrant workers tended the fields, housing conditions were wretched, schools inadequate, churches almost non-existent, and there was little community life. At the same time farmers in the Dinuba area lived in neat homes, either owned or rented, worshiped in good churches, and sent their children to fine schools. Tradespeople in this service community had shops that made their owners a living, and they too enjoyed an active community life.

Arvin, quite recently has been the scene of the bitter grape pickers' strike. I have talked with some of the participants. None seem aware of the greatest doublecross of the century. They knew what has been done to them, but they don't really know *how*. What has happened to many now filling the migrant camps in California is what is happening to corn belt farmers. Public policy and the failure of America to read that policy is permitting a tragedy equal to Stalin's liquidation of the Kulaks.

The Tale of Two Cities was the last USDA attempt to examine the value of the family farm as a business unit, and as a socially valuable institution in our social order. Shortly after it was published, the Bureau of Agricultural Economics found its budget cut halfway through the bone. A fantastic power struggle was coming to the fore in USDA. By 1952 the street walkers for corporations had gained beachheads. Bank of America Vice President Earl J. Coke became an Assistant Secretary to Agriculture Secretary Ezra Taft Benson, and although he stayed on only briefly he and his associates completely splintered research having to do with the first fact of economic life—people, and a satisfactory way of life for people.

Of a sudden, no one cared about people and the social impact of how they moved about. Production efficiency, labor efficiency—these alone counted. What happened to people and the social costs were declared outside the realm of agriculture. "Move more people out of agriculture" became the battle cry, and by the late 50s, only NFO was fighting back. In almost any year, a half million dollars was being spent by USDA to speed up production efficiency for the "great owners." Nothing was being spent to gear technology to the needs of millions of people still in agriculture.

All this, of course, was only part of the process.

It didn't take long for "the process" to have farmers on the run. Few in America ever expected to see a farmer fight for first class status in the nation's economy. Then came the big surprise of NFO and "militancy." The completeness of this surprise adequately measures the abject awe farmer and city dweller alike had for the power of giants.

No one doubts the power of the chains, dairy bigs and processing giants to crush a farmer's soul. Proud men have crawled before, and whole populations frequently have been shorn not only of justice but self-respect.

Yet those who watched NFO on the march should not have been surprised. De Tocqueville, writing about the conditions in France before 1789, told how "a people which had supported the most crushing laws without complaint, and apparently as if they were unfelt, throws them off with violence as soon as the burden begins to be diminished." Only one thing can diminish a well-fastened burden, and that is hope.

Farmers under the great estates of Karol Radziwill, the Potockis, the Czartorykis in late 18th century Poland were the most miserable in the world, whereas as the same time farmers in the United States joined a few leaders to form a new nation.

De Tocqueville was quite clear when he pointed out the great difference between discontent and hope: "The evils which are endured with patience as long as they are inevitable, seem intolerable as soon as hope can be entertained of escaping from them." It is quite correct to note that despair is a static factor. The will to battle is born out of hope and pride.

NFO gave farmers both. Always, farmers had known that they were being used badly when the powers that be paid them for less wealth than they produced. Always, farmers had seen the tide of economic balance drive them still further from prosperity. Short booms and long bursts had been the farmers fare. Farmers had known these things in a common sense sort of way, but before NFO they never knew *how* it was being done.

Now they knew both *how* and *why*.

This knowledge made the NFO member secure in his beliefs. It supplied the backbone needed for battle.

And so when dairy farmers started holding their milk in March of 1967, they were psychologically conditioned. They faced city folks who had been brainwashed into thinking that the only way food could be produced was on huge corporation farms. They answered the big lie. But the barnacles of unreason were still around. Some of the passages in this book quote contemporary newspaper editorials. Readers will note the striking similarity between H. L. Mencken's comment and the one on page 219.

This is basically a simple book. Much of it is based on my own field notes. I have not burdened the text with many footnotes, but the student can easily trace down citations from books and periodicals anyway. Nor have I burdened this presentation with complicated formulas on economics. Although my education is that of an economist, I am basically a journalist, and this is a journalist's approach to a story that isn't being told properly.

There are three opening chapters before the narrative takes up the holding action. Each of the regular chapters details the happenings in a single holding action day. In addition, there are three background chapters. One deals with "the economy," one with "the church," and one with "the law." These chapters are equally important, and each in its own way furnishes foundation insight into the social order that caused farmers to dump milk.

This is really not my book. It belongs to the NFO farmers. They lived it. They told their own story as they lived it. Lacking the perspective of the novelist, I have merely assembled the notes and written out non-fiction sentences from the vantage point of a journalist, so that others may know.

"Tell it the way it was," was the only advice anyone in NFO ever offered. "Don't make us any worse—or any better—than we are."

I have tried to obey this injunction to the letter. Yet I am the first to admit a certain bias. I find it impossible to be unbiased toward truth and falsehood.

I cannot say that I am satisfied with this book. It is not complete. The holding action is still very much a part of the scene, and therefore this book is but an opening entry, with so much of the story still to be written.

I would like to thank NFO President Oren Lee Staley for allowing me to be a privileged observer at pre-holding action and holding action sessions, and for the encouragement he extended this effort. Thanks go also to W. W. "Butch" Swaim and Martha Swaim, for providing helpful documents, and to NFO Vice President Erhard Pfingsten for encouragement above and beyond the call of duty. I will not name other NFO members who helped me, nor will I thank them in print, as is the custom. The list would be too long. But I will state my indebtedness to a few of the others who encouraged this book, and critically read either the draft or galleys. They are: Richard Calvert Sr., wine expert and proponent of a healthy agriculture, who insisted that readers outside of agriculture must be told this story; Arnold Paulson, Director, Citizens Congress for Private Enterprise, Granite Falls, Minnesota, who critically examined some of the calculations contained herein; Carl Wilken, Research Analyst, National Foundation for Economic Stability, Washington, D. C., who supplied me with 16 hours of taped interviews and superb instructions on the anatomy of parity; Ed Wimmer, Public Relations Director, National Federation of Independent Business, who made comments and suggestions after the book had reached the galley stage; Homer Jackson, Director, Production Credit Association, Rifle, Colorado, who provided me with new insight into ranch conditions and chain store activities; David J. Schwartz, farmer, Berne, Indiana (author of *The Sick Man of the American Economy*), whose correspondence and fresh ideas helped bridge the gap between the old and the new generations.

My greatest encouragement and help came from my wife, Anne, who not only permitted the solitude necessary to give form to the holding action story, but who saved me from errors no one who works with words should have been guilty of in the first place.

Charles Walters Jr.

Raytown, Missouri

st. louis post-dispatch photo

utside St. Louis milk plants, pre-holding action demon-
rations highlighted the farmers' demands. "Tell it to
SDA," the farmers were told.

Harold O'Neal, Charles Hartman and Everett Hartman, all
of Conway Springs, Kansas, poured milk onto a dry wheat
field in Butler County as the milk holding action got underway.

wichita eagle-beacon photo

NFO Dairy Commodity Department Director, during a Chicago-area pre-holding action briefing session.

NFO President Oren Lee Staley and Dr. Leon Keyserling, at a Washington, D.C. meeting "Find your allies," said Harry S. Truman's former economic advisor.

NFO Vice President Erhard Pfingsten.

Headlines of the day became window display material on the street end of the NFO headquarters complex at Corning. NFO Secretary Harvey Sickels and Public Information staffer Lee Elliott are shown here "fixing" a bulletin board.

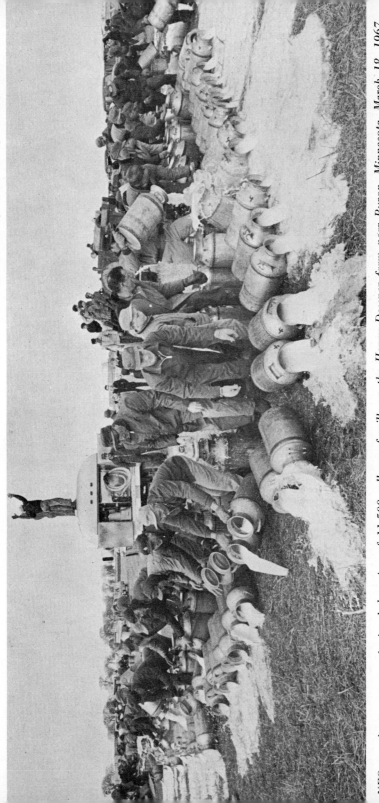

NFO members atop truck signal dumping of 11,500 gallons of milk on the Henry Dessner farm near Byron, Minnesota, March 18, 1967. It was MHA +3. Similar mass dumpings dominated the news that day in half a dozen states.

photo by author

A section of the Nerve Center in action. During the milk holding action, information was fielded by the Nerve Center first, then passed out to each of the counties in NFO's far-flung territory. A fast, accurate communications system kept the action alive long after a lesser effort might have sputtered and died.

photo by author

The Staley family received phoned threats during the holding action. Here are Oren Lee Staley; two children, Greg and Janice; and Mrs. (Ruth) Staley. A third child, Cathy Lynn, is not shown.

At 3:00 p.m., MHA + 6, milk hit the turf on the Gene Paul farm near Blue Earth, Minnesota. Farmers poured it from tank trucks and dumped it from cans. And (above) they sprayed it from tractor-drawn fertilizer applicators.

A ditch became a river of milk as farmers dumped 120 tons of the white stuff near Caro, Michigan.

NFO Headquarters at Corning, Iowa was a busy place during the milk holding action. Here is pictured a part of the crowd that witnessed a public milk dumping in the streets of Corning shortly before NFO officers flew out for negotiations during the second week of the action.

*red wing, minnesota daily republican eagle photo
by wally paulson*

Over 256,430 pounds of milk mixed with snow to form a giant milkshake at Ellsworth, Minnesota on MHA + 6. The milk would have sold for $26,547 at the grocery store. Had farmers hauled it to market, they would have gotten $12,948 (in terms of Class 1 prices).

NFO Chief Negotiatior, Gordon Shafer.

Milk was lost in the snow rather quickly during dumping in Herkimer County, New York.

eggy Kruse, age 3, recapturing the ost art of making butter at the farm, n this case the farm of her parents, 1r. and Mrs Harold Kruse, Loganville, Visconsin. Some farmers used wash- ng machines to churn butter.

Mr. and Mrs Jack Duncan, walking picket at the Kraft plant in Rupert, Idaho. "We are only asking 2 cts. a quart increase NFO" read the crudely lettered sign.

Flanked by attorneys Lee Sin
clair (left) and Larry Scalis
(right), NFO President Orer
Lee Staley responds to ques
tions from a newsman (with
microphone) after emerging
from the Des Moines court
room in which the U. S
Justice Department bombec
out the holding action effort

After the holding action had ended, this Phase 2 production (locked up in
Missouri during the hold) was loaded out of a Turner, Kansas storage cave in
boxcar lots. Each container holds several hundred pounds of cheese.

HARBINGER

---

the beginnings

silent revolution

IT CAME ON SILENTLY at first.

By the time cows started to freshen in March of 1966, it had already become a silent revolution. By the thousands, day in and day out, dairy herds were being sent to slaughter. As anger boiled up into desperation, many farmers refused to sell their dairy animals for replacement stock. "No, they're going to the block" became a *soto voce* injunction as the big Omaha Standards took on their loads.

Across the Dakotas and Minnesota and Wisconsin and Michigan, the silent revolution left a jagged scar. Herds that had become the pride of the country were suddenly gone; and a great sorrow filled the void. Sometimes the auction flyers went out—"Having decided to quit farming"—and with each thump of the hammer a bolt was being driven into the coffin of a heritage.

Between 1960 and the end of 1966, America lost 780,000 farmers, an average of 2,500 per week, or 357 per day. No clear-cut economic mandate proscribed the death of these independent units. But public policy for over 15 years made the result inevitable. Starting in the early 1950s, American farm parity was ever scaled downward. Always it was kept low enough and high enough to pace the rate of bankruptcy, to provide for liquidation of the family farm without embarrassment to the last three administrations.

The less-than-full parity policy not only paced the rate of farm bankruptcy, but did it in a very subtle manner. As the decade of the 50s wore on, thousands of farmers were forced to moonlight the job, the farm, or both. And when the end finally came, it was painful and swift, but not really embarrassing to the powers that be. Almost everyone was able to hold an auction, sell the land and the furniture, and attempt a fresh start in the city. Ironic as it may seem, Democrats felt

3

they were right in supporting even sliding parity, and at the same time many Republicans could defend their position in opposing government supported parity altogether. It depended on one's sense of perspective. Without sliding parity letting farmers down inch by inch, chaos would have brought the farm situation to a head a long time ago. Trauma requires action. A lingering illness gets boring.

At some uncertain point in 1965 or 1966, dairy farmers became aware of the fact that they were being buried one at a time. Behind the cooler, or in front of a tractor, one at a time, they started thinking. They could get as much for their feed as for their milk, so why process the feed into milk simply to be able to work without wages? By selling their cows as canners and cutters, farmers could liquidate some debt, get at least the "homestead 40" free and clear, and hang on to a buck or two for old age.

For most of them, old age had arrived. The average age of farmers had reached 53 years, according to *Kiplinger's* farm letter, and ten more years of working without wages started looking like creative insanity.

Grade A dairy producers in eastern Wisconsin were making 63 cents an hour, according to United States Department of Agriculture Bulletin No. 2221, but dairy farmers in the central northeast weren't doing that well. They were being paid a lavish 37 cents an hour in terms of return on labor. Even so, nearly 25% of the quoted hourly earnings were being developed as allowances for food or housing, and so the spendable income was never really what the government said it was, and the dairy farmers were going broke.

Nor were other farmers doing much better. The Georgia farmer who chose to grow poultry was losing 14 cents an hour on his labor after taking a loss on his investment. A New Jersey egg producer with $44,740 in his operation was losing $235 a year on his investment and six cents for every hour he worked. There were spot situations in which farmers were making at least the lowest wage paid to skilled workers in industrial America, but such operations—irrigated cotton production in the high plains of Texas, or cash grain farming in the corn belt—required $130,000 investment, or better, and the returns on such investments hardly matched the salaries of clerks at IBM.

Dairy farming is a seven day a week, twice a day job. For more years than most farmers cared to remember, they had gotten a scurvy pay for all their work. Early in April, 1966, the President of the United States in effect told farmers to abandon hope, that there would be no improvement in farm prices, that better farm prices were being viewed as bad public policy because the country needed cheap food, and that high pork chops and cheese and fluid milk meant inflation.

And so the silent revolution fell into full swing. By the spring of 1966, farmers had endured a depression since 1951. This had made the duration of their present agrarian depression longer than the debacle of the 30s. Individually, the milk producers looked at the rugs that had become threadbare and the homes that were old a decade earlier, and they didn't need USDA to tell them that they weren't making it. No one directed or encouraged them to slaughter their animals. Independently, one at a time, they took measure of spot economics. They appraised the public policy, and they began their revolt.

In Baron and Polk County, Wisconsin during April of 1966, 70% of the dairy cattle sold at auction went to slaughter. Only 30% served as replacement cows. In *The Minneapolis Tribune*, sales notices indicated that an average of 161 cows were being sold each day for a 23 day spot check period. In Wisconsin, some 12 herds were being sold out each day. In Oregon, the number of dairy cattle being phased out of existence had come to average 6,000 per year for at least several years.

Even without the overview of the aggregate that became available through government statistics, the average farmer could take a pragmatic appraisal and read the handwriting in the sand. The dairy farmer in Ohio could grab up sample flyers of auctions and read of cattle —herds of 70, 56, 40, 35—being sold out on a single weekend in a single location.

One reporter talked to Ron Ervin at a sale in Isabella County, Michigan during that spring. "We're selling milk for much less than we were getting ten years ago. At one time we were getting $5.10 a hundred. Now we get around $4.60 or $4.80, and your hauling comes off that. This cuts it down to around $4.30." In one six month period, Cass County, Michigan lost 1,000 milk cows. And a local veterinarian calculated that another 1,000 would go to the meat block every six months as "far ahead as you can see."

"I went to a sale and talked to probably a hundred farmers, and I talked to about a dozen I knew real well," Ron Ervin continued. "Of the dozen, every blasted one had sold his cows. In fact, two guys I didn't even know told me they've sold out. Maurice John was one of the guys I talked to. He had the best herd for five years in Michigan—the best production per cow, the best feed conversion, and he was awarded all sorts of prizes by Michigan State University. Maurice sold out the earliest."

When an economic structure tumbles, the best leave first.

The on-the-spot situation was no different in Missouri or Kentucky or Indiana. Farmers had been milking for nothing for too long. Many were showing signs of plain, simple battle fatigue. And it added up to the fact that veterinarians, processors, service communities, could count on losing a couple of herds per week in many areas.

As the months wore on, butter production dropped to the lowest in 57 years. Ever-increasing imports squeezed down the price of cheese to brand new lows.

So fantastic had the public policy of liquidating the family farm become that only those sound asleep failed to recognize that farmers were paying the highest price for inflation. As the months wore on the government continued its attack on the farmer, by curtailing pork purchases for military consumption, by dumping grain, by importing dairy products, by tightening export restrictions on hides, and by releasing through the appropriate government agencies official economic forecasts that farm prices would be rolled back from 6 to 10% in the next year. And the silent revolution continued. It had to go on because farmers were powerless to stop it. It continued to wear on because, in the main, the farm organizations did not even understand what was happening, or were not organized to do anything about it.

There was the National Grange, for instance, tooling to celebrate its first century in the organizing game. To have survived as an institution for a hundred years seemed reason enough for being. Oliver Hudson Kelley had left his USDA job a century earlier, "an engine with too much steam on all the time," and under his leadership the organization had fought some important battles. History has recorded in lines like these that the Grange wore down the opposition and cleaned up malfeasance in the handling of Land Grant College funds, and that the organization laid the cornerstone for the Interstate Commerce Commission. But the Grange took on the hammer blows that went with opposing institutional business almost to the point of its own destruction in the operation of tobacco pools, wool houses, and farm implement stores. Later the Grange regained some of its dominance in battles for agricultural experiment stations and pure food and drug laws. It may well be that the Grange survived because a part of each meeting is devoted to social activities. On the drawing board, circa 1966, was a handsome postage stamp, one depicting the century that had come and gone since the Grange came into being. There was nothing on the drawing board to cope with the assassination of the family farm.

And there was the Farmer's Union. Jim Patton had resigned as president not too many moons earlier, and now the faltering Union under Tony Dechant was hanging on to the government solutions that the passage of events had blown away.

And there was the Farm Bureau Federation. There were claims in the farm country—claims not entirely without jurisdiction—that the Farm Bureau had been organized to keep farmers from having an effective organization, and certainly the pronouncements from Charlie Shuman's Chicago-based office sounded like passages out of Manchester economics. Seldom unveiled in public was the fact that the Farm Bureau was actually an industrial-business combine dealing in life and casualty insurance, mutual funds, gasoline, fertilizers, auto supplies, auto rentals, trucking, real estate, veterinary supplies, accounting, and feeds and seeds, among other things. Hardly 50% of its members were farmers, some critics charged. In a world that saw industrial America bleeding agriculture to death, an organization with such widespread business interests was sure to get its cut. To justify what was being done, Charlie Shuman cited his love for the Newtonian purity of *supply and demand*.

As an abstraction, the idea of *supply and demand* found itself buttressed by its obvious excellence as a catch phrase. What could be more enduringly beautiful than the graph which shows that when milk production reaches here, then the price will drop to here? In the economic journals, and on classroom blackboards, *supply and demand* rivaled the government student's well worn diagram of how the Soviet power structure works. A defect exists, of course, in that neither *supply and demand* nor the Soviet table of organization describe anything in existence.

And, of course, there was the National Farmers Organization.

The NFO understood one quite simple proposition. *Prices are set by those who have the power to set them.* When NFO first started telling it that way, little waves of insight marched out from the corn belt, like ripples on a pond. The concept was dazzling in its purity. If prices are set by those with the power to set them, then *supply and demand* has to be a fiction. The new NFO phrase may not have been as breezy as *supply and demand* in an ad writer's way of thinking, but it nailed down the truth, and the farmer—with or without an education—could see this truth at every turn.

In the meeting places that almost always escape recorded history, the new heresy did not go unnoticed. There was such a meeting in Chicago on August 23, 1963 in which the NFO was given front burner attention. A few days later the substance of that meeting went out as "conclusions" over the signature of Donald E. Hirsch, assistant director, Commodity Division, Farm Bureau. NFO, the memo implied, had clearly become a danger. Farmers were listening to the message that prices are set by those with the power to set them, and therefore it was now mandatory that "Potential allies should be contacted and informed of the situation. These include (1) business and professional persons, (2) farm newspaper editors and farm news announcers on radio and TV, and (3) personnel of state departments of agriculture, and the agricultural extension service."

The NFO was talking power. It was, therefore, talking economic revolt. Such talk could be dangerous to an agri-business and industrial complex that equated agriculture with God's gift of raw materials as though it took nothing to produce them.

Supply and demand as an economic concept needed new life if it was to survive at all. The idea that farmers would go on producing because they had no choice, regardless of price, was going the way of all theories that fail to consider the economic process in which the community is involved. NFO leaders knew, if others did not, that the first general recognition of a farm problem would come when pundits and politicians ascended their podiums to cry crocodile tears about "babies without food," never mentioning the fact that the public policies embraced by almost all pundits and politicians had brought this calamity about.

1. *the innovator*

Halfway through the decade of the 60s, farmers who still had sand enough to fight knew that only one man would lead them. He was Oren Lee Staley, president of the farm group newspaper headliners liked to call "militant." Surrounded by loyal officers and commanding a personal loyalty usually reserved for a Bull Halsey, Staley was being looked upon by many as a prophet on a par with Elijah.

In the early days of NFO, Staley had gone so far as to predict that one day the organization would be known and respected the nation over, even by those whose interests caused them to be NFO's worst enemies. At that time not a few of the nation's farm editors and organization leaders thought this prediction absurd, and put it down to Staley's youth or the exigencies of his position as president of NFO.

Oren Lee Staley's success as leader of NFO had given him weight in the nation's top-level councils. Even so he was considered something of a maverick by those who did not know him. But farmers who were members of the NFO, and intellectual associates in and out of farm circles, did not consider him a quaintly impossible spokesman for an era forever gone. Not for one minute did the farmers in that active and viable group accept the idea that the family farm was obsolete, nor did they believe that there was clear cut economic reason for the elimination of the family farm. For a decade running, Oren Lee Staley had gone up and down the country iterating and reiterating this message.

An accomplished public speaker, Staley was sometimes ebullient, always dignified, a gentleman with a personality that was at once brilliant, versatile and adventurous. Before he was 40, his daring mind and almost melodramatic showmanship had accounted for an accomplished career as head of NFO, and figured mightily in building NFO to a position of national prominence. As the man who was to step to the front of the silent revolution, he seemed as something of a sphinx's riddle, as inexplicable as life, gravity and the swing of the stars.

Actually, there was less riddle than image in the makeup of Oren Lee Staley, and it was his image that helped distinguish him. There can be no doubt that the leadership and image he created for himself and the NFO are intricately interleaved. Despite, or perhaps because of Staley's enormous success, few rival farm leaders try to follow the Staley method, for not many can go the way of the innovator, the original view, the wildly improbable result.

Born in the home he and his wife Ruth and the three Staley children still occupied, Staley had missed few of the experiences that could have come the way of a farm youth growing up. The little country school in which he completed his first eight grades still stands, as does the King City high school where he was salutatorian and president of the student body.

Much of the rest around Rea, Missouri has changed—chiefly for the worse. Whitesville, a small town down the gravel road a ways, is now so small it has almost passed out of existence. Rea, Missouri has a population of 90, a white building over which flies an American flag because it is the post office, and a few frame houses—that's all.

Staley had gone to Northwest Missouri College, served as a Pharmacist Mate 3rd Class, and married Ruth Turner before definitely settling down to a farm career. The children duly arrived—Janice Lee, Greg Thompson and Cathy Lynn. Staley was growing Shorthorn cattle, and looking to a long career in agriculture. Leading a farm movement didn't even rate consideration in the family planning sessions.

Suddenly, almost overnight, something happened to farming. Farmers in southwest Iowa held protest meetings, and the meetings spilled across the border into Missouri. One night Staley went to a meeting in Maryville. "It was held in a sale barn in October 1955," Staley later recalled. "In those days volunteers were literally jerked to their feet and given offices" because farmers knew they had to do something, anything, about the cancer of low farm prices. Staley emerged as a regional vice president, and as such he helped organize dollar day NFO members in Missouri. He started to learn a great deal about farm economics.

2. *the social and economic mystery*

Farmers are the "meetingest" people in the world. They fill the high school auditoriums of rural communities and trample down grass in the parks because they love to meet other folk, talk about farming, about anything, because farming is essentially a lonely job. There was a time when professors could come out of the colleges and name their poison because there was almost no chance at all that a farmer would take issue with what was being said. The erudite airings became even more of a rural staple when farm prices started their long decline during the last year of the Truman administration. With or without powerful names, the meetings proceeded with the revival tent assurance that farmers would provide an audience before which the learned ones could demonstrate their wisdom.

One such affair held on January 6, 1960 should illustrate the point. Farmers in and around Upland, Indiana were invited to a very special meeting at Taylor University. "Certainly one of the most important social and economic mysteries of our time is the farm problem" said the opening sentence of the invitation, and on the agenda for a quick "look-see" at this problem were George Doup, president, Indiana

Farm Bureau; John C. Raber, president, Indiana Farmers Union; Robert J. Giltner, master, Indiana State Grange; and Dr. Earl L. Butz, dean, School of Agriculture, Purdue University.

These notable farm leaders had long been accustomed to a nice, polite crowd, and periodically they had all issued nice, polite pronouncements on the "social and economic mystery" known as the farm problem. Any thinking farmer had no real reason to expect anything new. Nevertheless some 350 came to the dinner that had been expected to draw 75. After the meeting was moved to the largest auditorium in Upland, one with a capacity of 2,500, the forum was again flooded out by over 4,000 farmers—and many had to be turned away.

What did these farmers hear on that cold January night? They heard that nothing could be done about this "social and economic mystery." Indeed, the master of ceremonies more or less indicated that he didn't even understand the problem in the first place. And, finally, as the meeting ended, someone said "things would have to take their course," and "finally the situation would resolve itself."

Translated into something everyone could understand, this meant that farmers could start looking for another round of inflation, more bankruptcy and more dispossession. In that entire gathering, there probably wasn't a handful of farmers who couldn't have handed Messrs. Doup, Raber, Giltner and Dr. Butz a solution to the mysterious farm problem: increase farm income. Every one of those horny-handed farmers knew that one of the longest steel strikes in history had ended only two days before the Taylor University conclave (with the steel workers getting what they wanted), but what really hit every farmer squarely in the eye the next morning was something like this: hogs, cattle, eggs—all had dropped in price from the day before. Not a few of those farmers left farm leaders Doup, Raber, Giltner and Butz forever that cold night in January 1960 and started looking into the merits of a farm organization that at least had a program subject to working. Officially it was called the National Farmers Organization. Most farmers settled simply for NFO. There had been other meetings, and each time a platform speaker begged the question, NFO picked up new members.

NFO had concluded a "test holding action" a few months before, and the very concept of farmers getting together to solve their own problems was in the air. After all, reasoned many a farmer, at least NFO knew what the problem was, and didn't waste time on seminars that ended on a note of "we really don't know what we're talking about." The problem was price, and prices are set by those who have the power to set them.

3. *a national farmer's organization*

NFO had come into being fully five years before the Taylor University meeting. The idea of a national farmer's organization, or at least farmers bound together in a program addressed to the real problem had been around even longer.

"There is still afloat among the rural population a slow-dying tradition of the 'Independent Farmer'," wrote economist Thorstein Veblen in 1919, "who is reputed once upon a time to have lived his own life and done his own work as good him seemed, and who was content to let the world wag. But all that has gone by now as completely as the other things that are told in tales which begin with 'Once upon a time'." It was a thesis Veblen repeated again in *Absentee Ownership and Business Enterprise* in 1923, because the farmer's income was being fixed and eroded by "those massive interests that move in the background and find a profit in buying cheap and selling dear."

By buying cheap and selling dear, the latter-day "massive interests" drove farm prices down approximately 30% between 1947 and 1955, while the prices of everything farmers bought doubled, sometimes trebled hard on the heels of "excess profit tax" repeal. Individual farmers who framed their discontent to spokesmen of the old line farm organization heard the Farm Bureau call for less government (a euphemism for *supply and demand*), the Farm Union call for government intervention, and all of them call for something or other without a hint as to how results were to be obtained. Before and since that day when a few Iowa and Missouri farmers founded NFO, the tragic-comedy of farm leaders shaking their head at "this social and economic mystery" had become a fixture on the lecture circuit.

As the cost-price squeeze became the farmer's personal property, he could pragmatically wonder whether an incantation might break the spell. If so, that incantation would certainly have to be, "two and two still make four." In other words, *the farmer could not go on forever receiving less wealth than he produced.*

It was a problem that had been attacked before, but always by others on the outside looking in, always by someone "interested," but either not interested enough, or unable to do more than "understand."

In the 1920s the Kansas State Board of Agriculture asked Wall Streeter Bernard M. Baruch to examine agriculture and to find a solution. The recorded findings appeared in a report entitled, *Putting Farming on a Modern Business Basis*. Baruch found that farming was uneconomic and inefficient because the farmer couldn't adjust his production to meet market conditions the way a factory could, and that the farmer was always at the mercy of nature. But Baruch's big point was that agriculture's troubles were "compounded by its organization, or rather its lack of organization." The individual farmer could not compete with the disposing end of agriculture, and every sale the farmer made was a forced sale: he had to take whatever he was offered. Those with the power to set prices were setting them.

Many of Baruch's associates shared his concern for agriculture. Out of Baruch's old War Industries Board marched George N. Peek and Hugh S. Johnson in the 20s, and the package they were selling was called McNary-Haugen. The McNary-Haugen bills insisted that farmers must be paid for as much wealth as they produced, and this meant that the production they sold had to be in line with the goods and services they bought. In a word, Peek and Johnson called for the same system of protection that American industry had enjoyed for over 100 years. There was yet another feature in McNary-Haugen. Farmers would have been forced to cooperate in marketing their production. They would have been required to erect their own institutional marketing power while at the same time enjoying protection from price invasion from foreign producers. Baruch supported McNary-Haugen, despite the fact that it ran against the grain of a true internationalist, and despite the fact that he was convinced there could not be a prosperous America while there was poverty in the world.

Out in Iowa, Dan Turner took the stump for the farmers. And on the Main Streets of rural America business groups supported the idea of a prosperous agriculture. And so, for the last time in history, farmers won the battle and lost the war. Twice, McNary-Haugen sledded through Congress, but Calvin Coolidge ("that little wart," Dan Turner called him a half century later) delivered the death blow via the veto.

Thus farmers did not get their McNary-Haugen measure in time to prevent 1929. Already, the credit base had been badly stretched, and by March 1929 the banks were taking in their sail. John Kenneth Galbraith was probably right when he later noted that the real debate was over a hard choice—whether to have a deliberate crash, or wait for an inevitable and more difficult one. Roger Babson saw what was coming at that time, but no one could buy his findings because no one understood the foundation ideas behind his reasonings—and besides, the professors who already knew all the answers had no reason to listen to anyone.

The farmers who had become the producing marvels of the world by 1955 had forgotten, if they ever knew, the broad spectrum economics that underwrote their plight. They did remember the long history of farmers trying to lift themselves by their own bootstraps.

There had been farm movements galore. After the Civil War farmers organized to repair their economic house. They ventured into buying and selling. They paid the price that went with mismanagement, and they suffered defeat at the hands of politicians. Yet organizations have a way of surviving their reason for being. Unless they continue to develop, they become merely dues gathering businesses, held together by group insurance and health plans. A few Iowa-based farmers had come to realize that much.

At least one farmer in southwestern Iowa, Wayne Jackson, sensed this drift of events. He wanted, in his words, "one organization represented by the farmer and for the farmer, solely for the purpose of seeking equality for the farmer and not for the purpose of being in business." As early as 1953 (when hog prices were $20 a hundredweight) Jackson convinced feed salesman Jay Loghry to "ask every farmer if they would be interested in starting an organization to combat the problems of price fluctuation." Two weeks later Loghry reported, "You can't organize farmers."

But Loghry didn't believe that himself. Two years later hog prices were in the process of tumbling from a high of $26 per hundredweight in April 1954 to a low of $10 a hundredweight in December 1955. Feed salesman Loghry was still about his business, and on September 5, 1955, in an Adair County schoolhouse, he once again suggested a new farm organization. The seven farmers who had brought their 4-H children to hear about Moorman's feeds were interested. The economic crisis had made Loghry's plea more appealing than it had been two years earlier.

In the days that followed, farmer Wayne Jackson left his silo unfilled and traveled around the neighborhood to set up a second meeting at Carl, Iowa. Some say 35 farmers attended. Jackson has since claimed that at least 80% of those he contacted were present.

Those were electric days—those first dozen days of NFO, when farmers met spontaneously to ask for Agriculture Secretary Ezra Taft Benson's hide, when word of mouth did the advertising, when a meeting proposed in the afternoon became a reality that night. Only after a while did anyone pause to log in the proceedings, to pinpoint dates and times where farmers met to "do something," to resolve the areas of effectiveness in which other farm organizations had been found wanting.

There were meetings at Greenfield and Corning, Iowa during which volunteers were "elected" to cover townships, to spread the word. Jay Loghry, the feed salesman, was well in the swing of things. As one observer said, "Jay had a sincere wish to help the farmers. He began to get fan letters, he was on TV, southerners thought he was Moses. At meetings, ladies flocked around him and wanted to kiss him. Old bent-up farmers said, *I want to shake his hand.*"

In those days farmers thought firing Benson for using ineffective medicine on the disease of low income was an answer, but a more mature sense of values told others that farmers themselves were to blame. They were, as Bernard Baruch had said, a disorganized mass. They fancied themselves rugged individualists. Rather than entertain "organization," too many had chosen to enlarge their constantly depreciating income by more and harder work.

Of a sudden, organization had appeal.

The whole movement had sort of a prairie fire spectacle about it. Former Iowa Governor Dan Turner, the old fire-eating McNary-Haugenite, was interviewed in the press, and he gave his prestige and voice to the movement. Loghry spoke of forming a farm group not unlike a factory union, and as Dan Turner later recalled, "Someone gave him the idea of leather markers. Then there was to be a deal so packinghouse workers wouldn't handle anything except marked livestock." Turner was visiting in the halls at Bedford, Iowa while Loghry held forth from the podium with what Turner called his "crazy scheme." A newsman from *U. S. News and World Report* came running back. "Governor Turner, the radicals are running wild."

The mere thought of illegal or violent action made Dan Turner shudder. He had been governor when Milo Reno's Farm Holiday Movement was in fullest flower. As chief executive he had been forced to call out the state militia. His political career had gone down the drain with Herbert Hoover, but he was still influential. Turner saw an opportunity to nip run-away radicalism in the bud. "You better get in there and stop them," the newsman was saying.

Turner did. He was duly introduced, and though 80 years old, he had lost none of his oratorical powers. He advised the farmers to petition their government. That was their right. He counseled against something that was not only illegal but ran "counter to common sense." Dan Turner could have a crowd shouting or pelting the floor with tears, all in good time, and when it was all over the farmers vetoed any "union" of farmers.

And so it was at Bedford, Iowa, on September 22, 1955, that a loosely knit group of farmers formed a Board, and the Board in turn met a day later to petition the government for 100% of parity under suitable controls, an immediate floor of $20 per hundredweight on hogs, and $30 per hundredweight on cattle. The Board also decided to adopt the name, National Farmers Organization.

NFO was an almost "no budget" organization from the start. Jay Loghry drew $100 a week salary. Volunteer workers were in the field, and NFO had a relatively clear purpose. But NFO had little of the know-how that goes with finding a reason for being and meeting the challenge head-on.

Still, NFO was fast moving. Between early September and the date of the first national convention at Corning, Iowa, December 15, 1955, NFO had gathered in some 55,000 dollar day members, according to newspaper reports of that period. Over 1,000 farmers (including 315 delegates) arrived to fill the old Armory on Eighth Street and Loomis Avenue. Caretaker president, Duane Orton, stood ready to turn the organization over to anyone the farmers wanted.

Oren Lee Staley had been drawn to NFO because of Dan Turner's reputation, not because he wanted a part in a radical cause. When he arrived at the small but momentous national convention at Corning, Staley was already well involved in NFO. There had been meetings at Corning, and not a little collective bargaining had already taken place. Dan Turner wanted the organization to headquarter in a rural town, not in Chicago or Kansas City or Omaha. He wanted it to keep in touch with rural America by observing the posture of rural developments day by day. Thus it was not by accident that Corning became the headquarters of NFO, a location cemented into place by constitutional mandate. In return for the Missourian's support of Corning at the headquarter town, Iowa delegates joined those from Missouri in naming Oren Lee Staley the first president of NFO.

The convention did more. It designed its structure: delegates to be elected by county organizations, NFO to act only as a service organization, NFO to stay out of business, the sole objective of NFO being to secure better farm prices.

The aims of NFO were clear. The "how" of how this was to be accomplished was vague. Within weeks after Staley was named to head the new farm group, NFO leaders headed for Washington. But the talk with Benson was about as effective as hollering up a drainpipe.

"It was very obvious," Staley later noted, "that politicians react, they don't act. They gave us their attention, but they honestly didn't think farmers could elect enough support, and therefore not doing anything created no problem." The NFO delegation returned from the nation's capitol. Even the most optimistic among them could see no help coming from Washington.

Although the organization continued to build, first to 140,000 members, later to perhaps 189,000 dollar day members, petitions were spurned. Benson stayed securely wedged in the saddle, and farm income continued its historic decline. And with the lack of instant showy success, the NFO, too, started down hill. There were many dark hours in 1956 as the dollar days passed into history. Only a handful of dedicated NFOers held the organization together. They did more. They started finding the answers to economic matters.

Through the years economists and scholars had placed on deposit great funds of knowledge. The producer marketing experiences of citrus growers, the counsel of bankers (when they were willing to talk) and professors (when they dared talk) were all taken into consideration.

It has been calculated that several hundred general farm organizations with over 100,000 members have passed from the mind and memory of man since the Civil War. In the main they were organized as protest movements, and then died a-borning. Historians and reporters, wise in the way of farm organizations, figured that was what would happen to NFO. Those high in NFO councils are now agreed that except for Oren Lee Staley, NFO would have gone by the board.

Although hardly past 30 at the time, Staley was an accomplished parliamentarian. He had become attuned to work with the gavel as a 4-H Club regular, and had studied *Roberts Rules of Order* the way some people study stock market quotations. As NFO emerged from its protest days and took on the idea of collective bargaining for agriculture, solidarity of purpose seemed to vanish. Getting the organization to adopt a meaningful program called for adroit skills rarely encountered among farmers.

"In those days," NFO dollar day-ers will tell you, "there were members who wanted to turn NFO into a political action group." The collective bargaining resolution was bottled up in Committee and the Committee was presided over by a member who wanted no part of "bargaining." Bringing a resolution before a convention without the sanction of a Committee is not usually accomplished with a wave of the magic wand. But it was managed.

Oren Lee Staley's farm lies amid the rolling hills not far from Savannah, a few miles from Highway 71. Fields are not large because of the lay of the terrain, but the ground is fertile and the bottom lands almost always produce bumper crops. Staley's farm is not as easy to work as a treeless spread in North Dakota, but you can still do your best thinking away from the staccato of phones and cacophony of office routine. While Staley was riding a cultivator through waist high corn he realized that there could be no solution to low farm income as long as farmers relied on either government payments, or individual marketing. Plain logic suggested that there had to be an overall premise— an overall structure. "I made my big decision that day," Staley recalled. "I'd either have to present the broad idea to the membership, or return back to the farm entirely."

For several months after the collective bargaining resolution had been adopted, NFO's leadership was hot on the trail of a workable mechanism. At first "we looked into the law and studied earlier attempts," and finally "we found a law on the books nobody knew existed," Staley reported. "A USDA spokesman told us we had all the rights we needed. The farmer has always had the right to use collective bargaining since 1922, but he has never used it."

Having the right to use collective bargaining and getting farmers to exercise that right were two different things. There was going to be a struggle in the 1958 convention over whether an instrument the leadership had written for members to sign would be accepted. The Board of Directors would have doubts. Again, it was time for decision, and the decision was in fact made at Maysville, Missouri, when NFO organizers and Staley signed up the first 17 NFO members under an agreement made possible by the Capper-Volstead Act of 1922. Only a few weeks remained before the annual conclave. Those who hoped to see NFO go down the drain calculated that this would be the last hurrah. Whispers in the cornfield informed those who cared to listen that NFO was out of funds. Those who opposed collective bargaining were sure that processors would never talk to farmers, much less bargain. Some feared retaliation.

Those last few weeks before the 1958 convention were busy ones for President Oren Lee Staley. Running on a few hours of sleep a night, and practically never stopping in any one place for more than an hour or two at a time, Staley covered the many Kansas, Nebraska, Iowa and Missouri counties, and the memberships geared to collective bargaining rolled in. The checks were held for later delivery to the convention. Indeed, at the convention the membership checks became bargaining power in the hands of the man who figured farm organization would be futile without collective bargaining for agriculture.

When the Board of Directors objected that the resolution which endorsed collective bargaining had been implemented without approval, Staley adroitly submitted the question to the NFO's highest authority, the membership. Perhaps the membership checks helped, but the point of enduring importance is that approval came loud and clear. Farmers wanted collective bargaining for agriculture.

In the fullness of time, the new post-protest program for NFO emerged, and it is essentially the program NFO has to this day.

1. Members sign a membership agreement for a three year period, naming the NFO as bargaining agent. Members pay dues and fees of $25 per year.

2. Master contracts are presented to processors of all types of farm commodities. In these contracts, NFO is named procurement agent. Processors agree to pay prices determined in advance through collective bargaining.

3. In order to obtain master contracts, NFO relies on controlling the sale of production before it passes into processing channels.

4. Contracts with processors are not to be activated until 60% of a commodity is under NFO through membership agreements with farmers, or enough processors have signed master contracts to account for 60% of the processed production.

Up to this point, NFO had been met with mild disinterest, if not an outright conspiracy of silence. But from the day that NFO adopted collective bargaining for agriculture and outlined its mode of procedure, the "massive interests that move in the background and find a profit in buying cheap and selling dear" sensed danger. There was no need to worry as long as NFO was content to present petitions, or issue notes of social protest, but the moment the organization became subject to succeeding because it had a program that was subject to succeeding, winds of resistance blew cold. In the public prints and on the air, lavish abuse was heaped on NFO and its leadership as "massive interests" started to cut down the ring-leaders before it was too late.

4. *test holding action*

Quickly, and with determination, NFO passed through its "test holding action" phase, periods when holding actions were ordered by the membership in order, the NFO said, "to gather data," "to feel out the flow to market," "to determine how the NFO membership could affect the flow to market." These, however, were hindsight explanations. Even in the early days, the NFO leadership had a finely honed sense of history. Staley and his associates knew that great moments become what they are when discerning leadership seizes those moments. It is a matter of record that NFO entered the first test meat holding action with the idea that as a catalyst the action would bring cohesiveness to the farm scene, and that farmers who were shown the way would respond and join. The holding action at St. Joseph, Missouri in 1959 failed to deliver that spontaneous joining, and NFO officials—after seeing a great flood of pork heading for the river city—"recessed" the action.

There were other holding actions. A test action probed the feasibility of the NFO approach when NFO had substantial organization in only Iowa, Kansas, Nebraska, Missouri and Illinois. By April 1961, Indiana, southern Minnesota, South Dakota and Wisconsin were in the lineup for another test. By that time NFO had come down out of the clouds. Primary and secondary objectives now became part of the plan. Miracles were no longer expected. Evidence gathered and evaluated clearly indicated that an all-out holding action would jar loose some processors and pave the way for contracts. Should the spontaneous "joining" take place, then, indeed, farmers could write the whole ticket. But secondary objectives were well worth the effort.

Thus battle lines were drawn by August 1962. At least 20,000 farmers muled their way into a steaming Des Moines auditorium for a meeting for action. Several hours later the first all-out holding action was voted into being.

Statistics are not facts. They merely reflect data fed into the gathering apparatus, and they can be converted into "fact" only after proper evaluation. When the 1962 holding action was called all basic data fed into stock papers, the Meat Institute, even USDA, came from processors, stockyards, people with a vested interest in keeping farmers divided. NFO countered this situation by establishing check points, by gathering information on its own. Although stoutly denied by central markets, NFO checkers believed they found truckloads of livestock being shuttled from market to market, and they most certainly found loads of livestock arriving from outside the normal shipping channels. What they didn't find, because they had no way of checking it, was that the commission men had phone bills that must have appeared as big as the national debt, and that those same commission men bird-dogged long and hard to find production to replace livestock being held by NFO members.

As the weeks wore on, nerves got thin. The NFO production was sizeable, to be sure, but there were other variables. Packers could cut down killing crews, truckers could go further, chain stores could turn customers to chickens for a week or a month with heavy advertising, and there was always the reality that even if NFO won concessions it had not constructed a working structure for delivering the goods. There was also the hard reality that many farmers, still drugged by the lotus of the times, didn't even realize they were in economic trouble, that they were consuming their capital, exploiting their own labor, or both. In any case, they did not turn a well led effort into a spontaneous success.

Too, members had become accustomed to thinking in terms of a big leap forward, whereas the leadership had changed its approach to careful building—block on block, inch at a time, and this would mean improving farm income a bit at a time—until full parity was reached—not reaching up and grabbing full parity in one clean sweep. When a recess was called in 1962, the NFO Board of Directors issued the following statement:

"The National Board of Directors has reached a decision that the recess on the meat part of the all-out holding action will be lifted at the most opportune time, and a definite timetable has been set to include other commodities if the processors do not continue to sign contracts in sufficient numbers. The NFO will not tolerate any drastic price drop and we will not be satisfied until we reach our goal of contracts with processors that assure our members cost of production plus a reasonable profit." Implied, but not stated, was the basic criterion, "on an average, well-managed farm."

5. *the great debate*

There was more to it than that. Staley, for instance, weary beyond comprehension, had decided to quit. The job was going to be a long, lifetime one, obviously. He had exhausted himself in what seemed a thankless task. He had consumed his resources, from automobile to shoe leather, without pay most of the time, and now he had decided to let other hands take over. The trouble was—which hands?

Keeping an organization on the path of its chartered regularity had been a Staley strong point. Others were constantly trying to get NFO "behind an alcohol program," on the path of "monetary reform," in the mold of other cooperatives devoted to piecemeal efforts—all approaches that history has found deficient.

The worst pressure of the lot came from the NFO Board of Directors. Many were opposed to the holding action as a tool, and were constantly looking for an easy way out, a short cut that would deliver fair prices without abrasive contacts with the social order. "We have to make small gains and consolidate" became the working catch phrase of this group, but it was not a plan being pressed in any meaningful way, because even small gains were unavailable to the embattled farmers under the atmosphere of intimidation that had them fenced in. Despite all this, Staley had been able to keep these diversionists at arm's length. Now, as the top secret of his voluntary retirement became common knowledge, new forces came to the fore.

NFO Vice President Bob Casper had never accepted the idea of collective bargaining for agriculture, at least not in Staley's view. In talks before farmers he aired other ideas and charted other courses. Now Casper threw his hat into the ring. And Missourian Harold Woodward did the same.

There were also other elements. Some wanted to have done with the holding action under any circumstances. One group was busily touting short spot holding actions, rather than all-out comprehensive efforts. Some of these splinter factions would merge for voting purposes, and the recipient of those votes would not always be aware of what some supporters were about. By December convention time, 1962, Staley's ideas on collective bargaining were really on the firing line.

As in all great shifts of power, someone made a mistake. Staley would have resigned and faded quietly from the scene. A "mistake" caused him to change his course of action. That mistake came from those who didn't think Staley would quit despite his announced intentions, and wanted to make certain his defeat. Fantastic charges that ranged all the way from incompetence to moral turpitude were leveled at the NFO chief, and a battle royal soon took form. For a time Staley didn't fight back because, after all, he had decided to leave the presidency. The attacks continued. But before long those who figured Staley would not fight under any circumstances had cause to regret their miscalculation. As some point between the end of holding action and mid-fall, Staley decided to run for president after all.

On the Board of Directors, in-fighting had reached the boiling point long before the election. There were closed door sessions, quiet caucuses, and noisy debates almost everywhere. One of the most meaningful developed in the basement of the LaConn-E Motel. One anti-Staley faction was holding forth when a well-known and likeable meat commodity man drove by. He spotted a number of cars he recognized and walked into the meeting.

The atmosphere was thick, not just with smoke, but with the acrid stuff that sometimes passes for determination. This cabal was making strides, no doubt about it, and in all likelihood the time for debate was rapidly fading away. Tomorrow, it might be too late. The hour was ripe.

With this judgment the meat commodity man tore into the dissidents, one at a time. In turn, one at a time, they apologized and excused themselves—all except two. Unknown to the conclave, Staley and Lloyd Fairbanks arrived at the motel while the man-to-man debate was in process. With paper-thin walls, Staley couldn't help hearing the discussion that was going on. The words that defended Staley came on in an unfaltering parabola, and though they weren't really that loud Staley felt certain the arguments could be heard as far as the Conoco station next door. Staley stayed only a moment, but he never forgot the man who was doing the talking.

The speaker was Erhard Pfingsten. Pfingsten had joined the NFO in the dollar days, but had remained more or less inactive until the "protest" drive had spent itself. When NFO adopted collective bargaining for agriculture, the decision served as a lodestone to the intellectual drive of Erhard Pfingsten.

He started with NFO as organizer. First he took on northwest Iowa, and translated the potential there into a strong phalanx of NFO strength. He wore his tires down to the cords organizing southwest

Minnesota, and after that he took on the demanding job of Assistant Organizational Director under Lloyd Fairbanks. In 1960 he had been named to the Board of Directors by the state of Iowa, and a year later he assumed the top job in the Meat Commodity Department. Staley saw in him the qualities of leadership, and now he was sure that Pfingsten was the man for vice president.

It was a hard fought battle at Des Moines. The campaign raged through the hotel lobbies and into the mezzanine meeting rooms. Various groups had pooled their strength behind Casper first, Woodward second. When Casperites scheduled a hotel meeting at the same time delegates had been invited to hear Staley, pro-Staley NFOers Butch Swaim and Ed Shima resolved the conflict by carrying most of the chairs to the meeting hall they favored, and soon that's where the crowd was gathering. Finally the battle spilled on to the convention floor.

On the convention floor it was turmoil. Woodward's supporters, with walkie-talkies, commandeered the seven floor mikes at one time, and a few Casper supporters worked the aisle like Bob Kennedy pros swaying delegates. There was a showy atmosphere about all this despite the fact that every man and woman in the audience knew the vote would be settled by debate. Debate did not start until late in the evening. The vote was also tardy. Not a soul left the big auditorium, and when some 8,000 delegates voted, Oren Lee Staley emerged victor.

He was a victor, but a long way from being winner. Staley still had a Board that rated well below the one he believed necessary to make collective bargaining for agriculture work. Nothing less than another go-round would resolve the issue. All the ugly charges were still choking the life out of NFO, and all the old enemies were girding for battle.

Things got pretty rocky in 1963. There were several attempts on the lives of Staley and Pfingsten. In each instance, fortunate happenstance prevented tragedy. There was the time Staley and Pfingsten unaccountably delayed flying home after an evening meeting. Sawdust had been added to the fuel, but since the flight had been delayed until daylight the pilot made an uneventful emergency landing. In the dark, that same landing might have proved fatal.

The second attempt was made when Staley and Pfingsten were flying in different directions. The electric system on Staley's plane had been tampered with.

And there was the time the engine sputtered out over Michigan when Staley was aboard. Sugar had been put in the gas tank.

These attempts were amateurish, and even open to question. It was hard to decide whether the really wild ones were after Staley or Pfingsten. The question was resolved when Pfingsten took Staley's plane, Staley's pilot and Staley's place at a meeting. Again the plane had been sabotaged.

"All these attempts seemed clumsy enough," Pfingsten later recalled. "We believe they were either trying to scare us, or should we leak the news, scare our leadership." So between Staley, Pfingsten and pilot Hap Westbrook there developed an agreement that word of these attempts should not get out.

What happened in Beloit, Kansas made this agreement impossible. John Gipple, one of Hap Westbrook's pilots out of Atlantic, Iowa, had just taken off from the Beloit airport with Pfingsten and a Federal Avaition Agency man named Fred Vorrath aboard. Less than five minutes later the Beechcraft Bonanza came down into a Beloit street. It struck a utility line and crashed within a block of the hospital. Pfink woke up with a broken jaw and a fractured skull, and other injuries he was too numb to count. The pilot escaped uninjured. Fred Vorrath suffered a broken leg.

When Federal Aviation Agency investigators finally pulled the engine apart, they found bearings etched and frozen by acid, and immediately ruled out malfunction. Because of proved sabotage, the FBI started looking into the attempts at foul play. As soon as the FBI started looking at the case, attempts to get Staley and Pfingsten came to a halt.

This, however, was not true in the political arena. All the old charges were still around, and Staley had resolved to answer them from the podium of the organization's annual assembly. In an unbroken session that lasted until 3:55 a.m., he not only defended his record, but gained from the delegates the mandate that collective bargaining required. A Board was elected that believed in collective bargaining, and had the guts to make it work. Those who had made charges against Staley withdrew them before the morning edition of the Des Moines papers hit the street. It was more than a personal victory for Staley. The 1963 convention was iron-clad assurance that NFO would not abandon the all-out holding action.

NFO's holding actions before 1964 proved beyond the shadow of a doubt that there is nothing mysterious or imponderable about the way in which farm production finds its way to the grocery shelf. NFO's leadership and the rank and file hoped that the organization would ultimately gain enough strength to write the ticket for fair market prices. There was also a realization that any faltering on the part of NFO might severely damage collective bargaining.

NFO leadership, for a long time, had tried to convince processors that they were missing a great opportunity by not letting organization members supply production on an even flow basis. Some slow progress had been made along this line, but the real jump forward came when Staley, Vice President Erhard Pfingsten, Chief Negotiator Gordon Shafer, Indiana Director Wayne Miller, and NFO Meat Commodity Director Bill Lashmett met with railroad executive Ike Duffy and meat packer John Hartmeyer (of Marhoeffer Packing) in Duffy's private railroad car on a Muncie, Indiana siding. On the agenda was the concept of "marketing arrangements" for NFO to be carried out on a test basis by some of the organization's most loyal members. NFO was to be given an opportunity to show that it could even out the flow of animals to market, that members could work together and build the future of NFO as a marketing and bargaining organization.

Staley correctly sensed that it would be necessary to go slow, to take this brand new experiment one step at a time so that wrinkles could be ironed out, marketing people trained, counties staffed, but above all a plan put into motion that would send an even flow to the markets as required by industry. The area around Hannibal, Missouri and Griggsville, Illinois started operating by mid-summer—but, first, there was other business in the wind.

6. *1964*

Through half of July and almost all of August, 1964, the carpetless floors at NFO headquarters in Corning, Iowa thundered to the tune of comings and goings. Time and again officials held meetings far into the night, and marched off at dawn for even more meetings with NFO leaders and the rank and file in the then 23 NFO states. During the 17 days from July 14 through July 31, 1964, the word traveled out from the NFO hub at Corning. It went forth along each single spoke to all 23 NFO states, where individual and group informational and planning meetings were held. At times the leaders from two and three states were brought together for a meeting, but in the main the conclaves were statewide affairs, open to the rank and file. At some meetings, well over 6,000 were in attendance.

Thus it was at the grass-roots level that NFO farmers in election summer 1964 endorsed a holding action on cattle, swine and sheep. They endorsed it because they were living in a marketing world that was presiding over their economic destruction.

The action was announced by Oren Lee Staley on Wednesday, August 19, as "the greatest show of bargaining power that American farmers had ever made." Staley said: "It is time farmers forget their ties with farm organizations, their differences in political beliefs, and make this truly a farmer's effort to price their products at the market place."

Early in the action, there was evidence that farmers who had never joined NFO thought they should honor the action and help it along. The prices set by NFO were $32.25 per hundredweight for choice grade cattle, $22.75 for No. 1 and 2 hogs, and $29.45 for choice wooled lambs. NFO target prices may have looked strong when compared to Wednesday, August 19, 1964 prices in Chicago of $24 to $26 for cattle; $16.40 to $17.50 for hogs, and $23.00 for lambs, but in fact the NFO asking price was not as high as prices enjoyed in the marketplace 15 years earlier.

Opposition to the 1964 holding action was more vicious than ever before. Even the most hide-bound critics were privately admitting that NFO was a force to be reckoned with, and not a few were starting to adjust to the marketing arrangements that would follow.

The 1964 holding action was not without its sour notes. Governor Dalton of Missouri threatened to "call out the Guard."

At Bonduel, Wisconsin, NFOers Melvin Cummings and Howard Falk were killed when a truck driven by sometime barkeep, sometime truck driver Ivan Mueller ran over them in the presence of ten lawmen and several hundred farmers. Mueller had stopped his vehicle and waited for farmers to gather around. Then he backed up a few feet as if to leave, and without warning plunged into the crowd. Not everyone could get clear.

Even though lawmen took Mueller in tow, it was an ugly situation, and the farmers were in an ugly mood. There was talk of a lynching. Officials were taking precautions.

When Ed Graf and then Oren Lee Staley arrived at Bonduel, it wasn't even easy to talk to many of the farmers, so sullen had the mood become. Staley's first move was classic. He cornered the ring leaders of this reckless talk. He put it on the line. Did they believe in NFO? They did. Did they still consider Staley the legitimate leader

of NFO? They did. Then, Staley said, you'll have to take charge here
and see to it that none of these hotheads harm the prisoner.

Shouldered with this new responsibility, those who might have
sought vengeance suddenly became statesmen, and the talk of
vengeance evaporated.

But the holding action was over. Everyone knew it. It had been
killed by Ivan Mueller. It was only a matter of days before the rumbling showed up like a blip on a radar screen. Again, the primary
objective had eluded the embattled farmers, but their secondary gains
had come through on schedule. Also, on schedule, a year later, came
the jury's verdict on Ivan Mueller. He was held blameless in the
deaths of Cummings and Falk.

7. marketing arrangements

Nevertheless, the holding action had made a dent in the processing
industry's solid front. NFO proceeded to move full speed ahead with
the marketing arrangements.

The collection points at Griggsville and Hannibal, closed down for
the holding action, promptly started doing business again. Across Wisconsin, Minnesota, Iowa, Kansas, Nebraska, Illinois, Indiana, Ohio and
Michigan, NFO marketing arrangements points sprang up as if by
magic. So rapidly did the marketing arrangements build volume and
channel this volume to cooperating packers that the drain out of the
usual channels became significant. Packers who had come to count on
production as a matter of course felt the same pinch they experienced during a holding action, except that now they felt it on a
continuing basis. The economists and the farm journals, through 1965,
applied the old formulas, and joined the time-honored litany that the
"social and economic mystery" of farming had again eluded them. With
a rare singleness of purpose, many refused to admit that NFO marketing arrangements had injected a new variable into the usual pricing
structure. It mattered not—because NFO members kept building volume and gaining new members because members averaged better
money at almost all NFO collection points.

The spot benefits of marketing arrangements accounted for added
$1.5 billion to farm income in 1965. Nothing less than lower world
commodity prices could erode that gain.

If the Meat Commodity Department could lay claim to broad spectrum gains, the same was not true in Herb Goodman's Grain Com-

modity Department.

NFO's grain program had always been geared to the proposition that harvest-time sales are distress sales, and that "in position" storage was mandatory if better prices were to be achieved now, bargained prices later. To this end, Goodman developed a more than modest program for "in position" storage, either on the farm or in commercial facilities. NFO farmers who entered the voluntary program remained free to state the sales period in which they required income and wanted their grain sold.

The grain program could thus deliver an advantage to NFO farmers, but no one could doubt that the Board of Trade was really in charge. Dealings in Chicago's pit wrote the prices on the surface, and in the subterranean passages there was the world price, which was in line with $35 gold. Former mining engineer, now farmer, now NFO Grain Commodity Department Director Herb Goodman could view the world of grain with disarming candor. It cost the American farmer on the average well-managed farm more money to produce a bushel of wheat than any other producer in the world, and yet the American support price—in line with $35 gold—was the lowest in the world. An engineer's calculations indicated that Goodman's grain farmers were being paid about half as much as their stuff was worth.

Accountably, the grain program at NFO had not taken on top stature simply because NFO had still to organize the big wheat country from Texas to Kansas to the central Dakotas, and therefore grain had a long way to go.

But NFO, in 1966, had solid organization in the dairy country. The pressure had been mounting for a dairy effort, but none had been forthcoming. There were several reasons.

milk in a rigged economy

NFO DAIRY COMMODITY DEPARTMENT DIRECTOR Albin Rust knew all the facts. One at a time he could run them up the flagpole, but before the end of 1966 not many in NFO were saluting.

Take the surplus bugbear. As a matter of fact, this country hasn't had a surplus since 1910. In other words, consumption has pretty well matched production. We process most of our grain through livestock, so when 15% of the red meat consumed in this country is imported, we have a dislocation. It takes seven pounds of raw feed to make one pound of red meat. We took horses off the farms, and this released production that once went for tractor fuel, so to speak, but we forget the variable. Production hasn't kept pace with the expansion of population in any area, but no one seems to look down the road by as much as a quarter of an hour.

Take milk. Farmers used to separate cream, and as late as 1940, 38% of the production was marketed that way. Now only 3% of the production is sold as cream, with the skim milk staying on the farm. As a matter of fact, dairy farmers increased their marketings some 20 billion pounds between 1950 and 1965 just that way.

Take milk equivalent. This means all the dairy production in terms of butterfat, regardless of whether it ends up as powder, whole milk or neufchatel. In 1965 this amounted to 120 billion pounds.

Take cows. We've lost 500,000 cows a year for the last decade. Sure, production per cow had gone up, and they think they can get the average production up to 10,000 pounds a year compared to the 8,080 right now. Maybe the Dairy Herd Improvement Associations can do that much. But you can't double and re-double production forever— not with hummingbirds, rabbits or Mexican jumping beans. And you're not going to start having calves in litters.

30

Take farms. We used to have over 2.6 million farms selling milk or cream as late as World War II. Now only 600,000 farms sell any milk or cream at all. We've watered the milk and stretched the supply. We crowded farmers with health regulations that are two inches thick in any community despite the fact that there hasn't been a milk-borne health problem in the country in ten years. The farmer picks up the tab. As recently as 1960, we had about 141,000 bulk tanks on farms. Now that's up to 217,000, according to American Dairy Review. The transportation is further. It's nothing to be 100 miles from market.

Take interstate shipment. Fifteen years ago there weren't even 175 certified shippers in 17 states. Now, there are 1,429 in 46 states and D.C. With Ike's Interstate superhighways, they can really burn up the cement shuttling milk back and forth. Maybe a spot holding action would have had a chance 15 years ago. Today it'll take an across the board effort.

1. efforts started with the co-ops

Marketing channels for milk and dairy products are complicated in the extreme. A farmer sells to a processor. This can be an independent business, a fluid milk co-op, a butter and cheese operation, or a combination thereof. The fluid milk processor overloads his "surplus" to a manufacturer, and the manufacturer can sell his butter, powder, cheese, or ice cream to a cake mix maker, wholesaler, chain store, or to CCC for export and PL 480 programs. No neat package encompasses the system. The farmer co-ops in Wisconsin and Minnesota overlap. The flluid milk co-ops around the cities buy and sell to manufacturing co-ops. Class 1 milk can become Class 2 and vice versa, in the twinkling of an eye.

NFO's Dairy Commodity Department efforts started with the dairy country co-ops. Rust put it this way.

It takes maybe $300,000 to capitalize a fairly good size bulk processing plant, a plant that can handle between 250,000 and 500,000 gallons of whole milk daily. Such a plant has to operate at about 50% capacity to stay in business and make a little money. On the other hand, this same plant can handle capacity production of 500,000 gallons with little or no extra out-of-pocket cost over and above the cost required to handle 250,000 gallons. Almost all plants are geared for high production, low per unit profit. Thus they need volume more than they need the dairy farmer in an inferior position. Many NFO mem-

bers, on their own initiative, have picked the plants to sell their milk that were willing to recognize the farmer's right to price his products.

The reason is simple. Suppose Plant X needs 250,000 gallons of milk a day to operate at a profit. It cannot alienate enough farmers to lose 50,000 gallon of that production, or it will be in the red.

NFO members, because they watch the marketing policies of their dairy processing plants, have taken on an importance undreamed of by co-op managers in less sophisticated days a few years ago.

When NFO signed its first milk plants, the charge was handed out that NFO was signing only marginal processors, plants without enough bulk milk a day, plants that would in time go broke. It was a very difficult charge to answer because, unfortunately, it was true. But many NFO members, on their own initiative, decided to sell to the signed plants because they apparently felt the signed plants were willing to recognize the right of the farmers to price their products. Today these plants are strong, moving ahead, helping write the ticket. The early signers made it necessary for others to sign. It is now evident that the last plants to seek NFO contracts will simply pass from the scene because the production will have already been sold when master contracts are activated.

The trouble was, attrition was whacking hell out of the farmers faster than it was bringing co-ops to terms. The 84 herds liquidated in Wisconsin each week meant that NFO was taking it in the neck because, obviously, some of those dairy farmers would be among the 2,500 farmers quitting altogether in the U.S. each week.

The NFO geared its master contracts to 60% of production. Contracts were written with plants on the basis that the instrument would be made operative when NFO had signed up 60% of the Class 1 (bottled) milk production, and 60% of the manufactured milk production in the 12 state area that has the lion's share of the nation's dairy production. These contracts were to be good indefinitely until activated for the purpose of naming a price. After that they were to run 12 months. After 12 months, bargaining with processors was again to take place.

2.   the theory was beautiful

The theory was beautiful. Accomplishment proved a bit more difficult.

"We'll be talking ten years from now," was the way Albin Rust put it, "if we rely on talk alone." Rust had wanted a milk holding action ever since 1964. He mentioned the idea while NFO leaders were in Washington to lend grass roots support to an REA re-financing bill in August 1966. During two days in the nation's capital, NFO leaders from several states heard Dr. Leon Keyserling detail the posture of American agriculture. Keyserling had been Harry Truman's economic chief, and he clearly recognized the foundation nature of agriculture, but somehow couldn't get himself to see that the problem was price.

Keyserling told the farmers to find their allies, which he said comprised 60% of the American people. "The farmer is being treated so miserably because we live in a rigged economy. The only way back is to change the rigging—and this makes it a fight for plain democracy and economic morality." Despite his obvious love for government programs, Keyserling told the NFOers that collective bargaining by producers of farm commodities "may ultimately be the only sound approach by the farmers." Keyserling was colorful that night. "If farmers try to go it alone, they will continue to eat the crumbs that fall from the table of those being luxuriously fed by the farmer. Those in charge will continue to do most for those who have most and least for those who have least."

The farmers thought long and hard about this injunction as they made their ways through the monoxide miasma that hung over the streets in Washington. They talked to each other about this curious relationship as they ran the gamut in the Congressional office buildings. At the hotels the first order of business for a visiting delegation: "Don't walk around after dark unless accompanied by someone else." Down the street a ways from the White House, the Potomac River glimmered in the moonlight, but in the white light of high noon Washington was dirty. Farmers in town from NFO counties U.S.A. could only comment on how inappropriate had become the lines, ". . . how you gonna keep em down on the farm after they've seen Paree. . ."

Bright lights were not luring the farm boys, but poor farm prices were making it impossible for them to stay. In the south the Negro was being expelled because the world commodity prices farmers had to live with were too low, and while the well-meaning might think of emancipation, no sociologist worthy of his salt considered this expulsion as other than a tragedy.

The lawns in water-short Washington were as burned out as a Kansas stubble field in August, and a few Washington-based ideas got singed the same way. Under Secretary of Agriculture John Schnittker appeared before some 400 NFOers in the big USDA Auditorium and assured everyone that the farmer was not the forgotten man, but rather "an uncommon man." When the questions got a little too sticky, Schnittker turned to Graceville, Minnesota farm wife Doris McElwain, who cut through the doubletalk like a ripsaw. It wasn't a "cookie" question, and Schnittker had a hard time explaining how government maneuvers to knock down farm prices squared with his "obvious concern." Schnittker agreed that the nation has never owed the farmer as much "as right now." Poor as the answer was, those in the audience nodded in agreement, possibly wishing that they could collect cash instead of accolades.

More important, NFOers learned that "working Washington" was equally as difficult as plowing the north 80. They learned, too, something about the wear and tear on cells and protoplasm when a man packs, hotels, unpacks, taxis, flies, busses, walks, walks, walks for hours on the hard marble floors of Capitol Hill. And they learned that a farmer stands as tall as any Congressman intellectually, but there was a damning futility about it all.

Some 40 years ago there was the farm bloc, 250 Congressmen from districts whose populations were at least 20% agricultural. Now the farm bloc had evaporated, four-fifths of its strength having been laid waste as low prices continued to gut agriculture, sending the farm population packing to the cities once and for all. "Having decided to quit farming . . . " read the crude letterpress flyers posted in filling stations and sales barns, and at the universities the Don Paarlberg and Earl Butz types talked of an "agricultural revolution" when in fact there was no economic mandate for the changeover at all, when in fact it was all a matter of the institutionally strong raping the institutionally weak.

["What do you want now?" a Cleveland-based Congressman came on when NFOer Frank E. Black walked in. "I'd never vote for anything you want. If you don't like it out there, why don't you move into the city? I buy nothing but Danish hams. You don't know how to raise hams and you don't know how to cook hams. We can import all the cheese, dairy and hams we want, and we don't need you farmers." "And to think," NFOer Ed Sasey said, "the man doesn't even have a guardian."]

It was one thing for a Keyserling to blueprint "telling the story," but telling the story wasn't accomplished with the wave of the hand, not by NFO or anyone else.

3.   the double standard

There were 1,754 daily newspapers in the United States at the start of 1967, decreasing in number and quality rapidly. Of these, only 452 had duly designated farm editors, the same as 1965. Total daily newspaper circulation was 61,407,252. Newspapers with farm editors had a total circulation of 20,112,000. It mattered not. They weren't and wouldn't tell the story. Men like Rod Turnbull of *The Kansas City Star* pandered to the big millers and traders who supported balderdash like the American Royal, of which he was president, where curly-hided critters were led into show rings like pug-nosed bitches at a dog show. And why not? The Hereford people had their pylon on Quality Hill— "the bull on a stick," Harry Truman once called it—where it served as anchorman for the Kansas City, St. Joseph, Omaha breed farce, setting the pace but not the profits for a badly bruised beef industry.

In Washington the adroit Council on Foreign Relations and Committee for Economic Development knew how to handle its public information job, just as it knew how to cozy up to whoever happened to be in power this year. If a base like Guantanamo was to be abandoned, you could bet your copper-core Kennedy half dollar that articles would appear in *This Week*, in the Luce publications (both the one for the people who can't read, and the one for the people who can't think), and others until the trial balloon either passed the length of the nation, or got shot down in shreds. The writers were usually clean as a whistle, and the trail lead to nowhere.

But what could farmers do. What could NFO do, not a full time writer on the staff, so young it had still to learn the ropes in which raw cash dominated, so green it had yet to learn that words are the artillery shells that have to hammer and discredit a prevailing system.

Albin Rust, dripping a little milk into his coffee at the Congressional Hotel in Washington, had read the double standard for years. Over at the Department of Health, Education and Welfare the *Report of Import Detentions* got pretty thick at times. The cheese may be full of fly eggs and maggots, mite infested, or full of insecticides or dieldrin, but imports would increase until a holding action forced them back.

Item: Colby Cheese, 170,240 lbs. Country of Origin, New Zealand. Manufactured by New Zealand Dairy Board, Wellington. Reason for detention: contains an unsafe pesticide chemical.

Item: Swiss Cheese and Gruyer Processed Cheese, 6,490 lbs. Country

of Origin, Switzerland. Manufactured by Weitifurrer International, Zurich. Reason for detention: unfit for food, Dimethyl Anilene present in product and containers.

But who the hell reads some 52 plus pages of detentions, or bothers about the ones that slip through? Who the hell bothers if it will keep a Wisconsin dairy farmer working for 37 cents an hour?

4. *as much sense as chinese music*

When Jean Nicolet first landed at Green Bay, Wisconsin in 1634 while seeking a Northwest Passage to China, he reportedly put on mandarin robes to greet the "Chinese." A lot of history has gone by the board in Wisconsin during the centuries since Nicolet failed to find the Chinese—including all the John R. Commons reforms, the foundation of the Republican Party, and the development of this nation's dairyland after Swiss immigrants arrived at Glarus in 1845. In almost every area of activity, Wisconsin is a gem of a state, a clean-cut entry in the spectacle of America on the march. In agriculture, Jean Nicolet would be more at home, because things today make about as much sense as Chinese music.

Wisconsin is still billed as America's dairyland. It might well be billed NFO's Dairyland. Together with Minnesota, the Badger state presumably holds the price-making potential on the nation's dairy products.

Dairying in Wisconsin came to the fore hardly a decade after the Civil War, when it was encouraged by men such as William D. Hoard. It was Hoard who helped organize the Wisconsin State Dairyman's Association in 1872, and figured in the development of the cooperatives. Today, a sizable share of all farm co-ops are in Wisconsin.

Recent statistics indicate that there are about 118,000 farms in the state. Not all farms figure in the dairy picture, still it is safe to say that dairy production predominates. So far there has been little vertical integration in the dairy field—at least not down to the primary production level. "Dairy production," says Albin Rust, "is a seven-days-a-week job, a labor of love, and a job you either will work your heart out at or won't do for any amount of money."

In an earlier era, the farmer turned to co-ops to process the production. In almost every town of any size, co-ops came into being. What happened was this. Farmers reached into their hip pockets and produced the money for initial organization and "borrowing power." When a farmer came up with, say, $100, he was given a share in the co-op. With enough $100 shares logged in, the co-op developed "borrowing power," and found willing ears at the tables of money lenders. Co-ops bought trucks and equipment and went into the manufactured milk business.

From early days to the present, the key to dairy processing has been transportation. Transportation killed the super-plant from the very beginning, and yet volume remains the key to higher prices and profits. There are several hundred dairy processing plants in Wisconsin alone. Fifty would do the job. In the big dairy areas there are 750 to 800 plants selling largely to nine buyers—Borden, Kraft, Sealtest, Beatrice Foods, Carnation, and companies of similar standing.

Initially, dairy co-ops were organized to do a job that the farmer needed done if he was to find markets for his production, and escape having to separate cream and waste or feed skim milk.

Each co-op was a separate selling unit. This pattern has continued largely because there has been no unifying force in the co-op movement. Competition between co-ops has been even more vicious than between co-ops and privately owned companies. The co-ops still perform a necessary function on the processing end but they divide farmers' bargaining power rather than unite it.

Presumably, farmers own the co-op, but this does not mean that farmers can serve their own interests through the co-op mechanism. Like John Kenneth Galbraith's technostructure, co-op managers tend to emulate the mature corporation and serve the power structure—that is, those in charge, not the farmers.

Sometimes, when farmers try to take over the real management of their own co-op, they are met by a suave-tongued lawyer from up the line a ways who springs *Roberts Rules of Order* at every point, and in general establishes an atmosphere of intimidation by adroit use of parliamentary procedures. Should a group of farmers break through and name a Board of Directors or officers to such a co-op, chances are there will be an error in the proceedings, and the election will be overturned upon appeal.

The logistics of how all this happened are not without interest. As the decision-making function passed from the hands of original managers, either through death or attrition, some co-ops became almost the personal property of business people who had only shallow feeling for the farmer. Slowly, by degrees, a part of the co-op structure be-

came stratified. Through organization and power structure manipulation, base co-ops suddenly found themselves under a ring of upper-
strata co-ops, with the Boards of Directors no more responsive to the
wishes of the base co-ops than co-ops had been to producing farmers.
In essence though not in form, local co-ops are in the same position
as member banks of the Federal Reserve System. Member banks are
allowed to pay the bill, but any real voice in money and financial management has somehow become *delegated* to those above, and there is
no way of getting it back.

The local co-op is helpless to affect price or even marketing potential under the present structure because it relies on so-called sales
associations to find markets. A local co-op that fails to "play ball" can
find that it has no place to sell. After all, most of the dairy production
in Wisconsin must move out of state because it cannot be consumed
locally.

Nor are things any different for the so-called independents. A dairy
plant like the one in Almena, Wisconsin, for instance, sells 99% of its
production to Borden, one of the dairy bigs. Obviously such a plant is
in no position to pay NFO a fair price because it would be out of
business within 24 hours. Sometimes farmers can't understand this.
Why couldn't Twin-Town pay the farmer the price and then recover
when selling to Borden? The small manufacturing plants couldn't—not
unless the dominating force among them, the co-ops, joined together
in an NFO-like structure called Agencies in Common. They could do
this legally under the Capper-Volstead Act, of course, but for some
reason manufacturing co-ops were dragging their heels.

The big Turtle Lake plant in Wisconsin is a co-op, but the Board of
Directors are all NFO members. Presumably these NFO Board members could give the farmers a raise, but again this would prove impossible unless the industry did the same, otherwise Turtle Lake would
lose its markets entirely, also within 24 hours.

Actually, the dairy bigs, the Bordens, Krafts, Arden-Mayfairs are in
the saddle, just as chain stores are in the saddle in setting red meat
prices. The price of cheddar is allegedly set on the Wisconsin Cheese
Exchange, which in effect means that parmesan, romano and the rest
are pegged in relation to cheddar, all in a half-hour trading session
each week, but a mature valuation of this enterprise suggests that the
Exchange serves merely to sanctify collusion, because anti-trust enforcement has been written off for all except those who have not yet
achieved its status. The Exchange sets the prices in terms of the world

market, as do all Exchanges, and in world trade goods flow to the high
market. The cheese flooding the American market was causing heart
attacks among second-strata processors, and peptic ulcers among
farmers.

5. *with or without maggots*

Import data being revealed in early 1967 was not just so much idle
NFO chatter. According to the National Milk Producers Federation,
which probably drew its data from the National Commission on Food
Marketing, imports increased 567% since 1953. During the 12 months
before farmers started dumping milk, imports jumped 433% over the
year before. USDA was estimating that more than 3½ billion pounds
of milk equivalent would be imported before 1967 had flown.

In 1953 a Presidential Proclamation had established quotas on dairy
imports. The figure 189 million pounds of milk equivalent in the form
of dairy products was jotted down as the annual ceiling. In kinder-
garten, two and two still make four, but not in some government
circles. As it happened, imports were already well above 189 million—
525 million pounds to be exact. "The ink on the proclamation was
scarcely dry before exporters abroad and importers at home quickly
discovered that import quotas were easy to circumvent without repri-
sals," a spokesman for NMPF said.

As a matter of fact, it was quite possible to import dairy products
of any kind in unlimited amounts. Any 4-H-er who ever rigged a
champion steer could have noodled it out.

There was the matter of splitting loaves of Italian type cheese.
The original restrictions had specified "original loaves," and so Italian
cheese started arriving in "split loaves." What's in a name, after all?

There was the matter of colby cheese. Colby is so close to cheddar
most people can't figure the difference, but for some reason colby
wasn't restricted in the original order. This slight legalistic oversight
proved to be an open sesame to colby, which could enter the country
at a rate ten times the volume established as a quota for cheddar.

Butter was limited to 707,000 pounds annually in the 1953 order,
but who has not heard of butter oil, a product previously not imported.
There was much to do about that, and after the bickering subsided
the U.S. Tariff Commission established an import quota on butterfat.
Score one for the importers. But it didn't end there.

The hard won butter oil quota restriction paved the way for more subtle evasion—the butterfat-sugar mixtures.

And there was Exylon, an item developed to replace cream in ice cream and make the cone taste like frozen sawdust. Domestic cream was being churned into butter for government lockup at low returns to farmer, but Exylon with or without maggots arrived in the Liberty ships the U.S. government practically gave away a few years ago. It all got to churning up a nasty storm, so, presto, the quota for Exylon was set at zero. To the layman this would seem a victory for the American farmer. It was not. Getting a quota set at zero was really a victory for the importers, because in the process they got a legal definition of the product as containing 45% or more butterfat. Once something is legally defined, the road is wide open for evasion.

It came in the form of Junex. Junex contained only 44% butterfat and 55% sugar. In the year before NFO farmers started dumping their milk, some 104.5 million pounds of this stuff were imported, making the earlier import evasions seem like row boat rum running. Even scratchpad arithmetic indicated that imports were hitting 12 times the officially authorized quotas.

But how do you tell this to people who have written off the farm as something obsolete, who have been told that corporations are the wave of the future when in fact agriculture is headed for the feudal system?

Foreign producers, particularly those in the Common Market, were enjoying their stabilized prices, and dumping their butter on the American market at prices as low as 20 cents per pound. And a handful of dairymen behind the Dairy Import Act of 1967 sounded like some self-serving yokels to the provincials in the suburbs.

6.　*he had it first*

If the need for a dramatic effort seemed silently evident, the deficits screamed from the housetop. The need was rather simple. *NFO Reporter* carried it in terms of average milk prices over a period of years for 3.5 milk.

20 GOOD REASONS FOR ACTION

1947	$4.27	1957	$4.21	1952	$4.85	1962	$4.10
1948	4.88	1958	4.13	1953	4.32	1963	4.11
1949	3.95	1959	4.16	1954	3.97	1964	4.16
1950	3.98	1960	4.21	1955	4.01	1965	4.24
1951	4.58	1961	4.22	1956	4.14	1966	?

In the aggregate, or on an individual plane, the answer turned up the same. The Southern Minnesota Vocational Agriculture Farm Management program developed its records in terms of prices per pound of butterfat in milk sold, and therefore it included the price of skim milk. Over a five year period the figures read as follows: 1961, .96 cents; 1962, 93 cents; 1963, 92 cents; 1964, 93 cents; and 1965, 95 cents. At the same time the feed costs per cow were, less than static: 1961, $160; 1962, $175; 1963, $187; 1964, $184 and in 1965 the cost per cow reached a new high—$221.

The deficits came on in an ear-shattering crescendo. It takes about 100 hours of labor per year to keep a dairy cow in production. In a holding action the costs would go on and the labor would continue to be exacted, like a pound of flesh. In a day or two the cooler would be full. Assuming a farmer owned 240 acres and had a dairy herd of 25 cows, every day he would be required to dump $45 worth of milk. He couldn't turn the cows off, so he would have to spend money for feed—possibly $12 a day.

He would have an average investment of $28,000 in land, $9,000 in livestock, and $5,000 in equipment. He might have grossed $17,500 the year before, but his net profit—after paying out money for feed, repairs, breeding, veterinary service, testing, milk hauling, insurance, taxes, help—would be about $2,400, poor pay indeed, and likely as not this would be accomplished only after exploiting the labor of the wife and kids. Getting bigger was no solution at all, because the investment and operating costs would go up, and the advantage enjoyed by exploiting the kids would evaporate, because hired help doesn't exploit so easily.

The NFO Dairy Department knew that a milk holding action would make pale into insignificance the costs of a meat holding action.

All the factors in economics were running against the milk holding action, except one. The farmer had the milk, and he had it first. There was less than 24 hours of fresh milk in the supply pipeline, hardly a month or two of powder, calculated in terms of normal consumption.

The NFO holds its annual conventions in December, and in December 1966 the conclave had been scheduled for Milwaukee, the heart of the dairy country.

It had been a quiet summer and a quiet fall at Corning, Iowa. From all outward appearances NFO had become a dormant organization. But as convention time approached, little rivulets started running. By the time they spilled into the yawning oval of Milwaukee's giant arena, it was a foregone conclusion that a milk holding action would be approved by the delegates. NFO had had some signal success in this area. In Michigan the price had been driven up, and not enough milk could be spilled into Michigan from Ohio and surrounding areas to drive it down again. This was only temporary. No one figured these prices could be maintained over the long haul unless the general price level was given a shot in the arm.

Delegates jumped to their feet and sent a booming response into the delicate microphones when President Staley called for a vote. The resolution adopted by the convention read, in part, as follows: *"To raise the general price level of raw milk and secure same by contracts; which would necessitate a marketing agency in common for the good and security of the dairy processing industry; to insure an ample supply of dairy products to the American consumer at reasonable prices. Be it further resolved that NFO urge all members to hold their production on the farm and non-members to join NFO and hold to achieve these goals."*

The vote came late in the convention. The story the holding action was to hammer out started being told before that. It came to the fore when Staley and Rust both called attention to the shrinking dairy herds and the real danger that the milk shortage—being covered up with imports—would attain disastrous proportions if dairy farmers did not make a stand for higher prices and contracts immediately. The target prices were stressed: $6.05 for Class 1 and $5.00 for manufactured milk.

7. *the short end of the stick*

Even before the vote was taken, NFO was busily finding its allies. Number 1 was the American housewife. NFO Vice President Erhard Pfingsten used *Economic Indicator* to inform the delegates that farm income figures were largely fictional. Pfingsten noted, "The housewife of this nation is very, very fair if she's given the opportunity to know the facts."

She is. Mrs. Rose West of Denver, the acknowledged catalyst in the housewife movement, knew something was wrong. A jar of olives would double in a week or two at the store. Riding hard on the journalism of *Cervi's Rocky Mountain Journal* she had tilted with the chains. The battle got hot. In a few days even chain store ad carriers such at *The Denver Post* and *The Rocky Mountain News* had been forced to put reporters on the story.

Louis Hessler, an NFOer out of dryland territory near Wiggins, Colorado had made contact with the housewives. It was not long before Butch Swaim was sending bundles of information to the ladies who were raising hell with the chains. As new housewife groups were formed, they usually contacted Denver. As a result the housewife movement never jumped on the farmer's back. Mrs. Rose West had come to Milwaukee to agree that farmers had gotten the short end of the stick.

Her's was a pragmatic observation. NFO Vice President Pfingsten dumped the whole bundle.

First, agriculture as it stands today has an investment of $231 billion. For that $231 billion, a total of $14 billion was all agriculture received for both investment and labor. In this same year, the corporations of this nation, as represented in the ECONOMIC INDICATOR, *had an investment of a little over $300 billion, roughly between one-third and one-fourth more than agriculture. Yet these corporations, with just one-third more invested, turned a profit of $80 billion. Had the American farmer been paid at exactly the same rate of profit as these corporations, then the farmer should have had more than twice as much profit as his gross income turned out to be. He should have been paid $2.64 for his work in addition to that, because, keep in mind, the corporations had paid their labor bill before their profits were figured.*

Now let me give you another figure. It is estimated that corporation profits this year will be $87 billion. In two year's time, they increased their profits more than the American farmer receives in total, even with padded figures given. So I would say that if this nation is foolish enough to let the family-type farm be destroyed, farm prices to pay the same profits that corporations are getting now, will have to go up four times higher than they are today.

The housewives had better start to think what will happen when that takes place. If the American farmer were to be paid at the same rate of wage per hour as corporations paid, the labor bill alone would be $48 billion—$8 billion more than all the production in the U. S. brought today, and this does not count one single penny for the investment, and money for one single gallon of gasoline, or seed, or fertilizer. It's serious and it has to be prevented, and there's only one group that's seriously working at doing it—the NFO.

So spoke Pfingsten.

Viewed from the big front office at Corning, the growth of NFO suggested an approaching "high noon." But the Board of Directors knew in fact that midnight was drawing near for American agriculture.

The farm population was over 53 years of age. To the question, "Who will do the farming," Under Secretary of Agriculture John Schnittker had told a reporter at the Iowa NFO convention in Des Moines: "We'll bring them out from the city," and when reminded that a man named Castro had done that, John Schnittker refused to discuss the remark any more.

NFO could walk with fair-weather friends and sunshine patriots just as long as 'the organization made no move to succeed. Mused Pfingsten: *Maintain a dainty, correct approach, and every platform speaker in the country wishes you well. But pious platitudes and well wishing got the farmer nothing.*

"Do ideas have the power to affect the actual course of events merely by virtue of being true?" This question, posed by Clarence Ayres in the closing chapters of *Theory of Economic Progress* strikes terribly close to the heart of NFO during the hour of decision. Clearly, it seemed somewhat unsatisfactory to wait for the eventual triumph of truth when all around it could be demonstrated that the family farm won't be around eventually if the institutional arrangements of the hour went unchallenged. From the very beginning, from the day a feed salesman and an Iowa farmer talked about a national farmers organization, NFO has seen that waiting for the eventual triumph of truth and justice was uncomfortably like letting someone else do the fighting.

At Milwaukee, in convention, NFO chose to do its own fighting. The organization was promptly called militant, but the NFO member saw it as the militancy of a Loyola setting out with a handful of followers to reclaim Europe, a militancy that fought with ideas, with ethics, with conviction and with economics.

Nor did NFO members expect such a scope of operation to be appreciated by "those massive interests that move in the background, finding a profit in buying cheap and selling dear." The rank and file expected their organization to become the target of analysis, shallow analysis delving in personalities, trivia and the pre-judged conviction that NFO had bitten off more than it could chew, that in the end all of NFO's social criticism and work and accomplishment would have spent itself, leaving the old way of marketing and farmer exploitation still in command of the field.

as zero hour neared

THERE ARE 46.5 quarts of milk in a hundredweight. While some cows produce up to 30,000 pounds of milk annually, the national average is 8,080 pounds. The average tank truck carries about 50,000 pounds, roughly about 25,000 quarts. Thus 500 cows slaughtered, if they are average producers, account for 4 million pounds. In a given milk-shed, this may not be a large percentage of the total on a spot calculation, but a slaughtered cow does not withhold milk just a year, but from now on, and translates this non-existence to the calf that henceforth will not exist.

These are simple facts any high school student can understand. In formal economics, however, the first order of business is not to gather essential facts, but to coin a term.

The term of standing in dairy economics is "third degree price discrimination." The milk industry is an example of an industry where this device has been used as a basis for pricing policy. The application of third degree price discrimination works this way. The fluid milk market provides the inelastic primary market, and the manufactured products end of the dairy business—powder, cheese, evaporated milk —provide the elastic secondary market.

As worked out in Marshallian models, third degree price discrimination has accounted for one of those troublesome fictions, the Class 1 milk price, which is a dollar higher than the Class 2 price. In fact, there is no such thing. Farmers are paid a blend price. Their check varies according to the percentage of milk a certain plant used for the bottle trade, and the percent they sent out or used for manu-factured products. As usual, farmers have no audit rights.

The formal economic literature has always stated the case in terms of this model, and the troublesome realities have been abstracted

45

away. Indeed, up to the publication of *Demand, Supply, and Price Relationships for the Dairy Sector, Post-World War II Period**, in the *Journal of Farm Economics,* simultaneous equation estimates of demand and supplies had not been reported in a single study, not that it made much difference. Annual supplies had been assumed, and while the neat rows of formulas provided mute testimony to scholarship, they had nothing to do with the world in which farmers milked cows.

Oren Lee Staley, pouring over *Agricultural Statistics,* could pinpoint cow herds by counties, and this was helpful, but the erudition from the Agriculture Experiment Stations that came under titles such as *Equilibrium Analysis of Income-Improving Adjustments on Farms in the Lake States Dairy Region, 1965,* or the Fuller and Martin presentation, *The Effects of Autocorrelated Errors on the Statistical Estimation of Distributed Lag Models,* indicated that Clarence Ayres was right when he accused economists of hiding behind the complexities of their trade, behind scholasticism, the "last stage in the decay of the simple and obvious system" Adam Smith had lectured about.

1. *market orders*

The neat rows of formulas contained no entry for the fact that the Agricultural Act of 1949, now amended, requires the Secretary of Agriculture to set the minimum price for milk each year, starting April 1. Nor do they mention that as of January 1, 1966, there were 74 federal milk marketing orders, each charged with setting minimum farm prices for milk. In simple terms, these orders were set up to require dealers to pay a fair price to producers so that the average well managed farm could operate without consuming its capital or going broke, and also to assure a continuing wholesome milk supply.

---

*In the "Demand, Supply and Price Relationship," etc., article by Robert R. Wilson and Russell G. Thompson, cited above, the model was developed to explain the connection between the price the farmer got and the price tag at the grocery store. Variables ran from X_1 to X_{13}, and from Z_1 to Z_{17} (sample: X_1 is the number of milk cows on farms, ten million head; X_3 is the yield of milk per cow, 10,000 pound units; X_4 is the supply of milk produced.) With financial assistance and computer time from the University of Missouri, the writers were able to develop humdinger formulas (Item: Supply of milk in milk equivalent units is: $X_4 = X_1 \cdot X_3$) as well as other findings from the number of milk cows to the supply-demand identity in milk equivalent units, 13 formulas, each dazzling, except that none of them explained what maggot-infested milk from Italy was doing to the Wisconsin dairyman, and how prices were being set by institutions, over which the farmer had no control.

Presumably, order areas were set up by market size. Thus a 60 million pound area like Chicago or Boston was never averaged and calculated on the same basis as a five million pound area such as St. Joseph or Fort Smith. At any given moment in time, it would have taken only a stroke of a pen for marketing orders to give farmers the price they had to have to keep from posting their "Having decided to quit farming" posters.

Calculating the cost of production on the average well managed farm has never been much of a problem. NFO once ladled out several thousand dollars to Doane Agriculture Service for such a study, both for the pasture system and for the drylot system. The average herd and the average production in terms of 3.5% fat corrected milk had been calculated. In the study, costs varied from state to state, sometimes as much as a dollar per hundredweight, but the fact remained that nowhere were marketing orders setting prices anywhere near the cost of production.

In terms of the Doane findings, NFO's $6.05 target price for Class 1 stacked up as modest indeed. Failure to achieve a target price was making it necessary for farmers to work 1½ days a week for nothing, or one week out of each month for nothing, or three months of each year for nothing.

If what NFO was attempting looked gargantuan, the chances for success still rated well above what the average dairy farmer could hope for himself if he continued with the working arrangements that a complex marketing system required in early 1967.

When the delegates in Milwaukee voted for a hold on milk, they hoped for short action, and a quick one. They knew that the spring to June flush season lay hard ahead, and after that farmers would be working the field. At the same time, the next fall was too far away. Farmers simply couldn't be made to endure the seasonal declines in prices that would be hung around their necks no later than April 1. A breakthrough, or at least a standoff, had to be made now. The professors in the colleges would yammer about consumers switching to oleo and other substitutes, but NFO knew that a dairy victory would mean grain farmers would be hard on their heels in doing the same for soybeans, the intercommodity staple that was kicking butter into an economic cellar.

The natural problems of a holding action were big enough. Others were to come. Hardly had the convention ended before Staley was "called to Washington." NFO Attorney Lee Sinclair, Pfingsten and

Staley attended the interview in the Justice Department. After the usual "anything that you say may be used against you," the NFOers were handed a clipping from *The Wall Street Journal*. It told about how the holding action resolution had passed the appropriate Committee. The story itself had been published before the delegates had ratified the Committee's judgment in convention. It was on the basis of this clipping that NFO had been contacted, the Justice attorneys said. They did not mention telephone calls from USDA or other powerhouse areas in government.

As a former government attorney, Sinclair knew that usually it took several weeks before a development was brought to the attention of the Justice Department. Someone very influential was bird-dogging the intimidation that government people were about to try out on NFO.

The interview was polite, and came couched in the language of diplomacy, but out in the country farmers soon came to know that "they read Staley the riot act." They had in fact done just that. Staley would be held personally responsible for any violence or agreements with NFO allies. Anything that had ever happened in any of the holding actions would be laid at Staley's feet, the NFO chief was told. Staley, Pfingsten and Sinclair could hardly believe what they heard. Whether diplomatic or not, the tone of this intimidation could not go unanswered. Staley said that while he wasn't anxious to be a martyr, his first obligation as President of NFO was to give the farmer the opportunity to achieve fair prices under the provisions of the Capper-Volstead Act of 1922 as authorized by the Congress of the United States, and he was going to do just that.

It got pretty quiet in Justice that day, and the conversations ended with Staley's stand. But by the time the NFO trio had emerged from the briefings, the time-table for the holding action had already been delivered a blow in the solar-plexus.

It was a cruel, lonely decision—that one made in Corning in late December. In Washington, NFO counsel Lee Sinclair was giving himself a quick refresher in anti-trust law, despite the fact that he had served Packers and Stockyards Division as counsel, and was rated as one of the best anti-trust counsels in the business. The pressure was on from the highest echelon. Despite a mandate from the membership, NFO leaders were being pushed to "call it all off."

This NFO could not do. Farmers needed gains fast. Ideally, the action should have been "go" tomorrow. But this was clearly impossible, since organization and now the strictures imposed by federal edict had NFO trussed up like Batman on Thursday night. Really, there was only one way to run, the NFO leaders decided. They had to comply with the necessary groundwork, and they had to do it as rapidly as possible.

2. *the squealing force would be out*

It was breakneck work during the next two months. Even explaining the convention mandate required some doing. Not everyone understood what NFO meant by asking for $6.05 a hundredweight for Class 1, and $5.00 per hundredweight for manufactured milk based on the Wisconsin-Minnesota series. The series itself was developed by USDA in 1960 to represent the average price being paid for Class 2 milk, f.o.b. at the plant, based on a controlled sample of plants in the two big dairy states. Although NFO really wanted $1.00 a hundredweight raise across the board, there was always the letter or the long-distance call which explained, "But we're already getting this in our area." "Our area" was probably Michigan, or Oklahoma or Florida, but it wasn't many places in NFO country. Finally a common denominator emerged: two cents a quart. Two cents a quart times 46.5 quarts in a hundredweight wasn't exactly the same as another dollar a hundredweight, but it was close enough. During the next two months, Albin Rust followed the most grueling schedule since joining NFO. He spoke a rote speech and was careful to avoid giving anyone the idea that he was kidding.

"We can legally hold milk for a price and contracts. But our actions must be kept in the legal area where they can be protected."

The words weren't Rust's, but he spoke them. They had been hammered out by the lawyers in Washington, and were designed to do exactly what they said. In each meeting and in a great wave of meetings presided over by Rust or his associates, this message was reiterated until NFO almost choked on it. It wasn't easy for men who like colorful language to talk like mortgage holders in western movies, but they did.

Oras Kanerva, a National Director who also worked with the Dairy Commodity Department, was possibly the most colorful phrase maker in NFO, if Pfingsten be excepted. Born in Minnesota, he had completed high school in Finland, and returned to America for a farming career. He had tried the "other farm organizations" and jumped on the NFO ticket because the organization thought in terms of causes, not effects. Kanerva was busily buttoning up the meetings in northern Minnesota during the weeks between the national convention and the first day of the holding action, using stilted language when his own would have been more colorful, albeit less legal.

Allen Nunnenkamp's Yul Brenner head was recognized throughout NFO as one of the most knowledgeable. While he swept through the Kansas-Nebraska areas, his wife manned the milking parlor at the farm near Altoona, Kansas. Delbert Riley gave the rote readings throughout Missouri. Up in Michigan Ray Nielson recited the rules of the game. Through much of the Ohio, Pennsylvania area, Al Herman, an ex-Director from Ohio, performed the droll chore. And in New York, Guy Lewis did the talking. But the big Pure Milk Association territory of Chicago was considered Rust's personal property, just as every tough nut ended up on the plank desk Rust spent so little time behind these days.

Meeting with groups twice a day, and running on inadequate sleep each night, Rust and his associates fairly covered the milksheds—from Pennsylvania to Colorado, from Kansas to the Canadian lines. The message was always the same, a veritable recording so definitive in its language and phraseology that to report one meeting was to report them all.

"In collective bargaining," Rust and his associates told audience after audience, "farmers must abide by laws—fair trade acts, and regulatory acts. You as farmers must look upon yourselves as business groups and you must abide by the laws."

The laws were clear-cut, and the NFO leaders were making sure that ignorance of the laws would not undo the progress that a milk holding action could account for.

Almost reciting a litany, Rust's men told the farmers—

• Your local organization or members cannot talk to truckers asking their support, because that would be collusion between a bargaining unit and truckers.

• You cannot as county units pass a motion to have anyone visit with anyone in search of support for the holding action.

"If a holding action is won on this basis," Rust said, "the laws will chop down any of our gains."

Rust always called attention to the fact that during a holding action "people who should help the farmer will be fighting you." He reminded the farmers that those opposed to farmers gaining a fair price for their production would have field men out, "and they will be picking up firsthand information. I cannot stress too strongly that the NFO leadership will countenance no illegal actions. We can win this thing well within the law, and we can keep the gains we make."

Two groups would be fighting NFO, *Kiplinger's Farm Letter* was reporting.

The NFO holding action had already signaled a head-on clash with USDA and with milk marketing orders. The NFO bid for $6.05 on Class 1 was in open war with supports and marketing order guidelines (based on the Wisconsin-Minnesota series). Also, the NFO program would inevitably clash with the government's policy of keeping the economic kite flying by depressing raw material and food prices.

Rust commented: "Some co-op dairy marketing groups still do not understand that the NFO plan does not attack or weaken the co-op marketing structure, but strengthens it. Unless NFO teams can educate the leaders of these co-ops and convince them that they have as much at stake in fair prices for farmers as do farmers themselves some co-ops may battle NFO."

Also, certain observations had become evident. With or without conversation between NFO committees and truckers, the plain fact was that most milk haulers were tired of touring the country roads for nothing. Almost all would be on the farmers' side. If truckers, if other farm groups—acting on their own—decided to hold at the same time NFO was holding, well, that was their business! If members of another association voted to lend their voice to the NFO effort, even though some of the members of that association were NFO members, no Judge could consider it collusion under the law.

"But you can't get two groups together," Rust said. "There can be no joint meetings."

Thus out of Washington by way of the Justice Department, by way of Staley, by way of the lawyers, by way of the Dairy Commodity Department, NFO members learned that individually they could ask a non-member "to join NFO and support the NFO effort." "Make join every other word, and the NFO effort will never be endangered because of one individual talking to another individual. Just simply tell non-members NFO cannot advise them unless they join the NFO."

Across the many states, NFO members knew the squealing force would be out. They knew that there could be no violations of the law.

3. *delusion of the simple-minded*

The rumble that had been uncorked started getting registered here and there. An astute observer, even without the front door to the Corning office, might have followed any of Albin Rust's boys in the field. Al Herman had been conducting milk holding rallies throughout Order No. 2 territory in New York and New Jersey milksheds. In all his meetings, Herman repeated the prescribed litany about the law, gathering in the old dedicated zeal only when telling dairymen that the success of the milk holding action depended on preparation. Running 18 to 20 hours a day in early March, Al Herman ranged not only across New England, but turned up in Michigan as well. At Fowlerville High School in a town of the same name, Al injected as much fire as his tired tissues allowed as he covered the full scope of the NFO story. This was not a dairy meeting, but dairy had to be part of any meeting these days.

As Al talked, each premise fell into place, and the syllogism took form. *Chain stores and processors have brought about a managed economy in which farmers, acting as individuals in the marketplace, do not have the power they need for bargaining.* Herman used a blackboard that night to list the cases of government figure dumping, cases in which the government projected crops that were still to grow with the certainty that the extra bushels would disappear later on into the thin air from which they came, all after farmers had been paid low prices because there was a surplus. The farmers listened and nodded knowingly. They knew they were being defrauded at every turn.

Those attending the banquet sponsored jointly by the Livingston and Ingham County NFO chapters heard more economics in a couple of hours that night than most tax supported professors could turn out in five years. It was a rapid fire short course in both institutional economics and a sound refutation of the economic structure Karl Marx had called "classical." Herman was probably unaware of all this academic folderol. He was speaking from the heart, and he struck at the heart of the matter.

"In 1960," he said, "we approached the dairy co-ops, suggesting that they had all the power they needed to go after fair prices for milk producers. NFO had meat and grain bargaining units set up, but felt that the co-ops should do the job for milk. The co-ops did not respond. They continued to fight among themselves about who was to retain power, and who would have prestige. Meanwhile their members, upon which all else depends, are being paid on the average eight cents a hundred less than they got in 1949-1951."

"Impartiality is either a delusion of the simple-minded, a banner of the opportunist, or the boast of the dishonest," wrote Gaetano Salvemini. "Nobody is entitled to be unbiased toward truth or false-hood." This perfectly sound advice, possibly unknown to Reverend Harry E. Boyer, the Lutheran Pastor in Fowlerville, Michigan, did not keep at least this one man of the cloth from worrying more about what might be than about what is.

"Can you in NFO assure that your leadership will not get fat and rich off the members, as we see in so many other such organiza-tions today?" the good Reverend wanted to know. It was a question that caused the big banquet room to faintly crackle with hostility. Al Herman welcomed the question and answered it, but somehow not a few of the farmers present knew that this was one of the real trouble spots. The American public and those who shaped its public policy, never drew any issue as sharply as a dead issue. Tweedledum and tweedledee always accounted for the most violent altercations. With two-thirds of agriculture being gutted, with social problems being manufactured faster than wars on poverty could cope with them, the good Reverend Boyer had time to worry about whether a few farmers turned farm leaders might dip in the till. Later that night dairyman Bruno Budzek could play old piano favorites, but the crowd obviously reflected on the seriousness of Al Herman's message and the cloud of doubt that Reverend Boyer's concern provided.

4. *language of the court*

As late as March 1, some of the slick farm magazines were still speculating about whether there would be a holding action after all. But at the curd and whey level all doubts had vanished 30 days ago. Scraps of information were being filtered, and the razzle-dazzle of meetings in out-of-the-way places like Howell, Michigan with terse statements had uninitiated reporters wondering, because uninitiated reporters had very little idea of what it was all about anyway. William Mahaffey could talk about a "dynamic new approach," but this was the quickly concocted cow selloff program Corning had released in its leaders letters a scant few weeks earlier, and those looking for a milk holding action were quite confused.

Up in New York Dave Carrig of Herkimer County was in motion with the same cow selloff program, as were NFO members everywhere. Catching cadence and verse from NFO directives, Carrig told the *Cobleskill Times Journal* that the move was being undertaken to "bring supply and demand into more equal balance." It was a credo NFO regulars were to repeat with increasing regularity as the days rolled by. George Demeree, a Little Falls, New York dairy farmer probably nailed it closer when he said what every farmer in Herkimer, Montgomery, Fulton, Albany, Otsego, St. Lawrence and Jefferson counties was thinking: even with a rigged parity, producers were getting hardly 74% of what their stuff was worth.

Demeree was right. And a few economists, if they bothered, knew about it. But in the main, the American public had no more idea about farm parity than about who rated recognition as the eighth avatar of Vishnu.

During one sample week, NFO farmers across the country sold more than 15,000 bred sows. Cow sales were held at 50 collection points, and were averaging about 12,000 cows a week. One of the high points was logged in at North Central Service, Inc., a livestock sales outfit at Stetsonville, Wisconsin which then shifted the meat to Green Bay.

In the official statements, Oren Lee Staley said, "When we reach a given point we will say we've gone a certain percentage of the way and it's up to the non-members to go the rest of the way. We're not foolish enough to sell off all our basic stock to get them a price."

This was a Staley euphemism at its best. It was never meant to communicate anything to the press or the public, and it didn't. It was actually couched in the language of the court that held sway in Washington, and it delivered its message. USDA knew the background. Farmers were angry and determined. Those who dabbled in history saw them as the angriest ever, and NFO wanted to point out that they were not leaderless. Insiders at USDA knew, even if the public did not, that NFO leaders understood history. They understood that farmers had to *follow* if the milk holding action was to be successful. The fact that NFO members closed ranks behind the sow and cow selloff program set the current boiling. The temperature ran high. At Corning, there was no doubt that farmers would support the milk holding action as they had never supported a holding action before.

Long before March 1, the other holding actions had been put under the magnifying glass, each weakness logged in, each point of strength analyzed. It would be a massive error in judgment to think that NFO had entirely abandoned the idea that one day farmers—pressured beyond endurance—would respond, join and heave over the top a well planned holding action.

Thus the sow and cow selloffs in February and March were more than calculated reductions in pounds of pork and cattle production. They were probes to measure how fed up farmers really were, and they were communications to the powers that be, telling them that farmers were not leaderless and that it was brinkmanship in the worst form to allow 17 cent hog prices to prevail much longer, or milk price to continue without adjustments upward.

The NFO wasn't bluffing. The organization had over 250 seasoned topnotch platform speakers who could command vast audiences simply by staging meetings. Another 2,500 grass roots leaders were standing in the wings, all of them informed and capable speakers. Hardly a month earlier, farm leaders from the several organizations had been called to Washington, and the anger they registered at that meeting prompted the street walkers for the Chamber of Commerce to say hardly a word.

In the Dakotas and Kansas, the Farmers Union was dabbling with a "stop buying program," one that hammered home farmer discontent. In Kansas farmers were talking about a "plow-under" campaign, an approach that was seconded in the Dakotas where farmers were registering their intent not to plant new acreage allotments at all.

Thus there was no way of telling whether farmers might not catch up the sow and cow selloff program and make it their own. With hog and beef prices what they were, it might be speculated that NFO missed its mark by communicating too well with Washington and not well enough with non-member farmers. The same thing was not to happen in the milk holding action. Speaking editorially as early as December 1966, the *NFO Reporter* had told members that "It is a matter of high public duty that NFO is contemplating a holding action on milk . . . NFO farmers can bring the matter of ruinously low prices to a head in a matter of days if they act in unison."

NFO activity was churning in every direction, and members were working together as never before. Herb Goodman's Grain Commodity Department seemed almost lost in the shuffle as the milk action neared. Still, the action was to be a total effort, one that called on the entire NFO team. Across the organized states, Grain Commodity Department people were busily ramrodding a CROP grain movement, and seizing the opportunity to drum up NFO support.

The Community Food Appeal of the Church World Service, with the help of NFO, had arranged to have 70 elevators in 16 states receive grain for world relief during the first week of March, but so overwhelming had NFO's selloff programs and imminent milk holding action become that CROP hardly rated mention in NFO circles. There was to be a great deal of misunderstanding about NFO's cooperation with relief agencies, especially after it became apparent to the nation that milk was being dumped, but the records clearly indicate that NFO almost alone among farm groups had helped world relief.

5. *square wheel wagon*

Before March 1, the tempo of NFO activity had taken a new turn. The Michigan Milk Producers Association's receiving plant at Imlay City was one of the early anointed ones for "getting the message" via demonstrations. The procession was orderly. Ray Auvil, an NFO regular, was on hand to explain in ever-so-simple terms: "Dairy farmers are going out of business and herds are being sold because there is no profit in dairy farming." All MMPA had to offer was stoney silence.

The Imlay City demonstration, nevertheless, turned out to be impressive, and as papers picked it up and gave it coverage, it became clear that MMPA had to do something about it. Finally, in the monthly house magazine, MMPA printed a letter sent to Ethan E. Smith, who had asked MMPA to meet with NFO. The letter relied on the lawyer's device of clouding the issue, which in this case included asking questions that NFO would not answer as a matter of policy, chiefly one about how big the NFO membership was. MMPA correctly claimed that Michigan prices were above the prices being paid in neighboring milksheds, but no mention was made of the famous "Square Wheel Wagon" editorial in which NFO was castigated for suggesting that milk could ever be what it was now for Michigan farmers, an editorial once lavishly applauded by MMPA.

The experts could analyze it any way they liked, but for the average farmer on the picket line, NFO regular Robert J. Campbell spoke sense. "The reason for this demonstration is because MMPA has, an yet, refused to negotiate a contract. They are locking the doors to the NFO and the press, as happened before. I am personally tired of working for less than the minimum wage. I'm presently working for about 50 cents an hour." In the manner of the guard halting Caesar, Harold Hill, the local MMPA manager said he was "doing his duty" in keeping the doors locked, but outside the NFO farmers must have reasoned, as did Caesar in Shaw's *Caesar and Cleopatra*, that when small men do what they're ashamed of, it's always their duty.

Almost simultaneously, the price of Class 1 milk in the St. Louis marketing area dropped 31 cents a hundredweight. Outside two St. Louis milk plants—Sealtest and Sanitary Milk Producers—NFO farmers mounted hand lettered signs: "HAVE COW WILL MILK, BUT NOT FOR LESS," "If you don't get milk, Don't Blame Us, Blame Processors," "Handlers, Let's Make a Milk Deal. NFO." The dairies were not very receptive to talk. "Tell it to USDA," they in effect told Richard Rhine, the local NFO spokesman.

In Milwaukee, Borden drew pickets. NFO members wanted discussions. But, always, there was the brushoff. The brushoff came in various forms.

At Louisville, Kentucky, the three-man delegation to Kyana Milk Producers Association was received cooly by General Manager Burdette L. Fisher. Fisher said he'd relay the request for a meeting to the Board of Directors "without recommendation." Outside, possibly 1,000 NFO members waited patiently. When Pulaski County NFO Chairman Jack Hamilton spoke, he called the demonstration "just a step around the corner from a holding action." It was, in every respect, in time, distance and participation.

Almost on signal, editors across the country started dragging out their choice terms. Farmers were "disgruntled." They were "militant." They were "ridiculous."

In New York, the *Watertown Times* ran an article entitled, "Dairy Farmers Plotting 'Take It or Leave It' Edict on Milk Prices." In the main it was prophetic in uncorking a new dimension, one that was to prevail in the months to come. There was a time when any professor or editorialist would say almost anything on agriculture with impunity. That day had vanished, just as it vanished when Vernon Mullen of Gouverneur demolished the premise that farmers were gouging the public. Mullen simply quoted USDA figures: These figures revealed that farmers with capital invested to the tune of

$43,000 earned 37 cents an hour after figuring a modest return on investment. The 37 cents an hour was to become a battle cry during the holding action.

Those who demonstrated in front of the Miami Valley Milk Producers plant in Dayton, Ohio were charged as being "not dairy farmers shipping to the Dayton-Springfield market." Even the eggheads got into the act.

At Eau Claire, Wisconsin, an assistant chancellor of the University of Wisconsin characterized NFO activity as "senseless." It was a safe statement because Dr. Henry Ahlgred was speaking before the annual American Dairy Association of Wisconsin at the time. The executives in their Brooks Brothers suits could easily applaud such statements, and the one that followed: "We should be phasing government programs out and moving into a free economy. This is the trend. We are moving in that direction and should as fast as we can without disrupting agriculture."

Unfortunately the innane statements of professors sometimes become the pabulum for the nation's intellectual diet. Those in the rarefied atmosphere of big time management know better. As a matter of fact, NFO's suggestion to the dairy co-ops that they get together into an Agency in Common had scored points. According to the word that floated in and around the dairy business hardly a week before NFO called its holding action, a Chicago-based executive had said— *Considering the present situation with Borden, Kraft and the rest, anything more than one co-op for the country is one too many.*

But getting dairy co-ops to join together in an agency in common proved to be almost as difficult as bringing farmers together under one roof. There was, of course, the government. As early as March 4, eight dairy co-ops, representing most of the northern Illinois and southern Wisconsin fluid milk supply hadn't shared the good chancellor's prognosis. They had petitioned the USDA to conduct a hearing on a jointly made proposal to re-establish a federal milk order for Chicago which could combine the Milwaukee, Madison and Rock River Valley orders into one. The hearing had been requested jointly by Pure Milk Association, a Chicago-based co-op with most of its 10,000 members in southern Wisconsin and northern Illinois, and the Association of Operating Cooperatives, which included several Wisconsin groups.

In general, however, the daily press missed these signals.

And so the *Tulsa World*, or the *Omaha World Herald*, or a few hundred other papers, reported how "disgruntled" farmers sold so-and-so many dairy cows in that area, and the critics said that only culls were being sold. But Bob Rettig of Withee, Wisconsin told the *Wausau Record-Herald* that good producers were being sold, and Ray Purgett warned: "When milk goes below $4 per hundred I'm selling the whole herd."

At all the points cattle trucks had to wait to discharge their loads. Elmer Roland of Curtiss, Wisconsin probably didn't know about supply and demand models, but he did know that he sold a cow five weeks before freshening. At Stetsonville, Wisconsin, reporter Ben Luedtke caught up conversations back of the chutes, and they told all who wished to see that a great sorrow was hanging over the land.

"I took a $60 loss on my last two weeks milk check—who else gets a wage cut like this?"

"Where's the money going? Milk in the stores isn't any cheaper."

"Uncle Sam is taking care of everyone in the world except right here."

"I got $4.55 per hundred for milk last August—now I get $3.95."

And because milk had dropped from $4.55 to $3.95, a farmer from the town of Holton could report that the township had lost 15 herds during the past year.

A few discerning editors could sense, as did the *Herkimer Telegram* in New York, that "Some doubt exists as to whether the entire milk marketing system, as now set up, is the most desirable means of getting this valuable food product to the consumer."

Whether the present system was a "desirable means" depended on the vantage point. To the farmer, manipulated from pillar to post by institutional arrangements over which he had no control, any vantage point cried out for a remedy. To an honest economist, one who had watched with alarm as parity figures became rigged, the vantage point was one of disparity born of inequity. But the disposing end of agribusiness had hardly a whisper of a complaint. And the farmers on the surface were divided.

The Farmers Union, meeting in Oklahoma City, had heard from Vice President Hubert Humphrey and Senator Robert F. Kennedy, and had re-issued their ancient call for parity through government, but everyone knew the Union had become a minority in the farm field, drawing a mere 3,000 delegates from its 18 member states. As zero hour approached for NFO to call its holding action, Secretary Orville Freeman was winging his way to Tulsa.

Over at the Chicago-based headquarters of the Farm Bureau, President Charlie Shuman must have been thinking about what he'd say when the holding action was finally announced. His would be a "babies without milk" pitch, and that gem of originality—"They're going about it the wrong way"—according to odds available at NFO Headquarters, odds seldom in error.

6. the anchor word was violence

Of all the meetings that NFO crowded into the few weeks between the convention 1966 and the milk holding action, none rated higher in importance than the one held March 8, 1967. None more clearly reflected the burden that had come to rest on the NFO leadership, and at none could one better read the intimidation etched into every face.

NFO's chief building on Main Street, Corning, Iowa, was once a grocery store, one of the casualties as chains got big. High-ceilinged, and dull, a maze of fluorescent fixures seemed to smile down on rows of desks for the office force, all locally recruited. The office force had gone home that night, but a few sparks of activity could be read in the Meat Commodity Department and in Butch Swaim's Public Information Office at the back of the building. Staley's office, a corner partitioned off from the main building, was lined with extra chairs for the overflow crowd.

Eleven people attended the conclave. With a few exceptions*, they were the close core, the spark plugs at Corning who had run with NFO since the 1962 holding action, and who now were discussing strategy that would change the course of American agriculture. The odds they faced and the hyperbole of expression they were to be subjected to had not been equaled in a century of farm organization. Of the eleven, at least nine were to figure prominently in changing overnight the bucolic picture megatropolis American had come to have of the American farmer. Within weeks, they were to shake the very foundation of the tightly-knit, impregnable, unconscionably rigged dairy marketing system. Each was to run to the brink of exhaustion in the weeks to follow.

There was, of course, President Oren Lee Staley, the Shorthorn breeder who salvaged NFO after its protest days had spent themselves, and there was Staley's secretary, Mrs. Doris Peterson, who

*The writer was a privileged observer at this meeting.

had been with NFO since the protest days of 1956.

Chief Negotiator Gordon Shafer was there. Shafer was a realist. Mere purpose and faith and dedication were not enough for this ex-school teacher from Warrensburg, Missouri. As with most realists, he carried his formal college education with modesty, and his even greater self education with even more modesty. He had been with NFO from the first. Indeed, it was Shafer's rapport with reality that gave a weight of quality to the collective bargaining agreement under which NFO was now operating, an agreement Shafer gave direction during the writing stages.

Seated next to Shafer was the organization's Secretary, Harvey Sickels. The title was more or less a formality since Sickels spent most of this time in Washington as NFO legislative representative, and not at his farm in Iowa. He had grown into the job and through several years had mastered the art of diplomacy as practiced in the nation's capitol. In testimony before Committees, Sickels exuded quality rhetoric, but it was under questioning that he displayed flashes of brilliance. More important, he was well in touch with official Washington, understood its every nuance, and the probable direction of official action. It was the latter that was very much on Sickels' mind as he settled into a leather chair at the start of the meeting.

Directly across the room from Sickels, NFO Treasurer Earl J. Thompson seated himself on a wooden collapsible chair. A dollar day member of NFO, Thompson looked more like a small town banker than a farmer from Nebraska. Always eminently correct in dress—a rarity at the NFO office—Thompson allowed his personality to speak through his image. He understood more fully than most the requirement of compromise, and even in the sudden-death business of holding milk there would be need for much compromise. As in all conferences, Thompson would wait for the right moment to make the necessary observations.

Bill Lashmett was there. A product of a rural Illinois upbringing, with a University of Illinois and Western Illinois University education, Lashmett was forever an enigma. He could speak the idiom of the quarterdeck as easily as the syntax of theodicy, and he had ranged all the way from Navy duty to coaching football to running NFO's Meat Commodity Department, a role in which his talents were being tapped only partially. To the discerning, Lashmett had executive qualities, qualities which came through best when he was training bargaining committees or handling knotty bargaining problems himself. Lashmett read a sheaf of teletype messages as he shifted in his chair, waiting for Staley to start the meeting, then handed one to Lloyd Fairbanks.

Lloyd Fairbanks had been NFO's Organizational Director (now Field Staff Director) since NFO adopted collective bargaining. In fact, Fairbanks had been the second man to sign the collective bargaining agreement at Maysville, Missouri, when he affixed his signature right under Oren Lee Staley's. Fairbanks and Staley had been close allies in NFO on the march since the dollar days. Both lived near King City, Missouri, and both became pioneers in the grass roots revolt that became NFO. Fairbanks had helped Staley and the "Committee" author the original collective bargaining agreement. Fairbanks could look back at Kansas University days, back at World War II bomber pilot days, and now forward to a milk holding action, realizing that a lifetime had been more than half spent, and that the farmer had hardly advanced beyond the inferior economic position he had endured when Fairbanks was still a youth. The size of the job and the time available for its accomplishment provided a Parkinsonian dilemma for Field Staff Director Fairbanks, one that caused his hairline to take a beating.

At Fairbanks' left sat Grain Commodity Department Director Herb Goodman. A graduate of Colorado School of Mines, he had been with the Exploration Department of Shell Oil, and had served in WW II. Goodman understood organization, synchronized movement and *espirit de corps*. He sensed the need of each as preparations for the holding action kept building, and as the tempo of headquarters work kept him from his Coin, Iowa farm. Goodman knew how to block out field work in segments that permitted systematic accomplishment. His knowledge would prove invaluable in the days to come.

W. W. "Butch" Swaim came late to the meeting. Butch had been Public Information Director since 1960 despite the fact that his office once had a different name. A Superior Farmer Award winner in Iowa, Butch had been in and out of agriculture during his active lifetime. He had spent many working days in sales and almost all of his spare time studying economics. The ideas Butch Swaim picked up are the ones that hone close to reality, but they are also the kind that live in the underworld of economics until a man with academic stature—like Keynes or Galbraith or Ayres—arrives to sanctify what common sense people knew all along. Butch Swaim knew dairy.

He had seen it move from a low cost-of-production cream separator era into the high cost-of-production bulk tank, milk parlor, milking machine era with little change in price, and with increased efficiency picking up only half the tab, the rest coming out of the farmer's hide. Butch told this story over the some 50 TV programs he managed, on the countless radio tapes he commanded, and in the *NFO Reporter*, which was nominally under his control. All this was enough work for ten men, and Butch Swaim worked at it at least two shifts a day. His presence at the meeting represented after-hours work.

The last of the nine was Albin Rust, NFO's Dairy Commodity Department chief. Rust had headed the Dairy Department since 1962. A native of Barron County, Wisconsin, he grew up in the dairy country and learned dairying from the one-squirt-at-a-time level on up through association work in the Farmers Union, the American Dairy Association, and in setting up dairy co-ops. Rust had carried the lion's share of the ball up to the March 8 meeting. So far the pace had been inhuman. Before midnight, the holding action would leave the planning stage and go into full-dress organizational motion. After that the pace would be even more inhuman.

As each man opened an area for discussion, the topic made its way around the room, finally coming to rest as a conclusion or a big question mark. Mrs. Doris Peterson took notes, but the gist of a recap could hardly be reconstructed without remembering that small points sometimes flower into blockbusters a day or two later, and big points at midnight sometimes wake up as over-rated paeans the next day. In organizational activity, durability is what counts. Staley chaired the affair from the big seat behind a cluttered desk.

Despite their sometimes varied backgrounds, the NFO leaders all had one thing in common. They were not weighted down by intellectual commitments. Compared to farm experts in the colleges, they were not subservient to the "public policy" of a "grant" seeking institution.

As usual, Gordon Shafer came right to the point.

In the aggregate, about half the fluid milk sold by farmers ends up in manufactured products—butter, cheese, powder, or condensed milk. The minute farmers start holding, co-ops will stop routing their "surplus" to cheesemakers, and fill in the holes created when NFO members dump. The manufacturing plants will curtail production of power and the' like in order to re-route milk to fluid markets. There was a time when fluid milk went out to the public the way it came from the cow, high butterfat and all. Look at what's happened. Look at the big push on 2% milk and on all low butterfat products. From 1950 to 1965, the large gains have been for low butterfat products almost across the board. Ice milk has racked up a 458% gain; sherbet, 114%; nonfat dry milk, 62%; cottage cheese 48%. With the entire industry geared to a fictional two price policy, Class 1 milk will get first attention. So what's going to happen? In Wisconsin, Minnesota, Michigan and the big dairy areas, we'll end up closing the plants that are exclusively manufacturing first, and those are the plants we ought to keep open. Now I mentioned low butterfat products. What's to prevent the dairies from watering the milk, from putting a percent of powder in the milk, from selling it at less than 3.5 butter fat? These things are against the law, but who is going to enforce the law? These are problems we have to cope with and police, or a least try to.

That a holding action would close the wrong plants first had been evaluated, but the fact remained that NFO could do nothing about it. Dairy Commodity Department regulars were convinced that it would be impossible to sell milk for a hold and have honored the stricture that this milk not be forwarded to Class 1 shippers during the holding action. To start with, the manufacturing plants wouldn't sign an appropriate contract — at least not now. As the holding action progressed, perhaps! If it is possible to calculate a risk, then Rust was taking a calculated risk that the atmosphere would change as the holding action moved along. It was also a calculated risk that the holding action would last long enough to permit a working arrangement with the manufacturing plants to be effected.

Everyone had been digging facts and digging facts.

Earl Thompson, his suit correctly buttoned, his tie impeccably knotted, took the floor.

Let's start with one fact. Kansas State University food specialist Robert M. Schoeff estimates (on the basis of 1965 storage figures) that the U. S. has no fresh milk reserve, and condensed and evaporated milk for 25 days. But just because there's no reserve doesn't help NFO write its ticket. The industry has always been "no reserve." Now, let's look at the trade, according to the National Commission on Food Marketing, there were 5,041 firms engaged in fluid milk processing in January 1965. Some 3,364 were characterized as proc-

essors-distributors. The other 1,677 were producer-dealers. Producer-dealers accounted for about 2% of the sales and were considered dead or dying by the industry. The heart of the industry was represented by the 3,364 processor-distributors. Of these, nine firms were national: National Dairy Products (Sealtest), Pet Milk, Borden, Beatrice Foods (Meadow Gold), Fairmont Foods, Foremost Dairies, Carnation, Safeway Stores and Kroger Company. These nine firms operated more than 7% of the fluid milk processing plants in the United States. Below them in economic stature were the eight firms that operated regionally: Arden-Mayfair, Bowman Dairy, Dean Foods, Hawthorn-Mellody, Southland Corporation, Consolidated Foods (Lawson Milk Company), H. P. Hood and Sons, and Cumberland Farms. These firms racked up another 2% of the nation's fluid milk plants. Further, these 17 firms had contracts with the fluid circuit and with the proprietory plants, and with the co-ops, both those in the dairy surplus areas and those that feed milk into the cities on the fluid circuit.

These facts were not new, but they need retelling. Here were 17 firms that could control the entire industry and use their economic power to drive farm prices down.

Damning in their finality as these statistics are, the Big 9 meant even more to NFO. In federal milk market order areas, they accounted for 32% of the total sales. Without unfolding more of the details, it became at once apparent that the Big 9 wrote the ticket for the industry with or without the lesser eight. They were institutionally strong. They had the funds to ride out almost any storm. They were, in a word, what Galbraith called "mature corporations." In America, Justice Department no longer concerned itself with mature corporations in enforcing anti-trust, but only with firms or groups or agencies that aspired to become "mature."

The situation is the same as in red meat, Bill Lashmett said.

The hours wore on as the range of the problem endured examination and re-examination. Finally, Albin Rust took the floor. As Rust recapped the fluid circuit in NFO territory, he made it clear that even a well-meaning manager or president was rather helpless, that the dairy industry at the bottom was helpless unless co-ops joined together to make their stand, or—failing that—that farmers did it the hard way.

At Fergus Falls, Minnesota, the fluid milk operators were Fergus Dairies and Cass-Clay, but this was one of the smaller areas. The Minneapolis area fell into the 40 to 60 million pound category, a *sales ticket presided over by Twin Cities Milk Producers and Land O' Lakes, a federation. (Land O'Lakes handles poultry, cheese, ice cream, farm production supplies, feed and plant equipment in addition to fluid milk). Twin Cities paid $4.35 for milk during February, down a nickel from January. Look for a real skid if we don't make a showing with a hold. The general manager is George Pederson.*

[Hardly two weeks later, Pederson was to worry about bookkeeping. "We are as interested as anyone in getting high prices for dairy farmers," he said. "But even assuming we could get a higher price from dealers, we would still have the problem of distributing the proceeds to our farmer members."]

The Duluth-Superior area is a 5 to 7 million pound market. Fluid milk here is strictly in the hands of Indian Head Co-op and Twin Ports. Moving down to eastern Wisconsin, you're in the real dairy country—Consolidated Badger and Lake-to-Lake. Madison, Wisconsin, you have the Madison Milk Producers, and at Chicago, of course, PMA. PMA claims a nice, neat, round membership of 10,000 and supplies 13 midwest milk markets. It has membership over most of Illinois, Wisconsin and northern Indiana. This is real important. A. L. McWilliams at PMA claims that efforts have been underway for some time to improve blend prices in Chicago and surrounding markets through market orders. There's a blend price here of $5.22. About a dozen plants involved.

The Dairy Department Director fairly raced across the country, touching minor areas and co-ops, detailing capacity and managing personnel. A fast note taker could catch only basics as Rust moved on.

Western and central Wisconsin, you have Western Wisconsin Dairies and Rochester Co-op Dairies. New Ulm, Minnesota— that's 5 Star Dairies, a big fluid and manufactured milk combination co-op. Carlyle Hansen has really fought NFO in the past, but we've got the production. Several plants, everything from canned cream to bulk tanks here.

Moving west, the Sioux City Milk Producers at Sioux City, Iowa. Omaha—the Nebraska-Iowa Milk Producers, and at Des Moines, the Des Moines Co-op. At Des Moines, you're talking about 2,000 producers in 71 Iowa counties—about 30 million pounds a month class. Move down to Springfield, Missouri, you have MFA, and at Kansas City, PMA. At Wichita, Kansas producers are fenced in by the Southwest Milk Producers Association, and at Tulsa the Tulsa Milk Producers Association. These co-ops blanket the entire territory. They'll be rough on producers because they're fringe area.

St. Louis, Missouri—Square Deal and Sanitary Milk Producers. At Springfield, Illinois, its Prairie Farmer—all in the same boat, all will be fighting tooth and nail.

In the Evansville-Louisville area, it's Kyana. We've had our lecture from Burdette Fisher, Kyana's general manager. Fisher told our boys the real answer to the problem lay within the power of the dairy farmer—with his ability to increase production. This is strong NFO country.

We can run through them all, and the story is much the same. At Cincinnati, there are two co-ops — French-Bauer and Cincinnati Sales. Dayton milk is commanded by Miami Milk Producers Association. At Fort Wayne, the Fort Wayne Milk Producers Association. Toledo, Northwest Sales Association. Michigan, MMPA, which is really two independent co-ops. That's Glen Lake's outfit. Lake is president of Great Lakes Milk Marketing Federation and he's already told us "the federation will meet its marketing obligations." GLMMF deals in eight states, and they're lining up contracts in Tennessee, Kentucky and Indiana.

Move over to Akron, you have Akron Milk Producers. At Columbus, Central Ohio, and Athens-Maryetta. Go over into Pennsylvania, and you have the Erie-Crawford Milk Producers, all well in good organized NFO territory. It gets a little thin in parts of New York. Northeast New York, the Eastern Milk Producers and the Dairy League hold sway. In eastern New York and Pennsylvania, Northeastern Milk Producers. These co-ops can be counted on to do a lot of swapping, a lot of milk re-routing, a lot of trucking. There isn't a researcher alive who could get the figures.

That pretty well winds up the majors in the territory, except Tennessee, which is synonymous with Nashville Milk Producers Association. And Denver, Colorado. There's only one secondary supplier left in Denver, the Denver Milk Producers. Intermountain went broke about four months ago.

The recital was clear. Unless co-ops got together, they were both numerous and as helplessly divided as farmers. Their contracts with the Big 9 were the cudgels over their heads. They had to fight NFO because they were too thick headed to get together themselves. Their only safety valve was to push prices downward, because, obviously, the Big 9 put their sales making ads behind low butterfat products, and had no intention of rebuilding the image of butter or fluid cream products or even full strength fluid milk when more profits could be made out of soybean concoctions that rated as substitutes. The issue of the holding action was not two cents a quart, but new institutional arrangements that could serve the farmer.

Herb Goodman had the floor at one point.

How do we get from where we are to where we're going? The instruments and the timetable have to be ready. If we're not going to let our plans out of this room, then at least we have to work out an instrument for distribution later on. This means communication, and a communication system.

And so the judgment was made that certain psychological moments set the stage for change-of-pace action. Oren Lee Staley's sense of timing could be rivaled by few. He had displayed it at every convention, building each meeting to a perfect climax, just as now his guiding hand was building the psychological moment for a holding action. Within the action itself there would come another psychological moment when NFO could uncork what was later to be known as Phase 2, but plans for this could not emerge for days, partially because they were still to be refined, partially because surprise would be the most important element of all. Finally, Congressmen would be home for the Easter holiday while the holding action was going on. Should L.B.J. relent and haul back import quotas, the concession would only be temporary. It would take Congress to impose restrictions. While home, Congressmen might as well find out what's going on in rural America, Staley reasoned.

The meeting wore on, and the details on the agenda were scored, one at a time. Harvey Sickels had just returned from Washington. The anchor word in the nation's capitol was *violence*.

And it hung like a pall over the conclave. It was an ever-present threat. In earlier holding actions, NFO leaders had published strictures against the use of violence, but there had been incidents. NFO later explained that rural delinquents had accounted for many of these incidents, being triggered into motion by the opportunity much as bomb nuts get the idea to blow up an airplane after reading about another blast in the papers. And, undoubtedly, some incidents were manufactured by those who opposed NFO, hoping that NFO would get the blame. But the fact remained that some NFO members had been caught making mischief. National headquarters had never defended any of these misguided members because they had departed policy, but the publicity deficit led straight back to Corning, and it was hard to live with.

NFO knew this, but no one understood the anatomy of violence until James Riddle Hundley came along. Hundley was an Ohio State University student working on a doctor's degree in sociology. He had ranged across the NFO territory more than many of the most traveled leaders. He had accumulated some 50 hours of taped interviews, 8,000 to 10,000 pages of papers, notes, minutes, periodicals and documents. He had examined the field data collected by sociological researchers in Missouri, Ohio, Michigan, Wisconsin and Minnesota, all basically data that juxtaposed the NFO member along side the non-member.

Hundley defended his dissertation and got his doctor's degree. Not everything he had to say was kind to NFO, but he was a scholar with the scholar's scruples, and so he passed a copy of his dissertation on to Butch Swaim at Corning. Some of the details in Hundley's report were published in the *NFO Reporter* long before the membership had voted a holding action.

Now as the holding action neared, and the word *violence* was being whispered by shadowy characters in dark corners, those who had read the dissertation recalled some of Hundley's findings. NFO had lost most of its wild-eyed radicals after the early holding actions. "We found that the bulk of the NFO membership could not be categorized as *impotent or deviant, chronically discontented, or determinedly isolated.*" wrote Hundley. NFO's appeal was large enough not to attract a majority of particular personality types.

Not only members, but non-members rejected intimidation and violence. In the counties where Hundley interviewed farmers, he found the holding action the big bone of contention. Sometimes 75% of the farmers voiced disapproval. When really narrowed down, it developed that violence was the element that made the holding action unacceptable. "The point we wish to make is not that there was widespread lack of support among NFO members for participation in the holding action . . ." Hundley's passages in effect argued that the radical approach of rough stuff could not possibly achieve results, certainly not among non-members, and probably not among members. And still, NFO had to find a way to make the holding action socially acceptable.

NFO could not have paid for this kind of research. It told the officers something they needed to know. It put them in touch with Neil J. Smelser's *Theory of Collective Behavior* and with Ralph H.

Turner and Lewis M. Killian's *Collective Behavior*, both of which became mandatory study for a quite obvious reason. There had been incidents in the early holding actions. Rarely could blame be fixed. Did the pattern of incidents have to repeat itself? If so, NFO might just as well fold its tent and quit the fight. Intimidation and incidents of scope would obviously put to death the holding action.

But, as Turner and Killian pointed out, the program of change, gratification of membership and external power are all present in a movement. With the hot-heads largely gone from the ranks of NFO, with an adequate orientation program, and with a mature overview of the degrees of success available, NFO leaders believed social acceptance for the holding action had finally arrived.

Indeed, the growth of NFO as an organization would have been impossible without this transition. One of the main points in George Brandsberg's book, *The Two Sides in NFO's Battle*, assured the organization that the evolutionary process would quietly dry up the "extreme direct action" that rural sociologists liked to talk about. If NFO had in fact achieved this departure, then the holding action would have excellent chance for success.

Things were going to be different this time. The Dairy Commodity Department had wrapped up all the orientation meetings, and now the multilith machines in the back room were spitting out codified sheets of instructions.

Everyone in Staley's office that night knew that even one serious incident could blast the NFO effort out of the saddle. In the rough, the statement Staley was to issue was thus worked out: "We believe all farmers will join to support our efforts as soon as they understand our programs, and we believe they are now beginning to understand."

Still, everyone realized that a simple statement would not flush away the haunting spectre of an incident and government intervention. Some of the governors in the several states were friendly. Some were not. All would get letters from Staley spelling out NFO objectives, and naming local representatives who had been charged with seeing to it that an atmosphere of calmness prevailed.

Minnesota was pegged as a "danger" spot from the start.

"If there's a serious incident—if the Guard is called out, we get clobbered," Harvey Sickels said.

And so the word went out that NFO Headquarters would not tolerate even a single minor incident. "Don't even jaywalk—just hold milk," was the way Earl Thompson put it. And Staley added, "If any county has an incident, then the County Chairman is hereby instructed to cooperate with the authorities in tracking down the source of the incident, whatever it might be." It was about as forceful as you could get.

Around 11:00 p.m. a tray of Cokes arrived, and a few minutes later the meeting ran the gamut of considerations that had to go with a holding action. Drawing nourishment from previous experience, counties with herd strength were outlined so that field offices could be set up, roughly, over 15 county blocks.

The metes and bounds for the holding action thus came into being with startling rapidity. All Department heads were to name their best people for special duty, and before hardly an hour had gone by a structure and a communication system had been set up and blocked out like a military phalanx. Years earlier, Butch Swaim had worked out a minuteman phone system, one that enabled county groups to reach each member in less time than it took Paul Revere to make his ride.

There were other details:

A backup structure was developed, handbills and membership forms (the scarcest item in NFO) were scheduled on the press, and a few midnight calls to leaders in the field were made on the spot to take reports. The architects of the "freedom to go broke," as Butch Swaim characterized the Farm Bureau, were asleep by now, but at NFO headquarters the kilowatts were still burning.

Yet the work-a-day details fell into place quite easily. A working rapport with men in every county in every state had put grass-roots leaders on a first name basis with Corning, and therefore recruiting a special force was no real chore.

7. *no human can say*

Sometime during the next several days, preparations for the holding action were completed. A semi-secret Board meeting was held to set the date. It was to be March 15, and would be announced to the members late in the afternoon. In the meantime, more "prepare for action meetings" were scheduled for after Easter as a ploy to throw those watching NFO off guard.

A few days before March 15, Staley could view the psychological warfare, and say, "This is building perfectly. The dairy farmers will

never be readier for a holding action than right now." The NFO
Board* agreed.

Staley had a few bad nights as zero hour neared. He allowed, "Anything can happen. No human can say what the outcome will be." At
his farm the Saturday before March 15, he could work off the tension
with a chain saw, for on the following Wednesday the holding action
simply had to be. It had to be because the institutional arrangements
under which the farmers sold their products were driving not only
NFO people, but two-thirds of the corn belt farmers into bankruptcy.

8. natural scoop of the decade

It came as the strangest and most unforgettable irony that on
Wednesday, March 15, NFO members reached an agreement with
Pure Milk Association for PMA to market its milk from the three
pump-over stations at Fond du Lac, Madison and Cuba City, Wisconsin. These three pump-over stations were part of the Elroy Co-op,
which was under NFO contract. Dave Miller of Beaver Dam went
through the motions of announcing that the deal was effective immediately, and that immediately the producers shipping to the three
pump-over stations would agree to sign PMA membership contracts.
At Chicago, A. L. McWilliams, the general manager of PMA, was
delighted. It was a breakthrough in getting farm organizations to work
together. John Butterbrodt, PMA's second vice president called it a
"first step." Al Rust took a moment from his schedule in the Milk
Commodity Department to issue a very correct statement: "Since
PMA has stepped out in the lead to correct the Chicago milk market
situation, NFO agreed to join in with a cooperative effort."

*The NFO Board of Directors at the time of the 1967 Milk Holding Action, by
state and community, included the following: Idaho—William Hepworth, Rupert.
Illinois—Merle Willard, Pittsfield; Gene Potter, Sterling; Bob Kessler, Louisville.
Indiana—Glen Utley, Fort Branch; Don Myers, Waterloo; J. W. McKinsey,
Thortown. Iowa—Harvey Sickels, Fontanelle; Jim Stewart, Columbus Junction;
Willis Rowell. Edgewood. Kansas—Chris Walker, Mayetta; Don Evertson, Mel-
vern. Kentucky—Earl Hatcher, Hodganville. Michigan—John Kuch, Union-
ville; Eldeen Jones, Charlotte. Minnesota—Oras Kanerva, Zim, Ralph Kittelson,
Appleton; Pete Nagel, Amboy. Missouri—Fred Deardorff, Auxvasse; Rhea Hack-
ler, Long Lane; Elmer F. Bell, Jr., Warrensburg. Nebraska—Val Akerlund, Val-
ley; Bill Sellhorst, Dodge. New Jersey—Henry Douma, Hackettstown. North
Dakota—Clarence Stockstad, Milnor. Ohio—Ralph Hoover, Fostoria; Raymond
Zumbrum, Union City, Indiana; Art Phillips, Greenfield. South Dakota—Kenneth
Stofferahn. Humboldt; John Oster, Ethan. Wisconsin—Robert Manke, Arlington;
Ed Graf, Tomah; Robert W. Rettig, Withee. In NFO states are represented
on the Board according to strength of the organization in that state. A state
can have no more than three Directors.

NFO members who had dropped out of and spurned PMA were re-enlisting again. This had always been a sore point. Farmers were flatly told by Rust that they had to grow up, they could no longer afford the luxury of a grudge. The dotted line beckoned. At Columbus, Wisconsin, Eugene Rake, Chairman of the Dodge County NFO, allowed that in the past NFO members had been reluctant to work with PMA, "but PMA has opened the door to cooperation."

Almost alone among knowledgeable press, the *Beaver Dam Citizen* correctly appraised the situation. The PMA was holding a convention in Chicago over the weekend. Many dairy farmers and NFO members would be there. A week after that would be Good Friday and Easter Sunday, an unlikely time for a holding action. ". . . . and after that farmers will be busy getting machinery ready for spring field work."

Unfortunately the *Beaver Dam Citizen* went to press early in the day Wednesday, March 15, 1967. The holding action was not called until late afternoon, and the greatest natural scoop of the decade went down the drain.

9. *ex-captain paul gauthier*

Among the rural publishers, only Paul Gauthier's *Adams County Free Press* could rely on more than mere speculation. Gauthier published his weekly hardly a block from the NFO office. Ever since the dollar days, he had been on top of the story. Indeed, as a guiding hand behind *NFO Reporter*, he had given the organization's house journal direction, and had helped shape it as a magazine with dimension. In recent years he had helped Staley recruit new blood for the NFO's five W and feature needs.

Now, the evening before MHA Day, Gauthier calmly put his *Adams County Free Press* to bed without the MHA Day story. Ethics required it. And certainly, NFO could use all the help it could get.

Of all those who had coached the forming NFO story, Gauthier was the most philosophical. He had been a briefing officer for General George S. Patton Jr. during the war in Europe. He still admired that soldier's excellence and fight. In the old days it was Patton's refusal to smile on mediocrity that caused the electricity of comradeship to flow between this Iowa editor and the deeply religious, tough, poetry writing, blood-and-guts fighting general. On Gauthier's office wall hung a portrait of Patton, one that smiled with determination. A full measure of that determination was staffing a fight down the street a ways, where farmers were machining to battle the odds, scrounging for resources the way Patton once scrounged for gasoline. Lesser men had brought on the fight because they in fact lived out a line in one of the general's poems, the one that said "all men pay homage to me, I am fear!"

It was blind fear that made lesser men seek to deal with effects, not causes. Lesser men were content to think in terms of low income housing, guaranteed minimum income, paid compensatory education, and the bureaucratic octopus called welfare—all measures that accepted poverty and made its continuance a certainty. Of the lot, the concept of low income housing was the worst. It institutionalized poverty for the city just as surely as low farm prices institutionalized bankruptcy for the rural towns. Now the lack of farm income and a tax base was drying up local school systems, beating the life out of local governments, and driving state treasuries to the wall.

"The female flea walks backwards," Gauthier once said. "No forward locomotion is either possible or considered acceptable in the best flea circuits. Except for that farm group down the street, it looks like the entire country is making like the female flea."

First agriculture acquired the characteristics of the flea. Somewhere along the line the entire industry decided it could not climb uphill, or even join the drones who stumbled downhill. For a decade and a half now, agriculture had emulated the female flea and moved only enough to jump backwards.

The agrarian impulses must have fed to the highest level, because the nation was doing the same thing. If the men down the street had the sand to fight and change all that, then ex-Captain Paul Gauthier could do no less than lend moral support and technical know-how, and perhaps a pungent line or two. He knew he would get plenty of chance during the next several days. Lesser men would attack NFO like the vandals who sacked Rome. And Paul Gauthier, standing in the wings, would look at the enemy, smile and say to himself, "I am *underwhelmed.*"

NARRATIVE

---

holding action

mha day

It seemed that Kansans had to be larger and
    stronger than life, even to survive in that old
    Kansas,
Let alone to subdue it.
So that they put on pride like an overcoat that is
    donned to hide the patches beneath
And when the haughty princess asked Dorothy
    of Oz:
"Are you of royal blood, by any chance?"
Dorothy tilted her small snub nose just one tilt
    higher than the princess',
Her sonsy face glowing with honest pride,
And answered in her forthright prairie twang:
"Better than that, Ma'am! I come from Kansas!"
And so the state grew character, as well as
    characters:
John Brown, Jim Lane, John J. Ingalls who once
    called Kansas the navel of the nation;
Sockless Jerry Simpson, Edmund G. Ross, Carry
    Nation, Victor Murdock, Arthur Capper,
    Charley Curtis;
Mary Elizabeth Lease, she who adjured Kansans
    to raise more hell and less corn;
And William Allen White, Bill White of Emporia,
Who began by demanding that Kansas raise more
    corn and less hell, but ended by raising more
    and hotter hell than anybody. *

*Quoted from the poem "Kansas," by permission of the author, Roscoe Fleming.

When Mary Elizabeth Lease stormed across Kansas around the turn of the century, she told farmers to raise less corn and more hell, but in fact it mattered not at all whether Kansas farmers raised any corn at all. There was always Iowa, Nebraska, Missouri, half the nation, in fact, that could and would raise corn. That no farm state could operate in a vacuum was the single concept that had failed all farm organizations before NFO.

It was not a case of "less milk, more hell" with NFO. The fluid milk traffic was too "fluid" for that. The entire market was like a giant tank. Take a million gallons out of one corner, and every milk producing area in the nation would, directly or indirectly, contribute toward making up the deficit. Lower the level of the tank and the trade rolled into action. The trade swings the big stick in the dairy business.

There are a few old timers in western Kansas who still remember the "dollar wheat bulletins" of 1903, in which sometime editor J. A. Everitt told farmers to hold their crop until they got at least a dollar a bushel. It worked that year, and a year later the dollar wheat bulletin was asking $1.20—but then trouble set in. The wheat elevator was like the milk tank, and you don't catch the trade napping twice.

In 1964, dairy production dropped off 2,794 million pounds from the previous year, and in 1966 it dropped off another 3,943 million pounds, but "less milk" had been neatly balanced by more imports: 900 million pounds (in terms of whole milk equivalent) in 1965 and a whopping 2,800 million pounds in 1966. Imports that skirted the law took up the rest of the slack. And the trade set the prices in the end.

Of a sudden farmers were coming to their senses, one at a time. Kansas NFO Director Don Evertson was an intensely practical man. He could sum up the situation in a sentence, a word, or even a nod of his head. NFO could dump enough milk to cancel out the imports, surely. And NFO could raise enough hell to adjust the institutional arrangements that made driving farm prices downward the name of the game these days.

Once before, men like Evertson had been goaded beyond endurance by the four horsemen of Kansas, "Drouth, Grasshoppers, Railroads and Bankers," and had gone Populist to the last man. Things were different now. With a farm population that had become paper thin, NFO believed farmers could fight only one way—with the power of their production while they still had that production. The Kansas corner of the national milk tank may be small, Evertson reasoned, but it's going to hold tighter than a snare drum.

1. *the endless days*

"The first inkling I had of the holding action," wrote Mrs. Ellis Kitchen in her diary, "was when Chris Walker called us this morning about 7:00 a.m. and asked if we would be home about 9:00. He drove in and I could sense an air of secrecy as he sat down in our den . . ."

Ellis Kitchen was NFO legislative representative in Kansas. With three phones installed for the action, his home would be headquarters, not just for phone calls, but for NFOers who were too tired to drive after each of the endless days. "As we talked," the diary entry continued, "Ervin Stoneback drove in, so we told him of our plans and swore him to secrecy. Don Evertson stopped for a chat after dinner."

Shaded by circumstance, this scene at the Carbondale, Kansas farm of Ellis Kitchen was being replayed at the home of Charles Barbay in Andover, New Jersey and at Bill Hepworth's farm near Rupert, Idaho, in a hundred homes from North Dakota and Minnesota to Florida and Georgia, in motels and hotels, and in sundry locations where NFO leaders could get office space. Through the early day and mid afternoon, calls over hastily installed phones went out from Corning, to district people, to the action staffers who each had been assigned a block of counties. In Kansas, for instance, Fred Killian of Wamego had been assigned eleven counties in the north-central part of the state. Helped by Marvin Miller and Fred Seibert, the Wamego triumverate would operate from a small trailer at the local NFO meat collection point. Kansas NFO Director Chris Walker had been handed 13 counties in northeastern Kansas. During the holding action he would keep in close touch with these counties from the den of the Ellis Kitchen farm. Monte Johnson of NFO's Field Staff Department lived at McClurg, Missouri, but he had spent nearly five years organizing in Arkansas and Missouri as well as Kansas. Now he logged in his phone number at the Ferguson Motel in Augusta, and settled down for a quick appraisal of his southcentral holding action counties. In the meantime, Don Evertson took a slightly bigger bite of counties for his southeast Kansas territory. He would keep in touch from his home at Melvern.

"March 15 . . . Ellis and Chris both arrived at 3:00 p.m. to set up the office," the diary of Mrs. Ellis Kitchen recorded. "I took their picture as they were unloading the car. They came in and began calling the helpers for a meeting here and at Chris Walker's place for 6:30 p.m. The men were eager and excited to get started." They would work full time in each county for $15 a day plus mileage. They were to report to headquarters each day and hold meetings at the county level every night.

As the ladies and PR secretaries made the opening entries in their diaries (". . . we saw a Shawnee Milk Producers truck going north with a large snowplow attached to the front of it . . .") NFO President Oren Lee Staley finally tipped the press. Simultaneously, on different trunk lines, the wire services were told that the holding action had been called. The announcement was terse in the extreme. Within seconds after the "release" chore had been completed, the big switchboard lit up like the panels in a futuristic movie. The official time was 4:00 p.m., C.S.T. On the switchboard, the call-back tickets piled up.

As Staley worked his way through the calls, a few first glimmerings of the story that was to come took form. Reporters had questions. To each, in turn, Staley predicted "tremendous support" because farmers "are not in a mood to take these low prices any longer." Some farmers, he said, had the facilities to keep their milk cool for a few days, but after that they would have to feed it to their hogs or dump it.

The questions were mundane and very predictable. The answers were direct and to the point.

Yes, the milk holding action would be held in every NFO county in the 25 state area. Yes, county meetings would be held every night except Good Friday and Sundays. Did Staley expect it to last until Easter? "We'll have to wait and see." Possibly for the first time, reporters from such citified papers as the *Chicago Tribune* and the *Wall Street Journal* learned of the action that had been prompted by a desperate situation in dairy farming, a situation that "really threatens the future milk supply of America."

"Farmers are simply putting a price on their product in the same manner every one else prices the product they have to sell," Staley told Associated Press and United Press International. To NFO members the statement meant simply that farmers could no longer endure their inferior marketing position and would henceforth require contracts, but the copy editors quickly found a misleading common denominator: farmers were striking for more money—end quote!

As a matter of fact, farmers were not merely holding for two cents a quart more at the farm. They were holding to secure contracts, because without contracts a two cent increase would evaporate as quickly at it came. Staley tried to sell this message, but he was talking a language well removed from the common reporter's orientation.

Pencils fairly flew across the paper. "We are convinced we would still be talking ten years from now and not get a single penny increase in price for the farmer unless we take direct action," Staley was quoted as saying, and he said it—but he said much more. His sharpest barbs were aimed at the insipid doctrine of supply and demand. Whenever a reporter would permit it, Staley would point out that the Big 9 in dairy sheltered themselves on both ends of the famous dichotomy. They controlled their prices. They controlled their costs. Their operating profits were not set by the market, but by the power of the firm. In essence, though not in form, Staley argued that the degree of rigidity evident in one sector of the economy must be matched by a similar degree of rigidity in another, both in its institutional content, and in the final reward for the creation of wealth. The pencils moved, but they were merely distributing carbon on scratchpads, not getting to the heart of the story. Later, when the stories headed for the linotypes, there was a sameness about them all. Farmers were striking for two cents a quart at the farm, no more, no less. NFO's pursuit of contracts, of adjustments in the institutional arrangements, were rarely mentioned.

2. *project 80*

Calling the holding action did not give newsmen action—not at first. It would take a milking or two to fill the tanks. It would take several hours to inform all the NFO farmers, even with a good minuteman system, and some would not learn of the action until after milking early in the morning. By that time even the farmers without phones would know. Farmcasters would have it, regular newsbeats on radio and TV would at least mention it, and likely as not industry spokesmen would hand out judgments that the action was faltering badly and would die a-borning.

In the meantime the business of building NFO would go on. The NFO bureau speakers—men like Glen Utley, Erhard Pfingsten, Gene Potter, Oras Kanerva, John Kuch, to mention a few—would be telling the NFO story before rural audiences, and they would also carry the word that as of 4:00 p.m. C.S.T. a holding action had been in effect. As a matter of fact, Michigan NFO Director John Kuch would be speaking at Dearborn, Missouri that night.

Kuch was an unusual speaker. He didn't handle the King's English half as well as he handled his topic, but farmers like to overlook the fluff and get at the real filling. The press had been invited to the Dearborn meeting. Half a dozen rural weeklies were there, and even Rod Turnbull of *The Kansas City Star* had materialized as Kuch reached the podium.

Kuch was born in 1908 in Vienna, Austria. His parents were poor people, but somehow they managed to come to America in 1911. They did not have sufficient funds to bring their two children with them, so the children were forced to remain in Austria with an aunt. It was still the era of Ellis Island immigrants and penniless foreigners working their fingers to the bone and borrowing the limit to bring their loved ones to America after them. John's parents did just that. By 1914 they managed to borrow $1,400 to defray the passage expenses of the children. When the money arrived in Austria, WWI broke out, and the dream of coming was shattered, not just for a fortnight, but until 1921.

"I can tell you, my friends, that in that time I became the richest boy on earth, and also the most humble. I saw times when I did not see bread for more than a month, when we lived like Indians, and picked berries to survive. How could this be with that kind of money? That money would have bought castles, that's how valuable the American dollar was at that time, but money won't buy the other man's only meal if he needs it to live." It was an era of incredible hardship. Farmers would flail their grain and nurture its volume, only to have the government take two-thirds. And when they took the rest to a grist mill to have it ground, they again paid out a third. As John Kuch told the story, many men cried softly.

"I saw days when I would try to catch fish with my bare hands in preserve streams. Had I been caught, I would have been shot. In 1918, I saw the flu epidemic sweep through Austria. People died like flies." His relatives, school chums, all fell.

Then came inflation. In 1919 a man could make 25,000 schilling a day in wages, money which had to be spent before the sun went down. A suit of clothes for a 13 year old boy, weighing 60 pounds, cost eight million schilling. "I saw when one chicken egg was priceless. The water that an egg was cooked in was not dumped away, but was soup. I saw human skeletons walking." But the day finally came, and when John arrived at Cassville, Michigan he saw a groaning board full of food only a hungry boy could behold.

"No one who has seen hunger can take lightly the destruction of food," Kuch said. Only one thing can justify the destruction of milk, and that is the certainty that we will lose our ability to produce milk if we do not win this holding action, the NFO Director from Michigan concluded.

John Kuch had been appointed to the Steering Committee of Project 80 at Michigan State University. The Purpose of Project 80 was to project the complexion of agriculture by the year 1980. As Kuch detailed the scope of developments—synthetic cheese, synthetic frankfurters, artificial meat—he arrived at the questions that present themselves.

Can synthetic meat be processed in volume? Yes. How much does it cost a pound? $1.78. From what commodity is it processed? Soybeans and corn.

To John Kuch, and to any farmer who tumbles out of bed at 4:30 a.m., the prospect of doing away with milk and meat production should seem "Utopia arrived." "Just think," Kuch told the learned ones. "Our farmers will not have to get up at 4:30 a.m. to milk cows or walk in the barnyard feeding cattle. Farmers can grow soybeans and corn, and for the first time in history they can take a vacation. They could if you were right. But you're not."

The discussions ran into and out of economic box canyon after another, but in the end the learned ones on Project 80 concluded: the projection is that we will go into vertically integrated corporation farming. We will have to have bigger farms and fewer farmers and lower farm prices to bring this about. Two million farmers will have to be eliminated. This process will start in 1968 and it will be completed by 1980. The family farm is obsolete. It has to go.

But where will the farmer go?

Don't bother us with that. You work it out. We're the surgeons. You have become a cancer to the economic order. We will excise you.

And so the surgeons operated on the body economic, but the

healing did not follow. The farmers held their auctions, and the carbuncle in the country became a boil in the armpit of the city. The theories of the learned ones admitted no mistakes, but mistakes lay like carrion over the land.

The first fact of economic life is people, 3 billion of them in the world today, projected to reach 4.3 billion by 1980, and 6.1 billion by the year 2000. The United States will have 340 million people by the year 2000. Yet the nation is losing some of its best farmland to highway and urban expansion, to recreation and conservation projects.

It takes 40 acres to every mile of superhighways, as high as 178 acres for intersections, and we've just begun to build highways.

We will have to triple the bushels per acre within the next 33 years, and that will not be sufficient to feed the people. Corn has responded to research, but soybeans seem to have topped out, and the only way to get more production is to plant more acres.

If we were to take away the polar regions where nothing grows, and if we were to take away the desert we hope to irrigate, then we would have a production strip of good soil around the world about the size of the island Cuba. By the year 2000 this will be a fraction of an acre per person.

Men like Dr. Georg Borgstrom at Michigan State University could see in this dilemma an open sesame to world peace because "man can only afford one war today—the war for human survival . . . the Golden Rule is not a question of compassionate action, but the supreme of prudent policy." Those not living in the sheltered tranquility of the ivy halls saw it differently. William and Paul Paddock (*Famine 1975*) saw only a Time of Famines lasting several decades in an atmosphere of widespread political turmoil. Likely as not, the U. S. would turn to "triage," not the Golden Rule, and peoples perceived to be antagonistic to the U. S. would be cut off, starved, kept out of the steppes and other food producing areas by force, if necessary. As usual Pollyanna saw peace, but Cassandra predicted turmoil.

Stark as this projection is, offset as it has been by the efficiency of the small unit farm, the family farmer who has gotten more milk from each cow, more meat from each animal, more potatoes from each acre, the only solution Project 80 planners could arrive at was the judgment that the family farmer had become surplus.

The "80" judgment had been made before, and it has been made since Project 80 hammered out its last "finding." As early as 1962 The Committee for Economic Development published its policy paper,

An Adaptive Program for Agriculture. The report, written with one farmer in tow (Robert J. Kleberg, Jr., president, King Ranch, Inc.) concluded that the economy's payment to agriculture was quite satisfactory, and that the trouble was too many people in agriculture. The CED counseled moving some two million farmers out of the then existing farm industry. The Food and Fiber Commission report of 1967 counseled the same thing.

In terms of the first fact of economic life, people, the "liquidate agriculture" advice, by early 1967, was already duplicating one of history's most disastrous blunders—Stalin's clumsy liquidation of the kulaks. If the process seemed more refined in the United States, it remained just as lethal. The initial impact could be read within months after the policy first went into effect. The rest has still to follow.

As early as March 1963, *Nebraska Farm and Ranch Economics* evaluated the impact the CED report would have on Nebraska alone. Developed by Department of Agricultural Economics workers in the College of Agriculture at the University of Nebraska, the report detailed how 45,000 farmers, or 150,000 farm people in Nebraska would be affected. The mean of 3.5 members per family was used for the calculations. The human multiplier did not stop there, the report held. In Nebraska, the ratio between farmers and rural townsmen for the purpose of providing goods and services was about one for one. Thus removal of 45,000 farmers required removal of 45,000 other people in rural Nebraska, all involved in farm-related occupations. Even in a state like Nebraska, the CED policymakers required liquidation of 90,000 farm jobs, and removal of some 300,000 (over 20% of the state's population) into industrial towns, ostensibly to compete for jobs and make more necessary "job opportunity setups," "great society programs," and to further add to the nearly 40 million in the nation's defined poverty class.

All the "gut agriculture" seers of the 1960s had embraced certain tenets of conjectural economics. These tenets had been best stated by Dale E. Hathaway of Michigan State University in *Problems of Progress in the Agricultural Economy:* "Essentially, there are four contributions that agriculture can make to a nation's economic growth. First, it can provide the food and fiber base necessary for a population growing in numbers and in wealth. However, it is important that this be done without an increase in total resources used and/or in the relative price of farm products. In fact, economic growth is stimulated if farm prices decline so that [other] people will have more money to spend on other goods and services. Second, agriculture can provide workers to produce other goods and services by releasing them from the production of farm products. Third, agriculture can provide a market for non-farm goods and services, enabling the gainful employment of people in their production. Finally, agriculture can provide a source of capital that may be invested in improved productive facilities in [other areas] of the economy."

Hathaway's concept of "a decline in the price of food" having the effect of permitting consumers to expend more for other goods speaks of a short-run observation, and takes on the intellectual bent expressed by Pareto, who would have agreed that cannibalism could be justified on the same grounds.

"The farm sector of the United States," Hathaway continued, "provides a classic illustration of the contribution that may be made to economic growth, although this contribution may have been less than was possible. At the same time economic growth has created problems within agriculture."

It may not have been his intention, but Hathaway set it out for all to see that agriculture can serve other sectors in the economy by patriotically allowing itself to be exploited simply because it has something to exploit. It is to perform the same function as usual, for more people than usual, but for less pay. To stress the last point, Hathaway pointed out that farm prices should really go down a little every year so that people [other than farmers] would have more money for color TV sets, power boats, automobiles, hair dryers and other goods and services, rather than to spend it on farm products, principally food.

Neither Project 80, the CED paper, nor the Food and Fiber Commission spoke pure economics. Without exception, they represented institutional arrangements speaking out with policies they perceived to be to their institutional interests. Hence the endorsement, for instance, of CED's *An Adaptive Program for Agriculture* by the American Farm Bureau Federation (serving industrial America in the name of far right individualism), the American Meat Institute, the Board of Trade, the National Association of Manufacturers, and the United States Chamber of Commerce, and hence also the endorsement of the concept by institutional government branches subservient to the above, namely the President's Council of Economic Advisors and the Land Grant Colleges. Only rarely do business people rise above their class principles, as did J. M. Symes of the Pennsylvania Railroad Company and a trustee on the CED Research and Policy Committee, in rejecting the CED report. Having some time for thinking is a first requisite. The vice president of great establishments rarely can pause for thinking in depth.

Sometimes, however, the presidents of rural enterprises not only think, but communicate their ideas to all who will listen. When Hartington, Nebraska banker Vince Rossiter first hit the lecture circuit for NFO during the organization's formative years, he found that ideas gain acceptance on the basis of who endorses them, not on the merit they contain. Before the meeting for action in 1962 and before the Minneapolis convention in 1964, Rossiter detailed the scope of agriculture's debauchery, but for really concise statements, informed NFOers read Rossiter's articles in the *Independent Banker*. In article after article, bank president Rossiter developed these points—

This lack of participation in the well-being of the economy by agriculture is no accident, nor is there any compelling economic mandate for it. It is entirely due to the deliberate acts of calculating people who want to achieve the following:

• *The assurance of an abundance of relatively cheap and readily available farm raw materials.*

• *Comparatively cheap food, shoes, beverages, clothing and tobacco, all made from farm raw materials, to relieve the upward pressure on wages and salaries paid by large employers.*

• *A surplus labor force, amply supplemented by the influx of hundreds of thousands of dislocated rural employables annually.*

• *A comparatively docile union labor force, properly chastened by an abundance of willing non-union workers who are capable of innocently, or maliciously, disrupting the traditionally unionized labor force.*

• *A farm raw material price level that can be manipulated from 100% of fair value to less than 50% of fair value so a profit can be made on both the purchase and again on the sale.*

These are the real accomplishments of the farm programs since 1952, and this is what they were intended to accomplish.

Unfortunately, the road to hell is paved with sweeter intentions. In early March 1967, NFO farmers could look with alarm at the effect of the cause that may or may not have been part of the policy makers' intentions.

Those who heard John Kuch on that cold March 15 evening were thinking in terms of causes, not effect, but *The Kansas City Star's* ace reporter was not one of them. Early in the evening he had walked out of the meeting.

3. *the illusion of milk*

Only eight hours separated the announcement of the holding action from midnight. As the hours tightened, and the journalists started assembling the points against dairy farmers seeking a higher price, the tanks filled to the brim, and the milk cooled. By feet and inches the drain was still the same distance from the valve, but it was getting closer, in time.

Hardly a dairy farmer could be told about pricing himself out of business. He had heard too much about corporations buying into agriculture as a tax loss to produce those low cost soybeans, and he had been told about how the magic of modern technology could turn starch into meat or milk, even how water was being added to non-dairy milk in Florida so that when the cartons were put on display the illusion of milk remained.

And so when the Cresco, Iowa *Times* laid it on the line a little later that "the public would not pay sky-high prices for butter," that the public would turn "to substitute spreads such as margarine" farmers instinctively knew that typesetters were turning to cold type too, not because it was more efficient than hot type, but because bargained wages prevailed in the latter, and not in the former. If non-fat powder from corporation grown soybeans puffed up with advertising could turn more of a profit while independent farmers were joining the 2,500 going out of business each week, then this could make the dairy farmer inefficient in "conjectural" economics only, nowhere else.

In Gainesville or St. Petersburg or Miami you could get liquid "milk" that way, especially from restaurant coolers. To start with, Florida is not self-sufficient in dairy, and having Glyn Johnson set up a High Springs holding action post was more or less perfunctory. Florida probably had many more NFO farms than there were dairy herds in the state, but the fact remained that too much of the milk was being imported from unorganized territory. A come-lately in the organization, Florida had entered NFO in an unusual way. An NFO farmer "from up north" had driven through northern Florida. The farm he visited at random turned out to belong to Bill Herndon, the youngest farmer in Suwannee County. Unavoidably, the conver-

sation got around to NFO. Later that year a few farmers got up
enough money to send observers to the NFO's Minneapolis convention. Two farmers, Kenneth Smith and Larue Tippette, reported on
what they saw, and not long after that Winnebago County, Iowa
farmer Glyn Johnson arrived in Florida to do some organized organizational work. He knew how. He had put his farm in grain. He had
hit the organizational trail in such widely separated places as Pennsylvania and Minnesota. In short order Florida counties were being
chartered. Now men like Earl Jeffords were helping Johnson cover
the organized counties, which were reaching well down the great
peninsula.

Northern Florida is a land full of tin roofs and broken down farm
houses. The splendid facades of resorts stand in awkward juxtaposi-
tion to abandoned rural dwellings, dwellings that do not last long
once a family moves out. As in most of rural America, these buildings
are pulled down fast, but farmers are leaving the farms even faster.
Viewed from almost any vantage point, there is very little difference
between the Florida farmer and his Iowa counterpart. North and
south, farmers have the same deficient income. North and south, they
are in the position of a man who says, "With friends like these, who
needs enemies?"

Upstream on the famous Suwannee River Stephen Foster didn't
know how to spell lies NFO's Georgia, roughly the two southern tiers
of counties. At Ocilla, in Irwin County, former state legislator, former
lumberman, now farmer Marion Green turned his kitchen into an
office and a field post. Holding action activity in the Georgia counties
would feed through his "office" to Corning, and news from Corning
would be recorded for delivery to county meetings each night. Hard
on the heels of the AP and UPI wire story that NFO had launched
a holding action in 25 states, Chairman of the Georgia Milk Commission, Clifton A. Ward, told local media, "As far as I know, the NFO
has no membership in Georgia, and if they did I think I would know
about it."

NFO had membership, and the membership had been growing ever
since Green first sent a $25 check to Corning after the 1964 meat
holding action. Green had learned about getting big the hard way.
He had been in the lumber and pulp business for 20 years. "All of
a sudden it wasn't the right kind of wood. They needed better quality,
and mine was now worth less. The last two years I sold $500,000
in logs, then I had to sell off $50,000 worth of land to bail out and be

able to quit." When Green saw the same thing happening in agricul-ture, he reacted "like most of us southerners do. I thought all the trouble came from Yankee-land, some 300 miles north. It never occurred to me farmers up north had the same problems." Up north farmers were holding for a price in 1964. "When I saw that I said to myself, that's the organization for me."

After Green sent a $25 check to NFO headquarters, "a fellow drove into the yard." He was Harry Thompson of Hopkins, Missouri. Thompson had a very pertinent question for former lumberman, for-mer State Representative Marion Green. Would Georgia farmers help themselves? Green said he didn't know. He'd find out. "I went with Thompson. The more I helped NFO, the more I woke up and realized I was working at organizing NFO full time." Farmers had to help themselves because those in charge of public policy seemed oblivious to the conditions in agriculture. Despite the fact that NFO organiza-tion ranged across an entire end of Georgia, despite multi-page articles about NFO in the *Georgia Farmer,* a man like Georgia Milk Commission Chairman Clif Ward was unaware of what "his" farmers were doing. He did not remain unaware for long.

One of the first calls to Lloyd Fairbanks after the holding action got underway came from Green. He had been asked about allowing a cameraman to film milk dumped. Fairbanks thought a moment. NFO is an open organization. News belongs to the man who has it. Georgia's TV viewers might just as well find out right now what was happen-ing. "It's up to you," Fairbanks told Green.

4. *the last minutes of march 15*

Even at a few minutes to midnight, March 15, it was early. Farmers were still being given the word. As headquarters regulars sounded their way around the territory, they detected spirits that were high, determination that was enduring. Leo Williams pulled into his Akron, Colorado driveway to report. The word was on the way. Before milk trucks arrived for their every-other-day pickups in the morning, Colorado, Wyoming and western Nebraska farmers would know of the hold, and they would hold.

At Grand Island, Nebraska, John Oster ran through a test call from his Conoco Motel headquarters. Across NFO territory, U.S.A., well over a hundred of NFO's top leaders were readying their reports, a routine act, because during the last minutes of March 15, there was very little to report. The news would arrive in a few hours. Either farmers would hold or they would forever abandon the idea that they could either help themselves or bring the nation's attention to the tragedy of the hour.

5. *on the periphery of action*

Oklahoma rates as a self-supporting dairy state. In the Tulsa area, farmers were getting a blend price of $5.53, which at mid-March was two cents lower than it had been in January. The market administrators were already making their calculations. Producers had averaged 48 pounds of milk a day more in February than in January, but the number of producers had declined in a year from 1,590 to 1,479. In Nowata County, Chairman Cliff Gowen personally knew all the NFO dairymen. They would hold. In the days to come, the Sooner dairymen would buy milk and hand it over to the Osage Nursing Home and to Hays House for retarded children, and a top producer could calculate that it was costing $90 a day to hold.

Seated on the periphery of the action, Oklahoma NFOers knew that they could not dent the local milk supply. "But," commented Herb Karner of the *Tulsa World*, one of the nation's best farm editors, "they feel strongly about the national action and said they will do all they can to cooperate with dairymen in other states to get higher prices."

This meant that John Fuller would dump the milk from his 45 Holsteins, and that Joe Swanson would feed the milk from 27 cows to the hogs (". . . what we used to do before we had refrigeration and rapid truck transportation, but now it means something . . .") and that artificial insemination technician and dairyman Art Delmas would have his wife churn butter and hold it in the family's freezer, and that Leo Glenn would be riding Ottawa County's dusty roads and hold, and that all the rest would hold, and when necessary dump. This was the least they could do, the Oklahoma farmers knew. The big dairy states would have to write the ticket.

mha + 1

LIKE THE SOUND WAVES in a sonic boom, the thunderclap of NFO on the move rolled across the land. As when the nation is in the grip of storm, there had been a few hours lag between the fact and the realization. In the production of milk itself, there had been such a lapse between the fact that farmers were giving their milk away and the realization that many were going broke. Yet to Idaho farmers who spilled their milk over the edge of Snake River Canyon near Twin Falls, it made just as much sense to dump in the wilderness as to dump it on the market in town. At the prices they were getting when they sold to processors, it amounted to the same thing.

And so farmers piled their 10 gallon milk cans into about 35 vehicles for a run to the canyon's edge. Coming as it did in Idaho, the dumping of 127,500 pounds of milk was more symbolic than anything else, but as former Idaho State NFO Chairman George Juker put it, we are living in a world of symbols in which the symbol of power means efficiency, and unrecognized farmer efficiency takes on sack cloth and ashes. That farmers would no longer endure this inequity was dramatically displayed as the white liquid whitened the ground on the north side of the Perrine Memorial bridge. It made a good show for the second holding action day, and farmers immediately planned to bring out the big tank trucks the next morning.

There are 8.5 pounds in a gallon. Thus 127,500 pounds spilled near Twin Falls meant that about 6,000 quarts had been kept off the market. Actually, that is only a calculation. Processors cut milk to 2.5 or even 2%, and milk doesn't come from a cow that way. Water stretches the supply—as NFO farmers were soon to be reminded.

1. *capital of yesteryear*

The Associated Press did most of the milk action reporting on March 16. Only here and there did a local paper bother to haul in the story, and still more rarely did the mindless minds of the fourth estate appear. The "brilliant ones"—that is, the wiseacres of journalism —were not to hand out their holy ordinances until much later. The mediocre immediately lived off the capital of yesteryear, which in reporting NFO meant "violence." This time NFOers were ready.

To a man they had come to realize that even a small incident could bomb the NFO effort, not enhance it. This intelligence was bound to clash with one of the few absolutes almost all reporters believed. Violence made news. It was good for the front page, *ergo* it must be good for the NFO effort. Men denounce it, but love it, and pack the stadiums to see it. Isolate a man and he knows that there isn't a thing in heaven or hell worth dying for. But put him in the theatre of action, and he stumbles to the slaughter chute like a sheep. "The eyes of the world are on you," the field commander tells his troops. If a man has to die, he surely doesn't want to die alone. Newsmen see enough death and destruction to drink a conclusion from the sorry distillate, but the conclusion has little to do with the dimensions of a social movement. Individual mayhem is not war, and war is not social protest. NFO had researched what made social movements tick, and violence was not an enhancing element. In the face of steps taken to prevent even an incident, the organization's leaders had every reason to believe the past would not repeat itself.

But the questions were there. At Mandan, North Dakota, the *Pioneer* sought out Conrad J. Kalberer, Chairman of Emmons County. "We definitely don't want any violence. We're taking all precautions to avoid violence." Over at Valley City, the *Times Record* picked up and rehashed the wire service report. A reporter talked to Gerald Gerntholz, Chairman of Barnes County. The questions were the same. The answers were the same. Orientation had paid off. Across the country, spokesmen were counseling against incidents and reciting the story of agriculture.

If "low farm income" was a common denominator, the elements were never the same. North Dakota NFO Director Clarence Stockstad ran through those elements with every chance, whether on the road or fielding a phone call at his holding action office at Edgerley. Danny Downs and Lawrence Beitz were doing the same at Hillsboro. The action had to do with milk, but NFO in North Dakota was even more worried about CED's fast ripening dream of corporation farming. The entire state had only 12 cities with a population of 5,000 or more. The farmers who remained were bigger and poorer than their neighbors to the south. Their land sprawled so that on a clear day, one could literally see forever. Rare, indeed, was the wheat farmer who could take in his holdings with a single sweep of vision from north to south, east to west.

Milford Odegaard of "imperial" Cass County, who had helped NFO organize ever since it crossed the border, had sold his cows nearly two years before the holding action, but Sylvester Radermacher still operated a dairy farm, over 2,000 acres worth of it, having taken another couple of sections the year before. As NFO headed into the milk holding action, Radermacher and his son Gene knew that taking over more land was no answer, because no variable, absolutely no variable could substitute for poor milk prices, just as Woodrow Nelson having his wife plow his 2,560 acres near Berlin was no substitute for low grain prices. This was the story. It had to be told to the public, the politicos, the customer. The processors already knew it by heart.

The grass-roots ingenuity used in handling both information and maintaining image reached new proportions at times. At Alexandria, South Dakota, for instance, the Community Room in the Security State Bank served as an NFO information booth during the holding action, open until 8:00 p.m. every night except Sundays.

As the news of the milk action exploded across South Dakota, a lot of people learned for the first time how the industry is run. NFO furnished a great deal of the information, but citizens who read statements by Don Culhane, the owner of the Culhane Dairies and a past president of the South Dakota Dairy Association, found themselves looking at the storm that was breaking with abject disbelief.

"We're in a marketing area in which the federal government sets the prices to be paid to farmers," Culhane said. If that was the case, even the assertion that farmers were being paid 20% more than last year could not keep people from asking how come farmers had been driven to such desperate measures. Joe Klug, the manager of Armour Creameries at Mitchell, could not dispel such doubts with a "too soon to comment" remark, nor could a "spokesman" for the James Valley Milk Producers Association when he asserted that farmers shouldn't hold, and that 26 farmers of that group would continue to deliver because, in his words, "We are obligated to deliver because we are under contract to the processors." To the other farmers standing in the wings, this sounded all too much like, "We'll let NFO do the fighting."

NFO was doing the fighting on March 16, but it wasn't the kind of fighting headline writers liked to report.

Like early Christians who expected the world to come to an end very soon, South Dakota NFO members did not look for a long hold-ing action. They looked for a peaceful one. Richard Minnaert of Lake County said: "This holding action will be run different."

South Dakota's counties had been blocked out and placed under holding action leadership to make sure. Vince Spader's home base at Oldham was his farm. It was here that he received action instructions, and it was from home base Oldham that he methodically kept track of milkshed, farm and county activity, in that order of importance. Bill Nafziger lived at Spencer, but the holding action office was set up at the Larson Manufacturing Company in Woolsey. At Salem, Warren Stofferahn and Richard Feterl turned Room 9 of the Home Motel into a special MHA field office. More information was to clear through that office in the next few days than was handled by many a secton command post in Europe during WWII. Early on March 16, reports started popping like firecrackers. It was that way from the very start.

For one thing, people around South Dakota were good and mad. They had been sore ever since a *Madison Daily Leader* article the summer before had told of the low prices at the farm and the 100% spread between producer and consumer. There had come about a growing realization—at least among small town folks living in a rural setting—that people were willing to pay the farmer a fair price for milk. This idea had been fanned into flame by hearsay reports that people were paying up to $1.50 a quart for milk during a Chicago blizzard hardly a few weeks before the holding action was called. The short end of the stick, after all, was the short end of the stick. In a way it had never been any different.

History records that agricultural settlement in South Dakota began in 1856, when a handful of pioneers from Iowa and Minnesota started farming near present-day Sioux Falls. Indians were still very much in possession of the land, yet land-starved farmers considered the hostile territory "free land." Later, in 1858, a treaty between the Sioux and the federal government remanded all lands between the Big Sioux and the Missouri to the U.S. government, presumably so that victims of the recent depression back east could get re-capitalized out west.

It is one of the ironies of history that the United States stood alone in the new world as the only government that started by giving no free land to settlers. France, Spain and Mexico handed out free land from day one. The emerging United States perhaps offered freedom to men, but it sold its western lands to wealthy speculators.

At a time when wages were 25 cents for a 12-hour day, the United States government was handing out blocks of a thousand acres of the world's best land for $5.00 an acre. American land was thus the speculator's gamble, and underwrote fantastic booms and crashes, with the farmer getting cleaned out in the process. After the fertile acres had been settled, and only the plains remained, and the gambling had moved off into railroad stocks, the Homestead Act came into being. The year was 1862. The Act was repealed in 1935.

The great period of homesteading did not come in the era called "the timeless west" by movie makers. It came from 1913 to 1926. During the 1913-1926 period, homesteaders took title to nearly 101 million acres of the total 276 million acres passed out during the homesteading period, 1862-1935. As late as the 1930s, land was being homesteaded at the same rate as in the 1860s Homestead title was given to more than one million acres in 1934. Homesteaders held approximately six million acres in 1935, at the time the Homestead Act was repealed and 197 million acres were withdrawn from home-stead entry.

Looking history squarely in the eye, one can almost understand why early pioneers feared neither Indians nor the wilderness, but shook in their boots when dealing with speculators, land agents, marketing interests, railroad men—in a word, with the emerging business com-plex that farmers were not even to understand before the advent of NFO almost a hundred years later.

With or without NFO, South Dakota is a land "full of distance." Half the state, particularly out west, is pasture land. Field crops take up almost all the acres between the Missouri River—that more or less halves the state from north to south—and South Dakota's eastern border. South Dakota's farmers have never lacked courage. Fighting dust storms, droughts and blizzards, they have always taken the worst of nature in stride. And when the chance came for farmers to fight the worst features of a system that paid them for less wealth than they produced, not a few climbed aboard immediately.

2. *capillary action*

They were in the biggest battle of all time now. And so the tanks filled up. With and without fanfare, farmers opened the valves, and thousands of pounds of the lacteal liquid spewed out on the spotless concrete floors. The more enterprising of the daily papers sent cameramen into the fields, and the party lines carried conversations, "When are you going to dump?" and "Will you let us take a picture?"

At first there were mixed emotions about this. How the dumping and the pictures were to be handled had never been resolved. Two schools of thought had been aired at NFO. One was that dumping would enable every editor in the country to fish out a picture of a hungry looking kid and run it next to milk going down the drain. This might damage the effort beyond repair. Some counseled hidden dumping. And still there was the necessity of driving home the point. The dispute had never been resolved. A problem that isn't resolved usually finds an answer anyway. NFO in effect dumped an ink well on blotter paper to see which way the capillary action would take it.

Milk trucks usually pick up at the farm every other day. Farmers who had been skipped the morning of MHA Day found their tanks full the following morning. For them the moment of truth arrived first.

John Zurfluh, whose picture had appeared as early as Wednesday, made the UPI Telephoto transmission cables, and across the nation bureau cylinders were spinning off screened copies. On MHA + 1, editors who didn't see this dramatic shot as satisfactory had to shoot their own pics. This is what the *Free Press* at Mankato, Minnesota did. The reporters went after the NFO leaders, but they could have asked any individual member to equal effect. C. N. Tachney taped a

NFO

MILK HOLDING ACTION

NOW IN EFFECT

sign to the stanchions where he milked 31 cows a day, and readers who saw it could be allowed to infer what they would from the demand for $1 a hundredweight, but for sheer drama there was nothing to equal a picture of milk going down the drain. Inch by inch the real message made its way into print. Robert Sorenson of Blue Earth County, Minnesota warned of milk shortages down the road a ways, and found his words quoted, but pictures were worth a thousand words.

In the Austin, Minnesota area, the details started coming in. *Bloom-ing Prairie reported holding; Vernon at Hayfield was starting to count the customers who weren't shipping; Adams chalked up the milk that wasn't there, and at Brownsdale managers were going through the same motions.*

Robert Stier, NFO Chairman of Mower County, started working up the check sheets, but the weekend was dead ahead, and he hardly expected a real pinch before the weekend.

It was, in that much quoted phrase, "too early to tell." If there was to be a run on milk buying, it hadn't developed. Most of the creameries were operating. And, NFO regulars didn't expect a long holding action. There was, in the words of Gerald Goldschmidt, NFO Chairman of Brown County, "power in this kind of holding action." Goldschmidt had handed out the announcement of the holding action itself at a district meeting in Sleepy Eye. And at Sleepy Eye the manager of the local drying plant reported "no change."

Everything was more normal than normal. Dutifully, the questions were asked of the dairy associations and creameries, and just as dutifully the managers entered denials. Milk was coming in as usual, they said.

But there were the pictures and the TV cameras. And there were the statements by farmers. "Our milk is for sale at a price," Homer Mote of the Winona County NFO said, and there were some few references that this was a holding action, not a dumping action as nurse May Ann Beetz had told the Milwaukee-based NFO convention. Yet everyone knew that the difference was merely a matter of hours, and advance intelligence indicated that processors weren't going to strike their colors in any matter of hours. There were always the "on schedule" statements. Milk supplied into the Twin Cities was said to be arriving on a normal basis, and over at Ellsworth Co-op it was "too early to tell." The rundown statements of creamery managers were quite complete early on Thursday, but any discerning analyst could detect a change of pace by the time late editions hit the city lawns. Joe Woelfinger of Goodhue County could count the "members dumping right now," and right now had to be considered in terms of a holding action hardly 16 hours old.

At Welcome, New Ulm, and at Northrop the eyewash said "normal." From Rochester came what was possibly the first honest reporting job in Minnesota. The story was headlined:

NFO MILK HOLD ACTION
HAS SOME AREA EFFECT

Housewives in Fergus Falls added it up correctly, and reports started floating in that the ladies were "obviously stocking up with several half-gallons of milk." Otter Tail County NFO dairy committee head Elmer G. Johnson had warned of the farmer's stand-pat attitude. "We will not go to the creameries to initiate contracts. They have to come to us."

Despite the "no effect" litany that had come to reverberate from the airwaves, there was the simple fact which could not be shrouded in a spate of words.

Rock Dell Cooperative Creamery, which averaged about 150,000 pounds daily, expected to process no more than 50 to 75% of that total on March 16. Farmers on one entire route called and told the bulk driver not to turn out, and this was a route that usually accounted for 30,000 pounds. The manager at Stewartville said he was short 4,900 pounds, but the rest of the processors admitted nothing. Either they were holding to the party line or in fact getting their milk.

3.   *down the road*

Spinning the wheels of its calculators, NFO soon came up with figures, by plant, by county, by state. During the early hours of the action, charges and counter charges filled the air and created a picture, an image. Examination of the process in a single state should suffice.

None of the press coverage in any state hauled out the skeletons of the past as did the reports in NFO's home base, Iowa. The two Bonduel, Wisconsin casualties of 1964 somehow became the villains, not the victims in the piece, and the alleged bombs of yesteryear were lobbed again, at least in print, as though an insurrection had arrived. Not a few NFOers recalled the *Des Moines Register* farm editor's "half exploded sticks of dynamite" with a chuckle, but a chuckle would not dismiss the damage shaded reporting could account for. At NFO headquarters determination tightened. The goal was to prevent even a single incident in the entire holding action, and there were prayers that if some hothead became uncorked it would be anywhere except Iowa.

The Des Moines Co-op claimed to sell milk for nearly 2,000 dairy farmers in some 71 of Iowa's counties, as well as four counties in

Minnesota. In terms of volume, this came to 454 million pounds a year, or really more than a million pounds a day.

Iowa co-op managers were among the first to put the heat on striking farmers. The Des Moines Co-op president issued a statement, one that was to be copied, improved upon, and refined as the action wore on. In a nutshell he told farmers that if the milk volume doesn't come in, it will mean increased costs. As everyone knows, costs are the farmers' personal property. "We must assume that the members causing such costs through violation of their contracts with the dairy cooperative will be liable for such additional costs."

Threats didn't matter. Ray Weber, NFO Chairman of Dubuque County, promptly had himself photographed by the *Dubuque Telegraph* dumping milk into a hog feeder. In the Newton area, Robert Buckles, Hollis Adams, Harold Hoksbergen, Ray Vander Linden and Gib Bandstra went down the road on a membership drive, asking farmers to join NFO and support the action. Henry Norman in Whiteside County took his role in NFO seriously and started telling the NFO story—how improved milk prices would improve the economic posture in rural America.

Across Iowa, like tenpins tumbling, a schedule of meetings came into being. There would be a meeting every night. It might be in the Clinton County NFO meeting hall at Delmar, with Chairman Sam Thompson of Lost Nation and Lyle Doty of the Dairy Commodity Department presiding, or it might be held in the Whiteside County Bank or Coliseum with Don Bush and Henry Norman in charge. It took a minority to lead the way. It took NFO Chairman Thomas H. Williams in Johnson County and some half dozen of his close associates to start the ball rolling, "no pressure," just plain talk about joining NFO and as members refusing to let trucks pick up the milk.

At Mason City, Robert Jellings of the North Iowa Cooperative Milk Marketing Association took up the call sounded at Des Moines. Holding farmers would lose their membership, he warned. With 100 Grade A producers, this Co-op sold about 80 to 85% of its production to Carnation. Farmers viewed the fenced-in position of the co-ops with disdain, and held anyway. Everywhere, the green printed NFO handbills, carefully worded, showed up "down the road." They stated that the organization could not legally advise or solicit support of non-members. But NFO could ask farmers to join, and the immediate reason for joining was front page news in 50 states.

Always, a small group led the way, because, in the words of Wilbur
Garrels of Des Moines County, "A relatively small number of people
cooperating can do wonders." Such a message was essentially the one
John Kuch, Oras Kanerva, or Erhard Pfingsten gave in other rooms
with other voices.

Don Smith of the *Spencer Reporter* promptly seized on "small
numbers leading the way" out of context and reported that farmers
"are not going along with the milk holding action . . ." The conclusion, he said, had been fielded from drivers and officials at the
O'Brien County Creamery and at the Hartley Creamery. As an Iowa
assessment it made the AP wire service.

Iowa NFOers pounced on such reports. Cemented into place,
"negatives" could destroy the holding action before it was well
underway. Likely as not, farmers hearing such billingsgate over the
radio and reading it in the public prints would tuck their tails between
their legs and quit. It would take a lot of screaming by men like
Fred Deardorff to change that.

4. *nfo wire service*

Missouri NFO Director Fred Deardorff was one of an even dozen
usually available for duty in the holding action Nerve Center. The
Nerve Center had been set up in the big Board of Directors room at
Corning. It had 17 phones and looked very much like the news
bureau of a big city paper, or at least a command post in the Battle
of the Bulge. It was both. Over a hundred men had been handed
blocks of counties in the organized states. In turn, each had been
assigned helpers to cover the counties, "down the road" territories,
and to report. As reports came into the field offices, they were
handed on to Corning's Nerve Center by direct wire. Anything
really important rated "hot line" status.

The Nerve Center functioned 24 hours a day, seven days a week,
and the lines would not be taken out until after the phones stopped
ringing. From the far-flung territories the details came forth. Scraps
of information, case reports, all were filed by this hastily recruited
"NFO wire service."

Fred Deardorff was not the only man in the Nerve Center, even if
he was the most vocal. In fact, there were times when even that
point was moot. When Lance Johnson, Clarence Thatcher, Bill Lashmett, Albin Rust, Ralph Meek, John Kalainoff, Allen Nunnenkamp,

Herb Goodman, Gene Potter, Lloyd Fairbanks and Don Zmolek all talked on different lines at once, the Nerve Center became a veritable boiler factory.

The operation indeed had all the earmarks of a command post. Rollaway bunks had been carried in from the alley. Here and there limp forms, directors, officers, field men, President Staley himself, could be seen catching a few winks amid the roar of activity. To clear the way for foot traffic, chairs had been stacked in a corner. Cartons of milk lined the tables usually reserved for personal papers of Board members. Overhead, wires had been strung on insulated hooks, festooned like balcony decorations at a pep rally.

As the information flowed in, handwritten, cryptic in the extreme, but correct in detail, it was fed into a nearby Smith-Corona portable. Minutes later those same facts flowed out again, this time to all the field people, who not only reported in, but took down the details Corning had to offer with each call.

The job proved to be impossible. Sometime during the second day, someone dropped a suggestion, two words: *tape recorder.* Of a sudden the messages got short. "Get a tape recorder and know how to use it, then call back."

It was a refinement that was to put the Nerve Center in the forefront of activity, and if informed opinion is correct, saved the holding action time and time again. The calls got shorter. In half the time it takes a secretary to write a few notes, Nerve Center workers could spiel off an entire tape. These tapes—while poor quality by studio standards—could be reproduced in the field and played at county meetings in the evening, or transcribed and handed out as mimeographed newsletters.

As fast as county groups could lay their hands on tape recorders, a new scene was born across rural America: farmers with their eyes glued to a tape recorder listening to the battle news as it came in. "It reminded me of the old radio days," Vic Holst reported after a tour through Minnesota counties.

Understandably, some reports were of marginal importance. Some were too germaine to be re-issued without first being checked.

Individually, and a half dozen at a time, the phones clattered, day and night. The shifts changed, and morning relieved night, and afternoon relieved morning. Milk, paper cups, and a spartan tank of coffee stood well out of elbow reach on a table in one corner. Papers flooded the tables and floors in an ever-swelling tide, and still more

papers and notes were racked up by the hour, the day, so that anyone interested could reconstruct the entire action in the fullness of
time.

5. *the nerve center*

The Nerve Center. Three men in charge. Lloyd Fairbanks. Bill
Lashmett. Herb Goodman. Phone numbers on the wall. Legal sheets,
single spacea. States. Names. Addresses. Ohio. Art Phillips. Area.
Zanesville. Phone 614-453-5392. Ohio. Don Lowry. Ken Jones. Names.
Names. Names. Phone numbers. Phone numbers. Phone numbers.

Whirr! NFO. Lloyd Fairbanks. Who? Joe Hobbs. What's going on
in Kentucky? Kyana's manager said on the radio he would furnish
trucks and protection for those who wanted to bring in milk. Nobody's
bothering anybody. Just talk. Trying to sell the violence bit to the
public.

Pink sheets. ATTENTION. Who called? Norbert Conners. Where
from? Wisconsin. Hour: 8:30 A.M. P.M. [Circle one.] Northwestern
Co-op Creamery (formerly Blair) down 80%—daily over 1,000,000
pounds. Other plants in county down 25 to 50%.

Clip boards. Ball point pens. Coffee cups, paper cups, Styrofoam,
plastic, glass. Did you make this stuff, Potter? I've seen better
coffee come out of a crankcase. Strong coffee, mature coffee, plenty
of milk to water it down, plenty of sugar lumps to sweeten it up.
Cokes. 7-Up. Vess.

Write it down, boys, we'll all know. Give it to the "journalist." Feed
it through the Smith-Corona. Gawd, what a typewriter. It must have
been old during the Hoover administration. Tap-tap-tap-tap-tap. Look
at that speed. The machine's smoking! What a typist. I know, if you
had it all to do over again, you'd buy a new ribbon. Item: Twin
Fork, Wisconsin trucks not out. Who? Ken Linquist. Write it down.
Get the facts. Five W's. Who. What. When. Where. Why. And How.

Phones ringing, Red phone. Black phone. White phone. All together, 17 phones. Some for in-coming calls. Some for out-going calls.

Spell it out, boys, spell it out. Oras Kanerva has a question: Why
do they bury Finnlanders with their heads above the ground? Answer:
Cheaper than a tombstone, lasts longer. Conversation. Listen, Oras,
that's the way business operates. They like to appear brighter than
they are. They've got to have "competition" even after they've rubbed
it out. Everybody employed has to become convinced an enemy will

wreck the firm if they get into the saddle. The air has to be lead-heavy with suspicion. Any employee who sympathizes with farmers, out! Can't have stooges for the competition in this company. The boss bungles, so someone else gets fired. The reason the company went wrong was because an enemy got within. Tap the phones. Read the mail. Keep the employees in line. Suspicion is the cement that holds the big industrial complexes together. Can't let the farmer have allies. Keep 'em dumb. Don't let them hear this farm story.

Papers under the phones. Notes in shirt pockets. Reports on clipboards. Clipboards on nails. Waste baskets full. Boxes overflowing. Keep your hands off my report. Anyone caught taking my spiel will be shot. The penalty for stealing this poop sheet is death. Signed John Kalainoff.

Whirr! Ken Schmidt, Evansville, Wisconsin reporting. Roy's Sanitary Dairy received 10% of the normal supply this morning. They contacted every farmer and that's all they got. Jenny Brothers at Platteville got 8% of normal supply. The Cuba City Pumping Station, no milk at all. Look up the capacity. Make the calculation. Get the figure. Where are we? My gawd, she's building. Man, are the boys holding. Boy, what a holding action.

You want a holding action, then have a holding action. I know you've got Nervous Nellies out there. How many? Four. How do I take it? How do I listen to it? Just a minute. I'm splitting my gut laughing. Four Nervous Nellies. I'll tell you when you've got a holding action. You've got a holding action when she's bone dry. Now get those Nervous Nellies lined up. Hold. Quote me. Fred Deardorff.

Ed Graf on the line. Wrights Town Plant in Green Bay, Wisconsin, driver says down 50%.

Cigarette butts. Air blue with smoke. Ashtrays full. Ashtrays overflowing. Camels. Benson and Hedges. Who's smoking that cigar? It'll never stand up under chemical analysis.

Willis Rowell reporting. Manchester Cheese, no milk this morning. Rochester Dairies, in conference. What are they saying? How the hell should I know? OK, just kidding.

Coffee boiling. Milk sour. Sugar cubes gone. Who's got Sucaryl?

Start the run-through. New Jersey. Charles Barbay. New York. Guy Lewis. People in the field. Henry Specht. Max Douglas. Just got back from down the road. The non-members are signing like mad. Get some membership forms out here. The scarcest thing in

NFO. Membership forms.

Whirrr! Leo Hutchinson. Versailles, Missouri. Sealtest at St. Louis warned trucker he'd better run or forfeit his contract.

Delbert Riley on the line. Missouri. Around the horn. Dave Sudsberry. Bill Talbert. Rhea Hackler. Henry Shimek. Wally Larson. Ed Taffe. Bob Arndt. Dick Suntken. Write it down. Don't tell me. Write it down.

Clarence Schuchmann, Charles City, Iowa. I'm having individual farmers call radio WHO telling how many cows they are milking and that they're holding milk.

Whirrr! NFO. Leo Buehler, Piqua, Ohio talking. Sidney Dairy called my wife and asked what we meant by keeping the milk out of Sidney Dairy. They're out of milk and have to go to Furrow Dairy, which is between Sidney and Dayton. Sidney and Furrow are supplied by Miami Valley. Sidney stated that his supply was cut only 3.8%. It appears to me that he's either careless with the truth or a poor mathematician.

Whirrr! Ernie Knock, Fremont, Michigan. Radio Station WSHN, Fremont, had an hour-long call-in program with Ernie on the panel. Rundown: 75% of those who called in were in favor of the holding action; 25% didn't understand why there was need for a holding action.

John Engel in the Nerve Center. Got to leave boys. Nerves getting jaded. OK, spell him. Tired eyes, tired nerves, tired bodies, sleeping bodies on rollaway bunks. Don't leave a man on the firing line if he's dead tired. A false move out of the Nerve Center and the news runs like wildfire. You're worn out. The action's still strong. One sour note, and they'll think you're down at the mouth because the action is going bad. Psychology. Mass psychology. Truth. Loud, rumbling, groaning, screaming, ear-shattering noise. Boiler room noise, Nerve Center noise.

6. embattled farmers

And so the scraps of information arrived. (Wisconsin NFO Director Bob Manke's wife drives a schoolbus in Columbia County, Wisconsin. She said she saw a lot of strange trucks in the local area this morning.) And the scraps are put together. (Ed Shima was talking to the company in Chicago that makes NFO TV tapes. The lady said stores in North Chicago were out of milk last night and this morning.)

Across the dairy country, milk was filling the coolers. Charles King of Owosso thought his milk was going to stay in the tanks, but this was wishful thinking. No tank could have held the milk that was to build up. Bill Mahaffey, NFO President of Sanilac County, Michigan could store 400 gallons of milk, and after that it meant hitting the frost covered turf. Michigan was tough territory. It was MMPA territory.

MMPA markets milk for 8,539 members, and on cold morning Thursday, March 16, they "couldn't tell" whether the action would have any effect.

"No Action" came on like a chorus in a Greek play. Michigan Milk Producers in Bad Axe, Michigan Producers Company in Sebewaing and Nestles in Ubly all reported "no activity" by noon Thursday.

But Edwin Riethmeier of Frankenmuth, Chairman of Saginaw County, reported it differently. At least 98% of the NFO members were holding. Non-members were joining NFO and the action.

In the face of reports fielded by the Nerve Center, NFO leaders could only stare in abject disbelief when they read.

NFO ACTION NOT FELT YET IN THIS AREA

in the *Bad Axe Huron Daily Tribune.*

In much of the rural press, the story shaped up differently. Carl J. Buehler of the *Jackson Citizen-Patriot* reported embattled farmers staking their futures on the holding action. "If this doesn't work, we're done," said Mrs. Reginald Miner, who with her husband kept a 30-cow dairy herd.

Harold Seifert, Jackson County NFO Chairman counted most members as holding, and many non-members, while not responding to the plea to sign a formal membership, holding milk anyway. Seifert figured it would be a short action. Elmer Rohrback Chairman of Lenawee County, could report member participation in his area at 100%.

Early polls among the dairy industry tended to downgrade the effect of the holding action. But piecemeal reports of individuals, pounds dumped, all sent the calculator wheels spinning. It was like trying to catch gossamer threads in a strong wind—but the farmers at Corning tried. They tried. They did that. You could read in the moods how it was going. The spark was there and yet it wasn't hitting on all cylinders. On MHA + 1 the big city press was trying to hammer the holding action to death.

As the Nerve Center became overloaded, some of the report reading passed imperceptibly into Butch Swaim's Public Information Department. Don Mach had been an announcer at WIBW in Topeka, and he had never lost the knack.

This is Don Mach reporting from NFO Headquarters, Corning, Iowa. As the milk coolers across NFO Country, U.S.A. filled to overflowing today, milk dumping picked up volume. James Watson of St. Clairsville, Ohio dumped 2,000 pounds today.

Elsewhere tonight, Leo Buehler, a regional supervisor in Ohio, stood by his estimate that 50% of the farmers are holding. Ohio NFO Director Ralph Hoover has reported a hold running higher than the membership.

In the meantime, Ashland County, Ohio, NFO Chairman Wade Puster reported dumpings ranging from 12,000 to 13,000 pounds. And from across the state comes word that over 50 NFO members and non-members were reported dumping 50,300 pounds. Non-members had been asked to join NFO, but some didn't pause to sign the certificate of friendship before throwing out thousands of pounds of milk.

As the holding action continues to build, attempts are being made to stop the action. Affidavits have been filed in Athens Municipal Court against two farmers who were dumping on a road west of The Plains . . .

Reports read out of Corning were always condensed. There was hardly room on a tape to spill the details on what many a farmer was investing $3,000 in a month of dumping to tell. Locally, the story was gaining a hearing, depending on the mood and interest of the local editor. There was always something poignant in a man like Robert Shininger brooming milk down the drain in Defiance County, or Walt Chumney of Love City sending 4,250 pounds down the drain. Twelve hours earlier, such items would have rated top priority. Now they had become mundane. In the early hours of the milk holding action, the *Bellefontaine Examiner* tapped all the pictorial possibilities of milk dumping with three massive photographs on page one, showing Bill Haynes, John and Ralph Shoots and Bill Robson, all dumping in the milkhouse. In the days to come milkhouse pictures would no longer do in Ohio.

mha + 2

HARRY STILES, general sales manager of Bowman Dairy Company, Chicago, told *The Wall Street Journal* reporter: "I don't see how farmers can survive at $4.90 (a hundredweight)—that's what we're paying them."

Circa 1967, farmers couldn't survive on low raw material prices anymore than a nation or the world can survive by earning less than parity at the foundation level. As commodity indexes sink—in the U. S. or anywhere in the world—whole populations become strike-bound much of the time. Social programs are bitten to pieces and digested by inflation. Cost of living indexes rise. And if national income goes up, it is awkwardly juxtaposed against the fact that poverty multiplies. A nation out of tilt is not a happy one, and certainly on MHA + 2 much of rural America realized that 40 million people had been "shared out," and they weren't happy about it.

The businessmen—who think only in terms of buying and selling milk, and little else—geared their organizations to riding out the storm. Pure Milk Association in Chicago supplied more than 40 milk companies in the windy city. Avery Vose, president of PMA, told the press that the supply would run low by late in the day if the holding action continued.

It would continue, of course, and the new and subtle pressures would be brought to bear on farmers who were holding. The Omaha-Douglas County Health Department led off. In letters to farmers, Harold Irvin, Chief, Milk Sanitation Section, flowered forth in the finest martinet fashion: "*Effective immediately your Grade A Milk Handling Permit is revoked for the reason you are no longer sending milk into the Omaha market. Prior to reinstatement of your milk handling permit, it will be necessary that a representative of this*

*department inspect your milk handling facilities. At the time of the
inspection, it will necessary that the bulk tank be emptied so that
it can be properly inspected along with the rest of the milk handling
facilities."*

The tactic couldn't work in Minnesota or Wisconsin, but in an
area where farmers had no alternate outlets, removal of a permit
was tantamount to closing down the farm. Some farmers capitulated.
They were immediately reinstated. A cryptic note scrawled across
the bottom of the threatening letter was sufficient. "Reinstated . . .
Harold Irvin, 3/17/67," read one document hand carried to NFO
headquarters.

South along the Missouri River, a similar communication had gone
out to farmers in the Kansas City area. In the front office at Corning,
Chief Negotiator Gordon Shafer fell hard on the task of "straightening
it out." It is difficult to straighten out something that hasn't happened
by accident. The trail led Shafer to Dr. Philps, who was the top
regulatory official in Kansas City. Philps was reached in California.
Shafer politely detailed the nature of the milk holding action, the
necessity for it, and the general economics of what a cancelled permit
would do to the NFO farmer. Ever so tactfully, Shafer suggested
that breaking a holding action did not come within the purview of
a regulatory official's office. Philps wasn't even polite. His answer
came like the bite of an axe. "Didn't you think of this before you
started this thing?" In California a phone receiver was slammed down
hard.

It was not an unusual position for a regulatory official to take.
Every city has an inch-thick milk code. Those who enforce the codes
do not attend farm organization meetings in the main. They go
to processor conventions and golf at the clubs where processors
lunch. Their orientation and thinking is cosmopolitan, not rural, and
being an unsophisticated lot they made the judgment that they
were indeed choosing their side, or at least staying on their own
side, when in fact they were working at their own destruction. NFO
officials followed through on everything. A call to Mayor pro-tem
Vic Swyden of Kansas City drew a promise that His Honor Ilus
Davis, who was away from the city, would be appraised of the NFO
situation upon his return Monday morning. Swyden promised NFO
would be called Monday, which to NFO would be MHA + 5. The
call never came.

It wasn't missed. Activity was racing the length of the NFO office, and the length of NFO country. Without time to eat, Butch Swaim existed on Gus Glaser Old Smoky Summer Sausage, and staffers with phones propped to their ears like so many added appendages simply drank milk. Milk was plentiful in Corning, Iowa. The corner supermarket had filled its big back room—several times the usual trade requirement—because it simply would not do to let NFO run home base Corning out of milk. During the first hours of the action, when the word had gone out, and not enough time had elapsed to let the word come back in, restless NFOers had bought plenty of milk. On the drafty floor of Butch Swaim's Public Information Department, it kept as though it were in a refrigerator. Swaim's desk was a regular W. C. Fields scandal. Usually knee deep in papers, it had been cleared for the holding action, but at MHA + 2 the papers had built up again. Now a half gallon spilled in the middle of Butch Swaim's desk might not have been discovered until fermentation set in.

The shelves in the PI office had been filled to the ceiling months before—TV films, projectors, tapes, reprints, newspapers. Halved from the entrance by the cabinets for telephone rheostats, PI was a friendly place, albeit a hectic one. Maps adorning the walls pinpointed over half a hundred TV stations serviced by Swaim's office. Assistants Lee Elliott, Hugh Crane and Don Mach worked the mail if only to keep it from stacking up during the holding action, and spent their hours bouncing out with reprints, data, magazine articles, an ever increasing flood that tried to keep pace with the acceptance NFO was gaining across the country. Even Martha Swaim, recently recovered from heart surgery, put in several hours a day during the holding action.

If the tempo in PI outdistanced the imagination, the terror in the Nerve Center evaded instant comprehension. The signs of both doors were securely taped into place: *Authorized Personnel Only*. It didn't matter. Walking into the Pentagon to pick up top secret items would have been child's play compared to entering forbidden territory at NFO during a holding action. Everyone knew who belonged. Security was no problem.

1. *processors gave the pledge*

UPI was on the line. Staley handed out a few details, but newsmen weren't interested in details, yet! They wanted a statement.

"The milk holding action is beginning to snowball. Farmers realize this is their chance and they are making the most of it." For 6:57 a.m. it was a pretty good statement, and as the hours unfolded that Friday, it would prove to be an accurate one. As the sun moved from east to west, NFO activity rolled with it.

A change of pace was bound to come. TV cameras, always hard up for decent film clips, sensed the pictorial possibilities in milk going down the drain, and farmers—who at first suffered no little emotional trauma while dumping, must have decided that misery loves company. A reporter who knew a dairy farmer or could find an NFO officer's name in the paper's library had his work cut out for him. With or without cameras grinding away, the milk had to go. By MHA + 2, the difference between holding and dumping had already been decided. Time had decided it.

Oscar Knaggs, Vice Chairman of the Albany-Schnectady NFO unit, took one last look at the scurvy pay his milk had earned him these many years and marched to the milk shed and dumped. Down the coast a ways, New Jersey state Chairman Henry Douma echoed determination. "I'll drain the milk out of the tanks if I have to," and on MHA + 2 he had to. The New Jersey Milk Industry Association, Inc. represents 75% of the state's processors and sellers, a nice monopoly position, and Dan Wettlin Jr. played it for all it was worth. "No threat to supplies for consumers," came the refrain. But on the TV screens thousands of gallons were sinking into the snow.

Across the line in Pennsylvania the newspaper editorialists wasted little time in calling the hold a "tempest in a 10 gallon can." Always behind the times a decade or two, the city-bred writers would think of milking cows only in terms of illustrations in outdated texts. Cartoonists would draw bib-overalled farmers on milk stools, instead of milking machines and stainless steel tanks fed by polyethylene tubes.

On MHA + 2 processors gave the "pledge." Like a Boy Scout oath, it rushed to soothe the chain store customers. "Consumers will have an ample supply of milk," came the word from the Delaware Valley's largest co-op.

Leave it to Big Brother, the subliminal voices seemed to say. This holding action is Iowa stuff. Forget those plains blizzards. They always loose their strength as they blow east.

Inter-State claimed about 3,500 producers in Pennsylvania, south Jersey, Delaware and Maryland, and supplied most of Philadelphia. Inter-State could breathe a sigh of relief. NFO's strength had not spilled over into Delaware or Maryland.

In western Pennsylvania, things were different. Mercer County NFO Chairman John Stull could report that 90% of the country's dairymen were holding milk, not always without misgivings. Al Eilerman, for instance, could see his way clear to feed milk to livestock, but "It's morally wrong," he said, "to dump a cup of milk." It sounded strange coming from an NFO member. It was a sentiment that would be fanned into a mighty crescendo in the days to come, but today, MHA + 2, farmers were still too numb, and the public was too shocked to know what to think or say.

Still the NFOers knew they had to dump. It was that simple. Ashland County, Ohio NFO Chairman Wade Puster had seen a lot of dumping by noon. He could calculate that 212,500 pounds had been dumped in his county alone, and had watched a great deal of it go down the drain personally. At the Ray Hall farm, for instance, one needed boots to avoid the white stuff as it skated across the concrete, hunting a drain. The 212,500 pounds was no figure out of thin air. It was calculated, and within the standard deviation permissible, was probably correct.

2. *watch the amazing details*

There had been a small incident early in the day. "Just some of the neighbors having fun," one farmer later recalled. The neighbors had arrived at the NFOers farm and had blockaded a truck belonging to the Akron Milk Producers. The driver continued after NFO Director Ralph Hoover gave the errant funsters a good talking to. That was all. But it was an incident.

That was the way of the action. An observer could take the overview, or he could watch the amazing details. The details, in written form, stacked up, and the stacks had to be moved to make way for more.

Item. There are 1,300 dairy farmers in Wayne County, Ohio. NFO is not strongly organized in that county, possibly only 10%. Yet the hold is much better? Why? Farmers hear about the NFO action. Many would like to talk to NFOers, but members are too busy. What a farmer does with his milk is his business. He dumps.

Item. In solid Belmont County, Ohio, NFO Chairman Ralph Griffin reports a hold that is 100% effective, an easy calculation, since there are 100 NFO dairy farmers, and all are holding.

Item. Auglaize County, Ohio, holding 50,300 pounds a day, according to the best calculations.

Item. J. Frank Michaels, a dairy man in Warren County, has earmarked 5,100 pounds for dumping. "I'm going to keep it up until this thing is over."

Item. Walter Albers of near Dayton dumped over a ton of milk.

If you're a milk inspector, you never worry about the farmer. Milk is a gift of nature. It belongs to the people. A good, wholesome supply on a continuing basis is a sacred goal, and a farmer should be willing to realize this. How can they think of dumping when we need the milk?

In Dayton, Carl Williams of the milk inspection crowd was worried. A successful hold could affect the milk supply in three days.

So far, Milk Producers Federation, MPF, northeastern Ohio's largest operation, was supplying milk as usual. In the Dayton-Springfield area, where the Miami Valley Milk Producers Association held sway, Leslie C. Mapp cautiously counseled consumers not to push the panic button, to just buy milk in the usual manner. There was logic in this. Masters of traffic management, the secondary suppliers would know how to re-route milk into deficit areas. All they needed was time. And there was a blessed Sunday dead ahead.

But the Sunday would not save the disposing end of the dairy business from the reality that was taking form. On the buses city people read of that reality. There was the photo of Trumbull County NFO Chairman Lawrence Moore in the *Indianapolis News,* big as life, dumping milk into the drain system before the last of the white collar workers had arrived at work. It had impact, drama, pathos, tragedy rolled into a few columns of screened metal for a cylinder press.

But the cameramen couldn't be everywhere. They couldn't cover Walter Albers every time he emptied his tank, and they couldn't always make it to John Cochran's place in Seneca County, where John and two other producers dumped more than 8,500 pounds of raw milk. They couldn't be everywhere.

3. *the multiplier effect*

Farm income has a duality no other type of income has. It serves as a basic operating and living income for the farmer, and for the townspeople who provide services to the farmer. And it goes on through the economy, obviously. Perceptive economists have always had an inkling of the multiplier effect, the strange phenomenon which dictates that money injected in an economy must turn over several times. As early as 1908, a man who has come down in history simply as N. Johannsen published a complete anticipation of the multiplier effect now part of the Keynesian theory. Johannsen worked with a schedule: savings=1/7 income.

In other words, the total new earned income in an economy could be no greater than 1/7 of the net income.

It may be happenstance, and it may be a reflection of the enchantment man had for his technical accomplishment, but at the time of the milk holding action the duality of farm income had been forgotten. Hardly anyone in business or government remembered that in addition to serving the farmer and townspeople in service areas, farm income is the lion's share of the total new wealth created in any given year, and also the lion's share of the total addition to the existing money supply. Farm income—together with other raw material income—is the source of investment and expansion, and it is the total savings of an economy. It thus has a foundation quality. Income generated by industrial America does not have this quality.

Through generations we have added annually the gross value of the raw material production of the world or the nation—one year on top of the other—and each year we have been able to build so many homes and so many schools and so many churches and so many miles of highway, and then we have to wait another year for another crop to get some new wealth to expand some more. It's bigger now. It's more glamorous. We've learned how to use credit. We can have the highway the same year we clear the right-of-way. But ultimately we have to harvest the next crop to pay for the cement.

Yet the money is not created if the raw material price is scaled downward below its cost of production. It is not created if the production is lost. It is not created when the production is destroyed.

Thus every pound of milk Indiana farmers dumped cost the economy a loss in income. It cost the farmer who dumped 1,000 pounds a day some $55.30, but it cost the national income possibly seven times that much. The Central Indiana Dairymen's Association could gloatingly estimate receipts down a scant 10% as it collected milk from 63 of the state's 92 counties, and the Fort Wayne Co-op could team with the Dean Milk Company is chopping the shortage into half, but they could all gloat only because they did not understand the multiplier. The farmer may not be better than the processor or the steel worker, but his money is. His income has the highest multiplier. As farm income goes down, that multiplier goes with it.

In NFO, men like Loyal Berkholder, Chairman of St. Joseph County, Indiana, knew about the multiplier, and they also knew that the rhythm of arithmetic works both ways. Reduce a dollar of income at the farm level, and you reduce the national income fully $7. Only people who patronize small loan companies think they can shore up income losses with new borrowings forever.

For a decade running, NFO members had been telling some parts of this story, but the men who buy cheap and sell dear know little of all this high falutin' stuff. Sidney Wanzer and Sons in Illinois knew only that, boy oh boy, orders were coming in fast. In the front offices, the prospects of rationing rated mention. And here and there a merchant could lick his chops in anticipation. If a blizzard can get you double your money in a couple of days, maybe a real hold on milk can do the same. At Hawthorn-Mellody Farm Dairy, Inc., it was noted that "the demand for supplemental orders began late yesterday."

Dwight Clouter was NFO Chairman of Christian County, Illinois. He was one of 14 county chairmen summoned to Mattoon, where the holding action for Illinois was announced. Clouter knew, as did most Illinois dairy farmers, that the action would shape up the minute milk stopped arriving from Minnesota and Wisconsin. He knew that most of the milk produced in those two states was exported, and that much of it was tanked right into Illinois.

4. *the heart of the fight*

NFO members in Minnesota and Wisconsin knew it too. No little effort had been expended in seeing to it that members knew exactly where the heart of the fight was to be found.

Late in the day, March 17, the Zumbrota State Bank community room was quiet. Elmer Hintz had a little information. He hoped to have more by the next night. Richard Steffenhagen, who farmed near Red Wing, was the seventh stop on the milk hauler's route. "Out of seven stops only two shipped milk," he said.

That's the way it was. Information came in scraps. The mosaic was too complicated to be analyzed where it was happening, too disjointed to be reported except through the medium of estimates and guesstimates. Each county could count members like Roger Larson pouring milk to the hogs in Nobles County, but what did it all mean?

Milking was finished at 6:30 p.m. at the Gerald Durst farm on the Goodhue-Dodge County line west of Pine Island. About 2,000 pounds had gone through the pipeline milker system into the 5,400 pound stainless steel storage tank in the milk house. Shortly after 6:30 p.m. Durst opened the valve on the tank, and the white stuff gushed across the floor, out the drain and into the farm yard. "If this doesn't bring a price," Durst said, "the cows go next."

You create the foundation for money, but you don't get any of it, and because you don't get any of it, the rest of the economy fails to get its share. It sounds crazy, but that's the way it is. Except the bright boys don't understand it that way. The economy is a poker game to them. The money is fixed, or static. Isn't the price of gold fixed? The new economists say all government has to do is fix tax policy and monetary policy. Pick up the winnings from those who get too far ahead, and redistribute them with "programs" so more can stay in the game. The world? What about the world? The government takes a cut out of each pot, then ladles some of the dough to the onlookers outside the game. Trouble is, we're all playing for scraps of paper now. The dairy farmer is tired of producing simply to trade in some of his equity for more money to keep on producing for less.

"We've laid our organization on the chopping block. It's do or die," John Hermand told the Olmstead County, Minnesota NFOers. This was common talk. It would be bad enough to create wealth for others, but the way this thing's rigged, farmers weren't even doing that.

And so Merle Bany of Olmstead County could empty the milk cooler into a manure spreader, and Alvin Tegtmeier who farmed along the southeast shore of Otter Trail Lake could hoist the cans hip high and drain 3,000 pounds of milk. It was costing Tegtmeier $70 a day. Somehow the public had to learn it was costing them even more, both when he dumped and when he was underpaid.

Minnesota farmers understood the action in a sophisticated way. And the action was building. Redwood County NFO Chairman Gilbert Koller knew exactly how many of his 425 members were holding, but he also knew the news of the hold was out, and there was nothing he could have done to encourage or discourage sympathetic farmers to do likewise.

One by one the Minnesota action workers had located offices. Brynolf Grahn and Ernie Stock had turned the Mahnomen area into a finely honed holding operation. Ed Taffe, Ted Schwank and Glenn Shannon could always be reached at Clinton. In Minnesota it usually took three men to a station, even though Pete Nagel, Henry Schimek and Wally Larson handled St. Cloud, Rochester and Brainard on a one-man, one station basis. Over at Tracy, Minnesota, Bob Arndt and Melvin Klein kept in touch, both with the territory and with Corning from Elmer Klein's place—because it was more convenient and because it was cheaper. Kermit Bottke and Jim Dububik did the same at Faribault from Bottke's home.

The staffers knew it. The farmers knew it. Minnesota and Wisconsin, more than any of the other NFO states, would write the holding action ticket this time. The leaders in those states had no intention of letting the effort fall apart.

5. *the daddy of them all*

Even though Minnesota NFOers sometimes didn't agree, Wisconsin was the daddy of them all in milk. All day, MHA + 2, Wisconsin had experienced every charge, countercharge, and psychological gimmick in the book. The atmosphere had become defined early the day before, both on the give and the take side, and so far no one was budging an inch. Hour by hour, all day long, the rumors and data and facts and information and misinformation churned in the milkhouses and the prints.

In Green County and Outagamie County, and in all the counties, NFO members hurried through their chores to get on with it, to go down the road and ask dairy farmers to join NFO and to dump. On the radio men like Truman Torgerson of Lake to Lake were being quoted on the "no effect" bit, but there was nothing opaque about words. It was different with milk, and farmers were pragmatic enough to discern this. Karvin Neuenschwander of Evansville had authorized his milk drained from a truck after it had been picked up by mistake. A lukewarm member would have shrugged his shoulders and let it go. Not Neuenschwander. It wasn't what he liked to do, but it had to be done.

There was indeed something opaque about the milk. There was something real about the partial monetization of the production that had come to characterize the farmer's creation of wealth. Only part of the money was there when the check came. Now none of it would be there.

And as Ashland County NFO Chairman Ken Lindquist assumed direction of the 12 northern Wisconsin counties, and as Steve Pavich move into the 11 county area centering around Rice Lake and Barron, the farmers who responded and dumped their milk knew exactly what they were doing. They were destroying real wealth, not so much to increase money income, but to adjust the institutional arrangements under which they operated. Few of them really believed in spot economics, in short supply, more demand, *ergo* more money. They really knew better than that. At the foundation level they knew that farmers had to write their own sales ticket, or perish, and take the companies and co-ops with them.

Early in the morning, a group of NFO leaders met at the Ben Klismith farm east of Stevens Point on Highway 10. It was the same farm that had been the rendezvous point of a tractor caravan the fall before, one that drew some measure of attention to the personal sacrifices of men in Viet Nam, and ever so subtly informed the powers that be that sagging prosperity brought on by low farm income could not be repaired by the public works project called war. From the Klismith farm, NFO regulars fanned out. Before the day was done, 90% of the non-members in the area had been offered the NFO membership agreement. If they were in sympathy, they could sign and hold. Many did.

It was, after all, America's dairyland. And in America's dairyland the question was bound to be posed whether in fact farmers were not holding against themselves. Did they not own the co-ops? Yes, farmers owned the co-ops, but the co-ops were not working for the farmers anymore. Farmers were not working against the co-ops, but the co-ops were working at their own destruction, and they didn't know it.

"There's been a 40 cent drop in three months," Larry Brostowitz, an NFO Field Representative, reiterated. "And I understand it will drop to $3.83 a hundredweight next payday."

Brostowitz had ten children. He could recall the first delivery, some 14 years ago, which had cost $50. The last delivery in February, hardly a month before the action, cost $150. During the same period the room rate at the hospital had gone from $7 to $22.50 a day, and nursery charges had jumped from $1 to $9 a day. "Yet they expect the farmer to feed the baby for the same milk price. It just doesn't work."

Everyone knew it. (And so 50 farmers took their milk to a farm near Dodge Center and dumped 50,000 pounds in a big ditch.) Calculated in any way, it couldn't work.

6. *the last resort*

It wasn't working in Kentucky, where Warren County Chairman
Curtis Lightfoot was telling farmers about the "only hope" of farmers,
and it wasn't working in Tennessee, where NFOers spoke of NFO's
Paul Revere message—*we're trying to warn the people before serious
food or milk shortages occur.*

To those who had never looked down the road by more than a
quarter of an hour, the NFO warning made little sense. Certainly,
it wasn't a message people were used to hearing, despite warnings
in *Ill Fares the Land,* a paperback that had been making the rounds
and was being read by a few NFOers, despite the hatchet job author
Dan P. Van Gorder did on the NFO organization. It was, however,
a message Hal Herd, farm editor of the *Nashville Tennessean* could
run with. Low milk prices were transmitting disaster like a disease,
east and west.

At Buhl, Idaho, NFOers had developed a flair for the dramatic.
Standing like so many tin soldiers on Buhl's Broadway, NFO members systematically tipped over 100 cans while 17,000 pounds of
milk flowed from a large milk tanker. At Buhl some farmers were
not NFO members. No one had asked them to dump. They had
heard about it and showed up, and the townspeople understood.
Several businesses had closed in Buhl during the previous few months.
Every time 13 farm families were forced out, the calculation ran,
another business went down the drain. Townspeople understood that,
too. The large milk tanker had come from Banquet Company, and
Clifford Ward, its owner, was an NFO sympathizer. Ward said he
would match each gallon withheld, and no one could stop him.
And as 12 tons of milk ran down the slanted main drag, women on
the curb felt their husbands were doing the right thing.

At Corning the leadership knew NFO was doing the right thing.

Staley's basic philosophy had been sounded to Doug Kneeland,
the Kansas City-based correspondent for the *New York Times.* Staley
had become convinced that the American farmer reached a cross-
roads during the depression of the 1930s—and cautiously took the
wrong fork.

"The farmer could have gone either way," he said. "He could have
organized, like labor, and fought for a price, or turn to government.
He chose the government."

He turned to the government, and the government paced his rate of bankruptcy. Suffocation is easy and painless. It puts to sleep not only the victim but those watching the tragedy—thus the abiding tragedy of the public press failing to comprehend what was happening. Those on the scene more frequently missed the signals than those far removed. Even now, in the holding action, it was happening that way.

As far away as Inglewood, California, the *Daily News* would show Lebanon, Missouri farmer Allen Sharpe dumping milk under a legend, "The Last Resort," but the *St. Louis Post-Dispatch* and the *Kansas City Star* would carry only the blandest of the wire service offerings.

At the end of MHA + 2, the diary at the Ellis Kitchen farm, near Topeka, Kansas wrapped up the day in nine lines. It was St. Patrick's Day, of course, and that rated mention, even if the holding action was not a base for merriment. "It is hard to keep the men's spirits up. Dairymen are pretty tough in many ways, but are downed easily too. Homer Nixon called and had six teams out on the road. They bought 42 gallons of milk at three stores. Two members dumped six ton in Leavenworth. Bernard Uhl dumped 600 plus 200 gallons to date . . ."

The big battle map on the wall outlined the counties under NFO organization. The map was easily 6 x 8 feet, framed and covered with acetate. A 16 mm. Bolex shooting ASA 400 captured the scene without extra light while Nerve Center regulars responded to Laverne Eldred calling from Michigan, Don Lowry calling from Pennsylvania, Danny Downs calling from North Dakota, all at the same time.

The milk cartons and cans of Butternut coffee seemed to stay full and the Ritz crackers remained uneaten. The Nerve Center, taking a cue from Butch Swaim's PI Department, subsisted on sausage and tomato juice.

Dick Fout could report a dumping in Ohio, pounds dumped, and the number of cows being milked, but this was getting to be mundane stuff. In an early hour any scrap of information was welcomed. Now it took a blockbuster to excite a Nerve Center regular. The data was logged in, that was all. And the report for the hour was read out while the line was still open.

Keith Emenhiser, Ohio, signing new members. Auglaize County, dumped 50,000 pounds . . . Hillard Waller, Missouri, Central Dairy at Jefferson City laid off all employees at noon yesterday (official). Franklin Simon, Kansas, reporting. KTVK and KAKE, Wichita, were

on hand when Dale Thompson dumped . . . Pete Nagel, Minnesota—
Businessmen at St. Cloud asked non-NFO members to hold their
milk. Some took it back home . . . [And always the long sheets of
details, this creamery out of milk, that truck not running, this creamery
closed, that truck arriving at a farmstead empty at 11:00 a.m.]

Bob Wilson was taking calls in the Nerve Center at 5:30 p.m. Bob
Arndt, reporting . . . Two Vulcan, Michigan (upper peninsula) bankers went down the road to encourage non-members to come out
to the meetings.

John Engles out of the Grain Department was taking calls at the
same time. Howard Vail was on the line from Indiana. "A milk hauler
claims he got 73,000 gallons from Beaver Dam today."

And suddenly a trend emerges from all the scraps of information.
Fantastic re-routing was shaking the dairy industry, and the non-
stop Interstates thundered to the tune of tanker traffic.

Clarence Thatcher was weary, but he was still in the Nerve Center
close to midnight. On the line was George Stiles of Kentucky. *St.
Mary's Catholic Seminary has 100 plus cows. Father Thompson thinks
it is right and moral to dump milk.*

7.   *sculptured stone calm*

The Country Club at Corning is a euphemism for an old farm house
and several acres of pasture punctuated with well kept greens. Sometimes, when not pressed too hard, NFO officials go there for a quiet
meal, one away from the interruptions that almost always attend
supper in any of the town's dining rooms. With the exception of NFO
Vice President Erhard Pfingsten, all the officers and Department
Directors joined Staley at the Club at 7:00 p.m. on St. Patrick's Day.

The talk was quiet and speculative, and Staley more than the rest
seemed imperturbed. If grave doubts slumbered in his soul, no hint
of emotion showed on his face. He had come a long way by mastering
his emotions, by clocking every move, and shifting emphasis on the
shaved part of a second.

Former Iowa Governor Dan Turner walked in with a few friends,
and at that moment Staley's sculptured stone calm broke. The governor had been one of Staley's best advisors back in the dollar days,
and the two men obviously admired and respected each other.
Independently, each would always credit the other with saving NFO.
"If it hadn't been for Dan Turner," Staley would say, "there would
be no NFO today." And Turner, the old battler who rarely bowed

to anyone, always reminded newsmen, "If it hadn't been for Staley, there would be no NFO today."

Staley got up, and with him the entire NFO delegation walked to Governor Turner's table. It was Dan Turner's 91st birthday. Staley introduced each of the men, and each in turn wished the governor well. It was a prophetic moment, this being taken back to the days when Dan Turner rode the county roads talking for NFO against all odds, and the memory of the dining room incident would take each of the weary staffers through the trying hours ahead. As they shook hands with the aging scrapper for farm parity, each drew from that salute the will to battle the odds.

The problems seemed to multiply geometrically. When Herb Goodman, Lloyd Fairbanks and Bill Lashmett returned from the Country Club dinner, they had a decision to make. NFO was sitting on top of an information explosion. Passing more than a few scraps of that information on to the field had become humanly impossible.

The decision came fast. Henceforth, a bulletin on the hour would be sufficient. The bulletins had to be terse.

SUMMARY, HOLDING ACTION REPORTS, 10:00., March 17 . . . Milk, up 2 cents a quart in Omaha. Four of largest non-members dairymen in Washington County, Nebraska dumping milk and working. Anderson-Erickson Plant at Fort Dodge, Iowa received no Minnesota milk today. Des Moines Co-op on the radio saying it will take legal action if members don't start selling. Grant County Kentucky, 32 new members yesterday. PMA transfer, Fond du Lac, no milk. Sheboygan County Cheese closing down. Garnett, Kansas plant, normal 37,000 pounds, down to 5,700. MMPA, Grand Rapids, reported using powder to bottle. Wright County, Missouri, 20 new members. Batavia Dairy, Batavia, Illinois, closing down. Leroy Orangeburger dumped 1,500 this morning at Salsberry, Missouri . . .

The facts piled up, but facts are not the story. The story was still out there where midnight was only minutes away, where holding action meetings were hardly over, where reports were being readied for reading into the thunder of the Nerve Center.

mha + 3

". . . exploitation of the weak by the powerful, organized for the purposes of economic gain, buttressed by imposing systems of law, and screened by decorous draperies of virtuous sentiment and resounding rhetoric, has been a permanent feature in the life of most communities that the world has yet seen." So wrote R. H. Tawney in *Religion and the Rise of Capitalism* in 1926, an era that saw raw material producers the world over exploited as a prelude to a world depression.

It was not by accident that the institutional spokesmen for acceptable exploitation came up fighting from their chairs the day NFO started holding milk. By early morning, MHA + 3, the defense advocates for the status quo were spewing out words in great geysers. Yet almost any farmer on the land, laborer in the factory, or freshmen in college could observe the quite simple fact that farmers were dumping milk because exploitation had been sanctioned by law and custom.

A year earlier, economists and social leaders had celebrated the 20th anniversary of the 1946 Employment Act, which proclaimed full employment for industrial America as official federal policy. It had been a lofty aim, but the vision had become tarnished for those in rural America.

Years of grinding unemployment during the 1930s had convinced Congress that even a viable democracy could no longer endure unemployment. Unfortunately, the law handed to three economists the task of constructing a system that would do away with enforced idleness, and—almost immediately—the President's economic advisors chose badly. Late in the 1940s they made the judgment that raw material production did not shape the level of prosperity in a tech-

123

nological age. Stabilize the big corporations, the thinking ran, and you stabilize the economy.

It didn't work that way.

But in the late 40s, with farm prices nearing full parity, the nation had a solvent economy. In 1948 there was an $8 billion surplus in the federal, state and local budgets, and reconversion from a war economy accounted for hardly $16 billion debt expansion.

Farm income had returned to the 1929 level hardly a year after the beginning of World War II. The general level had been balanced since 1942 by supports on the one hand, and—during the war—by OPA controls on the other. During the early months of the great, great war, the House Banking and Currency Committee had in effect monetized basic farm raw materials. The Committee was calling wheat, corn—the basic crops—by their correct name. The U. S. Constitution had given to Congress the power to create the money and regulate the value thereof. In the middle of the war, no one doubted that unless the government regulated the value of basic raw materials, it could not regulate the value of money, and therefore couldn't maintain economic stability.

But 1948 was a year of another color. The war was over and business was straining at the leash to get back to "normalcy." The House extended the price support bill at 90%. The Senate voted a 60-90% sliding scale. Finally, both measures were passed, and President Truman signed both bills. Thus the 90% bill continued monetization of farm crops at near full parity until 1949, and the second law provided for 60-90% parity to take effect January 1, 1950.

The minute 60-90% parity went into effect, farm prices started to slide. As commodity prices hit the skids, national income declined on a ratio of seven. When the Korean War broke out a few months later, a few in Congress wanted to go the World War II route again. They realized that without parity raw materials, the United States might well have suffered a liquidity crisis (gone broke) in the middle of WWII and lost the war. They wanted to monetize raw materials again, but the move was blocked because things were supposedly different.

There was war work to be done, the public pronouncements ran. And the 1946 Employment Act required the economic advisors to maintain full employment. New earned income from raw material production had been scaled down in homage to international trade. Therefore, there was only one way to operate. More debt had to be created, $40 billion of it a year to fight the Korean War.

When the war ended, debt creation was scaled back to $30 billion, which immediately canceled out $25 billion "unearned income" debt expansion had accounted for, and the 1954 recession followed.

Full employment could not be maintained without either parity raw materials, or more debt expansion. In 1955, $72 billion of credit was injected into the economy. President Eisenhower was promising the nation a $500 billion income. It couldn't be. On the basis of $300 billion of national income, $72 billion debt creation represented twice as much money as the nation had a right to borrow based on profits and savings. Savings started running out in 1957, and debt expansion fell down to $36 billion, or half the rate of 1955. The 1958 depression followed.

By this time the mandate for action had become clear. The small confederation of Cassandras supporting sound economic procedures argued for a return to parity raw material prices, but they failed to carry the day in the general's tent.

In 1959, $69 billion debt was created to shore up the faltering economy, whereas farm prices drifted downward, and Agriculture Secretary Ezra Taft Benson handed out maxims attributed to Brigham Young. But by 1959 the operating loss of the economy had increased to a point where $69 billion was barely enough to keep the momentum. A year later, 1960, the presidential campaign was fought against a background of "we've got to get the country moving again."

Kennedy did that. He duplicated Ike's tactic simply because he was taking advice from the same school of economists. By years, the gross debt injection mounted rapidly.

1961...$ 79 billion.
1962... 80 billion.
1963... 84 billion.
President Johnson took over and . . .
1964... 94 billion.
1965... 104 billion.
1966 (estimate) .... 110 billion.

A war can throw all the rules out the window, and the war in Viet Nam was doing just that. Keynesian economists pooh-poohed all concern over the burden of debt by saying, "We owe it to ourselves," a euphemism for "We owe it to a few," and "We're working to feed the interest mill," but the fact remained that too many people were being shared out in the process, and wars on poverty were not picking up the deficit. Farmers who were dumping milk had been shared out in the first year of the crazy game, and now their frustration had been distilled into spectacle-making desperation.

They believed that in an economic sense, if not legally, the 1946 Employment Act was "unconstitutional" because it failed to extend equal treatment under the law to those who lived and worked in rural America. Not a few of the dairy farmers who were dumping milk that cold Saturday morning, MHA + 3, knew that farmers were being used badly so that industrial America might prosper. Government manipulation of import quotas, crop estimates and surplus disposal were ever designed to drive farm commodities in to line with $35 gold. When basic crops arrived at 69% above the 1910-1914 index level, they reflected the difference between pre-Roosevelt gold at $20.67 and New Deal gold at $35. The trouble was, farm prices in line with $35 gold meant that farm earnings remained at the 1943 level—half high enough to cover the cost of production. Uncanny statisticians in the USDA had rigged the parity figures to show farmers getting 74% of parity, but any farmer who knew eighth grade arithmetic could calculate the real reward—hardly 50% of parity. Any way you figured it, on a 1910-1914 basis, or on a 1948-1950 basis, that's what it was. And the anger that went with knowing the facts made dumping milk all the easier.

1. *without passing through the intervening space*

The first report in the Nerve Center was typed at 9:00 a.m.

Don Lowry, Pennsylvania, reports that Crawford County members and non-members held 85% yesterday, and are going for 100% today.

As the new data was fed into the Smith-Corona, new patterns emerged. The hold was tightening. It was tightening in its image, effectiveness and durability. In New York, seven farmers loaded manure spreaders with milk, used oleo to grease the wheels, then ran the machinery up and down the fields in front of TV cameras. Oleo was cheaper than regular gun grease. Across the country, the catalog of participation had run well beyond the imagination of individuals. In every county, in every state, members were dumping milk, and the leak in the dike was being felt in the fluid circuit, and that's what counted. More important, non-members were joining NFO and then dumping. In Webster County, Missouri, for instance, the Cologna Brothers signed an NFO membership agreement in the morning, and by noon they were dumping 7,000 pounds of milk before the KYTV cameras. The individuals, names and pounds, were important, but they were no longer news.

What really perked up the ears of talkers in the Nerve Center was the fact that Fort Wayne, Indiana was rationing milk, one quart to a customer. MMPA at Grand Rapids, Michigan was reported using powdered milk to bottle, and suddenly, like a big *whoosh*, reports arrived from other states that powder was being fed into the fluid supply. This was clearly against the law, but it was being done, and on Saturday, who could get enforcement from the otherwise hell-on-wheels health inspectors! Using milk and water to stretch the supply became the order of the day. It was reported that the Central Dairy at Jefferson City, Missouri was down 82% the day before, but milk was still being fed into the stores. The NFO gumshoes went to work. By the time the 11:00 a.m. report was being written in the Nerve Center, it was to contain this line:

". . . . Grade A plant in Missouri using 1,000 pounds whole milk to 100 pounds water and milk powder for bottling."

An inside report from an employee at Milgram in Kansas City told NFO that the trade considered the next Tuesday to be critical, that retailers figured they could beg, borrow, steal or manufacture enough "Grade A" to get by until then. But it was tight. Trucks were picking up milk on off days in the Kansas City area when farmers were not at home.

Immediately the word went out of the Nerve Center to alert farmers. Hardly had the word gone out before a Michigan Producers Association member reported the same thing. An MMPA truck had arrived at the farm while he was gone. The sheriff was notified, but for every instance in which a sheriff could intercept an errant pickup man, countless others managed to squeeze their loads into the plants. Albert Nase at Lennox, South Dakota could write a warning on the blackboard in his milkshed ("THIS IS NFO MILK—HANDS OFF—DON'T PICK UP"), but in the main farmers would have to stand guard. Those who didn't want to stand guard could simply dump the minute they finished milking.

In the fullness of time, farmers would get paid for milk picked up "by mistake," but mistakes didn't help the holding action. The tactic of "mistakes" would not be good the next day, but for the moment across NFO country, U.S.A. it was working.

There was no way to salvage the milk that hit the dirt. Near

Minneapolis, snowplows cleared a field north of town for dumping of milk by a bunch of manure spreaders. TV and news media were on hand.

In the Nerve Center, the hot line was ringing. "Sauk County, Wisconsin is falling apart. A non-member was begging people to go down the road and work. Only one member would go with him. Trucks are running like crazy. What the hell's the matter?"

The Nerve Center flew into action. Bob Manke was back on the line with Bob Wilson by 12:39 p.m. "Ok, ten teams are out. It's been a little flat, but it's going now." A Spartan chewing by the king of Spartan chewers had shaken the apathetic farmers and puffed life into them.

As with the Nervous Nellies who wanted to break ranks, there was always a little repair work to be done. The pressure from some health departments eased somewhat while it picked up steam from others. In Kansas City, the Dairy Section of the Health Department reiterated its stand that farmers not shipping for three days would be de-listed. But the communication added that inspection would be made more promptly than indicated earlier. In Omaha, intervention by state representatives gained the same concession for producers. While the matter died down south, Bob Arndt in dairy-rich Marshall, Minnesota, could report that Schwan Dairy was threatening to cut off farmers if they didn't ship their milk forthwith.

With or without threats, the dumping continued. At the intersection of highway 55 and 19 on the Lawrence Vasser farm, six ton loads, one can truck, and four pickups dumped 112,000 pounds of milk. Minnesota's KSTP and WCCO were on hand. WCCO farm editor George Tice immediately scheduled a meeting for the next Tuesday to discuss the problem. The spectacle was big. But it was no bigger than the one at Waupaca and Shawano Counties, Wisconsin where bulldozers opened holes in the ground so that the two counties could have a contest to see which one could fill the hole first.

From every quarter, reports carried the omen of success. NFO Director Clarence Stockstad enjoyed complete rapport with the membership in North Dakota. There were deficit areas and good areas, but Stockstad could hand out only one word, "building." Deliveries were dropping at Cass-Clay Creamery in Fargo—the largest dairy in North Dakota. Ernest Malmskog, Cass-Clay's procurement manager, admitted: "We had about half our normal receipts today." One hauler, Malmskog said, normally picked up about 100,000 pounds. He had brought in only 20,000 pounds.

The Jamestown, North Dakota *Sun* wrapped up the holding story in a superb four column headline:

MILK HOLDING SAID GETTING NEAR
UNANIMOUS SUPPORT FROM STATE

On Saturday, MHA + 3, farmers in the field paused to take a reading on what they were doing.

No, statistics are not facts, and facts are not the picture. Nevertheless, the 11,600 pounds of milk dumped by McHenry County, Illinois farmers Alvin Tinberg and Harry Tinberg mean something, because neither were members. No one put a gun at their heads to get them to dump. No one spoke crossly, and they weren't afraid of their weight in panthers. But they were dumping. They were Farmers Union people, and they were dumping. They were not alone. Glen Paulson of Berwin, Wisconsin was a Farm Bureau member, and also a PMA Director. He attended an NFO evening meeting and possibly for the first time understood what NFO was doing. By 10:15 a.m. on Saturday, he was on the phone with Raymond Keck. He told Keck he was going to call Farm Bureau members to get them to join NFO for the hold.

Across the 25 states, the message remained the same. Ask farmers to join NFO and dump. BULLETIN: *"W. W. Worthington, NFO Chairman of Kenton County, Kentucky signed 55 new farmers, chiefly dairymen, by Saturday. This was accomplished because NFO chapters met each night, invited non-members in, and stressed non-violence."*

In Colorado, *Rocky Mountain News* photographer Mel Schieltz got up early to make his way to the Manuel Silva dairy farm. The picture was a corker. The white stuff spread out like a blanket before it started soaking into the ground.

In the meantime, farmers over the organized counties, from the Kansas line to Denver, were dumping, not because they themselves could change the course of history, but because they wanted to help the NFO effort. Even without the Colorado Dairy Products Association telling them so, they knew that the local shortage would be shored up by tankers arriving from Utah and points across the Continental Divide.

Saturday had its moments of levity. Diane Mishey, age 17, took a bath in 400 gallons of milk at her dad's Mt. Vernon, Ohio farm. In a bathing suit, she wasn't going at it *Playboy* style, but it made the prints, grimace and all. The milk was really too cold for genuine frolicking anyway. During the holding action others in NFO—Mrs. Leah Brooks of Waupaca, Wisconsin, and Mrs. Judith Ann Reed and Mrs. Devon Godwin of Daleville, Indiana—donned bathing suits for a bath in the lacteal liquid after the manner of Nero's wife Poppaea, possibly on grounds that milk was milk, whether from the she ass or not.

But, first, last and always, Saturday was a time for dumping milk.

Chester Wyatt of Lomax, Illinois was typical. The tractor he had purchased four and one-half years ago cost $4,060. Now he needed a replacement at $7,700. Working 18 hours a day had not created enough money to pay the tab. Worse yet, a new squeeze had materialized. Farm youngsters are drafted into military service on the basis of a population pattern no longer in existence. A lad of draft age in the farm country rarely escapes military duty, not the way the card burners on college campuses do! Wyatt had a son of draft age who would be leaving soon. The other two boys were too close for comfort. Without free family labor, hardly a dairy farmer can stay in business, and Wyatt—with a 200 cow operation—could read the handwriting on the wall. He dumped. He dumped 12,750 pounds of clean milk from the big dairy tanks into a fertilizer pit, and then he transferred the liquid into fertilizer spreading equipment for distribution on his farm fields. Milk made good fertilizer, and wasn't completely wasted that way.

Oliver Mennens of DePere, Wisconsin earned his total income from milking cows. On Saturday, he drained his tanks again, this time for the third consecutive day. This meant 1,600 pounds down the drain to the fluid circuit, and "putting your money where your mouth is" to Mrs. Mennens. Pouring money away to make a point may have been cruel, she realized, but it was the only way.

NFOers were erecting their rationale that way on Saturday. The loss of the paycheck hurts, but it's the "only way you can talk to some people," William Lancalle of Oneida, Wisconsin said.

Donald Sixel, the outstanding farmer of Door County, Wisconsin for 1966 was dumping 1,700 pounds a day. It hurt. No farmer could afford the action. And no farmer could afford not to cooperate either. "I don't like it," the farmers said, but "it's necessary."

In the minds of many farmers, a great deal more than milkshed dumping was necessary. Alvin Jeanquart of Brussels, Wisconsin purchased two half gallons of milk from a Sturgeon Bay store, then proceeded to dump it into the storm sewer on the corner of Third and Kentucky Streets. Women stopped and shook their heads in amazement, and cars slowed down almost to a complete stop to witness the incident.

And the incidents of "store boughten" milk dumping increased and multiplied. The idea seemed to go from one end of NFO country to the other without passing through the intervening space. Like a subliminal impulse, it popped to the surface in Oklahoma and Pennsylvania, in Michigan and Kansas, everywhere. No magic of communication could tie the impulses together. They just happened. Farmers got to thinking, and package dumping happened.

At Cook, Minnesota the NFO farmers had looked at the long lines of milk cartons on the grocery cooling racks, "and it kinda ground them," Pete Nagel reported. They chipped in and raised a kitty of $115 to purchase milk. Ideally, they wanted to give milk directly from the farm to institutions that couldn't buy milk, but there was the law. Milk had to be pasteurized if it was to be sold or given away off the farm. The way the laws were written, farmers couldn't give away the milk if they wanted to. They had to dump. If they wanted to give the grocery store its profit and then hand milk over to the poor, they could do that, but it hurt doubly hard.

2. *"garbagemen of the fourth estate"*

On Saturday, the first of the serious editorials started to appear. There had been a small spate of "it's a sin" balderdash, but those who were morally offended were still too numb to do much beyond "being offended."

The Yakima, Washington *Eagle* came to grips with the real problem. Farmers, in short, were tired of milking cows for the fun of it. *With an average investment of about $1,000 per cow, and an average of 50 or 60 cows, welfare pays better.*

Earlier, Doug Kneeland of the *New York Times* had voiced some of the same kind of thinking. Now the *St. Louis Post-Dispatch* saw the holding action as the mechanism most likely to "lend fuel to the fire of the direct-actionists." Direct action, in *St. Louis Post-Dispatch* parlance, was to be eschewed at all cost, just as "price rigging" was to be avoided. (During NFO's 1965 convention in St. Louis, the *Post-Dispatch* had demanded to know what farmers meant by suggesting fixed prices. And farmers answered, what did the *Post-Dispatch* mean by fixing the rates on advertising.)

At NFO headquarters, President Oren Lee Staley and his officers watched the editorials out of one eye, and the dumping record out of the other. Inquiring reporters were told that NFO was ready to "go for broke." And there was always item for item "proof." (*Item:* Martin Vander Heide, Jr., Orange County, New York, reporting: 117,250 pounds dumped.)

The bugbear of violence had all but died down. The pallid incidents of the first few days had been consumed in the retelling, and now city editors were getting pretty jaded by it all. Pre-fab incidents rubbed most honest editors the wrong way in any case.

Iowa State Chairman Clarence Schuchmann was pleased. Not a single minor incident had been reported in the state. The work to prevent arrant nonsense was really paying off, and die-hard hunters had to content themselves with rehashing alleged incidents of the day before, or pillorying the two dead farmers of Bonduel again.

If there were incidents, no one could fix the blame. A man had allegedly put cyanide in a milk tank at Ravenna, Ohio, but the culprit had eluded the posse. It was always that way. Unidentified men stopped trucks, bullets came from nowhere so that drivers could go home early on Saturday, and vandals obligingly supplied the information that they had been hired by NFO. Most of it had the earmarks of a W. C. Fields movie. There was always the possibility that maverick holdovers from more radical NFO days had emerged, having lived underground these many years, but sound sociological evaluation argued aginst this. More likely, the incidents were coming from truckers, who were tired of hauling for next to nothing, and who were at least mildly disenchanted over the fact that Jimmy Hoffa was in the clink, and their union faltering in every direction. And from processors came the stone of blame, because no one believed that violence and incidents either helped NFO or drove the holding action even six inches closer to victory.

A clear reading on this concept emerged from the daily press. The anatomy of news writing required every incident to be built up, of course. A quarter of a million people doing nothing was not news. One man hammering another into the ground was. But the press treatment went further. A reputation for incidents could blast to pieces any effort.

In discussions at NFO before the holding action, a staffer had analyzed the Negro situation. For a decade running, Negros had gained stature by passive resistance. Many of the gains were erased by

riots in Watts and elsewhere. In communities where the good will
of the press marched with the Negro, editors played down street
incidents, or failed to report them at all. It was probably no happenstance that Kansas City riots never spread, although there had
been many. Press coverage could have fanned the flames. Instead,
Kansas City media merely allowed silence to drown the fires.

Much of the metropolitan press didn't understand the holding
action, and therefore lavished abuse on the NFO movement. This
general policy required every city desk to take isolated incidents
and make capital of them. Most of the *press* supporting the farmers
was printed in the rural towns. And in the rural towns the isolated
incidents rated the coverage they deserved. Had the little press
been against farmers gaining a fair price, rural editors would have
exploded fiction bigger than reality, as did the "garbagemen of the
fourth estate."

Puffed up news stories, after all, had prompted Wisconsin Governor
Warren Knowles and Michigan Lieutenant Governor William G.
Milliken to appeal for law and order, as though law and order no
longer prevailed.

Staley knew the atmosphere of intimidation under which both
executives proceeded. The eye-wash effect had branded NFO. This
public affront could never be atoned for by a private apology, even
if one were forthcoming from a governor's office.

Staley was correct, as usual, when he picked up the tone and content
of each executive's message, and responded:

"Our leaders have been instructed that this holding action is a
business action that must be carried on in an atmosphere of calmness." It went out that way, and the wires use it that way, but the
mere fact that the holding action was still going made up-grading
of the NFO story necessary.

Of all the farm writers hammering out holding action copy Saturday, Bill Zipf was one of the most far-seeing. He was too attuned
to the reality of low farm income to work the morgue and make
incidental molehills into mountains. While others were drowned by
NFO's catch phrase, Zipf saw the picture clearly. He saw the holding
action as a "massive power struggle between proponents of two
different milk marketing systems . . ." NFO, on the one side, was
reaching out for contracts. The farmers wanted equal bargaining
power, not dominance, monopoly, or the upper hand. They wanted
institutional arrangements that would protect them from exploitation.

In an earlier era, the entrepreneur corporation proved to be the exploiter, but now the government had taken on the chore. And the government had powerful allies.

There were the milk-marketing cooperatives. Individually and as groups, they supported the idea of federal marketing orders setting the minimum price and curbing imports. Up to a year ago, they had been protected as co-ops because the government marketing orders had merely paced the rate of farm bankruptcy, and never really invaded the middleman's province. Now, imports had been cut loose, and the co-ops were taking a drubbing along with farmers.

The trend had become apparent, and co-ops had been joining together, not for monopoly, but to gain equal bargaining power. The mechanism was an NFO-like structure called Agencies in Common. If taken up by the co-ops, the job would not be difficult.

3. pma day

MHA +3 was PMA day. The Pure Milk Association was meeting in Chicago, and NFO would be there in spirit and opaque form. Many producers were NFO members, and they were pressing for a resolution putting PMA squarely behind the holding action. Such an endorsement could create a tenpin effect and resolve the holding action in short order. Earlier there had been rumors that the Board of Directors was in sympathy with NFO and could act on its own, but that the politics involved overrode convictions. The resolution had to go to the floor.

On the floor things got hot and heavy. Gerald Earleywine, a District 2 president of PMA, led the fight. He simply asked the delegates to support the holding action "in a true spirit of cooperation."

There was some spirit, but not enough. The resolution was tabled by over 1,000 votes. The Board had proposed remaining neutral, but sympathetic.

As the vote came in, delegate George Smith's face became rimmed with anger. "I think this group has fumbled the ball for the second time this week. I'm tired of being a member of the group that is always wearing the white hats. I believe we are doing too little." Smith sat down.

The bitter response came like a sledge hammer from another delegate: "I don't call that cooperation when they take one of our trucks and dump 28,000 pounds of milk. In the old days we hung a horse thief but nowadays we're supposed to sit down and talk with them."

The incident had occurred, of course. Who suggested, aided or a abetted it, no one knows. It was well reasoned, this incident. NFO had no corner on psychological knowledge. Whoever dumped that milk damaged NFO, and killed PMA support, and he knew what he was doing. NFO needed PMA support. Without it the fight would be as difficult as wars without allies usually are.

In the front office, in the Nerve Center, and in the field, NFO settled down for a long, hard fight.

All day NFO had held on to the idea that PMA might vote to support NFO and start the tenpins tumbling. All day a call from Chicago had been expected, and when it came the news was of the worst sort. As the word filtered through the Nerve Center and made its way along the streets of Corning, the NFOers slowly accepted the fact that they would be in for a long fight. Easter would come and go before NFO could make its points, and when farmers plowed their fields they would be looking back on a holding action hardly over.

Late that night, Staley settled down to pave the way for a harder fight than anyone had visualized. When the message went out to the counties shortly before midnight, it gave members something to hang their hats on:

"We are now just getting into the heart of the holding action, because they had to use up the supply that had been accumulated when the action started. This they have done.

"We have been getting feelers from the dairy industry about talking and appointments have been requested from important segments within the dairy industry for Monday morning. The next 96 hours will be crucial hours . . .

"Farmers hold the trump card because they're the ones who milk the cows. They are very determined to get their two cents per quart increase."

mha + 4

THE LAST of Allen Nunnenkamp's hair came out on Sunday. He had started dropping the thinly populated crop on MHA Day, and it had been coming out ever since. "I'm a regular Yul Brenner without tweezers," Allen said with a smile. Even so, the smile came hard. Allen's wife was dumping 3,000 pounds of milk that morning near Altoona, Kansas, while he was on Nerve Center duty in Corning. Not that the dumping was so unusual. It was a fact—that's all—just as 2,000 pounds being thrown away at Carroll Copeland's farm near Fairfield, Iowa was a fact at exactly the same time. A difference existed, perhaps, in that the tension was costing Nunnenkamp the last few stems of his hair.

Sunday morning news was arriving a little late in any case. The volume being dumped was up, the industry's trucks were making longer runs, and the supermarkets were running out of milk. The clipboards were filling up just as the details were filling pages. French-Bauer at Cincinnati was short three loads, and the Nerve Center knew it immediately. Volunteer State NFOers were reporting a 100% hold in Marshall County, Tennessee, and the Nerve Center logged it in.

From Wisconsin came word that Trempealeau County was dumping two million pounds a day. That too made the record.

And there were newly written pages called "individual items"— ("Ron Ervin at Mt. Pleasant, Michigan. Charlie Wilson is dumping 14,000 pounds a day.")—and there was the stuff from which legends are born ("In Kane County, Illinois, a PMA farmer stopped on the road to hear a tape made from an NFO telephone report. When I asked him to join, he didn't say a word. He just walked over and pulled the plug on 2,400 pounds. He's joined now and says he's going down the road to get 40 more PMA producers to join NFO and dump").

1. *the big plan*

In Staley's big front office, the door was closed. Top officials entered and left at long intervals, but Staley stayed on. No one at NFO headquarters doubted that the holding action would be a long one. All reports from the field indicated that farmers were hardly in a quitting mood. From the chair of leadership, this meant that the big plan had to be shaped up and readied. If it was known as anything at all, it was simply "the plan." It hadn't been named yet. It had been discussed, of course. Albin Rust had calculated its potential, and cross-checked its application by areas. And a draft instrument had been hammered out by NFO Attorney Lee Sinclair, who was working in Vice President Erhard Pfingsten's office.

Everything else about the plan was still hush-hush on Sunday morning. Although the general idea had been around for a long time, it had never been really refined. Now, as the holding action marched into MHA + 4, two important industry executives advanced it again, and Staley—sensing unusual interest—crowded its consideration forward on a well filled agenda.

The store and hold idea had a certain irresistable charm about it. It avoided the waste of dumping, true, but it was a long pull tactic and was not really workable in peripheral areas.

Nevertheless, the store and hold idea had merit. With proper timing, it could push the holding action over the top. So far manufacturing plants were carrying the brunt of the pressure because of the industry's nature. This seemed to many as something less than justice. Not a few plants had closed down. By Sunday morning, MHA + 4, not a few indicated that they would go with any reasonable intermediate step that NFO might offer, just as they would go with the increase farmers sought the minute the holding action went over the hill.

Albin Rust's pencil fairly flew over the scratchpads. Each calculation refined the earlier figures. There were plants that NFO could definitely count on. As to others, no one would know until the question arrived in fact. Under economic pressure, almost all would do what was reasonable. The big question remained. Had the psychological moment arrived when NFO could uncork "the plan" and expect maximum results? Staley believed it had not. "The plan" had to be kept in abeyance pending the right moment. Coordination and split-second timing would have to attend its announcement. In the meantime, any leak would be fatal.

Indeed, getting copies of contracts to NFO people in the field under security conditions became a fantastic proposition. Mailed out in advance, the multilith reproductions might account for a leak, somewhere, sometime.*

Erhard Pfingsten had been keeping his speaking engagements since MHA Day. Now he was in the office helping decide the prospects of the lockup program. He helped revise several drafts of contracts during the afternoon. By early evening he was on his way to Omaha, where he was scheduled for an impromptu radio interview. The radio station told Pfink that the program would be broadcast from "location."

The "location" turned out to be a crummy bar full of hippies. Pfink stuck it out—loaded customers and loaded questions—and was back in Corning a little after dark.

Pfingsten's image in NFO was second only to Staley's. He had earned every inch of his stature the hard way. In thousands of appearances he had transformed his lone voice in the wilderness to one that could command large audiences in all of the organized states. In formal debate, Pfingsten was lethal. Although Staley had written NFO's policy paper, Pfingsten by dint of stamina had possibly put it across to more people than anyone in the organization.

He could take spot economics and overall economics, and wrap them into a most convincing message. He was also something of an intellectual magnet, attracting diverse ideas into NFO, and NFO was the stronger for it. Pfingsten was particularly vitriolic when annihilating those who mislead. A tireless student, he had examined the range of history, and he had come to realize that the rationalizations of those in command carry more weight than they deserve because an atmosphere of intimidation always walks hand in hand with power.

In short, Pfingsten saw no real need for the keelhauling American life was receiving, nor did he admire the schoolmen who were

---

*A few days later, March 22, 1967, the Gonvick, Minnesota "Leader" editorially suggested the lockup idea (". . . channel the milk . . . into dried milk or cheese which could be stored rather than dumping on the ground at the direct expense of the producers . . .") but there is no evidence that the suggestion had leaked out of NFO. Apparently, it was arrived at by the "Leader" editor, who came up with the idea independently at the same time is was being discussed in Corning.

guiding it. Other men with other voices might trace the conspiracy of a brain cartel. Pfingsten saw only a Michigan economics professor here, a Foundation Chief there, and 300,000 + college professors everywhere, most of whom proclaimed deification for a few sanctified ideas, when in fact they were ratifying "laws" to justify what was being done to agriculture.

In his more cynical moods he saw a business world in which organization men destroyed their subordinates, an educational machine in which department worship had turned more Byzantine than life under the Varangians, and a government in which dogmatism became party loyalty, and idiocy a virture. Unknowingly welded together for mutual protection, this unholy triumverate seemed hell bent on whipping a free nation toward what they considered a fuller life. Profoundly confident in their own superiority, "they" had assumed power—even in their loose-knit collectivity—but Pfingsten never for once doubted that the real power rested in the hands of farmers. One day, farmers would tire of being left standing naked with their hides peeled off, their nerves and muscles opened to the winds. Then, and then only, farmers would stand up and be counted.

In the meantime, farmers seemed to want their independence without being willing to pay the price. Independence on the land simply had to mean bare subsistence, and so far only Amish and Mennonites were willing to pay out the kind of coin that could purchase classical independence. The fruits of civilization, the baubles of technology required collectivity. ["The trouble with the farmer," said John Haberman of Nemaha County, Nebraska, a Pfingsten admirer, "is that he hasn't adopted the ways of an exchange economy yet. His collectivity is communistic in the generic meaning of the term. His collectivity is for social, not economic gain."]

Frequently, Pfingsten left his farm untended while be busied himself educating all those who would listen. He was something of a maverick in this regard. Ideas had to stand on their own feet. They had to add up. They couldn't cry on someone's shoulders. And ideas had to be communicated. If there was one thing that disturbed Pfingsten, it was his observation that those attuned to the cerebral process were unwilling to soil themselves by trafficking with the less educated.

Pfink was not the first to make this observation.

Men of learning frequently see that the distinction of education is not enhanced by concern for the underdog. Circa 1967, a certain phoniness pervaded the American scene. Intellectuals frequently pretended concern, but careful analysis revealed this devotion to be that of the hobbyist, the pseudo-scientists interested in microscopic examination of the lower order. Those mightily concerned with the Negro problem took great care to preserve a clinical detachment, and those concerned with agriculture worked their formulas with little regard for the human being involved.

Economists were the worst of the lot.

"In recent decades economic orthodoxy has become increasingly recondite," wrote Clarence Ayres in *Theory of Economic Progress,* "and professional economists have barricaded themselves from criticism behind the formidable complexities of their trade. 'Oversimplification' has become a mortal sin. This is scholasticism, the last stage in the decay of the 'obvious and simple system' described by Adam Smith."

The fantastic indifference of the intellectual to the plight of the farmer became embedded in policy papers and laws during the last of the 1940s, and the early 50s, and farmers knew not how to fight so elusive an enemy. Only a handful of allies stepped forward during NFO's protest days. Only a few more joined the fight in the decade to come. Hardly any had credentials from great universities, and all but a few had nothing to offer other than native intelligence and a fine singleness of purpose.

2.   *the broadsword for farmers*

One at a time, Pfingsten and Staley welcomed them. There was Arnold Paulson, for instance. Paulson was a small businessman from Granite Falls, Minnesota. Always a live-wire town promoter and Junior Chamber man, Paulson was vitally interested in the future of "his town." He was prepared to work for that future. This took him the usual route—hunting for industry to bring into Granite Falls. In the early 1950s, Carl Rowan of the *Minneapolis Tribune* wrote a series of articles entitled, "Small Towns Grow or Die." Rowan's message was disturbing. If new industry for the rural community was not the answer, then what was?

Paulson ran a study on the effect of industrial payrolls on the per capita income in a community. Granite Falls is one of the most envied communities in southwestern Minnesota. It has more industry per capita than any other town its size, and more than many communities up to ten times larger. One industry alone, The Northern State Power Company, pays 52% of all the taxes, including school taxes. From all outward appearances, the picture looked bright.

Paulson took the total industrial payroll and divided it by the population of the town. He found that if Granite Falls was going to live on its basic industry alone, citizens could have only $400 a year per person. Immediately, Paulson wanted to know where the rest of the money was coming from. He searched each nook and cranny of the town's economy, but it wasn't there. Finally, taking the gross income of farmers on the local mail routes, he found that gross farm income contributed $1,600 a year per capita income to the people of Granite Falls, or roughly four times more than industry accounted for. In short, if Granite Falls were to attract four times more industry, it could achieve a $1,600 per capita income—except for one thing. The law of diminishing returns entered the picture. New industry means more streets, schools, services. A little pencil pushing revealed that Granite Falls couldn't do without gross agricultural income at the farms, not even if the town expanded its industry twenty-fold.

The finding was unnerving. Paulson started devoting less time to his Minnesota Business Industrial Promotion Agency, and more to the farm problem. He appeared at farm gatherings, and in a little while NFO groups started asking him to speak.

Much the same proved to be true of leading figures in the Independent Bankers Association, which represented 7,000 small banks in rural America. Bankers Harry Rash of Thayer, Kansas, and Vince Rossiter of Hartington, Nebraska started swinging the big broadsword for farmers. A few at a time, the corp of NFO "allies" grew. Lutheran and Catholic ministers became interested. They held seminars and discussed the foundation problem. Sooner or later they were led to Carl Wilken, an economist who had served on Senator Homer Capehart's Committee during the Truman days, and who had spent the years since the depression of the 1930s researching the American economy.

Wilken had never been paid one brass farthing from NFO headquarters, but he was interested in the welfare of agriculture and willingly gave Butch Swaim permission to use his material. Not only that, he made his material available to IBA, the Farmers Union, the Farm Bureau, the Secretaries of Agriculture and members of Congress.

NFO workers also made findings on their own. One at a time, these findings were meshed—gear for gear—with the foundation economics

Messrs. Rossiter, Rash, Paulson, Wilken, et al., accounted for. Hardly a month before the milk holding action, NFO had sponsored a seminar during which the problem was all but gift wrapped as a fantastically meaningful package. It carried the stamp of Carl Wilken's thinking much of the time.

Officially, the seminar was styled "a blue ribbon meeting of business, banking, professional, farm and church leaders," when it met at the Sheraton-Warrior Hotel in Sioux City. But part of the tab was mailed to NFO at Corning.

Attended by leaders from Chicago to Colorado, it ended with a resolution: ". . . that programs should be initiated immediately among business, civic and social groups of the central United States to request the support of our governors, congressmen, and senators to return stability and solvency to our national economy, and economic balance to the trade and commerce of the nation, by restoring 90% price supports on basic farm raw materials, with an accurate parity formula based on the 1946-50 average consumers price level."

This was not the NFO program. NFO had no real quarrel with 90% of parity. It was just that no one in NFO believed farmers could ever again go that route. It was for this reason that Staley and the NFO leaders kept the organization squarely behind collective bargaining. Everyone was agreed that farm raw materials had to be monetized at approximately 90% of parity. NFO figured farmers would have to do it on their own.

3. *commodities were monetized*

Through most of his adult years, Wilken lived in the underworld of economics, a limbo from which there was no escape. Had he accomplished his research under the auspices of Harvard or M.I.T. and then endured a lifetime subservient to the canons of acceptable economic thought, he might have survived to gain a hearing replete with academic trappings. As it happened, he had emerged from World War I as an officer with only a part of a college education in tow, and taken up economic analysis in the depth of the depression.

For fully a decade after the great collapse, the academic economists rated less than well in government circles. They had known all the answers, and yet the economy had collapsed. Congress in the 1930s wanted new and daring ideas.

The ones who had been so mistaken fought valiantly. They dismissed men like Wilken as "colorful cranks" or "talented amateurs." On grounds of credentials, they dethroned scholars like Foster and Catchings, Frederick Soddy, Gertrude M. Coogan, Irving Fisher and Vincent Vickers. At the same time men of good common sense dismissed many of these with credentials on grounds of ignorance.

In the final analysis, the intellectual failures of the 1930s accounted for Wilken getting his chance. Practical congressmen wanted practical answers, not more of the taxonomy associated with Marshall's *Principles*, which was then standard college textbook fare. Wilken appeared before hearings on the Pope-McGill bill in the late 1930s. Always he tried to upgrade the half-hearted, on-again, off-again New Deal attempts to solve the depression problem.

Wilken hinged his analysis to a very basic idea, one contained in the United States Constitution, one that said Congress shall have power "To coin money, regulate the value thereof, and of foreign coin, and fix the standard of weights and measures . . ."

Wilken reasoned that income for a nation boiled down simply to two parts, each equally important. One was the production of goods and services for human use. The other was the pricing of goods and services at the consumer level. Production times price became income.

In the case of physical production, Congress has obeyed the Constitution to the letter. The lawmakers established weights and measures, and all are guarded by a government agency, and kept very accurate. Corn is 56 pounds to a bushel. Milk is 8.5 pounds to a gallon. One hundred pounds of beef weigh as much in terms of specific gravity one year as the next.

Yet anyone who lived through the depression had seen the price of corn as low as ten cents a bushel, and as high at $2.50. Still, that corn had just as many calories of food value at a dime as it did at $2.50. Years later, in an interview with *Farm Tempo U.S.A.* Wilken detailed his method:

WILKEN: The first thing I did was to take up the farm production because the low prices were being blamed on surpluses. So I set up the record crop production in 1928 and 1932 and found that our crop production in 1932 was less than it was in 1928. And we had 4 million more people in 1932 than in 1928. Having operated a farm I knew that most of the grain was processed through livestock, so I set up a record of the production of livestock in 1932. I found that we had less meat production in 1932 than we had in 1928. So the surplus theory went out the window.

FARM TEMPO: The 1928 production was all consumed, was it not?

WILKEN: We were going great guns. I have a chart which covers a period from 1910 through 1950. It shows that during the time span represented, our consumption has pretty much equaled our production. In other words, we didn't have a surplus other than seasonal between 1910 and 1950. Now—due to our crop cycle, the law of supply and demand can't possibly maintain farm prices at harvest because at harvest we have full year supply and one day of demand. Even with half a crop, we'll have 180 days' supply and one day of demand. And without support prices everybody takes advantage of the farmer because they know he's got to bring it in and get some money to pay off his banker at harvest time. The next step was to take a look at the import-export situation. Because the theoretical economists blamed the low prices on the high tariffs. So I checked the exports of the United States and found that in 1929 our exports represented 5½% of our national income in 1929. Then I checked the imports. And after deducting the imports, many of which were the same products as those we exported, I found that 98% of our production is consumed in the United States. So it didn't seem possible to me that this small 2%, and the tariff situation, could have broken the price of the 98%.

Surpluses didn't break prices in 1929, and they weren't breaking prices in the depth of the depression. Those with the power to set prices were setting them, and in world trade this meant keeping farm commodities below or in line with the price of gold, the world's common denominator.

During World War II, and through the last of the Truman years, commodities were monetized at close to parity. Wilken at one time published a chart in *Agricultural Outlook* which illustrated the relationship between farm income, factory income, and national income. On the front page agriculture was represented as a gear driving the other segments of the economy. Later he sent a copy to each of the 48 State Commissioners of Agriculture, and to the executives of their powerful organization. It was this group that finally became the spearhead that induced Congress to enact a 90% price support bill in 1942, because without parity raw material prices the nation would likely develop a depression within a war—*and lose the war!*

The parity idea was never really in danger until the last part of 1947. At that time, a full-dress review of foundation economics was held at the Mayflower Hotel in Washington. Over 300 members of Congress were present. During the affair, Commissioner Tom Linder of Georgia took out after the fats and oils group. Then the roof fell in. R. A. Trovatten of Minnesota, Matt Dahl of North Dakota, Tom Linder of Georgia and J. E. McDonald of Texas together with Dr. John Lee Coulter and Carl Wilken were called in to explain why they were lobbying without registering as lobbyists. Finally Tom Linder and J. E. McDonald were indicted. They retained former Senator Burton K. Wheeler of Montana to represent them. Nothing happened. The indictments were later dismissed. But the process of intimidation broke up the organization and prevented it from trying to get a fair deal for agriculture.

Farm commodities immediately started their decline, and they have never stopped.

4. a babson-type approach

When the end finally came, a zone of silence came to blanket the area between the happening and its realization. The change of the surface power structure in Washington made the break complete. Wilken and his associates departed into oblivion.

A few years later, when Governor Dan Turner helped spark the NFO movement, the lessons of yesteryear had all but disappeared. No intellectual, Dan Turner did not understand the foundations of economic theory enough to help them surface in a revolutionary new movement called NFO.

The task fell to banker Vince Rossiter, who, with his father, had followed the unique corn belt research of the old Raw Materials Council in Sioux City, Iowa, a Babson-type approach so basic that the sophisticated set failed to understand it. By 1955, division of the economic discipline was complete. In the main, it dealt in air-tight compartments, cubby holes so circumscribed that no light dared enter. Indeed, so little light remained when Keynes' *General Theory* was finally sainted for its broad spectrum approach—macro-economics, if you will—that hardly an objection was heard.

By 1967, the front rank of objection could be found in NFO, and hardly anywhere else. Farmers in the holding action Nerve Center knew a great deal about foundation economics. Wilken's *Prosperity Unlimited* was high on the reading list.

5. *this isn't money*

You really couldn't think in the Nerve Center. You wrote it down. Dave Sudsberry of Missouri called. WHO DID WHAT: Leroy Ornsterger dumped 20,400 pounds to date. Sweat and blood to Ornsterger, but routine in the Nerve Center. Time 3:30 p.m. Elmer Ball called. Write it down. "Teacher at Golden City, Missouri reports Foremost delivered milk for Monday. Says can't fill contract next week. Can deliver reconstituted powder." Jim Horn called. LeRoy Kannas called. A hundred men in the field called. Gene Potter writing it down. Clarence Thacker writing it down. Don Zmolek writing it down.

Don Zmolek fingered several Johnson quarters between phone calls. He was pensive, and after each message he returned to clicking the coins. Soon a cluster of farmers inched their way on to the soiled bunk.

"This isn't money," Don said. "The real money is being poured on the ground out there. I figured that out a long time ago."

A question from a farmer followed.

"Oh, you have to understand the background," Zmolek said.

BACKGROUND

---

the economy

In EVERY EDITION of the *Wall Street Journal* are listed a daily Dow-Jones Futures Commodity Index and a daily Dow-Jones Spot Commodity Index. These indexes are based on the 1924-1926 average, which equals 100. The Commodity Indexes include all items regularly listed on the various commodity markets throughout the country. The Dow-Jones Commodity Indexes are accurate tabulations within the framework of the base period, and have more than passing value in showing price trends.

The futures are always more sensitive and active, but a comparison with the spot indexes will illustrate and confirm commodity price movements.

Reuters of the United Kingdom also lists data, but this index uses the year 1931 as 100. The United States government uses an index of 1957-1959 as 100. The Associated Press uses 1926 as 100.

Thus there are four major measurements of commodity prices—AP, Dow-Jones, Reuters, the United States Government—and unless the student knows the base period he simply has to get lost in the maze. With the proper conversion figures, of course, anyone can trace the condition of raw material prices.

Tracing raw material indexes is essential to the problem of understanding overall economic stability, because raw materials lead the way in enabling a nation to either export its unemployment or import its depression.

It may seem like a long jump from wheat in Hutchinson, Kansas to iron ore in Svappavaara, Sweden, but a full evaluation of the role of raw material is necessary if we are to understand why farmers everywhere are the anointed ones when it comes to suffering erratic price movements.

Data from the U. S. Bureau of Mines, and data from the Department of Commerce now tend to confirm projections worked out in the late 1930s by Carl H. Wilken and Fred T. Crawford of the then functioning Raw Materials National Council that raw material production in the United States falls into a 3-7 ratio. Approximately 70% of the raw materials used in operating the American economy come from agriculture. The Raw Materials National Council researchers also found that the basic farm production consisted of 12 nonperishable crops which are produced on 90% of the harvested acres.

Approximately 30% of the raw materials used in operating the economy come from mines and pits in the form of gravel, building stone, non-metallic ores, coal and petroleum, and of course in the form of metals (including the monetary metals), copper, lead, zinc, iron, manganese, tungsten. These preliminary findings have since been cemented into place through statistical verification.

The measurable economic cycle starts with raw materials, and accordingly, the economic state of raw material production in the measurable cycle precedes other economic factors. In a manner of speaking the energy and "working" capital contained in raw materials have all been placed on deposit or renewed by nature, and the laws of thermodynamics clearly indicate that when all is consumed there can be no more life—a distant projection.

1. *la terre est la source*

"La Terre est la source ou la matiere d'ou l'on tire la Richesse," wrote Richard Cantillon in Essai Sur La Nature Du Commerce en Genaral. "Le travail de l'Homme est la forme qui la produit: & la Richesse en elle-meme, n'est autre chose que la nourriture, les commodites & les agremens de la vie."

Cantillon's treatise described the source of new earned income at a time when John Law ruled the economy of France. Cantillon and Law clashed, chiefly over the real character of money.

Law established the Banque Generale in 1715, and had it converted to a state bank three years later. His every move was designed to drive raw material prices down while he, John Law, furnished substitutes to repair the deficit. In his own way, he developed a war against poverty, created make-work projects such as digging a canal at Briare, and he took steps to make Paris a seaport town. All tolls were abolished so that the grain trade could be "freed." Import duties were reduced on oil, leather, tallow and wines so that free trade could furnish France with cheap imports. Commodities fell in price. And new money issues were constructed by the Banque Generale, which simply monetized collateral. It took the economy only two years to explode.

After the dust settled about the only thing left was Richard Cantillon's *Essai,* the masterpiece that reached the purity of theory in one lesson, and limited itself to the possibilities of life in the next.

The problem facing the farmer here and now can be more easily analyzed.

Writing in 1957, Wilken prefaced his remarkable tabulations with the observation that "Unstable raw material prices, the forerunner of unstable income, rather than tariffs and import quotas, have been the key factor in disrupting both domestic and foreign markets. Tariffs and quotas have been attempts of different nations to protect their internal economy against violent fluctuations of price levels."

There is nothing very complicated about international trade. The low cost producer has to end up with the market. It's that simple. When world markets move higher than the wage and capital cost level in the United States, as they do when a depression has knocked the American economy down a notch or two, then American producers can export their unemployment by underselling in foreign markets. When the wage and capital cost level in the United States rises well above the world level, then foreign production will flow to the high market. This means that the United States under such conditions simply imports its depressions.

Needless to say, an economy only rarely moves as a whole. Usually, the various sectors manage to mangle each other first, creating an imbalance. Trouble is usually manufactured through imbalance at home, and unfavorable climate abroad—both at the same time.

The underdeveloped nations of the world have only raw materials to sell, and even among the most unsophisticated there is a growing realization that these nations cannot permit the profits from business enterprise to leave the country—because without capital profits the so-called emerging nations cannot emerge at all.

This faint adumbration can be read in the reports on raw materials. The relationship between copper scrap moving up, say, ten cents, and raw copper remaining the same, tells something of how institutional pressure—not the planetary system of the markets—writes the box score, for it is a matter of record that some nations control raw material prices through stockpiles, others administer prices, and still others submit the pricing decision to speculators. Aluminum, zinc, and certain other minor metals, have remained stable because they are under effective stockpile control, but they have been stabilized at a level so low that expansion of production is prohibited.

Farm raw material producers see most of their problem located in legend of the independent farmer who refuses to organize. Failure to organize is much of the story, but even an integrated industry can discover pains in the financial solar plexus because of the tendency to "import depressions."

Take iron ore production. F. E. Brantley and H. T. Reno of the Bureau of Mines estimate that captive mines comprise 80 to 90% of the iron ore industry. They point out that even the insulation of distance and freight charges cannot protect domestic iron ore producers from price invasion because "mines competing for the North American industry's market are only $3 to $6 per ton ocean-freight charges away through deep sea ports." Accordingly, iron ore mines in Brazil, Chile, Peru, and Venezuela supplied 10.6% of the North American market in 1964, even more in 1965 and 1966. Even iron ore from the big underground mines in Kiruna and Malmberget, and the open pits in Svappavaara, Sweden are a factor to be reckoned with in world markets. India, West African countries, and Australia, with lower labor costs and lower capital costs, are starting to produce substantial quantities for the world market.

In terms of the state of the arts in 1967, there was little likelihood that American producers could develop technological or other differential advantages over competent producers in the rest of the world.

In almost every quarter one can read the story of how institutions are at work, merrily upsetting the fondest abstractions of the economists. In early 1966, for instance, there was the example of tin. Tin prices had gone up slightly because speculators on world markets had assigned an ascending price to this raw material. This prompted the U. S. Government to dump tin at the stockpile price of $1.16 to keep the world market down.

In the work-a-day play of international institutions, raw materials are the first to field pressures of economic imbalance. This pressure at the raw material level short-circuits purchasing power through the full length of any economy, because in the final analysis gold and silver (the money) are really wheat, corn, lead, zinc—the basic raw materials that become the wealth of nations. If gold is to remain stable in a dynamic world, then there must be constant pressure to bring wheat and corn in line with the price of gold. If wheat and corn are to line up with the price of gold, then the wage and capital cost structure must submit to pressure to line up with the price of gold.

Thus an unadjusted price for gold speaks of a static world, but almost all economic pursuits of man speak of a dynamic world, one that will not be laid to rest at the level of a certain year in history.

To illustrate this point: The British pound was $4.86 in terms of $20.67 gold. When the price of gold for the world was raised to $35 by the Roosevelt administration, the British pound sterling became worth $2.80. Pride, the "going concern" of England as the world's financial house, and not a little tradition figured in England's decision not to devalue the pound at that time. Through the rest of the 1930s and all through World War II, England kept the pound sterling at $4.05. Some $10 billion in lend lease from the United States extended the British an assist in this endeavor.

2. *organized by countries*

The world is organized by countries. This is so obvious that to repeat it here might seem a reflection on the intelligence of the reader. Nevertheless, were this fact to be repeated about four times a day, most of the economic ills associated with depressions could be avoided.

Many economists like to think of Country A and Country B in terms of "the efficient producer," but the fact is that all these countries have different shapes, different resources, different stages of development, different labor costs, different institutional "going concerns." The interplay between countries cannot be controlled at the U. N. level. From the economic point of view, a country such as the United States must control its own destiny.

It must be remembered that ever since the Roosevelt administration pegged the world's gold at $35 an ounce in 1934, England had refused to bring the pound in line with $35 gold. During WWII, England expropriated foreign held securities of its citizens to keep from making this monetary adjustment, and after the war England showed more than academic interest in the removal of the American farm parity program. Thus when the U. S. Congress returned to 90% parity in 1949, English financiers must have abandoned hope of maintaining the pound at $4.05.

The British pound was devalued to $2.80—or 30%. A host of lesser trading nations followed suit. This action reduced the price of goods being produced in England by 30% to the rest of the world. Such a maneuver, however, could have only a short run effect, because after devaluation Britain could only buy 70% as much as previously for the pound.

As a result of the devaluation, the U. S. became the high market in the world. In the five years following the devaluation of the British pound, the U. S. imported $6 billion more in farm products than were exported. The American economy, in a word, imported its surplus. As a result of the British devaluation, and as a result of imports prompted by Britain's lead in devaluing its pound, American farm raw material prices were reduced to the world price level —where they are today!

In the meantime, Europe has set up a Common Market. The Common Market has protected itself from import invasion of its price level by setting up a support price for agricultural raw materials at approximately the 1948 level. And the Common Market has kept it there ever since.

On the blackboards and in the economic journals, economists work out complicated looking formulas illustrating the nature of inelastic demand, and at the same time governors and farm spokesmen look the world over for export markets for farm products. Yet world income is at a level that makes it impossible for foreign nations to buy American farm production at world prices, much less at prices that would return to the farm producer his cost of production as balanced with the rest of the American economy.

3. *the world level*

The fundamental concept that separates the approach being discussed here from the one being entertained at the policy paper level can be delineated historically, and it can be demonstrated arithmetically.

The advice to all four presidents since WWII—Truman, Eisenhower, Kennedy and Johnson—has been exactly the same. All four chief executives have been in favor of getting farm prices down to what is called the world level. This policy conforms to the Cordell Hull victory in achieving free trade via the Reciprocal Trade Agreements Act of 1934.

The post WWII effect of this public policy has been to drive farm prices down. As a result, business has lost its markets in rural America. It has lost new capital for expansion and has been forced to turn to Keynesian-type borrowed capital generation. When the going concern of business has to borrow its capital, it has to pay interest.

After paying interest and wages, private enterprise is now paying hardly 3% on stocks as dividends. When raw materials go down, business loses money for the simple reason that it loses the volume of market necessary to earn the profit to meet wages and capital costs.

Raw material prices in the United States are subject to constant and devastating price attacks from the rest of the world under a system of low tariffs simply because the United States is the high market. The low cost producer sells to the high market, and the high market buys cheap until the very process pulls down its own standard of living to comply with world standards.

In 1966 the Common Market price on wheat was about $2.64. Yet per capita income in the E.E.C. was less than half that in the United States. At the same time the U. S. support price was $1.25 for the same commodity. If the Common Market were to follow the leadership of the United States and reduce the support price for wheat to $1.25, the Common Market would collapse.

The chapter being written in international economics is not new. It is as old as the debate over an American tariff policy, which was not settled by Henry Clay's victory with the Tariff Act of 1824, nor by Cordell Hull's triumph in pushing through the Reciprocal Trade Agreements Act of 1934. Yet since 1935 the United States has stood committed to tariff reduction.

However, since 1934 the national income moved up from a low of $70 billion to $609 + billion by the end of 1966. Exports expressed in terms of a percentage have not changed materially. Thus the 5½% of the national income in exports has not improved the trade ratio, but has cost having the world determine the price level for American raw materials.

Prior to removal of tariff walls, manipulation of raw materials downward was accomplished through adjustment in the prices of monetary metals, principally silver. In 1800, the U. S. economy functioned under the concept of bi-metalism. Gold was valued at $20.67 and silver was valued at $1.29. In the U. S. this gave rise to the slogan, "16 to 1." In 1873 venturesome miners in Nevada discovered the Comstock lode, one of the biggest silver finds in the history of the world. Suddenly, as if by magic, the developing nation called the United States found itself with its own money store. With silver production in tow, the U. S. could create money the easy way.

The international financiers who operated in London at that time correctly sensed the gravity of the situation. A disparity between silver and gold production had developed. In one of those decision-loaded meetings that almost always escape recorded history, the world's money managers decided not to maintain the price of silver. So they made a commodity out of it. This cut the basic metal for money in half, because silver and gold had been equal on the differential in price.

The economic dislocation created in the United States can be gleaned from the campaign oratory of Missouri's Silver Dick Bland and Nebraska's William Jennings Bryan, a debate that culminated in the McKinley-Roosevelt election of 1896. Not too many industrialists listened when Bryan warned, "tear down your farms and grass will grow in the streets of every city," and perhaps not much grass ever did return cities to the countryside, but the fact remains that between 1873 and 1896, for every penny an ounce silver moved down, the price of a bushel of wheat in Kansas moved down a penny a bushel also. In the late 1890s, international manipulation did not wreak so much havoc simply because the U. S. had developed gold production to help pay international balances, and bankrupted farmers could get re-capitalized on free land out west.

After World War I, the price of silver moved back to $1.38 from about 60 cents in the 1910-1914 period. That, of course, increased world commodity prices because all the foreign nations on silver had more money. The American economy moved up from about $31 billion of income in 1910 to $79 billion in 1919.

Hard on the heels of World War I, there must have been another meeting that escaped recorded history. Again, almost as if directed by an "invisible hand," international financiers maneuvered to get commodity prices back in balance with $20.67 gold. To accomplish this, the price of silver in the world market was sold down from $1.38 to 65 cents an ounce in half a year.

Recorded history picks up the story again. In 1920-1921, the United States suffered another depression. And the administration in Washington changed. Henry Ford emerged in the post World War I era as one of industry's chief spokesmen. Ford pointed out to the country that the average wage would have to be increased to 50 cents an hour because—taking the cost structure into account—23 cents an hour would not enable a worker to buy the production of industrial America, chiefly the automobile.

The debate ended with Fordney-McCumber Tariff Act of 1922.

There was a 42 cent tariff on wheat; 25 cents on butterfat; 25 cents on corn; and in 1922-1929 the economy moved up to $87.8 billion national income. Statistics indicate that during the 1922-1929 era, the United States produced 98% of everything needed. The nation enjoyed about half the world's income in terms of dollars.

Christopher Hollis, writing in *The Breakdown of Money*, detailed the manipulation process. Hollis noted that the international bankers found that they could not convince the American people, or their Congress, that they should have free international trade by preaching the economics of Adam Smith and classical economists. So they found it necessary to break down the buying power of the American people to the extent that they could not consume their own production, and would have to look for markets elsewhere. Starting in 1925, the price of silver broke downward again. Silver started down from 69 cents an ounce and finally achieved a new low of 24½ cents an ounce in 1932. The break in silver was fed into raw material prices. The giddy speculation and credit expansion of the late 1920s constituted the usual reaction of people who do not understand what is happening.

When farm prices started down in 1925, the deficit in income was shored up by an advance in consumer credit. Stock speculation on margin became the hallmark of the era. The bubble broke in October, 1929. National income dropped by 54% between 1929 and 1933. An economic bubble always breaks after agriculture's last straw, because agriculture produces a year ahead of the economy. This adds credence to the theory that raw materials lead the way—up or down. As stated earlier, the American economy did not get back to the 1929 level of national income until 1941.

As late as 1940, the American economy was in a depression. Some 8 million people were unemployed.

4. *the income equation*

Richard Cantillon's *Essai* was first printed in 1755, although colleagues examined it in manuscript form during the John Law era. Cantillon, more than most, accounted for ideas that shaped the thinking of *Les Economistes* shortly before the American Revolution, and found themselves transplanted to thinkers like Benjamin Franklin and Thomas Jefferson.

Although the general thesis had been stated by philosophers as early as the ancients, Cantillon was probably the first to define wealth as such and to work out a system to illustrate that "all wealth comes from the soil," and that labor "is the force which produces it." Cantillon was also one of the first economic workers to try to trace the circulation of wealth. It was a formidable job. There were no statistical abstracts in 18th century France. There were no journals to codify day-to-day data. There was no communication system capable of detailing the hour-to-hour workings of economic traffic. Nevertheless, Cantillon worked out the first trace of an idea on how an economic system functioned in fact, not daydreams.

After that, the "great work" waited almost two centuries for the proper tools.

When Wesley Clair Mitchell went to Washington in the early 1920s, he had already completed his *Business Cycles*. He knew there could be no analysis without statistics, and he knew that practical statistics were not in existence. But to construct a system required a theory, one that would comply with both abstractions and reality.

Even uneducated men understood the anatomy of a business income equation. The businessman saves, borrows, begs or steals, and puts together the capital needed to run his shop. He pays out wages and capital costs. He handles expenses. And in the process of doing business, he recovers everything he has advanced from the market. If he doesn't he goes broke.

The income equation for an economy is much the same. It does not take an astute seer to observe that the gushing well that keeps the economic system moving is the private enterprise system. Individual capitalists save, borrow, beg or steal, and create businesses or farms. They advance the wages and capital costs to get a job done, and recover from the market if they are successful.

Mitchell and his associates didn't work out the details in ten minutes, but they finally achieved certain common denominators. And today national income is shown in the *Economic Report of the President* as six component parts. They are:

1. Income of unincorporated enterprises.
2. Income of farm proprietors.
3. Rental income of persons.
4. Corporate profits.
5. Compensation of employees (wages).
6. Net interest.

In terms of an equation, the balance must line up this way.

Income	*Costs*
1. Income of unincorporated enterprises.	1. Wages.
2. Income of farm proprietors.	2. Interest.
3. Rental income of persons.	
4. Corporate profits.	

Needless to say, income to one segment is expense to the other. Therefore, an income equation has to relate the working mechanism of the economy to the solvency of those on either side of the income equation.

The income achieved on one side of the equation has to stay at a level with the costs on the other side, even in a static economy. Thus corporate profits, income from unincorporated enterprise, farm income and rentals have to be sufficient to pay the wages and interest.

Hundreds of sub-topics feed into the economic equation, but all fall into one of the six common denominators.

In running the economy of the United States, the various sectors must move in a balanced manner. Each of the sectors must advance at approximately the same rate unless some compensating factor becomes evident. Usually velocity of money turnover is not of significant foundation quality to repair a fundamental imbalance.

Today the federal government spends millions gathering all the data needed to give its executive and legislative heads, as well as the business community, an income equation—a profit and loss statement of the economy. Yet for some strange reason, those in command of public policy do not feel it necessary, or politically expedient, to give the American people comprehensive statements on the economic health of the national economy. Private audits must intervene.

These audits, properly correlated, reveal that from 1940 to 1950—a ten year period—the national income increased 196%. For the same period the gross value of all farm production sold increased 195%. Wages increased 195%. Readily seen, for the five years of war and five years of peace, growth was equal for all the basic segments, and therefore for the aggregate. In simple terms it was a healthy balance, and this balance was duly reflected in the wholesale and retail indexes, and in the commodity indexes.

With the demonetization of farm raw materials and the abandon-

ment of the 90% price support law, imbalance set in. In the period
from 1950 to 1965 (Table C-10 from the President's 1966 *Economic
Report*), here's what happened:

The national income increased.........................130.0%
Corporation profits before taxes increased.............. 93.9%
Small business income increased...................... 67.9%
Rental income increased.............................. 97.8%
Farm income (gross) increased....................... 5.9%
Wages increased......................................153.4%
Interest (capital costs) increased.....................725.0%

In 1950, corporation profits after taxes were $24,900 million.

By 1965, the corporate profit structure had moved to $44,500 million
(after taxes). Everyone had been reading about the fantastic profits
of corporations, but under analysis it must be noted that national
income had increased 130% since 1950, whereas corporations increased
their profits only slightly over half of the ratio of increase in national
income during the pre-holding action period.

Translated into something everyone could understand, this meant
that private enterprise as a whole had earned only 62% of what it
needed to earn in order to keep pace with the growth of the national
economy during the 15 years in question. If this picture was weighted
upward by a few more-successful-than-usual corporations, it was
weighted downward by the sorry condition of agriculture and small
businesses. The surface manifestations could be seen by almost anyone: mergers and bankruptcy on the one hand, bargained wages
and high interest costs on the other.

For 15 years prior to the milk holding action, private enterprise
had not earned the returns necessary to pay the wage and capital
cost bill. For 15 years, this deficit had been hidden under an umbrella
of expanded debt. Private enterprise (including farming) continued
to function by consuming its capital, scaling back its earnings, and
substituting debt for earnings.

5. *machine efficiency*

Raw material production ideally should expand in advance of the
rest of the economy. Food production, in particular, is geared to
weather cycles, and must be made available a year ahead of consumption. Balance between segments on either side of the income

equation can be changed with impunity only when warranted by technological development, efficiency of capital, and a change in the state of the arts. Indeed, an entire segment can be erased as long as it is absorbed by a segment on the same side. Balance between different sides of the equation must be maintained (except for short term dislocation) at all times.

Thus still another premise has to be considered. There was a time when medicine lagged behind mechanical engineering, or farming lagged behind industrial production, but in mid-20th century America, it must be noted that technology has affected the economy evenly, visiting no special favors on one sector over the other. Labor in the factory is no more efficient than labor on the farm. This assumption, which bears up under critical inspection, must be openly stated, because labor (cost factor) is being paid for machine efficiency in factories, and labor (income factor) is penalized for machine efficiency on the farm.

This observation inescapably leads to the concept of parity, or equity for each of the sectors. In the United States, the period 1946-1950 is the only one in recent history when all parts of the economy moved in balance. Farm income, wages, interest—in a word—all elements in the national income breakdown were in balance during that period, and have not been in balance since. Wholesale prices in each sector were in balance also. In 1966 alone, agriculture found itself short of some $51 billion in income as compared to what agriculture should have earned had farm income advanced at the same rate as labor and capital costs. Since 1951, farm income has dropped from being 7.1% of the national income to about the same as it was in 1929—2.5% of the national income.

A lot of economists point to the shrunken human population on farms and therefore conclude that agriculture does not matter in an industrial economy. Again, what are the observed facts? Carl Wilken has assembled one of the most unique contributions to the economic literature of our time. His statistics reveal that $1 earned in raw material production moves on a straight line ratio with $5 of national income. A drop of $10 billion in raw material income means that $50 billion in income will be lost to the nation as a whole. Wilken has called this ratio a "trade turn." Trade turn, or multiplier, the turnover effect of money injected into an economy at any level has seldom been questioned by professional economists, and thus leaves no grounds for rejection of the general principle.

What determines the multiplier between raw materials and national income? The efficiency of labor figures in this, the development of the arts (technology) is a factor, and the part of the labor force required to feed the population (assuming equitable labor expenditure for equal work)—all affect the ratio. Loosely speaking, when the stage of development requires half the people in a nation to be involved in mining, lumbering, farming, fishing, etc., then the multiplier between raw materials and the national income remains very close to two. This means such a nation would earn $2 of national income for every $1 earned at the raw materials level.

As an industrial economy emerges, the multiplier between payments to raw materials and national income increases. Industrialization does not absolve an economy from the necessity of paying for raw materials on an equitable basis. Indeed, industrialization makes parity even more mandatory.

Raw materials can be broken down between agricultural materials and others for the sake of convenience, but the multiplier must be considered an off-shoot from the whole. Since agricultural production accounts for 70% of all raw materials, there exists a remarkable ratio of seven between the price paid farm production and the entire national income (on an earned basis). This is not to assign sole cause and effect, but merely 70% cause. The ratio itself holds because commodity indexes move with striking coordination, up or down, and the 30% of raw materials included in minerals, etc., seem to keep a consistent ratio to farm commodities as raw materials move in response to manipulation or speculation.

The syllogism thus falls into place. All new wealth has its beginning in raw materials. Since income is simply production times price, the price assigned to raw materials becomes the income generating force of the economy. Data gathered since 1929 indicate that each dollar injected into the economy at the raw materials level multiples itself five times before it is tabulated as income at the national level. Similarly, income withheld at the raw material level will never materialize at the national income level on an earned basis. Milk that is not paid for generates no income, either for the farmer or the economy.

On the firing line of real dollars, the $51 billion agriculture failed to earn in 1966 because it failed to maintain parity with the rest of the economy meant—on the ratio of seven—that the national income was short $357 billion. Still, it might be observed, the "general welfare" does not indicate a depressed condition of this sort. How has this so-called shortage been made up? In a word—*debt*.

The shamans of Polynesia had a theory of magic that "like begets like," as Jevons and others have pointed out. Their pre-scientific minds grasped the connection between rains and the winds. When they wanted rain they took up rags and waved them around to make wind.

The magic of today is not to fall back to the fountainhead of prosperity, and produce a profit of sufficient scope to assure continuing prosperity. Instead, the shamans inject still more credit into the economy and boast of the prosperity it has produced.

6. *the economic equivalent of war*

If credit injection falters, new devices have to be found.

This has given rise to the "solution" of the simple minded—*war*.

Economically speaking, what is a war?

Social philosophers have searched long and hard for the meaning of conflict, and they have found war to be "the gory nurse that trained societies to cohesiveness," a "permanent human obligation" made necessary by man's pugnacity. "War is the strong life: it is life *in extremis;* war taxes are the only ones men never hesitate to pay," wrote William James in *The Moral Equivalent of War.* James and also H. G. Wells lavish a great deal of praise on the "collectivity" made necessary by war. "All the qualities of a man acquire dignity when he knows that the service of the collectivity that owns him needs him. If proud of the collectivity, his own pride rises in proportion. No collectivity is like an army for nourishng such pride; but it has to be confessed that the only sentiment which the image of pacific cosmopolitan industrialism is capable of arousing in countless worthy breasts is shame at the idea of belonging to such a collectivity," wrote James.

But economically speaking, what is war?

Everyone seems to know that wars and preparations for wars lift an economy, at least temporarily. Money becomes plentiful. Activity runs rampant. People are on the move, and the economy is on the move. Arguing his underconsumption theory, H. Gordon Hayes pronounced war "a veritable orgy of consumption. It is collective consumption, not individual consumption, and hence it does not depend on the buying power of individuals but on the productive power of the entire nation." Only a very learned man could be as hopelessly and articulately wrong as that. In war and in peace, consumption depends on buying power, and failure to generate buying power damns in advance the economy "in process" to a rude adjustment, whether war consumes material or not. WWII lifted the American economy out of the doldrums, whereas the Viet Nam action continues to drive the nation deeper into bankruptcy. Why?

Social philosophers like William James have hunted for the moral equivalent of war, but what the nation really needs is an economic equivalent of war. David Friday, writing in *The Journal of Political Economy* in February, 1919, cited the problem:

"It seems that somewhere in the present industrial process there is a factor of retardation which is only occasionally cast out by such a holocaust as war. What is the secret of its casting out, even for the space of three years? If this secret can be discovered, we may indulge the hope of institutionalizing it and adding permanently ten billion dollars to our annual national output. We could then realize the high standard of living of which reformers have dreamed . . ."

There is an economic equivalent of war. Application of this equivalent made it possible for America to fight WWII and move ahead, and absence of this equivalent has kept underdeveloped nations equally as old as America from developing at all. To understand it we must go to the record of what has actually happened in the American economy.

The American economy experienced a stabilized depression between 1929 and the first year of WWII. WWII was essentially a catalyst. It provided a spur to get things moving, and became a destructive public works project. At the same time it created the psychology that enabled raw material prices to move up, and government to hold down wages and consumer prices. Between the incentive to produce, and the balance between wages and capital on the one hand and raw material prices on the other being maintained, the conditions of WWII—despite the waste and destruction—developed a new level for the economy with little inflation. It has been noted that from 1940 to 1943 gross farm income increased $12.4 billion, and the national income jumped from 81.6 billion in 1940 to $170.3 billion in 1943. Production jumped because war created the psychology that enabled the institutional "going concerns" to pay the price necessary to get that production.

Surpluses vanished because people had the money to buy the food production. From 1943 to 1952, farm production continued to command close to 100% parity. During that period the national income moved on a ratio of $6.7 national income for every $1 of farm income.

The observed facts of what happens during a condition of war fly heavily into the fact of orthodox economic theory.

Take the law of demand. It in effect says—other things being equal —that the higher prices will have the effect of regulating the amount to be produced, hence sold. It is often argued that industry takes all this into consideration when deciding on how much to produce. The amount of stuff to be manufactured or created is determined by what businessmen perceive the price objective to be. Under conditions of war, production is directed by official decree. No sector is asked to produce at less than the cost of production. Raw materials pulled from the ground, food and fiber harvested from farms, all of which start the chain, are priced to get the job done. The value judgment of "survival is necessary" prompts mining metals of strategic importance, and the price for this production is paid.

Farmers, normally used to producing what nature makes possible, and asking at the market, "What will you give me?", are freed of having to sell at less than it takes to produce. The cry, "We have to feed war workers and soldiers," is raised to the level of sheer patriotism, and all efforts are redoubled to produce more. More important, there is no lip service to the law of supply and demand during a condition of global war.

The economic equivalent of war does no less than do away with the theory of supply and demand. For there is an assumption embodied in the supply and demand theory that appears to be fatal in advance. It assumes that the fact of population is stable, which it isn't, and it assumes that farm production has outrun the requirements of the population, which it hasn't. Individuals no older than the half-way house of life can remember the so-called depression year surpluses, when granaries were full to the brim and people were going hungry. The contradiction does not square well with the theory of supply and demand simply because the classical catch phrase fails to take into consideration one of the basic realities of life—people and income, or the lack thereof.

If one recalls the words of Santayana that "those who will not read history are condemned to repeat it," then one has some idea of why a basic economic concept cannot pose as the definitive word without undergoing the rigors of being tested. During the 1930s a number of subsidy programs were started to pump income into the economy. These pump priming efforts undoubtedly generated activity, but the economy nevertheless failed to achieve full employment. Commodity prices stayed near the 1932-33 bottom. During this period the government programmed the income of factories with all sorts of ideas. The NRA attempted to cut back "over-production," but the courts rejected the idea. Nevertheless, the NRA idea stayed on and found itself expressed in programs designed to reduce farm supply to balance with consumer demand. Supply and demand would eventually raise farm raw materials income, the thinking ran. But the over-production continued. And millions of people, without income, simply did without. They did without proper food, among other things.

Farm over-production has always been considered a cardinal sin because the principle of inelastic demand has been considered too sacred to be tested. The demand for food, this reasoning runs, increases only slightly as prices increase or decrease. Despite the fact that it obviously contradicts the theory of supply and demand, this idea has remained enshrined as the most sacred of holy cows in farm economics. People can eat only so many steaks, so much oatmeal, so much bread, the reasoning runs. They can't eat all this farm production we're capable of if they stay up all night. Is this true?

For almost two centuries the concept of business cycles has been investigated. One of the first to present it graphically was Leonard P. Ayers of the Cleveland Trust Company. His charts reached back to 1790 and detailed 23 depressions, with the depression of the 1930s the worst of the lot. Even casual scrutiny reveals that there were really few normal years. There seems to be an almost equal division between years that can be termed "prosperity" and years that can be called "depression." The strange association of wars with prosperity and then depression is at once apparent. And aside from the fact of wars, good years seemed to be associated with new industrial opportunities. The depression of 1893 *seemed* to be overcome by the birth of the mass production industries, and this stimulant again seems to be in evidence in 1907 because of new technology, automobiles, etc. Recovery from the 1920-1922 depression correlated with the development of radio, a sensational invention that mushroomed into a billion dollar industry in about five years. Other developments included railroads, corporate enterprise, and mining. Still, periods in which there has been full employment are rare and of short duration, sometimes only a few months. During those periods, however, food surpluses vanished as if by magic, and when a downturn came it seems always to have been a drop in commodity prices that led that way.

The obvious observation to make is that want and demand are not coin with which men pay for beef steaks. Salesmen nowadays are told that to make a sale the prospect must have a need, a desire and the ability to pay. Without the ability to pay, the hamburger remains unsold.

"It is not because the wants of all of us are satiated that we fail to consume the product that is, or might be, available," counsels H. Gordon Hayes. "At least a third of the population are always underfed and shabbily clothed, except during a major war, and always poorly housed. Another third are far from having their desires for the necessities and comforts of life satisfied and know practically nothing of luxuries."

During WWII an OPA was required to ration food, not because the U. S. was feeding the world, but because the income of the community was large enough and distributed well enough to enable almost everyone to eat well. On the index of 1957-1959 as 100, the food output in 1946 was 84. In 1964 it was 111—an increase of 32.1%. The population of the United States during this period increased 35.8%, from 141,389,000 to 192,072,000 persons. By 1967, population reached 200 million, and production to keep pace with mouths to feed was no longer in the running.

Even for Americans, the richest farm nation of all has failed to keep production geared to population, and yet when income was available every bit of food disappeared, was paid for, with less being exported than at any time in history. The highly special concepts of inelastic demand, and supply and demand, fail to take into account the basic reality that surplus is not the cause of low farm prices, but the effect of them.

What, indeed, does war do?

Does war provide a "cheater," a new set of operating principles that systematically overcome obvious defects in the capital economic system, defects that require vacillation between boom and bust as a matter of principle? Is there, in short, an economic equivalent of war that could be used in economic management?

Since parity for agriculture was maintained for some time after WWII, the nation was not forced to endure a post-conflict depression.

Then came the 1953 slide—a case of manufactured prices going up, farm prices going down, the net result on the charts being stability. Down, down, down tumbled farm prices and raw material prices. To keep the full effect of this curtailed purchasing power from visiting its violence on the economy, all sorts of preposterous schemes became current coin. And without exception, they drew their nourishment not from the creation of new wealth, but from the tools Keynes had discovered: tax policy, credit policy and budget policy.

Any economy not based on production is indeed a Las Vegas economy and contains the seeds of its own destruction. Changing the rules for the dice hustling does not alter the fact that new money must enter the casino. So far the money managers have satisfied themselves with borrowing money and injecting this into the economy Keynesian style, and to the unsophisticated the turnover of this borrowed money has created prosperity.

It is true that institutional business takes a war economy as it comes, profiting handsomely, because earned income is reckoned as a matter of course, but hounds the body economics to death during times of peace because the collectivity of war is replaced with the dog-eat-dog individualism of peace that enables the strong to possess the weak.

By early 1967, the strong had driven farm prices into the ground, and that is why NFO farmers were dumping milk.

NARRATIVE

---

holding action

mha + 5

As HE DUMPED his milk, the farmer suffered, not in the historic past, nor in the abstract future, but here and now, today, this hour on Monday morning, MHA + 5. He could dump because he saw how his farm fit into the terrible mosaic of the whole. If he were dumping only as an individual, the act could rate as no more than a tantrum, but dumping as part of farmers' collectivity became meaningful, and this meaning made it possible for him to do something that ran against the grain.

Farmers who still saw themselves as rugged individualists couldn't dump at all. Allowing milk to slide across the floor to the nearest drain was to them like dying for a cause alone and unheard of, an absurdity no consideration in heaven or hell could make real. The overview of the rugged individualist ranged no further than the farm, this crop, that cooler full of milk, and all else "out there" was too complicated to grapple with. The individualist could only fall back on God and nature—and prayer—if his stuff wasn't fetching what it was worth. Like the die-hard in any pact with futility, he would suffocate never realizing he was being choked to death by the marketing system. He would look on those who banked at least a little hope on collectivity as less than "he men" because they refused to let themselves be chewed up and spit out by the powers that be.

The NFO member accepted a measure of collectivity, and with it came an overview that reached well beyond the farm, the county, the state. His overview slid west each day with the sun, and rolled around the world to start a new day the following morning. In the floodlight of that orbit, dumping made sense.

Yet it hurt to dump milk, and it hurt now. The milk was opaque and therefore real. If the white liquid soaking into the snow in

171

Pennsylvania offended the sob sisters and the do-gooders, it offended
the farmer who was dumping even more. "It's a sin to dump milk in
a hungry world," was being heard like a march cadence on MHA + 5,
and the NFO farmer agreed. But whose sin was it?

The individualists—on the farm and in the editorial office—worried
that sin along with all the trappings of indignation, but that same
individualist hardly considered the mature overview—a world building toward widespread famine while the ability to produce food was
being destroyed. The gallon of milk on the ground became a sin
when it arrived on the TV tube as an image. The herds being
destroyed remained an abstraction simple minds could not grasp.

Still NFO farmers could grasp that long view, and it enabled them
to dump milk, if not with a smile, then at least with an air of statesmanship. Dumping milk was all they could do when faced with
breath-taking economic illiteracy.

It was this illiteracy that nourished both the individualist on the
farm and his alter ego in the public life. Spoke the Waukesha, Wisconsin *Freeman:* "While repeated efforts have been made to repeal
the natural laws of supply and demand, they have usually returned to
plague those who flout them." The dairyman, the editorialist said, cannot expect "to be insulated against the rise and fall of prices in the
free market." Spoke the Beloit, Wisconsin *News:* "If the processors—
and the consumers—are adamant against an increase, farmers have
two choices: Accept defeat and resume marketing milk, or quit
dairying . . ."

Supply and demand, like the Ark of the Covenant, was too sacred
to be touched, at least by farmers. Everyone else could have a go
at it. That the very proposition made agriculture as basic as God's
gift of raw materials and resources seemed to elude those who equated
the law of supply and demand with the law of gravity.

Truman Graf, a University of Wisconsin agricultural economist,
had issued the same sermon, more or less, countless times. He would
undoubtedly tell how overproduction was driving milk prices down
were he to mount a podium amid the starving masses in India.
As author of the Food Commission's Supplement No. 1, *Cheese Production in the United States,* Graf knew all the figures. He simply
couldn't milk a conclusion out of them. Earlier, at Janesville, Wisconsin, he had recited how since 1960 there had been a 22% drop
in cow numbers, with a 21% increase in production per cow. Wisconsin production had increased 8% the past year, and national

consumption had gone up only 1%. He concluded that production should be discouraged, not sales expanded. Had he given this advice to soda pop manufacturers, he would have been fired. Yet this was the advice tax-paying farmers were expected to swallow. How could they? There was a ring of systematic insincerity about all this supply and demand business. Even casual inspection uncovered a lot of it.

1. *dumping in silence*

During the milk holding action, reports from New York, New Jersey and Pennsylvania arrived at the Nerve Center first. Fred Young's partial survey revealed that New Jersey farmers were dumping over two million pounds a day, but henceforth they would be dumping in silence. Later on MHA + 5, CBS was scheduled to cover dumping in Sussex, Orange and Warren Counties. Shortly before the dumping, NFOers got a call from the station. "You're sitting on a keg of powder," the farmers were told. "We won't touch it with a ten foot pole. We've been ordered to drop all this." When asked who ordered it, the answer came like a rifle shot: "The powers that be."

As a matter of fact, the powers that be, not supply and demand, provided the law for functional economics. In Commonwealth Court in Harrisburg, Pennsylvania, nine Pittsburgh area dairy groups were asking for revocation of a half cent per quart reduction in the maximum retail price of milk which had been in effect since February 14. Where was the law of supply and demand while Judge William Lipsitt deliberated? Indeed, where was supply and demand when the State Milk Control Commission decided to drive down milk prices in the first place?

How much did supply and demand affect the USDA judgment then being made whether 14 western counties would be taken in by the Cleveland, Youngstown-Warren, and Wheeling, West Virginia federal market order? True, at the hearings the experts talked the supply and demand game, and there were all sorts of references to "homogeneity of supply and demand conditions," "competition among dealers," and "movement of milk within the area." As dealers expand their distributing areas, there is need to consolidate market areas, Dr. Robert E. Jacobson of Ohio State University testified. The consolidation may mean certain groups of producers will be "deprived of certain advantages to which they have become accustomed."

In effect, the great and good servants of the farmers, The Milk

Producers Federation, the Dairymen's Cooperative Sales Association, the Erie-Crawford Dairy Cooperative Association, and the Northwestern Cooperative Sales Association were asking the Secretary of Agriculture to amend the northeast Ohio order to include the other areas, not so much to help farmers hold prices, but to enforce a common denominator beneficial to the co-ops. Institutional arrangements for doing business, not supply and demand, were writing the ticket.

As the sun picked up another hour in its orbit, the flow of reports from the field moved with it. A hauler at Athens, Ohio picked up milk while farmers were busy going down the road. Later the farmers caught up with the hauler and made him empty milk from his tank truck. "They're out on bond," the report ran.

If it took a bond for farmers to dump their own milk, then at least they were willing to pay the price. The price, after all, was merely an extension of the price that had been exacted before. Ohio farms had been liquidated until now there were hardly 130,000, according to the detail merchants. There was a reason for this. Dairying had long been Ohio's greatest source of farm income. With low milk prices hanging on for too long, Ohio had joined Michigan, Wisconsin, Minnesota and other states in watching helplessly while dairymen sent their herds to slaughter. In Tuscarawas County—one of the several Little Switzerlands in the American farm country—they made Liederkranz cheese, and presumably the milk was still available, but north, around Akron, there was no secret about milk being imported from Pennsylvania, while Pennsylvania was fighting to keep the milk from leaving the state. As co-op contracts expired, farmers moved their milk west, and now a change of market order territories would put a stop to farmers seeking better spot situations.

Dealing as individuals, and on their own initiative, NFO members had been moving their milk to plants that recognized the right of farmers to bargain for fair prices. They had been doing this almost as fast as the signup news leaked out. Since NFO did not publish the names of plants that signed, the grapevine was sometimes a little tardy in spreading the word, but once the details became common knowledge a measurable movement became evident. The advantages had been spot advantages, nothing more. The entire milk problem could not be solved piecemeal at the local level, yet it was at the local level that individuals had to do their work.

Keith Emenhiser was on the job, MHA + 5, working at the individual and local level from his Monroeville, Indiana holding action post, yet covering an Ohio territory. NFO Director Ralph Hoover was doing the same from Wooster, Ohio. Together with action workers Leo Buehler, Dick Fout, Leland Walker and Richard Roberts, they formed Ohio's half dozen, and by 10:00 a.m. MHA +5 they all had their hands full.

Increasingly, the trade was looking to the law to stop NFO. Here and there a co-op would seek a restraining order, and usually the judge signed the legal paper. A local order had only local effect and usually involved only a single individual, or a handful of individuals. The local orders could hardly be translated into a stick of judicial dynamite for all the 25 states, not by a judge, the press, or the TV cameras. Nevertheless, the injunction was a nuisance.

One of the early ones in Ohio was issued in Wood County Common Pleas Court in response to a request by the Northwestern Cooperative Sales Association of Toledo. The writ named Floyd and Maurice Dewese "and other unknown defendants in Wood County." It gave the sheriff the right to stop any action that prohibited the pickup or delivery of milk anywhere in the county, including action on private property. Its legal language was well drafted, yet everyone knew the writ was for eyewash only and had no more meaning to the holding action than the "yer honor" in front of Judge. If its headline value in Ohio was negligible, it was nevertheless a new move, and a very prophetic one.

Those who planned on obscure action in a Common Pleas Court in Ohio soon learned that NFO was a veritable Hydra. There was no single head on which a state court could deliver a death blow. Nevertheless there would be tries.

Throughout Michigan, various plants loaded out their Class 1 milk to Michigan Milk Producers Association. Almost across the board, they all admitted that volume was down 10%, and MMPA's Glen Lake was buoyantly confident when he said that his organization would meet its marketing commitments, and that in effect the hold was suffering a dismal failure.

NFO Director Eldeen Jones watched each statement and each movement with care. Though loss of production was being stoutly denied, several "fortunately placed" developments had the effect of stretching the supply. There was the well-publicized phone call, for instance, in which an anonymous voice warned that milk tankers were loaded with poison. In the big city press, MMPA took on the air of the good guy in the white hat. Someone exploded dynamite, someone telephoned, and someone put oil in milk tanks (in one NFO member's tank, in fact), and MMPA was "forced" to place shotgun guards on each of the milk trucks. Photographers recorded the events of the day for posterity.

Eldeen Jones and Dick Suntken watched the proceedings from their Four Leaf Clover Motel office at Homer. There was a strangeness about the reports. The bullets that zinged into trucks at Rosebush, Capac, Sandusky, Swartz Creek and Pontiac always came from nowhere. The poison note was anonymously called. The only thing concrete seemed to be the precautionary steps taken my MMPA.

These steps reached the ultimate when MMPA filed a $1 million suit against NFO, its members, most of the Michigan leaders,* and President Oren Lee Staley, and asked for a restraining order against "vandalism and terror, stemming from the NFO milk withholding action." Judge Marvin J. Salmon of Ingham County Circuit Court entered the action and gave NFO 20 days to respond. In 20 days the holding action would be over. In the meantime, the headlines were big, but not very convincing. A million dollars was really too much. Hardly a farmer, in or out of NFO failed to think, "You can't get blood from a turnip." Not even the institutional power of government could do that.

Ernie Knoch relayed the news to Wayne Mathews, and someone told Charlie Rice and Mike Reed, who were all too busy running around Michigan to listen to TV. Finally, Lee Wery picked up the phone in his West Bend, Wisconsin home to call the Nerve Center at Corning. The response was electric. A million dollars—even in the abstract setting of a lawsuit—is a matter for wonderment. Finally someone in the Nerve Center, one of those ever-talking voices, relayed to Michigan a suggestion, at least 45% of which was jest: "Have the members of MMPA procure an attorney and attempt to file an injunction against Glen Lake and the MMPA Board of Directors for using the farmers' money to hold down prices."

"If all we had to do was deal with supply and demand," said Oras Kanerva, "we'd be home free. But, man, we're dealing with institutions."

*Michigan members named in the suit were Ford C. Hawkins, Stockbridge; Ernest J. Knoch, Webberville; Charles J. King, Owosso; Ronald Ervin, Mt. Pleasant; Ray Nielsen Jr., Saranac; William R. Mahaffey, Brown City; Matthew Satkowiak, Grand Blanc; Lee C. Shepherd, Hemlock; Hal E. Hash, St. Charles; Hursel R. Mier, Prescott; Lyle Schmidt, Hemlock; and Alton Tolan, Columbiaville.

2. *the power system*

Next to supply and demand, no word or set of words in the English language is more vaguely used than *institution*. The church, the state, the corporation, the family, marriage, property, machine technology even divorce are institutions, in a loose manner of speaking. Ever so vaguely, they all have one thing in common. They define the power system which makes rights and duties meaningful. From time immemorial, textbooks have described property as the institution through which the physical plant of the community is organized for production. In business, institutions set out the rules that attend transference of values. Whether farmers are paid for as much wealth as they produce is determined by institutions, not by supply and demand.

The world is populated by men who presumably ask of themselves, *Is this right? Is this just?* A civilized society is not inhabited by men who do business by referring decisions to Newtonian abstractions, or economic symbols lifted from ecology.

For many centuries running, the road to civilization has led away from the stagnant marshes of animal cunning or nature's survival of the fittest. During several centuries, the sciences have hypnotized the world with brillant displays of creative genius. Only in economics has evolution to a higher order failed, largely because the chief spokesmen of an entire discipline continue to set up questions without answers.

The questions are never answered because the only answer to supply and demand is allegory.

In the jungle there were two types of beasts, the herbivores and the carnivores. The herbivores ate plants, and the carnivores ate the herbivores. Nature prescribed a working balance. When the rains failed, herb eating animals endured a depression. They became weak, for they could not run very fast, and they provided many easy meals for the meat eating animals. For the moment, carnivores enjoyed prosperity. Of a sudden, however, the race of herbivores seemed to vanish. Deprived of their food supply, the carnivores endured hunger and starvation. Too weak to run, they failed to catch even the remaining herbivores, who obeyed the biblical injunction to increase and multiply. As herbivores prospered, so did the carnivores. Herbivore depression also meant carnivore depression.

Ecologists tell us that the world of insects provides a perfect laboratory in which supply and demand functions. Oddly, it does not seem a lesson applicable to the world in which farmers, co-ops, corporations and government flex the muscles of power over what happens to the price of milk.

On the roster of institutions, the government always comes first. Its judgments and sins are visited unto the seventh generation. Sometimes far-seeing planners have the vision of a Lincoln, and sometimes they are as blind as a mole. Sometimes the accidents of history correct inbred stupidity, and sometimes the visionaries burn every rung of the ladder they believe they are climbing to a theoretical perfect society.

Officially, the government said farewell to the frontier with the census of 1890, but the fact was something else. As late as the depression of the 1930s, the safety valve of free land still existed. Indeed, the decade-long farm depression that preceded the liquidity debacle of 1929 was eased somewhat by the fact that bankrupt farmers were being recapitalized on homestead lands out west. Claims were being filled by those who had been shared out by industrial and business institutions in America.

By design, accident, or stupidity, those who saw a rising industrialization as a foundation for economic stability seized the opportunity the great depression provided. The Homestead Act was repealed in 1935. After that, the design, accident or stupidity boys endured the greatest era of statesmanship the nation had ever seen. Starting in 1942, and for ten years after that, Congress in effect monetized farm raw materials. It was not until the end of the 90% of parity days that the deterioration of agriculture could be sent on its way again, this time without a safety valve.

Support prices were scaled down to pace the rate of farm bankruptcy. New and subtle pressures were brought to bear on farmers to increase efficiency, to get bigger, to develop the ruinous competition that alone could force prices down and drive farmers from the land.

Experts who had forgotten, if they ever knew, the foundation nature of agriculture, hardly hesitated to upset the balance of the economy. The income equation that ultimately governs boom and bust alike was declared obsolete. Those same experts, with no knowledge of the only supply and demand under the sun, suddenly perceived it wise and expedient to upset the balance of nature as well. If a steady stream of rural employables was to be kept arriving in the cities, agriculture had to deteriorate steadily, and at the same time it had to keep on producing more.

Technology was flung into the breach. Elixirs that dealt efficiency and death out of the same package were sprinkled over the crops, and the consumer was never the wiser. A Soil Bank came into being. By paying lavish sums to the big holders, it placed greater pressures on the small holders, who could not afford to keep pace. In 1953 *The Yearbook of Agriculture* devoted its pages to insects and use of chemicals for efficiency. If natural selection and mutation bring on strains resistant to the chemicals that can send crop dusters into convulsions, "More applications or greater quantities of the insecticides are needed . . ."

It has been estimated that the top eight inches of an acre of soil hold nine tons of microorganisms, the foundation life of the earth that enables man to grow crops, feed dairy cows, and harvest the renewable resources of agriculture. In the most fundamental terms, the rhythm of life depends on these microorganisms, just at it depends on nature's balance in insect, bird and wildlife.

Yet if one, two or three million farmers were to be kept scurrying into the cities, those remaining would have to reap bigger crops. They would have to introduce machine efficiency to rival that in the factory, and forego any reward on the investment. Further, they would have to drive nature to the wall and outsmart the balance that centuries of evolution had accounted for. Man has but three generations in a century. Insects sometimes run through that many generations in a week. Thus insects adapt faster than man. That is why the USDA told farmers to use "More applications or greater quantities of the insecticides . . ."

And so carcinoma-forming arsenic was dusted over the tape-measured tobacco patches to the extent that residual arsenic would be taken in until lung cancer became the plague of the land. The blind, deaf and dumb could go on looking for a lung cancer cure when prevention was well within reach. As the pressure to produce more and more for less and less fell into full swing, even family farmers backed their Omaha Standards into the loading docks to take on "store boughten" efficiency—chlorinated hydrocarbons, organic phosphates, systemics of all kinds—until the very environment became contaminated and the foodstuffs adulterated. Family farmers, desperate to survive, ravenous to survive, pushed this new efficiency to the hilt, but never as far as the corporations. The big spreads owned their own airplanes. They could dust whole sections, and drop enough arsenic on the orchards to last several centuries.

The chains owned cattle operations in Australia, New Zealand and South America. With liberal import quotas, they could pour enough red meat into the country to break cattle prices, and as cattle prices fell the ranchers were crowded to the wall. "Get efficient" became a battle cry. As farm prices inched ever closer to the world commodity price level, big chemical firms secured price protection from import invasion.

The debauchery of agriculture has never proceeded on a straight-line basis. Always there have been ploys, strange maneuvers, because wrecking agriculture to provide full employment was never sound and never really worked for more than a season or two at a time. Employables arrived in the cities, and they got the jobs. But the three million employables out of the deep south were black. In the cities they became indigents that cost the community four times their rate of keep in a rural setting. At intervals, the powers that be sought to stem the flow, so disastrous had the program for bankrupting rural America become.

3. *stronghold of the family farm*

At one time President Eisenhower appointed task force groups to study new crops the American farmer might grow. The strange thinking of the strange thinking set rejected the idea of stability through monetized raw materials. A free market for strange new crops was perceived to contain an answer.

The experts duly recommended American farmers turn to Korean lespedeza (a forage grass unfit for northern climates); Oriental bamboo ("for paper manufacture, structural material, specialty products"; castor beans (which are poisonous to human beings and animals and require air-tight fences); sesame (for "many feed and industrial uses,"); jojoba simmondsia (for the oil and wax industry); candelilla (again for the wax people); canaigre (a vegetable tanning material for the leather industry); dioscorea (a medical specialty which could keep at least a handful of farmers busy); guar (used in making gum for paper manufacturers); and kenaf (a jute-like fibre with little by way of market potential). These were the crops farmers were told to grow in 1956 as NFO got underway. The stronghold of the family farm, the dairy country, however, continued to produce milk.

Even now, the milk producer was responsible for nature's purest food. If trace elements entered the lacteal liquid, they were as nothing compared to the residue in corporation grown apples or carrots. In the heat of the holding action, farmers were even conscious of the pure food status milk enjoyed.

On the 10:00 a.m. report, Monday, MHA + 5, no less than two items were of signal importance:

NOTICE: Members are cautioned to be on the watch for reconstituted powdered milk blended with whole milk and passed off as Class 1. This is a violation of Federal Drug Administration regulations. Call this to the attention of the FDA man in your state. Have this milk analyzed. Ask for appropriate action.

NOTICE: Reports from all points indicate that Class 2 milk is not being processed. It is being tanked out of plants. Urge complaints be filed with Food and Drug Administration when concrete evidence can be furnished.

If NFO had become a Hydra, an organization that would not succumb with a single blow, the range of NFO activity produced equally as many heads. No summary could nail down each point, no recap could touch each phase. Yet the Nerve Center tried. The hourly reports on MHA + 5 started with an editorial someone had taped off KLIK at Jefferson City, Missouri. As field regulars checked in, they in turn recorded a few lines from the editorial:

"If a farmer has the courage to destroy his milk, to literally destroy some of his own money, in order to correct an unjust situation, then we can only applaud his courage . . .

"We strongly urge, however, that the process begin and end with the holding action. Let there be no road block, let there be no violence, for while the good wishes of the public go with a man who will stand on his own feet and defend a principle in which he believes, the anger of the public will be directed at a man who uses violence to accomplish that purpose and his course will be lost."

As the hourly reports indicated, the cause was far from lost. Individual entries indicated that the will to win ran high.

10:00 a.m., MHA + 5.

100 NFO members are helping Golden Guernsey producer Howard Stern clean up the mess caused by a bombing Sunday at 9:00 p.m. The blast tore a three foot hole in this NFO member's milk house. The vestibule door was blown across the barn. Bert Davey, also a Golden Guernsey producer, is dumping $100 worth of milk a day

and will continue to the end. He has offered a $1,000 reward to anyone with information that could lead to the apprehension of bombers at the Howard Stern farm. Address: Ixonia, Wisconsin.

11:00 a.m., MHA + 5.

Texas milk trucks are reported coming north into Kansas, loaded. This is a reversal of the usual flow.

12:00 noon, MHA + 5.

District 9 of PMA in Illinois voted to participate in the holding action. This district represents 450 to 500 PMA producers. Verified.

1:00 p.m., MHA + 5.

Dan Heiss, an NFO member, reports that a hauler for Page Dairy in Toledo stated that Page got 8,000 pounds milk from a surplus milk supply plant at Goshen, Indiana. This emptied their tanks, and from now on they will have to run on their daily supply if and when it comes in. At the start of the hold this outfit had several truckloads stored in anticipation of the holding action.

2:00 p.m., MHA + 5.

NFO Director Val Akerlund reports that two Nebraska state senators have intervened with the State Department of Health, which had threatened farmers with suspensions. Officials are now contacting members telling them they are free to hold and will be reinstated immediately.

3:00 p.m., MHA + 5.

Secretary of Agriculture Orville Freeman stated on the radio: "Farmers are well within their right in the holding action as long as it is conducted in a non-violent businesslike manner."

4:00 p.m., MHA + 5.

NFO farmers at Roseau, Minnesota are going to dump into a pit at the edge of town. They received a call from a Canadian Farmers Union member at Steinbeck, Manitoba, who would like to come down and watch the milk dumping. Canadians are making every effort to keep milk from being shipped into the U. S. to break the NFO effort.

5:00 p.m., MHA + 5.

Dave Sudsberry reports that the Kansas City Health Department has struck its colors. When NFO farmers are ready to ship again, inspection will be made immediately.

6:00 p.m., MHA + 5.

Embarrass, Wisconsin. Farmers dumped 550,000 pounds before the Huntley-Brinkley cameras. Anyone not dumping should be embarrassed.

7:00 p.m., MHA + 5.

Pleasant Hill, Missouri. NFO farmers dumped 28,000 pounds in a pasture before WDAF TV cameras.

On the hour, each hour, sometimes each half-hour, reports were fed through the portable in the Nerve Center. By supper time, even the big spectacular became commonplace. News had to be of a different stripe to rate attention.

All day President Staley had been on the phone, to every state in NFO, to industry spokesmen, to negotiators inside and outside the the dairy trade. As the last few minutes before midnight drowned amid the roar of the Nerve Center, one of the trade probes came to a head. Tomorrow, certainly no later than the next day, Staley told workers in the Nerve Center, an NFO bargaining team would fly out for what might be "meaningful negotiations." Even the limp forms behind the phones sat up with the news. They talked a little faster and took calls with a little more snap. And—imperceptibly—MHA + 6 had already arrived.

mha + 6

IT TOOK FANTASTIC FAITH for NFO members to continue dumping milk. From almost every quarter, they were being reminded of a world shadowed by malnutrition as though the pangs of hunger would somehow vanish if farmers simply agreed to go on selling their milk a little cheaper. Someone brought a *Kansas City Star* cartoon into the front office on MHA + 6. Labeled NFO, the outsized farmer had a head approximately the size of a kumquat and was dumping milk against a backdrop of human skeltons labeled "world famine." The editorial message said, "That'll Give Those Milk Buyers Something to Think About."

The first available impulse was anger, but when Albin Rust floated through with a grin on his face he brought an air of levity with him. Immediately someone took time to label the kumquat head "Star Brain Trust" and the caricature itself "Paper Boy." The milk can, through hellishly ingenious artwork, became a newspaper—a *Star*, in fact. It didn't hurt to laugh. Indeed, a laugh enabled NFOers to read the editorial a column away, one entitled "A Milk Strike That Can't Be Won," and smile. With or without humor, there was enough doubt laying about to test the faith of Job. And yet the members kept right on dumping.

Oren Lee Staley and Albin Rust had plenty to tell the membership, but they didn't dare. Bargaining sessions usually fell flat when someone talked out of school. The probes being fed into NFO headquarters depended on members tightening the hold on the one hand, and utmost discretion in leadership circles on the other. It would have been a simple thing for the Dairy Commodity Department to scotch all the misinformation being bandied about simply by pouring some truth on it. The trouble was, instant vindication wouldn't carry the day at the bargaining table.

It has been said that the chief qualification of a diplomat is a "willingness to be bored." Only the cynic would put it that way. A true diplomat, or a leader in collective bargaining, would substitute "patience" for "willingness to be bored."

NFO's leaders were all patient men. Each of their moves had grown out of patient study. The oblique bids for dialog that arrived on MHA + 6 indicated that NFO's analysis of industry trends were well on target.

1. the fluid circuit

For one thing, a trend in the fluid market was being confirmed. The fluid circuit, in fact, was breaking into three large marketing groups. Marketing orders were steadily combining territories, and co-ops were forming "associations." Basically, these associations were forming along geographic lines. One was beginning to encompass the eastern end of the nation and the big metropolitan centers on the seaboard. A second bloc was forming to include Michigan, Ohio, Kentucky and Tennessee. The third major bloc would include everything between Ohio and Omaha, and from the Canadian line to Texas.

These blocs of Class 1 co-ops were lacing together a trio of fluid groups that would one day vie for dominance, and with that dominance would go control of the dairy industry.

A fourth unit taking form was already being characterized as "the unregulated Class 1 bloc." This group took in dairyland producers whose production in the main found its way into manufactured products. Nationwide, an Agency in Common, had taken a leaf out of the NFO notebook and was busily organizing these co-ops into an unregulated Class 1 structure. The "unregulated" part always took a bit of explaining.

"What do you mean by unregulated," barked the Wisconsin dairy farmer who endured as many as five milk inspectors from as far as Chicago each month. The dairy farmer was right. His milk was Class 1, but he only got Class 2 prices for most of it.

The unregulated Class 1 bloc fed production into the manufacturing plants, true, but co-ops involved never missed an opportunity to ticket a tank into the big city fluid market. It was this overload that co-ops like PMA at Chicago relied upon to a great extent. And it was this overload that wrote figures in black ink on the co-op books.

Without the fluid trade, well, there was the cheese and butter business, and there was the by-product trade.

2. cheese economics

There were over 400 varieties of cheese, which was complicated enough. Yet these many products of the lacteal liquid were being distributed under twice as many names. Many took their names from the locality in which they were first developed—Edam, for instance which originally came from the region surrounding Edam in The Netherlands. Sometimes the same product had alternate names from the same locality, thus Manbollen, Katzenkopf and Tete de Maure were simply other names for a regional favorite, in this case, Edam.

Cheese and wine—two products of agriculture—have parallel lives. Both are foods that "live" in the literal sense of the word. Both use bacteria cultures, or starters, to activate fermentation, and both achieve the finished product through processes strikingly similar. Both are charged with romance, carry exotic names and rate as specialties. In the case of cheese, the product has a reputation as a complete protein food and as one of the seven basic foods. The parallels end there. Vintners take a hand in selling their products, in making varietal names household words. In dairy, the search is on for substitutes.

In a very real sense, NFO now found that it had to sell collective bargaining in order to really sell milk. If Wisconsin could not sell milk, then its farms would have very little to sell.

Wisconsin is rough country. You hardly see a big tractor from one end of the state to the next. Rolling hills, untillable patches of ground, and cool weather have made it America's dairyland.

In a very real sense, also, animal husbandry accounts for not only Wisconsin's agriculture, but also for much of America's farm efficiency. The nation has the equivalent of 200 million head of hogs and cattle. These animals are the biggest manufacturing industry in the nation. They work 24 hours a day with no wage cost except the capital investment of farm operators. In translating farm production into meat and milk, these animals increase the nation's caloric intake about six times the need in terms of grains. The staple diet of classical Greece was a sort of corn mush because that was the only way the people could be fed. Should America continue to pursue it ruinous farm policy and lose its meat and dairy production, the nation could very well have to return to mush to survive.

Certainly the corn crop could furnish enough calories to more than feed the American population. Each pound of corn has 1,500 calories, which is approximately the level of consumption in China. It requires about 42 pounds of corn to produce six pounds of beef in the feedlots. After this is done, and the dressing loss is accounted for, a rare steak delivers 1,275 calories. Thus if the American people are willing to live like Chinese on corn, the Wisconsin dairyland, the cattle producers, the hog belt—all could be liquidated with impunity.

Red meat production required individual attention, individual care. Under the existing wage structure, corporation agriculture would be required to go out of this type of production. As more and more farms went to corporation status, much of the efficiency of agriculture would vanish simply because animal production would be greatly reduced. First to feel the impact, undoubtedly, would be dairy production. The twice-a-day, seven days a week job would be too much for corporate agriculture to field.

Animal husbandry requires personal attention, and industrialized agriculture would unquestionably see the liquidation of a great deal of this type of production. And with liquidation of red meat production would go diminished efficiency. It has been calculated that red meat animals on American farms process more raw materials than all the rest of American industry put together, if the most vital of raw materials is included—namely water. The red meat animal thus becomes a labor force, working day and night, without strikes, at the job of harvesting crops, processing raw materials and manufacturing meat.

Meat is thus the great variable on the American farm scene. During the 1930s Secretary of Agriculture Wallace destroyed meat to alleviate surpluses, and thereby destroyed, rather than created wealth, yet on MHA + 6 experts still did not understand the role of meat as related to feed grains. H. F. DeGraff, in his book called *Beef,* illustrated that there is a seven for one ratio between dry feed and one pound of meat, all things considered. In short, it takes seven pounds of forage, grain, etc., to create one pound of red meat.

As the public policy of liquidation of the farm labor force arrives at its goal, and as population continues to grow, restriction of red meat production becomes a decided possibility, since seven people could be fed on grain in place of one on meat. Such a lowering of the standard of living in a nation like the United States was not likely to be accomplished without radical reorganization of the nation's economic and political structure.

There always has been stark tragedy in the kind of reckoning experts were pursuing, because corporation farming would return a state like Wisconsin to wilderness. Even casual inspection revealed that much of the acreage could not even be harvested without animals. It is this realization that made Wisconsin hard-hitting holding action country.

Fluid milk plants overloaded their "surplus" to manufacturing plants and manufacturing plants in turn shored up a fluid plant's shortage by pouring milk the other way. As farmers were quick to discern during the milk holding action, Class 2 milk can become Class 1 milk with alarming ease.

With little or no promotion, manufactured products became either raw materials for further manufacture, or they moved on to the market as the rarest of rare products—natural cheeses.

Unfortunately, economic pressures have driven the art out of almost all American cheese-making, and remanded the industry to a low common denominator. At the time of the holding action this meant turning milk into a few base products, notably cheddar and cottage cheese. This type of cheese-making was simple. Lactic acid cultures added to pasteurized skim milk turned out cottage cheese in the twinkling of an eye. Cheddar making became so standardized that it attained assembly line status.

The big Western Wisconsin Dairy Co-op at Blair was under NFO contract. A recent merger with Holman Co-op, and a little juggling of plant names, had turned this operation into one of the cheese-making bigs. The Holman operation handled Class 1 milk, and routed all "surplus" to the home operation at Western. Instead of bottled fluid for the home refrigerator, the lacteal liquid suddenly became cream, cheese, whey—and, in turn, whey products and powder for bakeries.

When NFO production arrived at Western there were two big 42,000 gallon tanks to take it in, and there was also a smaller 18,000 gallon "little tank" to hold the production. It wasn't held for long, not in normal times. In a matter of hours milk was pasteurized. Next it flowed into stainless steel vats. The ones commonly used in the industry held over 8,000 pounds. The ones used at Western had a capacity of 25,000 pounds each. It took approximately 11 pounds of milk to make one pound of cheese.

After lactic acid bacteria were added to each vat, big automatic paddles stirred to speed the ripening (fermenting) process. The art of cheese-making is an ancient one, yet it wore certain modern refinements as practiced in Wisconsin. Still the addition of rennet extract (a substance mined from a calf's fourth stomach) had not been bypassed by technology, no more than had the ancient techniques for separating whey from curd. Knives speed the process, as they slice and dice the curd. Workers in most plants work the curd to each side of the tank, allowing the whey to drain away. And they still turn the curd by hand in almost all plants. They sprinkle the salt by hand, and frequently they load and stack molds the old muscle way. A plant that can capitalize automated equipment—much like the farmer getting efficient—presumably has a differential advantage over the others until they too steal patents to prefab new equipment or buy expensive inventions that will roll the works without the burden of payrolls or human hands.

Obviously, a high cost economy cannot afford the luxury of inventories, not in cheese, wine or pretzels. Thus American plants have in the main abandoned the idea of aging cheese for great lengths of time. The pressure to turn the inventory has pushed cheese-making into fewer and fewer categories.

There are about 18 varieties of natural cheese. These are usually classified as soft, medium or hard, and mild, medium or sharp. Soft products generally include such ripened cheeses as Bel Paese, Brie, Camembert and Neufchatel, as well as unripened products, such as Mysost, Primost, cottage cheese and cream cheese. The mediums usually include Munster, Limburger, colby and brick. The hard ripened cheeses include Swiss, Edam and cheddar.

Even plant managers know very little about the range of cheese-making these days. "We make cheddar," is the usual statement. "That's it."

Mention Tamie as made by the Trappist monks, and you draw a blank. This is no criticism of American cheese makers. They do what the economics of their craft makes possible. Under different circumstances, they too could vary the salt, temperature, moisture left in the curd or curing time to create matchless products (as a few small operations still do).

3. *process cheese*

However, in 1917 a new development entered cheese-making for better or for worse. The word is "process cheese." Aggressive manufacturers took to blending natural cheeses with other elements to create process products, products that melt evenly in cooking, keep indefinitely, and are remarkably uniform. Initially, this new market allowed co-ops to sell the unaged product at a good price. Later, inch by inch, farmer co-ops allowed the balance of power to shift into the hands of the Big 9, so that now companies with monopoly status frequently buy the entire production from a Wisconsin co-op plant.

A plant like Western Wisconsin Dairy Co-op could update its operation, answer bargained wages with automated equipment, but the fact remained that two million pounds per day production was sold to a single buyer, Borden at Green Bay. No bargaining power attended this arrangement.

In turn, the price for cheddar was presumably set each Friday in one half hour of spirited bidding on the Wisconsin Cheese Exchange, although a more mature evaluation indicated that the Exchange served to no more than ratify what had already been decided.

At the time of the holding action even plants that were slow to move realize that an Agency in Common was required, because without it the cheese bloc in the dairy industry remained nothing more than a cheap source of supply for the foundation product needed in making process cheese.

Process cheese is advertised, its sales are pushed to the hilt. And the profits roll in from both ends—from the consumer, who pays the tariff, and from the farmer who sells his production for less than it is worth. Process cheese was making use of cheap colby imports, because colby is sold within 30 to 90 days of production. Technically, it is stopped in process at the curd stage, or a little past the cottage cheese stage.

4.　*the dominant bloc*

The so-called unregulated Class 1 bloc was in about the same boat as the farmer. The Big 9 told them what they would be paid, and they made this position secure by importing ever-increasing amounts of colby and Junex. In the final analysis, the co-ops paid the farmer what the Big 9 allowed them to pay the farmer.

NFO had consistently pointed out that it took production to price it. Thus the prospect of dairy co-ops following the NFO lead in forming blocs had become one of the most reassuring on the farm scene.

So far NFO calculations had proved correct. It had taken the threat of a holding action to drive the co-ops into meaningful blocs. Now the bargaining power of farmers would improve as scattered co-ops in the fluid circuit pulled together for a more stable home base. Obviously the bloc that attracted NFO production would become the most dominant in the dairy industry. With NFO production in tow at the farm level, this bloc would be able to negotiate on an equal footing with the monopolies in charge by virtue of their strength.

Sailing NFO into the treacherous winds of such an economic convulsion was no mean chore, and the leadership could hardly risk telegraphing intentions. On the water or in collective bargaining, you really don't sail best with the wind at your back. Nor can you sail directly into the wind. You have to tack into the wind and arrive at a goal over a most elusive route.

So far the route had meant a holding action. On deck for implementation was the new Phase 2 program. There was considerable debate over just when it would be thrown into the battle. Some of the staffers favored an early entry, but Staley and Rust were adamant in holding the lockup and store plan for a kicker, a big shot of institutional adrenal that would put the action over the top. The feelers that were coming in indicated that there would be bargaining sessions. When such sessions bog down, it takes more than weary hours to break a stalemate. Phase 2 could very well prove to be the breaker.

5. *like a rattail file*

Bill Lashmett hadn't slept much during several night shifts. There was something diabolical about the way in which the phone calls arrive after 1:00 a.m., MHA + 6. The intervals were just long enough to allow the night shift five or ten minutes of sleep before that insane bell clanged again. Like a rattail file on a sore tooth, the irritation of being awakened every few minutes usually drove the night shift to the coffee urn and to a half dozen sleepless hours before new voices took over.

It took new voices to cope with the early morning traffic. Clarence Thatcher couldn't possibly mistake the southern voice of Marion Green, "Well, suh, we're pouring it out to the hawgs in southern Georgia. Weren't having much effect till this mawning, according to radio and TV. Now they're saying there's beginning to be a milk shortage, that's on WALB-TV, Albany."

There were other messages that morning. One, a telegram,

    THIS AREA WILL SUPPORT NFO OPERATIONS. NEED YOUR HELP.

      WILL START ORGANIZING. REPLY URGENT. PAUL X GAUCHER.

had Lloyd Fairbanks pulling on his non-existent hair. In the entire Field Staff Department there wasn't a man not doing the work of two men, and sparing someone for special duty at Spencer, Massachusetts had never been considered. With a little shifting, and recruiting in New Jersey to fill Roger Kayhart's shoes, maybe, just maybe, Kayhart could head for the Bay state. Certainly the situation was desperate.

"Almost all the area farmers are interested in having the NFO come here," Massachusetts dairy farmer John Klem said. There was plenty of reason. Not a month earlier, Massachusetts Commissioner of Agriculture Charles McNamara had told *Farm Journal:* "I don't know how long some of our dairymen can hold on."

The dairymen didn't either, and that's why Lloyd Fairbanks suddenly found himself talking to people with John Kennedy accents, and why, predictably, a Farm Bureau man with the unromantic name of Good said he did "not condone" the actions of the Spencer group because farmers have bargaining power if they use economic weapons rather than strikes. Presumably the weapon of choice was the Farm Bureau's recommendation that farmers accept prices at near 50% of parity (in line with a moving average of world prices), a state of affairs that had caused Gaucher to send his wire in the first place.

As a matter of fact, telegraph offices across the country were getting a workout on MHA + 6. Earlier, a blast had been leveled at NFO from the office of Governor Warren Knowles of Wisconsin. Instantly, NFOers like Tom Schaller, Chairman of LaCrosse County, had uncorked letters to set the record straight—"If it is right for the Teamsters Union to call a strike and stop the movement of trucks without any interference from a governor's office, then the farmer has the same right in exercising economic forces to bring about justice to the farm producers"—but this was the least of a Wisconsin dairyman's worries. Public pressure was handling the governor.

In the Nerve Center, Cliff Oleson handled an early call from Wisconsin: "I asked the telegraph operator how long it would take to get a message to the Governor. He said just as soon as 40,000 similar telegraph messages ahead of it get there. You know what? I wonder whether he's kidding."

In La Crosse County, City Sanitation Director A. H. Schroeder suddenly found it within the purview of his office to break the NFO effort. His words were unequivocal: "Any farmer, now licensed, that participates in the holding action will be faced with a denial of license to trade with the people of La Crosse." Even with bad grammar, it hit where it hurt, doubly hard in Wisconsin because the Chief Executive had first established the tone for coercion, and the semi-private apology for the public affront had not undone the damage. (Some did not consider it much of an apology.)

The governor's "Dear Friend" letters were so neatly multilithed that they looked like originals—even the signature looked real. He had "personally read your letter," he said. He was "most sympathetic with the low prices received by the Wisconsin dairy farmer," he said. "I did not call the FBI into the milk holding action . . . At no time did I prejudge the effect of the holding action . . . " Attorney General Bronson C. LaFollette did a little better. He said, "The National Farm Organization is acting in the great tradition of midwestern Populism and Progressivism when it enables farmers to join together in an effort to gain fair prices through mutual self help."

Reports running out of the Nerve Center were up-to-the-minute only if they originated in Corning. Those originating in the field took a little longer—rather, the details took a little longer. The Bloomer affair was typical. It had been reported a day earlier, but the details were arriving now.

In a way, it was a typical dumping, if you can call dumping milk typical. In fact, a stylized form was rapidly shaping NFO public dumping demonstrations. This one began at Faneti's Livestock Market about a half-mile north of Bloomer on a very gray day, with mixed rain and snow turning the roads into a sea of slush. A red-lighted squad car led the parade down the town's main drag. It was a somber spectacle, and somehow the polkas and schottisches coming from one truck sounded like dirges. They were. At the dumping site, there was no shouting, no rowdiness—just the whine of engines and the muffled sound of milk sliding into the snow. As spigots opened, milk gushed out in streams as big as an arm. Still no anger, no horseplay, just the somber, funereal business of dumping milk. Everyone, absolutely everyone, who has ever witnessed such spectacle agreed that NFO made a powerful point.

Always someone had the data. In this case Chippewa County

Chairman Truman Bourget wrote it down: 80 trucks, 850,000 to 900,000 pounds.

Ken Lindquist and Henry Johns sheepherded developments from their homes at Marengo. It took ten regulars and countless helpers to handle the information in Wisconsin. Someone had to cover the ground, and this meant that Bob Manke and David Norrbon had little time to spend in the Wisconsin Kenron Motel holding action "office."

Everyone was answering questions. National Director Bob Rettig saw the action "tightening down." Marathon County NFO Chairman Martin Muzynoski saw the same effect, and pooh-poohed the violence bit that wire services liked to cabbage onto. "I keep in daily touch with the sheriff's office, and they are pleased with our farmers."

Quentin Ellingson, Chairman of Kenosha County, knew the members were "holding tight," but he figured it would all be over in a couple of days. It wasn't just wishful thinking. There was evidence and all of it was solid enough.

First off, in Sheboygan and Calumet Counties, NFO members were holding over 70 tons of milk a day. It added up to that. You took the 850,000 pounds spilled on Don and Frank Stoik's farm near Bloomer, and you took the individuals like Herman Sukowatey, and you did this county by county. Maybe it wasn't punchcard perfect, but it added up. Since the first day, the boys had simmered down a bit. Frank Stoik abandoned his $50 bond (for draining milk from his tank in downtown Bloomer) and just about everyone had come to agree that it was cheaper to dump on the farm—and better for the soil to boot.

There were other signs. PMA splinter groups were reported sore as hell about the Saturday night stand of the group in Chicago, and were holding on their own.

6. bits of the story

In Corning, Lee Elliott and Harvey Sickels took a page out of developments in China, and fixed up a bulletin board for the NFO's front window. There were plenty of headlines for such a bulletin board because across the country headlines were telling bits of the story:

BUY-OUT EFFORT

STARTED BY NFO

In Beloit, Wisconsin farmers decided to buy out the town, and Salamone Grocery said, "No," and limited sales to two gallons per persons.

On a bulletin board or in the papers, headlines made fascinating reading. Here are a few of those America was reading that day.

31,000 POUNDS OF MILK DUMPED IN GENOA AREA

The Lincoln Star, Lincoln, Nebraska.

6,500 GALLONS MILK DUMPED ON GROUND NORTH OF SIBLEY

Gazette Tribune, Sibley, Iowa.

60,000 POUNDS OF MILK DUMPED IN WINONA COUNTY

Winona News, Winona, Minnesota.

1,390,000 POUNDS MILK DUMPED DAILY

Public Opinion, Watertown, South Dakota.

DUMP TONS OF MILK

Detroit News, Detroit, Michigan.

FAMILY OF MILK STRIKE LEADER GOES IN HIDING

Chicago News, Chicago, Illinois.

OVER 29,000 GALLONS OF MILK DUMPED HERE, NFO MEMBERS REPORT

Hamilton Journal-News, Hamilton, Ohio.

$ MILLION SUIT FILED
AGAINST MILK GROUP
Philadelphia Daily News, Philadelphia, Pennsylvania.

FARMERS DEMONSTRATE WHITE POWER
Glascow Times, Glascow, Kentucky.

FARMERS FEEDING
HOGS MILK SUPPLY
Daily Ardmoreite, Ardmore, Oklahoma.

DAIRIES ACCUSED OF USING POWDER
New Ulm Journal, New Ulm, Minnesota.

MILK HOLDING ACTION CONTINUES
AMID TRUCK HIJACKING CHARGES
Chattanooga Times, Chattanooga, Tennessee.

CANADIAN MILK
SHIPMENT INTO
OHIO REPORTED
Bellefontaine Examiner, Bellefontaine, Ohio.

NFO MEMBERS IN STEELE COUNTY
DUMP 32,500 QUARTS OF MILK HERE
Owatonna Peoples Press, Owatonna, Minnesota.

HOGS ENJOY MILK HOLD CAMPAIGN
Dickinson Press, Dickinson, North Dakota.

INCIDENTS INCREASE
IN MILK WITHHOLDING
Stevens Point Journal, Stevens Point, Wisconsin.

FEWER MILK INCIDENTS: KNOWLES
Kenosha News, Kenosha, Wisconsin.

DUMP 17,000 POUNDS OF MILK A DAY
Knoxville Journal, Knoxville, Iowa.

424,000 SPILLED
IN AREA COUNTIES
Winona News, Winona, Minnesota.

And if there weren't headlines, there were pictures, $26,547 worth at the grocery price going on the snow at Ellsworth, Minnesota, 100,000 pounds in Faribault County, 57,500 pounds on the grounds (in color yet) in the Worthington, Minnesota *Globe*.

And there were other headlines:

POISON SCARE BOOSTS
POWDERED MILK SALES

Who wrote that note and mailed it to Madison, Wisconsin may never be known, but it was the greatest boost to powder sales in the memory of most people. For several days the powder traffic had been superb, and this had the effect of stretching the supply. NFO members merely tightened the hold. It was that way everywhere. If Fond du Lac County daily production of 1.5 million pounds was being cut by one-third, well, that was happening from New York to Colorado as well. If the soft-snow-covered earth on a Douglas County farm lapped up thousands of gallons milk on Tuesday, the same was taking place at Hopkinsville, Kentucky on the same afternoon. It was bigger when Douglas, Ashland, Bayfield and Iron County, Wisconsin farmers formed their convoy, but the act of dumping was just as deadly in Daniel Boone's old stomping grounds. Elmer Colby could estimate that "between 80 and 85% of the milk in Wisconsin was being withheld," and the news told Weston Edwards in Christian County, Kentucky, that Kentucky's bit counted more than ever before.

Ed Graf, Steve Pavish and Dale Burdick did much of the reporting out of Wisconsin, and Norbert Connors, Henry Fauske and Eugene Engh did still more reporting. In the Nerve Center Wisconsin rated a special phone, so heavy was the informational traffic. The pink sheets by Ken Schmidt stacked up, and they stacked up for all the rest, sometimes two for one when compared to areas such as Missouri and Kansas. Lee Wery was on the line at 9:30 a.m. "We had over a hundred men cleaning up the mess on Howard Stern's farm. That's right—he's the fellow they bombed Sunday."

7. *laments loss of lacteal liquids*

Across the nation, NFO's hold baffled the experts. They knew all the weak spots in NFO. They knew the damage dumping was doing to the supply. And they were baffled, partially because they knew much of the story, and also because they knew so little.

NFO had problems, for instance. "Lost some Sunday and Monday," was the sum and substance of the report from James McDonald at Mt. Pleasant, Michigan. But such reports—even from "million dollar Michigan"—were rare. It didn't take much to log them in. It took a great deal longer to take down the details Ken Lindquist furnished (256,460 pounds dumped at Pierce County; 90% hold in Duluth area, etc.) and it was always an easy calculation when a plant like St. Peter, Minnesota was reported out of powder, or when Tom Hook reported information on MMPA, where 100% of the supply was reportedly bottled. Normally 33% went for cottage cheese.

There was something strange about MHA +6. Usually reports started in the east and moved west. This morning they came on like a shotgun blast.

De Calb County, Tennessee—all Class 1 dairymen holding. All but two are NFO members. Herkimer County, New York—all 150 producers supplying Poland Creamery holding. Barron County, Kentucky —Straders Dairy reported not delivering milk in outlying areas today. Cold Spring, Minnesota—cafes out of milk. Only three glasses available in one. In North Dakota—state Senator Larson spoke in favor of NFO at a county meeting last night.

There was something grim about hammering out these facts, pounds dumped again as they had been dumped for a week running now, taking in that grim reality, living with it, holding on to it until it almost exploded. It was always a lighter moment when Oras Kanerva waltzed through. No tragedy could cause him to lose his sense of humor. Shown the amount of the Glen Lake lawsuit, he said simply, "Here's a headline—

LAKE LAMENTS LOSS OF LACTEAL LIQUID,"

and that's the way Nerve Center talkers sent it out.

Earlier in the day, UPI had asked Staley how he felt about the industry spending a million dollars to break the NFO effort. He told them.

On all fronts, the holding action was being carried off with an air of statesmanship. When a few of the boys let their humor get the best of them and decided to dump at Vice President Hubert H. Humphrey's home near Waverly, Minnesota, quick footed NFO leaders stepped in and stopped the horseplay. The matter of milk prices was much too serious to be used for a prank.

Across the nation there were milk suppers. Farmers were telling why they were dumping. As farmers sloshed through milk and snow they sometimes cracked jokes about the "darned expensive ice cream." Friends offered help and hope. The Wisconsin State Grange offered to arbitrate the hold.

Always, there was the economics of it all.

Keith Squires, NFO Dairy Chairman for Deuel County, South Dakota: "It costs us $4.96 a hundredweight to produce milk. We realize $3.79 after paying the freight to the dairy processing plant." You didn't have to use sigmas and quartile deviations to figure that one out. The figures changed from state to state. The names were different. At Mantua, Ohio the name was Jerry Cavanaugh, and he was dumping 2,500 pounds a day on his farm. At Caldwell, Idaho the name was Olan Grayson, and he was pouring 1,530 on the ground at the receiving docks of Dairyman's Cooperative Creamery. The names were different, that's all.

8.   *news out of tennessee*

The map on the wall in the Nerve Center detailed all the counties under NFO organization. Not that the workers needed this information. They knew their territories like the backs of their hands.

That Curtis Lightfoot was handling Warren County, Kentucky, and that 50,000 pounds a day was being held in that county, was no abstraction. Likely as not Curtis was a personal friend of almost anyone in the Nerve Center, and likely—too—Curtis was known to anyone in a position of leadership in NFO. Some of NFO's regulars literally knew thousands. Staley was said to know even more. Walking through the Nerve Center and catching up a pink sheet might deliver a name like John Cardin of Hardin County, Kentucky, where NFO calculated a 90% hold, and he too was real.

What wasn't real was the fact that powder was being fed into the fluid milk, and health officials refused to do anything about it. In Iowa the agriculture secretary denied it categorically. "We have ten men checking milk quality day and night," L. B. Liddy told Des Moines farm editor Don Muhm. The NFO hustlers, who were quietly having tests made, could only smile. State government workers, never a high target group in the heart attack department, weren't breaking their backs during Holy Week, not to help the consumer or NFO.

Equally unreal on MHA + 6 was the news out of Tennessee, where five trucks had been allegedly hijacked. Hershel Ligon denied that NFOers had anything to do with it, and informed opinion had it that Ligon was right. Tennessee was Jimmy Hoffa country, and Hoffa was in jail—unfairly, many truck-driving Tennesseans felt. Teamsters were girding for battle, and much as NFO needed help, leaders and members had been forbidden to even talk to Teamsters. All the happenings had a reason for being, NFO felt, but no one could put a finger on it.

Late in the evening, an answer of sorts started firming up.

Chancellor W. M. Leech had welcomed into his home certain representatives from the Nashville Milk Producers. A document was presented. There had been "four specific acts of violence," the request for an injunction stated. There were other details, but details were not too important at 7:30 in the evening. Chancellor Leech signed a temporary restraining order, one that would not be served on Hershel Ligon and Tennessee NFO until in the morning.

Earlier in the day, milk plant executives claimed that the NFO effort was ineffective. There had been no "squeeze in the milk supply until the hijacking began." The "four specific acts of violence" required a temporary restraining order, the executives said.

Ligon received a wire from the Tennessee State Labor Council:

THE OFFICERS OF THE TENNESSEE STATE LABOR COUNCIL HAVE DISCUSSED

THE WITHHOLDING ACTION OF YOUR ORGANIZATION, AND I AM AUTHORIZED
TO OFFER WHAT SUPPORT AND INFLUENCE WE CAN LEGALLY BRING TO
BEAR IN YOUR BEHALF. IT IS MOST REGRETTABLE IN OUR VIEW FOR
TENNESSEE FARMERS TO SELL THE PRODUCTS OF THEIR LABOR AT A PRICE
THAT WILL YIELD YOUR MEMBERS 50 CENTS AN HOUR OR LESS FOR YOUR
LABOR.

Now Labor was sending wires. And the powers that be were
obtaining temporary restraining orders. There was a deeper meaning
in all this, and those on the scene were trying to find the answers.
Something had to give before the unreal could be made real.

The milk being dumped was real, and on MHA + 6 it was just
about the only thing that was real.

Cincinnati Milk Sales was importing 300,000 pounds of Wisconsin
milk to shore up the deficit. The national milk tank was certainly
evening itself out. Farmers looked hard and continued to dump.
Their wives used washing machines to churn butter, tubs and tubs
of it.

On MHA + 6, the important became unimportant, and the unimportant became important. There was quite a to-do about a conservation official in Vernon County, Wisconsin, who told NFO members they could no longer dump milk on the ground because it was
against the law. And there was even more to-do about how the
bullet hole got in an Erie-Crawford Co-op truck while the truck
was locked in a Pennsylvania shop, because none of the windows of
the shop were broken.

In Iowa, a clerk in a court turned up a law that made it criminal
to destroy food. No one paid too much attention. Raw milk was not
food, at least not legally. It had to be processed before it was fit for
human consumption.

mha + 7

A MATURE SENSE OF VALUES told all who wished to see that nothing less than a continuing battle for agriculture would do. Exploiting the farmer had become a way of life. Had he been driven into virtual servitude, into the peonage of the great estates in South America, revolution would have remained unlikely. But—as every student of mass movements soon observes—rising expectations and the idea that "we're missing out on something" prompts men to revolt. Looking at a nation living in the lap of luxury, the farmer believed he had a cause. A thousand case reports could illustrate the point. One should do.

Vincent Georges and his wife Betty Ruth kept a 50 cow milking line on their Indiana farm. They started the dairying operation before daylight each day and worked until after dark. Three boys at home helped do much of the work—indeed, without the boys to help an operation of such scope could not function at all. In Indiana, all areas of the state are within easy mileage of industrial plants. Farm labor is impossible to find. "You do it yourself," Vincent would say with laconic disdain. "You do it yourself, and if you don't get a price it comes out of your hide." He joined NFO in 1959. "It was the only organization you could join if you really wanted to join something."

The paucity of controls protecting the farmer in dairy gave Vincent cause for alarm. "The test goes down every time there is an improvement in Class 1 milk prices. I've never figured out a way to check the test." The weight—that's something else. Vincent's $4,000 milk tank paid for itself, he figured, because it had a measuring stick and gave him an accurate reading just before the hauler made off with the milk. "But the test, I don't know what to do about that."

At the end of the milking line, it was "the test" that stood some of the rigging. At the end of the farm production line the word was "parity."

Merle Suntken and Bob Ayers were handling the holding action details in the Bluffton, Indiana area, just as Paul Schmucker was doing at Nappanee or Jack Vermillion at Greencastle. Although good speakers, they had neither the range nor the standing of a Dr. Don Paarlberg, whose enchantment over the death of "fundamental agriculture" knew no bounds. Doing their chores, farmers often thought about Paarlberg.

Paarlberg was a product of Purdue, and author of *American Farm Policy*, one of those "texts" that justified the disaster of public policy. In less academic moments he sang a treadnody about the Jeffersonian concept dying, about the old political power structure crumbling, about reapportionment shaking farmers out of the grass to make way for a more favorable corporation agriculture. On the podium and in the prints he saw the eclipse of the family farm with the sardonic cheer of the celebrated count from Bram Stoker's Transylvania. To make sure that pure economics had its way, men like Paarlberg devoted their energies to giving it an institutional push. Even while farmers battled, the intellectual set coined still more terms. Even while they dumped milk, the clockwork was ticking off the hours, and time was running out.

In Adams County, Iowa, NFO farmers had decided to dump milk in front of NFO headquarters. County Chairman Gary Botkin arranged it that way, replete with signed authority from the town dads. The spilling itself was a token effort limited to 20 gallons of watered-down milk. The rest of some 50,000 pounds was dumped at Mel Olive's farm near the Country Club.

The Corning demonstration was a natural, but Corning's Chamber more or less muffed the job. Here were wire services, network cameras, plenty of police officers and state troopers, and Staley on the bed of a truck talking to farmers—all ready to put Corning into the living room of every home in America, and none of the business people managed to much more than tolerate the dumping. Corning had always been a little sheepish about NFO. Without the organization, the town itself would have blown away by now, but the extra payrolls and organizational activity had come to the rescue. The buildings on the main drag were full. Things were humming. And the merchants, in the main, had never really forgiven NFO for coming to the rescue.

The dumping turned out to be a success nevertheless. It drew a handsome crowd from several counties, just at it drew news teams from Chicago and Omaha. The pickets and their signs were photographed, and later that day "Our Milk's For Sale At Our Price" flicked on TV screens from coast to coast.

Shortly before the spill, Paul Gauthier's *Adams County Free Press* had set the story. The front page was on the bed of the press, ready to go, except for a hole that would take the "picture."

An hour past press time, the picture had still to be taken. Finally, Staley and the officers arrived curbside, and the street spill was made immediately largely to satisfy the photographers. Usually a speech would have come first, but this time the milk hit the macadam before Staley told the crowd: "This demonstration indicates that these farmers want the NFO to keep on with the holding action in order to win a price increase."

While Gauthier disappeared into the darkroom with his picture, Staley went on. Farmers would fight until they won, he told the street crowd, and they were winning.

Pressed for details a little later on, Staley told reporters that NFO was ready for the first negotiations. In fact, Airplane Joe Phillips had been told to ready his plane. He had been furnished a destination, but he was one of the few. Neither reporters nor Nerve Center workers or those in field holding action posts could be told the rest. One slip on where President Staley, Chief Negotiator Shafer and Dairy Commodity Department Director Rust were going, and the trip might just as well be called off before they landed. The fight for farm parity was stranger than fiction.

1. *the boilerhouse*

On MHA + 7, NFO farmers in Indiana or Arkansas or New Jersey were baffled by dialog from the learned ones in Washington. The word had gone forth that parity no longer counted, and the farmer wondered whence comes this strange reasoning. Even the widespread economic illiteracy among American citizens could not wholly account for the strange concept that government provided the foundation under a sound economy. Certainly, it was a matter for common observation that the government had not yet absorbed the corporation, private enterprise or the farms. Despite the immense power for taxation and fiscal manipulation, the government was only an agency for social operation.

The private enterprise segment of the nation remained the boilerhouse that carried on its shoulders the responsibility for making the entire economic system move. It was this segment that had to provide all the capital to create every job in America, every payroll, every dollar of taxes paid regardless of whether it was paid by business or employees.

On MHA + 7, and for 15 years running, private enterprise had earned only 62% of the income it had to have in order to keep pace with the growth of the economy. The four walls of the economic system were corporations, small business, rental income to persons, and agriculture. And agriculture had fared worst of all. Obviously, should corporations take over all of agriculture and small business and rentals, they would still have to earn the parity necessary to pay the wages and the capital costs bills. Nor could this be avoided by efficiency of a corporate structure, because in the end a society must either employ or maintain on relief all of its people, and therefore failure to deliver parity to even a monolithic structure—such as Russia —cannot but become the cause of the effect in the end.

2. *the index price*

When George Peek and Hugh S. Johnson left Bernard Baruch's old War office after WWI, they sounded the basic call for farm parity. The year was 1922. It was the era of the Capper-Volstead Act and the Fordney-McCumber Tariff Bill, and farm welfare was very much in the news. Parity insisted that there should be a fair relationship between the prices for which the farmer sold, and the prices on things the farmer had to buy. The farmer sold his production at wholesale. He bought his tools and equipment at retail. If the prices on farm production at wholesale were not in balance with prices on tools and equipment at retail, farmers would either consume their capital and go bankrupt, or work for nothing, or both. When parity was first calculated, it was obvious that the mechanism through which a farmer got his income was simply "sale of farm production." Either a farmer on the average well-managed farm gained enough on the sale of farm production to cover costs, or he didn't. It didn't take a fancy formula to compute whether wheat, corn, rye or soybeans were high enough in the market at wholesale to cover the costs incurred by a farmer in producing them. It took simple arithmetic.

Thorold Rogers' *History of Agriculture and Prices* is eminently correct in seeking out a base from which projections can be made. Such a year has to hone close to an era in which there was no debasement of money, and no rupture of the price structure through imports. Should we follow Thorold Rogers, using 100 as the index price for 1541—a year before Henry VIII debasement of coins—we can read the sorry results, prices hitting 213.5 by 1556. Debasement, of course, is no different in principle than credit creation as practiced by the Federal Reserve System. Debasement, coupled with the flow of imports to the "high market," produces a double inflation, one that visits a heavy hand on the unorganized who are less able to fend for themselves.

Peek and Johnson knew this. It was not by accident that the first parity figures were calculated in terms of 1910-1914 as 100. It was a period when farm prices at wholesale were in balance with the commodities the farmer had to buy. The calculation thus became simple in the extreme:

1910-1914 average price = base of 100

CORN ....$ .642 per bushel
WHEAT ....$ .884 per bushel

Since 1910-1914, up to the holding action, prices of goods the farmer had to buy increased 240%. To compute true parity prices as of year end 1966, one had simply to multiply the 1910-1914 farm prices times the increase in commodity prices, or 240%. Thus the multiplier becomes 340%, because it is necessary to add the base period of 100. Thus:

1910-1914	CORN per bushel	WHEAT per bushel
	64.2 cents	88.4 cents
	× 340%	× 340%
Honest parity		
year end 1966	$2.18	$3.00

Therefore, the true 100% of parity prices as of year end 1966 for corn should have been $2.18 per bushel and $3.00 per bushel for wheat. During the base period years of 1910-1914 the total national income averaged $33 billion per year and industrial wages averaged 23 cents per hour. In short, it took several hours of wages to buy the equivalent of a bushel of wheat.

The span of time since the original 1910-1914 parity period has often been used to discredit the calculations, but this is an argument lacking in logical content. Indeed, many of the nation's leading educators pooh-pooh the idea of farm parity on grounds that the world has turned over many times since 1910-1914, that price relationships at that time might not have been satisfactory, that changes in production costs might have affected different sectors of the economy differently, that demand for food may have given way to demand for TV sets and other consumer goods, that farm production in kind and quality may have changed materially over a particular base period use for a parity projection.

These criticisms deserve to be answered. It is no argument at all that the modern John-Deere tractor far outpaces the Rumley Oil Pull tractors of many years ago, or that antiques on display at the Agricultural Hall of Fame have been replaced by more modern equipment, or even that beef and cotton and corn production nowadays are superior to the types of a few years back. The fact that ratio between any sector of the economy and the whole moves but slowly indicated how slowly technological improvement puts one sector ahead of the rest. In short, there is little evidence to suggest that technology has favored one sector over the other very much.

This is clearly shown by calculating farm parity on a later period, when, again, farm prices at wholesale were in balance with prices of goods the farmer had to buy. By using a series of balanced base periods, economist Carl Wilken clearly proved the honest parity idea as being one of enduring importance.

Taking 1946-1950 as a base period, farm prices average 99.5% of parity. Corn averaged $1.54 per bushel and wheat averaged $2.01 per bushel. From 1946-1950 through year end 1966, the consumer price level adjusted 43%. Therefore, it is necessary to multiply the base prices of corn at $1.54 per bushel and wheat at $2.01 per bushel times 143%, and thus determine the honest parity that corn and wheat should have been at year end 1966.

1946-1950	CORN per bushel	WHEAT per bushel
	$1.54	$2.01
	× 143%	× 143%
Year end 1966		
honest parity	$2.20	$2.87

During the 1946-1950 period the national income averaged $212.4 billion per year. The average industrial wage averaged $1.287 per hour.

Even the rank and file in NFO knew this much of the story. Don Myers had it on his mind as he answered phone calls from his Waterloo, Indiana holding action post. Given an opportunity, J. W.

McKinsey could make it a part of any evening holding action meeting in Indiana. Also in Indiana, Fred Lucas, Linus Wagner and Howard Vail hammered at it constantly, and throughout NFO members carried a matchbook with the true parity figures printed inside the cover. For the record, NFO had never gone much further than that. There was a reason. The rest of the story was so wild it would have been ruled from fiction because of its improbability.

In June, 1965, Carl Wilken published a study on the 12 central midwestern states covering the period 1951-1964, using prices from 1946-1950 as 100. Wilken at that time pointed out that as a result of America's failure to maintain parity prices for agriculture, the nation as a whole was short some $570 billion in income (on the income side of the income equation, see page 159). Of this shortage, $225 billion took place in the 12 states that produced 43% of all the farm production. In the publication itself, Wilken published a letter from Under-Secretary of Agriculture John A. Schnittker to Congressman H. R. Gross of Iowa, dated April 30, 1965. In the letter Schnittker admitted that the parity price paid for corn had been reduced from $2.04 under the formula used in from 1947-1949 to $1.55 a bushel under the so-called modernized parity. In changing the method of computing parity, government statisticians took 49 cents off each bushel of corn, in Wilken's words, "with a lead pencil."

Eric Hoffer tells us that those who dominate and remain unchallenged tend to retrograde evolution. The scribes of ancient Egypt and China, he says, did not work to develop a practical script, but labored mightily at complicating the art and keep it the personal property of the few. Apparently the art broke out of its backward movement because Phoenician traders needed something better to facilitate commerce.

Today, the strange manipulations in government records and systems must surely be the work of intellectual embezzlers, who are hiding behind the complexities of their craft. Having put the economy on a ruinous tack, they have sought to cover their miscalculations. Without a plausible theory or a meaningful story, USDA experts relocated the base period for calculating parity. The balanced years of 1947-1949 were perceived to be ancient, and therefore a new period 1957-1959 was called 100 and substituted in it place. The problem was, however, that 1957-1959 was not a balance period, either in terms of farm commodities at wholesale or consumer indexes at retail.

In terms of 1957-1959 as 100, the consumer price average for 1947-

1949 stood at 79.3%. In May, 1955, USDA listed effective corn parity at $1.82. Farmers who had the time could simply multiply the base price of corn in May, 1955 at $1.82 a bushel and wheat at $2.51 times the 22% increase in the consumer price level, and find the honest parity price for corn.

CORN $1.82 per bushel	WHEAT $2.51 per bushel
$\times$ 122%	$\times$ 122%
$2.22 per bushel	$3.06 per bushel

The multiplier, of course, is 122% rather than 22% because the base price of 100 must be added.

Honest parity price for corn should be $2.22 per bushel. Modernized parity is only $1.60 per bushel. This makes rigged parity 62 cents a bushel short of honest parity. The support price for corn today is $1.05 per bushel. Compared to honest parity of $2.22 per bushel, the equation is simple:

$$\$2.22 \overline{)\begin{array}{c} 47.3\% \\ \$1.05 \end{array}}$$

Therefore, the support price for corn was only 47.3% of honest parity price as of year end 1966.

The following table shows the wholesale commodity prices = 100 for the base period 1947-1949.

YEAR	ALL COMMODITIES	FARM PRODUCTS	PROCESSED FOODS
1947	96.4	100.0	98.2
1948	104.4	107.3	106.1
1949	99.2	92.8	95.7
Total:	300.0	300.0	300.0

By dividing each commodity by the three years one arrives at 100. During the three year base period 1947-1949, all commodity prices at wholesale were in balance at 100.

Using the same source of reference, the *1962 Economic Report of the President of the United States*, the commodity prices for the years 1957-1959 are as follows:

YEAR	ALL COMMODITIES	FARM PRODUCTS	PROCESSED FOODS
1957	117.6	90.9	105.6
1958	119.2	94.9	110.9
1959	119.5	89.1	107.0
Total:	356.3	274.9	323.5
Average per year	118.7	91.8	107.8

Prices were not in balance during the period 1957-1959. Farm prices were 26.9 points lower than all commodity prices, and 16.0 points lower than processed food prices. Farm prices were below prices on all other commodities.

Such lavish dishonesty could not possibly stop at the farm price manipulation level. It had to feed its way into the national records. When the supporting hanky-panky finally came, it was prefaced with a bureaucratic honey: "We're not satisfied with the accuracy of the figures." Any liberal translation would say it this way: "You laymen can't understand this deep, dark secret stuff, so why bother."

In any case, some elements in the government—we will probably never know which ones—became so dissatisfied with the figures in the *Economic Report of the President* that revision was indicated. Starting with the *Report* of January, 1966, all national income figures from 1929 to 1965 were revised. Indeed, every figure for interest for every year was changed all the way back to 1929. This change was made in August, 1965. In the prospectus of the *Report,* no mention was made of the revision. No mention of this sleight of hand was ever made in the newsprints. Hardly a year before the milk holding action, discerning NFO researchers saw in this "adjustment" a creeping alteration of the national statistics via the dishonest pencil, and the mere fact that such adjustments were being made without adequate explanation suggested that even the government was cognizant of the trend of events.

The adjustments had the effect of making the income equation look better than it happened to be, just as the rigged parity figures made farm income look better than it was. In one maneuver, interest was transposed from one side of the income equation to the other, thus raising corporate profits from $57.0 billion in the old report to $64.5 billion in the new, and when NFOers asked, "If this is a reality, why haven't the corporations paid taxes on this income?" they were ignored.

The adjustment for net farm income was a dilly. A new *net* came into being, one that delivered $14.3 billion for 1965 to agriculture—a big gain. The fact that farmers never got this big gain was abstracted away, out into the thin air from which it came.

The following statistics are taken from the *1966 Economic Report of the President of the United States.* They reveal how the price index = 100 was manipulated. This is the period now being used, years 1957-1959 = 100.

YEAR	ALL COMMODITIES	FARM PRODUCTS	PROCESSED FOODS
1957	99.0	99.2	97.9
1958	100.4	103.6	102.9
1959	100.6	97.2	99.2
Total:	300.0	300.0	300.0

Divided by three, everything averaged out at 100. Farm prices were brought into balance with all commodity prices with a lead pencil. Farm prices were actually 26.9 points below all commodity prices, but evidently USDA figured the farmers would never check, so they called everything even at 100.

Shortly before the holding action, All Commodities stood at 105.7; Farm Products were 102.0; Processed Foods were 110.2. Farmers noticed that farm prices were within 3.7 points of being in balance with All Commodity prices, when actually the spread was 30.6 points compared to 1947-1949 level.

3. *bulletin*

BULLETIN: NFO President Oren Lee Staley, Chief Negotiator Gordon Shafer and Dairy Commodity Department Director Albin Rust flew out of Corning for sessions with key industry sectors. There may be an important announcement. Progress has been made. Don't give an inch. Hold and tighten the hold still more.

Bill Lashmett logged in the name of each man in the field as he delivered that message, Paul Stolte, [checkmark], Ralph Payne, [checkmark], Paul Thomsen [checkmark], until he had read the same message together with the latest offerings of the Nerve Center to 23 far flung action workers. Other Nerve Center regulars did the same. The last contact got its checkmark before dusk, and by that time Airplane Joe had settled down for a long wait. The message had been delivered.

You couldn't drive a ten penny nail through that bulletin, but that's the way it was in negotiations. It told the members that the leadership was doing its best. That was all they could do. In the end, it depended on the members, and the members knew it. They knew that processors wouldn't pay two cents more. They knew that as farmers they could not afford to dump, but they also realized they had been giving away their production so long that a few days of dumping couldn't possibly matter. They shrugged off criticism about wasting food. It would cost farmers even more to give it to India.

Indeed, there was something quite unfair about this suggestion. One lady, through sheer persistence, had finally gotten Staley on the line. Can't you give the milk to India? Certainly, said Staley, we'd be happy to do that. Are you prepared to pick it up? Well no, can't you do it? I'm sorry, our farmers can't. It's costing them enough just to dump. But even if farmers shouldered the transportation burden, who's going to pay for the processing. Are you? Well no, can't you do it? I'm sorry, our farmers can't pay for that. It's costing them enough just to dump.

Albert W. Farmer, the national director for Christian Rural Overseas Program, had appraised the problem and issued an eminently correct statement. Processing and routing milk to India required coordination well beyond anything a "letters to the editor" protester could imagine. NFO's grain program had delivered much-needed food to Burundi, Ghana, Korea, Peru, Grenada and Taiwan, and "CROP is most grateful to NFO members for making available this significant contribution on behalf of people in need." As for milk, the agency head understood, even if others did not.

For a strange reason, those most likely to understand the passage of events were unable to grapple with them. And those least expected to handle the broad-spectrum crisis, came to terms with it. There was something poignantly unreal about intelligent people crying over spilled milk, much as Phil Harris might cry over Bourbon being destroyed by federal agents. And there was something penetratingly philosophical about people who had accepted the burden of their economic individualism suddenly dumping milk.

Such were the Amish Dutch in Pennsylvania, 500 strong, who started dumping on MHA + 7. Certainly they had accepted the economic consequences of their penchant for going it alone. They wanted no truck with the outside. They wanted only to do their own work, rear their children and care for their old. They had accepted low income as a status symbol, and willingly created their own furniture and homes with their bare hands. But even the Amish realized they were being crowded. They were being crowded by milk regulations, taxes on their land, burdens from civilization that meant they had to exchange some of the wealth they produced for wealth created in other segments of the society. Since they were not being paid for as much wealth as they produced, these exchanges served only to rob them of some of the fruits of their toil. They watched the NFO farmers around them and caught the signal. They dumped.

Every territory had its dumpings, public and private, and the pinch in the supply was being felt. But NFOers were getting impatient. The national milk tank was being lowered, to be sure, but tankers from distant territories could run across the country in a matter of hours. On the new interstate highways, it was possible to drive from the Mississippi to Pennsylvania with hardly a dozen stops. Even a decade ago, such a trip would have cost a trucker hundreds of stops and a dozen shifts of gears at each of them. Now trucks fairly sailed to repair deficit areas as NFO created them.

A day or two earlier, farmers had taken to buying milk in the stores and dumping. This hurt doubly hard. Here the hard pressed farmers were handing the chain stores their profit in order to dent the supply. The more fleetfooted took to going down the road and buying raw milk from non-member farmers and dumping. Economics didn't care about these details. The more realistic in NFO knew that the milk—either way—had to hit the ground. Others weren't so sure. Glenn Everett of Tuscarawas County, Ohio handed out his unit's reasoning: "We wanted to show that the waste of dumping milk is against our principles, too, but that it is our only means of protest." The county unit, one of hundreds, bought milk and gave it to striking industrial workers. In Minneapolis, Roger Citrowske and Aelgene Hoffman loaded milk into a refrigerator of a senior citizen home. At Maynard, Minnesota, Al Dybsand explained: "We wanted to give our dairy farmers a little moral support. And we wanted to do something to improve the NFO's image, to make a gesture . . . to prove we can do good things too." Thus in the eyes of NFO members, they had a two-pronged approach going. Ray Johnson could calculate that 18 million of Wisconsin's 34 million pounds of production each day was being dumped.

Despite the well-intended assist grain and meat farmers were handing their friends in the dairy department, it soon became a question for speculation how much good the buy-outs were doing. For one thing, the recipients of milk might have bought milk themselves. Shifting the burden for buying to NFO shoulders did not help this situation. Even the relief agencies, when presented with a free carton of milk, suddenly had no need to buy that carton themselves.

There was, of course, a second side to the coin. The impoverished old people at Iola, Kansas rarely got milk at all. The handouts around the courthouse square served as a damning indictment to the "cause" of local poverty, low farm income, and the free milk to old people enduring controlled starvation couldn't possibly hurt the effort.

The drivers of milk trucks turned out to be the most enigmatic of of all.

In Neosha, Kansas, a driver who worked for a plant that had been closed got bored. He went down the road on another man's route and bought Class 1 milk from farmers before the regular hauler arrived, and dumped it. Yet at Bell Buckle, Tennessee another trucker ran down NFOer Howard Hatchet on a country lane and left the scene of the "accident," leaving it for someone else to take Hatchet to the hospital.

4. a day for dumping

At Benson, Minnesota, businessmen who had been more or less oblivious to the changing farm scene suddenly started asking questions. The answers they got from NFO hit where it hurts—in the cash register. Before the meeting was over not a few asked the governor to apply pressure in the proper channels so that farmers could receive two cents more per quart at the farm.

Such help was appreciated, but the mature NFOer knew that only one pressure would suffice, and that was the pressure of production. The Red River Milk Producers Pool told the Crookston, Minnesota radio station that it was supporting the NFO effort. Said President Erv Vanik: "At least 70 to 75% of the pool members are actively backing NFO. I am holding and I have a big pool in front of my house." Those who supported NFO did so because NFO clearly demonstrated its strength. Those who contested the NFO hold did so because they believed they could wait the farmers out.

If Ray Johnson was correct, and NFO farmers were holding over half of Wisconsin's production, then the trucks would have to run hard. The water and powder would have to be added to the fluid until it ran out. One processor was reported using 400 units of powdered milk per carton, and labeling it as such. This made it legal. It hardly mattered. Up to MHA + 7, NFO watchdog committees had had little luck in getting law enforcement on adulteration anyway.

The law wouldn't act. Kids would. At Carson City, Michigan, children wouldn't drink the milk offered at school lunch. Such reports came like a shot of adrenalin to the tired NFO workers. Even a better shot was reported out of Minnesota by Ed Taffe. In Big Stone County a group of non-members had heard that NFO was being sued somewhere. They said they would raise money to fight the lawsuit if needed.

It was the little things that kept up spirits. A blockbuster series of millions of pounds dumped for some strange reason didn't mean as much as the Chat and Chew restaurant at Atlantic, Iowa being down to four pints of milk in the early afternoon, or the WXCO report out of Marathon County, Wisconsin, that of 40 farmers interviewed, 38 said they would sell their herds if they did not get their price, or Father Trizill, speaking in Linn County, Iowa, saying, "You're on the right track."

Good news had an uplifting quality, especially when it came from someone the members respected. Thus when NFO Vice President Erhard Pfingsten reported out of Minnesota: "No complaints, nothing but determination here. We're building, we're signing new members like mad," farmers believed it, because Pfingsten was respected, and because half a nation away farmers at Wooster County, Massachusetts were signing into NFO and fixing to charter new territory.

Moving east to west or north to south, it was first, last and always a day for dumping. Three of the largest milk producers in Howell County, Missouri—Harlin Dold, John Hahn and Louis Carl—were dumping. The local cost of $3,200 per day was sobering. Vince Closterman was counting 25% participation in the St. Louis area, and not all of them were NFO members. Some, seeing what was going on, just got into the act. "And nobody who has dumped milk has withdrawn from the program yet. It just keeps snowballing." It was that way everywhere. It was that way at Codington County, South Dakota, where the sparce dairy producers spilled 16,000 pounds, probably 145,000 pounds for the state. In a single demonstration near Salem, 90,000 were spilled alongside a highway. Roy Braunsreither, Chairman of Yankton County, as always, nailed down the reasons. "We're throwing away three months of the year anyway because of the price."

Barnes County, North Dakota, was dumping 12,750 pounds, and at La Crosse, Wisconsin, the rain of milk joined the fall of snow. Near Ellsworth, Wisconsin, farmers spewed 256,000 pounds on the farm of Haymond Hauth. Another 30,000 shot like a turret of white at Ozaukee County, Wisconsin. At Cottage Grove hundreds of Duane County NFO members converged on the Kerwyn Link farm to watch the dumping of 15,000 pounds. In Corning these scenes of human drama were statistics, but on the front pages of the dairyland's papers they came through like an epic—hundreds of trucks, thousands of gallons of milk, or the somber look on the face of Edmund Kuznia as he watched milk mix with slushy snow while standing next to County Chairman Lowell Lindermoon.

Milk isn't usually unloaded that way. Farmers usually attach a steam-cleaned polyethylene hose to the bulk tank and pump into a surgically clean milk plant tank inside. On the fields they simply opened the valves. In, say, Benton County, Minnesota, they simply dumped 50,000 pounds, and 50,000 pounds splattered the trucks, the license plates, the tires, and those who got too close. When Mower County farmers dumped on the Russ Stier farm near Grand Meadow, their many neighbors developed a slush fund to help dairy farmers really in trouble.

The organized dumping took on such fantastic proportions that that the press couldn't keep count. Even NFO couldn't get the data instantaneously. It was much easier to keep tabs on holiday traffic accidents than on milk dumpings in out-of-the-way places.

La Porte City, Iowa, wasn't Des Moines, but that's where they were dumping milk, cans of it lined and tumbled like a sidewinder rake. The milk dumping spectacular touched every state, but it never really rolled in Iowa. When Albert Wiener dumped 4,000 pounds near Le Mars, only Roy Kannas was on hand. Certainly it was much more convenient that way. Open the valve, let 'er roll. But the prints liked spectacle, and NFO farmers didn't like dying alone. One of the largest dumping operations was reported on the Jerome Schlader farm near Rockwell—50,000 pounds the day before an equal amount was dumped at Corning. This was as nothing compared to the 50 tons dumped near Superior, Wisconsin, but 50 tons in Wisconsin, according to Elmer Colby, "was only token." In Iowa it would have shattered the nerves of the Des Moines Co-op.

Regardless of circumstances, the dumpings made their point. At Falmouth, Kentucky NFOers got permission from the town dads and proceeded to paint the intersection of Main and Shelby Streets milk white. Louis Conrad Jr., Chairman of Pendleton NFO, estimated 2,500 gallons was washed down the drain a little later, when water hoses cleaned up the mess. The Logan County boys took their cue and did the same at Russellville, with 2,000 gallons, and NFO Chairman George Stiles warned housewives the dry-up was near. In

Adair County, farmers taking their cue from a *Life* magazine picture of Japanese farmers dumping from a high trestle, did the same off the bridge that spans Russell Creek.

Nebraska Governor Norbert Tiemann pointed to milk dumping as "waste," but farmers merely recalled how he had denied them the use of Farmers Hall in his home town. They had dumped in Jerome and Paul, Idaho, thousands of gallons, and they dumped near Wichita, Kansas, and the backwash of it all was feeding its way into the political arena.

In New Jersey, 200 dairymen marched on the state capital, and made their point. Agriculture Commissioner Phillip Alampi was urging Freeman to up the support level at least the 40 cents a hundred current law allowed.

The law was the thing, of course, in its scope, concept, enforcement and lack thereof. NFOer Ray Nielson had placed a 24 hour watch on his Michigan house and office. Earlier a caller had told him, "If your wife leaves the house she'll never return, or if you leave the house you'll never return."

The *St. Louis Post Dispatch* had never been sympathetic to the NFO action. Its words of wisdom were soon to see print, and it would have been a safe bet that they had been read *to* Washington, to be transmitted to the powers that be without going through the intervening space. The law, the scribes advised, could bring this thing in tow. There was after all the injunction.

A few minor test runs had already been made. Each time, however, the tattered banner had left NFO in charge of the field. Nashville was still up for grabs. Now, on MHA + 7, things were getting serious. The Cincinnati Milk Sales Association filed a suit in U. S. District Court against NFO asking that members be restrained from "withholding" milk from the Cincinnati market. The Association also asked for unstated amount of damages. The suit admitted that the NFO hold had cost Cincinnati Milk Sales $25,000 a day. Farmers named were Ed Sasey, Franklin Michels, Tom Conrad, Ralph Baumann, Richard Young, Dwight Fenner, Thomas Hudson, and William Attinger. NFO promptly retained counsel to handle the case.

5. *airplane joe*

Airplane Joe waited eight hours, possibily the toughest waiting in a lifetime. On the apron stood the Cessna, gassed and ready to head back to Corning. The sessions had turned into a stalemate. The names of the parties of the first part were privileged information, but they had been in touch with Washington.

At 5:00 p.m. the Nerve Center issued a terse bulletin: "Report from Gordon Shafer and Oren Lee Staley: Progress good in negotiations. Please, please tell everyone to avoid violence or incidents. Don't send our progress down the drain now. Repeat: don't throw away the gains now . . ."

The gains were not being thrown away. In Michigan there were no incidents to report by the state troopers. Instead, Ernie Cook could detail how grain and meat farmers had raised $600 and bought almost all the milk in Bad Axe stores. Melvin Zubrod reported from Mattoon, Illinois: Big dumping 3:00 p.m. 60,000 pounds. NBC and CBS TV on hand. But incidents? Absolutely none!

Against this background negotiators reminded Staley that the existing law could deliver a 40 cent a hundredweight increase to farmers immediately under marketing orders, but "first get the dumping stopped."

The fluid circuit would continue to develop into three camps, and the sailing of NFO was not being taken for granted. The primary objectives of the organization were still top agenda material, but the secondary objectives—in any negotiation—were rated by realists as up for the grabbing. But there was this business of dumping milk—and, face it, there were the hungry in the world. Never mind the institutional arrangements that will keep them hungry. It's the image that counts.

Not with NFO, Staley told the dairy executives. NFO wants the deal first, and the dumping stops on a secondary objective, for now!

The dairy executives agreed to carry the message to Garcia. If Washington wouldn't move, then they would add their names to contracts and give the NFO the big push. It was a big promise, possibly too big a promise.

Staley, Shafer and Rust arrived in Corning late that night. They did not hit their bunks in the LaConn-E Motel until 2:00 a.m. Later, hours later, when NFO was thinking of the holding action in terms of MHA + 8, the word came back from the emissaries. "We're black sheep up here," they told NFO officials. The maneuver hadn't worked. Now it would be a no give, no quarter battle all the way.

mha + 8

FOR NINE DAYS RUNNING now, it had been the Nerve Center *vs.* The Press. The Press was a nebulous entity that conveyed opinions and prejudices to every American capable of reading. Butch Swaim once totaled them up: 4,764 editors on daily and large weekly papers; 1,754 editorial page writers on the dailies; 230 editorial staffers on the mass news magazines; 726 editorial directors on TV stations and networks; 5,447 editorial directors on radio stations and networks, and 1,900 members of the Washington Press Corp. Of course, there were many more than these 14,821. There were the weeklies, the opinion molders for the rural set, and on the holding action they were divided just this side of down the middle. As the action wore on, their views and logic, or lack thereof, blended into the whole. Opinions of all shades diffused like gasses. Out of this mixture came consensus, or lack thereof, and this is what the powers that be attempted to read in Washington.

When newsmen knew only enough about their craft to report "happenings," such as the dance at the Legion, editors sometimes got pretty far afield, and NFOers chuckled. Cecil Goldsmith's diatribe in *The Leader Enterprise* at Montpelier, Ohio was essentially a throwback to the stuff H. L. Mencken put out in *The American Mercury* during the 1930s.

". . . The NFO (nefarious freeloaders organization) STRIKES AGAIN.

"Nothing arouses the sympathy of a nation like the erstwhile causes of the downtrodden farmer—save those of unwed mothers and abstemious Methodists. Without these three categories our great Republic would never have been blessed with its greatest legislation; Price Supports, The Mann Act, or Prohibition.

". . . let the farmer be damned . . . No more selfish, grasping dishonest mammal exists on the earth than those who claim to be the backbone of free enterprise. No organized group in America has supported the government handout, the unearned dole, the gimme-something-for-nothing gimmick like our farmers . . . These scalliwags, who have us all by the hind teat with products absolutely vital to our survival, have twisted and warped the whole concept of free enterprise until it is no longed free or enterprising . . ."

Unfortunately the ability to verbalize does not necessarily bestow an ability to think, as this example of creative stupidity indicates. Nor does the ability to use cheap labor earn a mail-subsidized paper the right to mouth off about economic concepts it understands no more than it understands ocean currents or brain surgery. Yet a few ignoramuses do not the journalism profession make.

There was, of course, the other side of the coin—the scholars who were in touch with the situation, who could report the holding action and tell readers what it meant in the scheme of things.

The Appleton, Minnesota, *Press* laid it on the line this way:

"Now it has become apparent to farmers they are the sacrificial lamb of this country's international trade and when domestic farm shortages appear, the import gates are opened wider to allow more and more foreign farm products to come in.

"For the import-export people, the corporations manufacturing to sell overseas, this works fine. More American made typewriters, computers, scotch tape, guns, etc., can be shipped to the countries from which we receive farm commodities. The farm imports help keep the balance of payments in line.

"Few things in this country take precedence over keeping factories going full blast and if a few million farmers have to be sacrificed to do it, not many will raise a hand to try to stop it."

Sometimes the Nerve Center ran with The Press. The Press meant a thousand friendly papers in NFO country, and it meant radio and TV stations batting 1000 at helping the farmer. At Hartford, Wisconsin, WTKM was furnished a half hour free air time each day for holding action news. Non-members would sometimes appear to urge farmers to hold.

The Press meant editorials supporting the farmers.

". . . It should be considered a national disgrace that farmers must take such drastic action to make their position clear," essayed the Thief River Falls, Minnesota, *Times*. "Why has affluent America been so reluctant to pay the producer of its food while making concessions to all business which handles the product between the farm and the table? An injustice is truly being done, and it appears that there will be no correction of it until the farmer organizes and forces the action."

". . . we applaud efforts on the part of the farmers to set their own prices in a businesslike manner," said the Trimont, Minnesota, *Progressive & Ceylon Herald*. The *News-Democrat* at Russellville, Kentucky, came right to the point: "We are not going to waste space joining the metropolitan papers in a hue and cry against violence . . . We don't condone the rough stuff any more than anyone else . . . But what we are more concerned about right now is relief for the dairymen whose condition is so desperate that they are willing to jeopardize bank and store credit by destroying their milk in the hope that someone will listen to their cause." *The State Journal* at Frankfort, Kentucky pointed to the double standard being invoked against farmers: "While citizens may be outraged at what the farmers are doing trying to protect their investment in their business, these same citizens have countenanced much more violent action in coal fields, the automobile industry and most any other industry you can name when the unions have called strikes . . . " "Sure we all deplore the milk dumping," noted the Willmar, Minnesota, *Tribune*. "So do the farmers. How tragic it is that this must be done to obtain an economic fair deal . . ." The Wheaton, Minnesota, *Gazette* handed out paragraphs that NFOers applauded. These were the sympathies frequently expressed by the rural press when it understood what was going on at all. "We think it's a rather sad situation when people must resort to sheer waste of a God-given bounty to obtain a just reward for their endeavors. But the dairy farmer will tell you they have tried every other means of getting prices boosted without success. As such, the city dweller has little right to criticize the dairy farmer for taking what action he deems necessary in his battle."

These were not the only views. There were countless tomes that spoke sympathy, yet chided the NFO for its foolish action. They accepted the institutional arrangements under which the farmer operated, and did not read the holding action in terms of changing those arrangements. The Davenport, Iowa, *Times* didn't understand the holding action. "Purpose of the activity is to secure a higher price for milk," the paper editorialized. The Carrington, North Dakota, *Independent* did. "Milk producers are seeking contracts whereby they will be assured of the price to which they feel they are entitled."

The Intermountain at Pocatello, Idaho, wrapped it up in one whip-lash sentence: ". . . we can expect some of the big-city press to be just as provincial about the economic right of farmers as much of Idaho is about the economic and civil rights of Negroes."

Editorial whining was one thing. Overt attempts to "call off" the action were another. The system was usually refined. A newspaper would pave the way by headlining the "failure" of the holding action. Frequently such headlines appeared over AP stories that didn't use the word. Next a radio station would broadcast the intelligence that the action had been called off—usually on the 10:00 p.m. news.

The Nerve Center's answer was smooth. If the announcement came on a TV or radio program, one of Butch Swaim's staffers would be on the phone to the station before the newscast had ended, demanding a retraction. Things were more difficult with the prints. But there were always the hourly bulletins, and they moved swiftly enough to kill off "holding action over" rumors before they got started.

1. *they are the poor*

At a question and answer session in a Nebraska school on MHA + 8, the teacher asked: "Why are farmers dumping milk instead of giving it to the poor." One NFO child answered: "Because they are the poor."

It took children to answer some of the questions that were being bandied about. Upon reading one of Don Muhm's articles in the *Des Moines Register*, one Corning, Iowa, youngster commented: "Aw, he'd of been against the Boston Tea Party too."

The old, tired lines about "babies without milk" had all but disappeared, largely because babies still had milk, even if it contained powder balls. Even the old saw, "They're going about it in the wrong way," vanished, largely because no one seemed to know what the "right way" was.

Fortunately, almost all human beings inject a little humor into everyday living. Indeed, without a little funny stuff holding action workers would likely have exploded under the tension. Thus when Jim Stewart overheard a Borden driver in an Ottumwa, Iowa, restaurant say that the "only way a hauler can make money today is to be a hog farmer living down the creek from an NFO dairyman," he wrote it down, and later farmers all over the NFO states heard it on tape, together with Jim's observation, "This region of Iowa is just getting in gear."

It was after 9:00 a.m. before the Nerve Center really got rolling on MHA + 8. Staley, Shafer and Rust had not returned to their bunks in the LaConn-E Motel until very late. Airplane Joe had landed on Corning's hilltop airstrip after dark, no problem, because Joe Phillips knew every lightbulb in NFO's headquarters town. The negotiations had run fully eight hours, Nerve Center regulars were told. Even without this meeting, they knew that Agriculture Secretary Freeman had been sitting on a milk marketing order hike of 40 cents per hundredweight for two weeks. The Secretary had felt himself in a dilemma. A market order increase to farmers might be construed as a bow from the waist to NFO because of the then threatening holding action. Now that the holding action was a reality, a market order increase would also be construed as homage to NFO.

The quaint oriental business of saving face didn't matter to the farmers. They had to have an increase, and they had to have it immediately. The farmers were willing to go on a handshake agreement with either fluid bloc, or with a government market order hike. The story was repeated time and again. If Washington wanted the dumping stopped, then all Freeman had to do was come through with the hike. The fluid bloc representatives were in agreement. They would go back to Washington and offer the terms NFO suggested. If Freeman struck his colors, then NFO would recess the holding action and proceed to work for contracts with at least one of the three fluid blocs through a different mechanism. The bloc representatives probably promised too much. They agreed to carry their message to the top. If there was no satisfaction from Washington, then they would return and support the NFO effort.

In the motel Staley, Shafer and Rust continued to talk over the situation. Unfortunately the membership could be told very little. That was the rotten irony of it. Yet some sort of a bulletin would have to be issued. When it finally appeared on the Nerve Center's 10:00 a.m. sheet, it read as follows:

OREN LEE STALEY, ALBIN RUST AND GORDON SHAFER FLEW BACK INTO CORNING EARLY THIS MORNING AFTER UNBROKEN SESSIONS WITH KEY INDUSTRY SECTORS. PROGRESS WAS MADE. REQUESTS FOR MEETINGS ARE NOW BEING RECEIVED FROM SEVERAL SEGMENTS OF THE INDUSTRY. NFO REQUESTS TIGHTEN THE HOLDING ACTION. HOLD AND HOLD STILL MORE. DON'T SLACKEN NOW.

The members had no intention of slackening. At Lamberton, Minnesota, NFO members told their story under a 72 point headline.

NFO AND YOU.

The heavy type recited the NFO credo that everyone in the business holds for a price, the grocer, the implement dealer, the supermarket. In Albany, Kentucky, farmers carried their story to the local businessmen in a 69 line ad. "Clinton County is a farming community, and the business firms in Albany are almost exclusively dependent upon the farmers and farm income for their livelihood. We have supported you—will you not now give us your support in this last ditch fight we are making for survival?"

Farmers were holding. "We have picked up through the trade the information that Wanzer in Chicago is extremely low on milk. This is the handler who is holding up the price increase to farmers in the Chicago area. We understand Lake-to-Lake is supplying Wanzer," read one paragraph in the 10:30 a.m. report. All morning the information flowed in, Pete Nagel reporting out of Minnesota, Val Akerlund reporting out of Nebraska, Bob Kessler reporting out of Illinois, Paul Schmucker reporting out of Indiana.

SCHMUCKER: A Whitley County, Indiana, hog producer took sows to market and made out the check to Whitley County NFO for a milk holding fund—For deposit only, $994.59. Eldon Cox reported, verified by Gaye White.

The phone calls had started slow, but by 11:00 a.m. things were really hopping.

Mike Summers, Texas County, Missouri. Two bankers, one from Cabool and one from Houston, Missouri, said: "Don't worry about money while holding action is on." One feed dealer was at our meeting last night. He is selling feed $2 per ton cheaper to members who are holding.

Daryl Krahling, Meeker County, Minnesota. One trucker with 26 patrons picked up milk at only four farms for the Grove City Creamery.

Tom Fagarty, Carver County, Minnesota. Says he has 4,000 bales of hay besides silage. Will dump until this feed is gone and if we don't have our price by that time the cows go too.

Viewed from any angle, the hold was building. The dumpings were bigger than the day before. One after another they were being reported in terms of gallons, not pounds, and in terms of tons, not gallons. Albin Rust, securely wedged behind the plank of his desk in the Dairy Commodity Department, found himself laboring through call-back tickets. A number of plants were offering to pay the two cents a quart increase if enough major cooperatives would go along. Eureka Cheese in South Dakota would sign, and several other South Dakota plants were reported ready to sign.

The pressures were building across the board. They came on in waves, and they stood in ranks, and the processors could not stare them down. Here and there a plant would openly side with the farmers. Bill Rozevic at Manchester Cheese, Manchester, Iowa, donated his radio time to NFO for as "long as the action lasts." In every state, radio and TV stations were telling the NFO story. WCOC at Albion, Michigan, handled the story by putting Jerry Boyce behind the mike.

This news marched north, into Canada, where Canadians were discussing rising their milk prices by 65 cents a hundredweight. It was hammered into viewable form by the Mason City, Iowa, *Gazette* with its headline,

AGRICULTURE IN CRISIS

MILK DUMPING DRAMATIZES UNREST

But what really drove home the message was the fact that a new wave of farmers was dumping. Sometimes they joined, and sometimes they missed that part of the message. In any case, they were dumping. These were not small come-lately farmers. They were the cream of the crop, the efficient producers, the operators by whose standards all others were judged.

Early on MHA + 8, Cash Bottema, a 500 cow producer in Indiana started holding. He would speak at the Poabt Horse Barn in the fairgrounds at Indianapolis in the evening, but this morning, MHA + 8 he was dumping milk. It was the same everywhere. In Mahaska County, Iowa, a 160 cow producer who was a non-member told his neighbors he was holding, and that he was contributing $500 to buy milk from trade channels.

The stories mounted and built and grew. Alfred Hall and Son, Ashland County, Ohio, said they would dump as long as feed lasted, and then the cows would go. These were not isolated cases. They were entries in a great wave of case reports. They took on scope when they poured their discontent into group action.

When the Jackson County, Wisconsin, Farm Bureau charged that farmers were dumping watered milk, NFO members insisted on a reading before DHIA tester. Results showed 5.2% butterfat, which was well above the 3.25 required. In short, dumped milk tested higher than any people could buy in stores.

2. *a short term agreement*

If the processors read the signals, NFO leaders were well ahead of the game. The Phase 2 program had been slated for Easter Sunday release. Nothing had happened to change that plan. But by late afternoon, an intermediate test was ready. It came in the form of a short term agreement. The announcement read out from the Nerve Center was short:

"Thursday, March 23, 1967.

"Because of the many requests which have come in the last two days we have prepared an agreement which we are asking members to take to milk processing and handling plants located in your area. This is an intermediate step. We are not pulling off of our master contracts in any way but this can be used as an intermediate step to break the log jam. The agreement is simply stated and if enough agreements can be signed we believe we could immediately start receiving a price increase. Call a special bargaining meeting somewhere in your area tonight consisting of one representative of each county bargaining committee. Use a minimum amount of personnel so this will not interfere with the holding action, but have all plants contacted tonight and tomorrow and give them an opportunity to sign the agreement. Call national office immediately reporting any success in signing agreements including amount of production covered by each signed agreement."

The instrument simply called for a two cent a quart increase at the farm as soon as agreements could be activated. "This contract shall be activated when the volume of milk under like contract is equivalent to the volume handled by eight of the major cooperative sales organizations in the midwest area." It was to run for four months, a term that would see farmers securely entered into a pricing program.

The minute the contracts were released, a new surge of energy entered the NFO scene. Staffers in the various blocks of counties took on new life, rehearsed their sales talks, wrapped clean cravats around their necks, and readied their schedules for a new run tomorrow.

3. *a simple message*

All day NFO had been churning the waters. Into business houses, presbyteries, homes and institutions went a simple message. NFOers, each in their own words, carried it, simply and with dedication. Its origin had been NFO.

URGE THAT YOU CONTACT ALL INTERESTED CONSUMERS, MINISTERS, BUSI-
NESSMEN AND FARMERS TO SEND TELEGRAMS TO GOVERNORS AND PRESI-
DENT JOHNSON ASKING THEM TO USE THEIR OFFICES TO SPEED UP NEGO-
TIATIONS BETWEEN NFO AND PROCESSORS. TELL THEM TO POINT OUT
THAT THE FARMERS ARE MAKING ONLY A SMALL DEMAND, AND THAT
CONSUMERS ARE WILLING TO PAY THE "2 CENTS" A QUART AT THE FARM
THEY NEED TO STAY IN BUSINESS.

There was a reason. From every quarter came word that national
officials were nervous. Foreign nations were alarmed and asking an
explanation. Religious and community leaders in several areas were
calling for immediate negotiations. They had already begun sending
telegrams to governors and elected officials in Washington. In Wisconsin, Attorney General Bronson LaFollette had asked Governor
Knowles to set up mediation meetings between the dairy industry
and the farmers.

By evening, the last ounce of credibility had been added to the NFO
claims. It came over the Huntley-Brinkley Report. Chet Huntley was
superb as he spoke his lines:

*"Thanks to the American news media, this current effort of dairy
farmers to secure a · little more for their labor and investment, is
receiving somewhat more attention than in former years. It is also
evident that the National Farmers Organization has hit upon a more
sensitive product to withhold from the market place. There is somewhat more drama and pictorial possibility in thousands of gallons of
milk going down a drain or being spewed out on the ground than
there is impact in the inexorable and non-dramatic withholding of
wheat or beef cattle from the market. Consequently, there is somewhat
more public interest in this current struggle of the dairy farmers than
there has been in previous efforts of the NFO to withhold other
farm produce from the supply lines of the economy. However, the
urban housewife is still pretty sanguine about the whole business and
is quite likely to blame the farmer the moment there is the slightest
increase in her grocery bill.*

*"The dairy farmer's return on his product is at an average of 10
cents per quart. At the supermarket the housewife is paying 30 cents
a quart for it. But milk is like all other agricultural produce . . . no
one is making a killing off it in spite of the fact that the mark up
between dairy farmer and consumer is an incredible 200%, to 250%.*

Actually the people doing better by farming produce than anyone else in the whole spectrum of food supply are those who belong to labor unions: the truckers, the retail clerks, the warehousemen, and so on.

"*Over recent years we Americans have been prone to criticize in the most vigorous terms, the archaic food distribution system of the French, in which produce comes into Paris and is then redistributed to the nation. It is time we take a look at our own system. Our distribution network is not archaic . . . it is overly sophisticated and specialized. All of that processing, sterilizing, packaging, and building in of convenience and guaranteeing of goodness costs money; but the housewife has not paid for it. The farmer has. These costs have been exacted from his end of the system, to the point where it is now criticial.*

"*Every farmer in the country, no matter what he produces, must have his sympathies with the dairy farmers. If the NFO wins this milk war the same tactics will be applied with renewed vigor to grains, pork, beef, and other products.*

"*The farmer has taken a cut in income over the past 15 years of startling proportion and you and I have been living on a handout from the fellow who produced our food.*"

4. *the message*

That, in a nutshell, was the message.

It screamed in the east, where NFO had hardly been known a few weeks before. At Spencer, Massachusetts, some 200 farmers from Massachusetts, Connecticut and Maine met with Roger V. Kayhart and started signing up. A day later the original nine who had autographed the NFO membership agreement had grown to 70.

It came like a sonic boom out of real Farm Bureau country, Illinois, where opposites lived and aspired side by side. Herbert Brantner was satisfied with the holding action in Carroll county and the fight farmers were making because "NFO is not a radical movement by a renegade outfit. Our goal is better prices, not trouble." It was a common goal among those who wanted to continue farming. R. A. Hesterberg of Gifford dumped his milk alone, and at Breese, Illinois, 10,000 gallons were dumped from trucks, tanks and cans on the Peek Brother farm. Erwin Wein saw it in this perspective, and the tragic scope of it all was driving farmers to do something they had never done before—picketing. NFO Vice President Erhard Pfingsten would be in the area because he was a spokesman NFO could rely on to make the point. A lot of points needed making in Illinois. A man named Charles Percy was making headlines, and smart money was betting he might one day be President of the United States. Not a few in NFO remembered the words Charles Percy used before a group of investment bankers in Hollywood Beach, Florida—"There is nothing wrong with farms but too many farmers." Farmers remembered—and they continued dumping milk.

Paul Stolte behind his phone at Dixon, and Bill Sinn fielding information in at home at Eureka knew the CED report like the ruts in a country road, and they had come to know the spokesmen for that report. Ralph Payne had helped set up one of the first marketing arrangements points at Griggsville, and now he was working the action from his Rushville home. "If a few farmers can do this much, what could a million do?" was almost a Payne aphorism as he toiled to make NFO work. Together with Jim Horn, Melvin Zubrod and Bob Kessler, they handled Illinois during the action—an action they had to win.

mha + 9

"THE CITY DWELLER or poet who regards the cow as a symbol of bucolic serenity is indeed naive," wrote Judge Jerome Frank in one of his celebrated opinions. "From the udders of that placid animal flows a bland liquid indispensable to human health but often provoking as much human strife and nastiness as strong alcoholic beverages."

Oddly, on MHA + 9, most of the strife and nastiness came from the very people who saw their bucolic tranquility in Elsie the Borden cow. Even that much was wrong. The real cow was in a dairy herd on a private farm. The farmer took that liquid one squirt at a time. He collected and cooled it in expensive union made tanks, and then paid union wages to have it hauled to the stainless steel facilities in a milk plant. There were still 8.5 pounds of milk in a gallon, and it had to test a specified minimum in butterfat content. The agricultural colleges could calculate to the penny just how much it cost to produce that milk, and the market orders were supposed to deliver a fair price to the farmer. But everyone, the Judge, the market order bigwigs, the farmer—everyone was living in a rigged economy. *Farmers were being paid for less wealth than they produced.*

That was bad enough. Of late, however, the USDA had leaked to the press information that a new government yardstick would henceforth measure the farmer's economic welfare. "Parity of income" rather than "parity prices" on production would be the new rain gauge. When it was still a hush-hush document, NFOers heard about it and saw that the concept was missing on about half the cylinders. The new government approach suggested that the farming operation is worthy of an hourly wage and a certain return on the investment. In short, a judgment on whether the payment to agriculture is satisfactory for the wealth agriculture produced would—under the new

230

USDA formula—be based on "wages" and a "return on investment," not the market value of basic commodities at wholesale.

At first glance, a sophomore in Ag school might ask: "What's the difference?"

Presumably there would be no difference if all computations were made honestly and if the payment for wages actually covered all the hours, not just part of them, and if the interest on investment matched the payment made on investment to other producers of wealth. In a word, if farmers were to be paid for as much wealth as they produced, it might not matter which method would be used to make the appropriate computation.

Unfortunately, the change-over from plain parity (even rigged parity) to "farm income parity" was not being made in good faith, or simple ignorance, but rather to comply with a thoroughly informed self-interest.

Failure to obtain farm parity these many years had meant one thing: farmers had not been paid for what they produced in terms of a fair relationship between the prices for which farmers sold, and prices on things the farmer bought. Taking the term "farm parity" and throwing it away could not change the real economic facts of life.

Adopting a new concept of "farm income parity" was full of promise for those who looked at economics from a mercantilistic point of view. A new term and a new concept at this stage of agricultural-industrial imbalance allowed those in charge of public policy to define away the low farm income problem and make secure an artificial technique for collapsing agriculture for the benefit of others. The fact of agriculture earning 4% on its investment and nothing for its wage bill in 1965 had been pointed up by both parity and arithmetic cost-of-production computations. Such an indictment had to be hidden if anyone was to claim that agriculture was approaching parity.

In NFO, farmers quickly saw that the "parity of income" formula allowed the USDA to redefine what constituted a farm, and therefore the number of farms that entered into parity of income calculations. It had already been suggested that having gross sales from $10,000 to $12,000 a year would put a man in the farmer category, and make his operation an "adequately sized farm." Thus, on MHA + 9, by definition there were less than 1,000,000 farms in the nation.

The production from "non-farmers" would still be production, but only those big enough to be "adequately sized farms" would hit the

USDA decimal system.

Actually, those experienced in governmentese felt that they occupied safe ground. The money price or exchange value of wealth could be calculated in terms of many considerations. The state of the arts, the laws pertaining to taxation, competition, trusts, monopolies, the growth rate of population—all figured in any formula. The average money-price relationship between wealth produced in different sectors of an economy was of utmost importance, and failure to maintain a balance in the payments made for wealth allowed an economy to mangle itself from within even at a time when it was being attacked from without.

A dominant class with political power could exact tribute from actual producers of wealth by arranging the market mechanism of an economy so as to accomplish that purpose. This had been done. The fact that raw material producers were finding out what was going on made it more necessary for the economic managers to hide the fact of this tribute-taking.

The rationale could have been predicted.

It was being argued that the old parity formulas were outdated due to new machine efficiency on the farms, and because the costs of production had not moved ahead on the same basis as costs of production in industrial America. Therefore, the argument ran, taking a base period when wholesale indexes were in balance with retail indexes for developing what the price tag on a bushel of corn or wheat should be had become an unsound procedure.

Machine efficiency had come to agriculture, of course. But machine efficiency had been introduced to industrial America as well. Calculated in terms of parity or in terms of plain, simple accountancy —i.e., gross sales less costs in production—it became at once apparent that farmers were being penalized for their machine efficiency, whereas factory workers were being paid for their machine efficiency.

As a matter of fact, honest parity had consistently pointed up this strange development, and the embarrassment it had cost both Republican and Democratic administrations had not been covered up entirely, not even with a flow of farm bankruptcies that removed millions from the countryside.

The idea of using a base period—when all indexes were in balance —to compute prices for a later period proved to be so accurate that the disparity it spotlighted simply had to be hidden. It was. NFO farmers still shook their heads over the fact of the index base period being changed so that statisticians could take 49 cents off each bushel of corn with a lead pencil. (Under the formula used when the 90% of parity law was in effect, corn should have been priced at $2.04. Under the formula being used on MHA + 9, one struck up when indexes were no longer in balance, corn was computed to be $1.55 at parity. From 1946 to 1950, the average industrial wage was $1.33 an hour. At years end, shortly before the milk holding action, the wage rate stood at $2.64 an hour. Simple arithmetic proved that an hour of labor could pay $2.05 for corn and buy 40% more corn than in the day when wages were $1.33 an hour.)

Surely it could not be argued that agriculture had become so efficient that it no longer had costs. Production costs for agriculture had increased from $17.5 billion during the 1946-1950 period to nearly $30 billion by the end of 1965—up nearly 70%. In the 1946-50 period, net farm income averaged $15.1 billion. In 1965 it averaged about $14 billion, even counting "paper income," the kind figured as "in kind" returns for killing a cottontail or slaughtering a chicken.

The parity story was really too strange for fiction. Everyone knew it cost a Nebraska farmer at least $1.50 a bushel to produce wheat, wheat headed for $1.00 a bushel in the next few years if the experts had their way. How parity of income could be developed out of prices like that eluded the farmers. For newspaper eyewash it would be possible to dump "non-farmer" crops in with "farmer" crops and conclude that parity of income had arrived, because "adequately sized farms" weren't being fed into the bankruptcy courts. And "non-farms" badly in need of loans could be denied farm loans as a matter of policy because they were non-farms in any case.

All this, of course, was doublethink, the last stage in the decay of administrative justice. Writer John Dos Passos had noted that it took bureau people 300 years to grind the Roman Empire into dust, but that American bureau people in government promised to do the job in less than 50 years. Perhaps! If so, the change in parity formulas will surely be seen by historians as one of these pieces of mischief that hid the truth so that a basic injustice could not be repaired.

NFO farmers weren't satisfied to wait for historians. They registered their objection now, today, MHA + 9. The entire business of not paying producers what their stuff was worth had to be brought to a head.

And it was coming to a head. NFO's short term milk contracts had been transcribed and refined during the long evening hours, and now, early on Good Friday NFO teams were busy contacting plant managers. On the long table in the Nerve Center, rosters were set up for each state: name of plant, location, Class 1 capacity, Class 2 capacity. The roster wasn't complete before staffers in the field started calling in. Brynoff Grahn called with the information that Waubun Creamery, Waubun, Minnesota, had signed, 855,000 Class 1, 997,000 Class 2. A few minutes later Weldon Willetts was on a Nerve Center line. Hastings Co-op Creamery of Hastings, Minnesota, had signed, and the Evansville Co-op Creamers Association had come through, and then Manchester Cheese in Iowa was reported on the dotted line.

2. *good friday*

Good Friday was not a likely time for contact work. Under usual circumstances, executives would be away from their desks, taking an early jump at the long Easter holiday. Things were different this year. Big co-op executives were reported keeping company planes busy between the midwest and Washington. In Washington, the temperature was mounting rapidly. Part of the fuel came from that vague entity known as world opinion, and part of it came in over Western Union from NFO's 25 + states. Farmers sending those messages weren't too concerned about the content. They sent them as individuals and kept them short. "Help, I'm drowning in milk," read one. Most of the wires were going directly to President Johnson. There no one bothered reading them either. But secretaries did take a count and likely as not they measured the temperature.

All morning and into the afternoon, reports came in. No question about it, the unregulated Class 1 bloc was signing the short term instrument NFO had offered. A few ducked, and a few more took refuge behind a non-available Board of Directors, but NFO was gathering in contracts, and the number was impressive. The hourly reports contained little else. Dumpings, bigger than ever, were methodically bypassed on Good Friday. Insignificant little anecdotes rated above the several ton spectacles chiefly because everyone was weary of heady statistics, heady numbers. A Class 2 producer in Tennessee dumped his milk—by flinging buckets of it out a window— he caught an artificial breeder who was in the wrong place at the wrong time. Everyone at the end of NFO's own information service heard about it, and it was just earthy enough to give everyone a lift. For some strange reason farmers remember the Tennessean's bucket and forgot the cumulative 500,000 pounds Ed Graf reported one Wisconsin farmer as dumping.

Things were off key across the board. Newsmen in Des Moines, Omaha and Minneapolis were burning up dollars in a conference call. No violence. They just couldn't understand it.

Senator Gaylord Nelson could. Farmers had justice on their side. Nelson wrote Secretary Freeman that NFO's milk holding action was dramatic demonstration of farm unrest, and had to be read accordingly. Senator Bill Proxmire went a bit further. He called for passage of his bill to put a ceiling on imports of dairy products.

These were not the details that were burning up the typewriter ribbons, however. NFO was interested in two things: contracts, and "how tough the pinch." The scraps of information that floated in told those keeping track something about both. The Wisconsin list led in signups, of course, because there was many more plants in the Badger state, but signups were being reported from the Dakotas to the Pennsylvania line.

There was a reason for this. Plants couldn't get hurt by signing the NFO contract. Either the industry went for two cents a quart, or no one would end up getting squeezed. In the meantime, the dumped tons of milk had knocked a big hole in the national milk tank. The fluid was leaking out on a continuing basis as long as the hold was on. Frequently the mosaic was pieced together from fantastic scraps. A friend of a friend worked in this or that plant. Someone at a filling station serviced a tanker from Utah. Marvin Sherber's friend worked at Red Owl in Minneapolis, and they were unloading a semi of bottled milk from Texas. The pieces fit—if you got enough of them. Even lies told the truth—if you got enough of them.

The big lie had it that no one was watering milk, but when the boys demanded an honest count at Jefferson City, Missouri, milk turned up with as high as 10.54% water added.

Out of Kentucky came six samples tested, all supposed to be Class 1.

1.7 BF.	3.5 inert matter.	Origin, Nashville, Tennessee.
1.0 BF.	3.6 inert matter.	Origin, Evansville, Indiana.
2.8 BF.	3.7 inert matter.	Origin, Hopkinsville, Kentucky.
2.9 BF.	3.3 inert matter.	Origin, Madisonville, Kentucky.
1.6 BF.	3.5 inert matter.	Origin, Mayfield, Kentucky.

All milk sold in that area was supposed to have 3.2 butterfat. Yet when the DHIA supervisor ran his tests, the results were as stated above. In Arkansas, a professor here and there would test and inform Max Douglas and Benton County NFO members, but—always—it had to remain "privileged information." A man could easily lose his job over the bland liquid called milk.

Even when figures finally hit the public prints, "they lost a little in the translation," was the way Elmer Bell Jr. of Missouri put it. Dr. E. H. Price, the Show-Me state's Director of Veterinary Public Health, said the first test results were high enough to cause concern. The manager of Central Dairy was "pretty unhappy about the whole situation," he said. But there was no chance that the water could have been added at the plant, he said.

Always, there were reports and denials. Al Tolen found that many restaurants in Detroit, Michigan, as well as food markets were running low, and were being rationed ten cases at each delivery. Iowa processors were reported hauling in milk from Colorado.

There was lots of hanky-panky going on. This led to speculation and farmlot lawyering. In Pennsylvania some of the NFO boys had a meeting with state officials. Federal orders statutes say that Class 1 price must be paid for all milk that is bottled. This meant that any secondary supplier who used powered milk in bottles would technically have to locate the original producers of the powder and pay them the differential between the bottling price and manufacturing price.

How the matter of extra water in milk would be resolved for farmers had the experts stumped.

2. *moral superiority*

You can't argue with moral superiority, and in the main NFO didn't even try. For one thing, enough allies were carrying the ball in that department to drive home the point. Dr. E. W. Mueller of the Lutheran Council didn't even equivocate: dumping milk was no different than holding back an hour of labor. Dr. Henry McCanna of the National Council of Churches of Christ issued a statement supporting collective bargaining. Many Catholic bishops and priests supported the farmers. The Catholic Rural Life Conference did the same.

But this wasn't really what the "it's criminal to allow waste when millions of people are starving" people were talking about. Unattuned to the problem, they wondered, why can't it be given away to the poor? A *Cleveland Press* cartoonist showed farmers dumping milk cans from a high place. As the liquid obeyed the law of gravity it spelled out, "Disgrace." "The children" complained the Lexington, Kentucky, *Herald*, "who don't get a vote on such strikes are the real sufferers in a milk war. Let's think of them." A lady in Dayton wrote: "When those men dumped that precious God-given milk which means so much to children, old folks and sick people in the hospitals, I wonder what their thoughts were. More money—not the fear of God."

Most of the "it's a sin" letters had been penned early in the work. By happenstance, the lion's share of them were being read on Good Friday.

"And it shall come to pass in that day that . . . the hills shall flow with milk," one man wrote the Ashland, Ohio, *Times-Gazette*, quoting scripture all the way. "Proverbs 30:33—Surely the churning of milk bringeth forth butter and the wringing of the hose bringeth forth blood; so the forcing of wrath bringeth forth strife."

Those who saw Satan doubled over with laughter still had the ability to define everything as black or white in a very complex world. They verbalized well. They were "fed up," "disgusted," "sick and tired," "shocked," and "ashamed." They took on the shame they believed really belonged to the farmer, or they berated farmers for not taking on that shame themselves. This one out of the Portsmouth, Ohio, *Times*, should illustrate the type:

"I can think of a lot of small things, but none of them are as small as I would feel if I were little enough to pour out and waste good milk just to try to pry the already too high price of milk a few notches higher when so many thousands of children are being deprived of the milk they need because their parents are not able to pay the present high price of milk.

"Furthermore, I would be ashamed to face any child, even my own if I had any, if I were so little. I would just try to find an abandoned ant hole and crawl down into it. I wouldn't go in an occupied ant hole because if I were that little the ants would either devour me in a few seconds or throw me right back out again.

"Shame, shame, shame on you, whoever you are, that will do such a thing when two-thirds of the world is starving and most of the other third is hungry. Are you going to ask God to forgive you the next time you ask His blessing at your own well filled table? I hope you will."

The letters came in waves, some sincere, some naive, all perplexed. Basically, the farmers defended themselves well, but that was not enough.

The basic moral question persisted. Steve Allen had asked it in *The Ground Is Our Table*, a book about migrant farm workers. "Which weighs more, a tomato or a person?"

NFO caught the tempo. Which weighs more on your scale of values? Nerve Center regulars asked. A quart of milk or a farmer? What worries the city dweller most: a slight rise in milk prices, or poverty and bankruptcy for those who produce the milk.

Later, refined, the same general idea would appear in *The Lutheran Witness:*

What angers you most: a gallon of dumped milk, or a farm family that is dumped? Farm production rotting, or rotten living conditions for farmers? What upsets you most, farm products a penny or two higher at the store, or farm families fed into city slums?

Answer those questions and you have your moral choice.

3.   *churchmen were not attuned*

If NFO farmers missed Good Friday services, it was not because they were in the habit. Almost all had church affiliations. Lutherans and Catholics were strong in NFO, according to Michigan researchers. The NFO itself never asked a man's religion. It only wanted farmers to say, "Yes, I am my brother's keeper."

The papers made much about a father-against-son situation in Urbana, Ohio. Richard Shipley and his dad, William, were at odds over whether they should support the NFO holding action. They milked 60 cows in the same barn. After the twice-daily milking operation, the son turned the spigot and ran his half out of the tank. His father sold his share.

Always there were men to whom religion had become a drillfield habit, and they soon lost track of the First Cause. In the oldsters on the farm this same habit meant responding to the intellectual left face and right face of supply and demand. In the editorial office it meant delivering space to paid advertisers at a profit, and carrying messages suitable to those same advertisers. In the Church it means proper decorum and a detached air about things that "didn't concern the Church."

Good Friday was the day that Christ died. No one in NFO drew a parallel. No one dared. They were too religious a lot for that. Yet the message was there.

Many citizens were calling on ministers, priests, and rabbis to ask for mediation in what had become a heart breaking ordeal. One lady* in the Kansas City area called the Catholic Chancery. Joseph Sullivan, the soon to be consecrated Auxilliary Bishop took the call. No, he didn't know anything about the milk holding action. Just what he read in the *Star* or saw on TV.

In any diocese, the bishopric is a powerhouse. Usually a bishop's activities are highlighted only when they pertain to "churchly" affairs, yet it was common knowledge that a bishop's persuasion went a long way. In the main churchmen were not attuned to the foundation nature of agriculture, and therefore did not understand how slum problems, ghetto life or man's affront to humanity was really an outgrowth of agriculture's low prices.

There were a few, of course, who saw the dimensions of what was happening, and understood how they related to the national problem. The few, one at a time, spoke out now as they had spoken out during NFO's formative years. "The time has come for our Lutheran Church to speak out in the silent struggle that has been taking place in regard to our farms," wrote Pastor Alvin P. Brucklacher in the May 1964 *Lutheran Standard*. "We can no longer remain silent spectators while the farmer is forced from the oldest calling known to man . . . The economic security of the farm family is the Church's concern." The few lined up during NFO's formative years, just as they lined up on MHA + 9, but the line wasn't very long.

Reverend Shirley E. Green, as spokesman for the United Church of Christ, had called on bankers to help erect a new marketing system years ago, and reprints of his *Independent Banker* offerings were still floating around. That helped. So did the published remarks of Lutheran clergymen such as Dr. E. W. Mueller and Giles Ekola, and the articles by Monsignors Edward W. O'Rourke and John Weber of the Catholic Rural Life Conference.

The idealism and realism of almost all churchmen had a way of going from home base idealism and home base realism without covering the space in between.

There were exceptions. Certainly James L. Vizzard, S.J., had called a spade a spade when he caused to be printed certain observations
*Mrs. Charles Walters Jr.

about NFO in *Catholic Rural Life:*

"*In my judgement,*" wrote Vizzard, "*there is no objective reason why the NFO should be such a cause of contention. Over the past several years, I have had long and frank discussions with leaders of all three established national farm organizations and of the cooperative movement. When pushed to it, all of them agree that there is no basic or necessary conflict between the NFO approach to farm problems and their own. They all admit that if the NFO idea had arisen and had been developed within their own organization it would by now be a major part of their accepted program.*

"*When you come right down to it the current conflict and the bitter personal . feelings arise primarily because of organizational competition and jealousy. It stems largely from a 'dog-in-the-manger' attitude of some established farm organizations and leaders. This new farm organization with its enormous vitality and initiative is seen as a threat to traditional leadership and old methods of doing things.*"

NFO members had applauded Father Vizzard's courage, but they had also noted that too many bishops considered Rural Life Conference as a poor child in the Church's bureau setup an unglamorous post of exile, and though a bishop in Omaha might take farm life and milk holding seriously, there were those who figured farmers rated a brushoff at best, as the lady in Kansas City soon found out.

"I don't see what the Church has to do with it," Kansas City's future Auxilliary Bishop said. "This area isn't affected by farmers."

BACKGROUND

---

the church

IT TOOK THE CHURCH to finally and unequivocably separate man from the nature about him. The process itself started with the ancient Hebrews, who discerned that man had been made to the image and likeness of God, and that he was therefore a partner in creation. The earth and all life—except man—might continue to obey the laws God provided for their regulation, laws later proclaimed "evolutionary" by biology and "supply and demand" by economists.

But no one with any intelligence ever really believed man could allow nature to take its course From the earliest order, man rose above nature's laws of survival which seemed to set the stage for the rest of "life." With his free will he could escape the lot of the beast. He read the depths of his own soul, and learned right from wrong.

Churchmen from time immemorial have seen man erect false Gods, but none of them became as distressed over the spectacle as Pope Pius IX. Writing a few years before Karl Marx, Pius IX could see that societies constructed on a foundation of *laissez faire* were necessarily unstable and liable to be washed out by communism. Taking his cue from the Pontiff, Karl Marx saw the same thing, and was delighted by what he saw.

The premise then being accepted was that capital accumulation required inequity, and without inequity an economy could not move ahead. Injustice and economic cruelty, in short, were a requirement of the system, a requirement men like Marx sought to escape by going to communism.

Writing in 1864, the Pope in his encyclical, *Quanta Cura*, asked: "Is there anyone who does not see and plainly perceive that a society of men which has broken from all the bonds of religion and true justice, can have no other object before it save that of planning for and amassing wealth and in its actions can follow no other law save the unbridled greed of a mind which is the slave to its pleasures and desires."

If greed were to be allowed free rein, and the rights and justice of men mattered not, then why should the poor pay homage to the God-given rights of the rich? The power of money had pulled priest and king from their exalted position. Why should not envy of money do the same to those now holding down the seat of power?

It has always been the job of the Church to sell the idea of justice—economic justice—and responsible leaders realized that they would do their job badly or not at all under communism, that strange ideology that rose to power on the fact of exploitation, and then proceeded to exploit people until they would no longer work.

Pius IX knew—if Marx did not—that there was really only one economic system. Under a democratic, socialistic, communistic or despotic social order, the economic system still had to be "capitalism." It had to produce goods and services for people. It was production of goods and services times the price at which they were exchanged that established the standard of living and the income of any particular system.

Should the government take over the private enterprise system of a country, it would still be unable to operate without a profit, as Russia and China and India have learned. Regardless of how the economy is run, it must earn a profit or it will not be able to develop and expand.

Unfortunately, the rate at which profits can be earned are narrowly circumscribed, first by the state of the arts, second by the distribution of the labor force between foundation raw material production on the one hand, and finished goods and services on the other. No nation can crank up a magical machine and take a giant leap forward by printing money. Growth can be paced no faster than the rate of profit. Communists, fascists and socialists must play out this game according to the same rules as capitalists, like it or not.

From a churchman's chair, men are more apt to perform well in an atmosphere of freedom. Freed of their despotic masters, turned loose to fend for themselves, Europe's misfits turned a virgin wilderness into the greatest standard of living the world has ever known, and they did it because of the American system of private enterprise. They did it because they had the freedom of individuals to take risks, to invest, to expand. It was this freedom that served up initiative, a quality sadly missing not only in communist countries, but in old authoritarian capital societies as well.

The Church—Protestant no less than Catholic or Hebrew—has sometimes been perplexed by the obvious contradictions that attend human existence. Freedom to grow served up initiative, but unbridled freedom put under a hobnail heel the rights of others. That no one could escape the dilemma distressed the Pope no end, just as it distressed Protestant reformers of that era. Even a nation that policed its internal business affairs was subject to economic invasion.

If the profit earned in a country like England was limited, then England could advance faster by exploiting the profits of its colonial holdings. Even a nation like the United States—one founded on the repudiation of *laissez faire* economics—could not protect itself entirely. Then as now, the proponents of a private enterprise system equated it with free international trade, a fantastic fallacy.

1. *free trade*

No less than four conditions underscored the existence of free trade, and fulfillment of these conditions was always fatal to world economic stability.

The first of these required "free contract" between employer and employee—in a word, no unions or labor collectivity. Economists of that age—Jeremy Bentham and David Ricardo—found "laws" to justify the harsh realities of the industrial revolution, but on the firing line of free trade low wages in industry simply meant that workers would be unable to consume the production they had accounted for. Low wages required England's industrialists to look the world over for new markets. Thus the first law of free trade required the second, which was freedom to export goods.

Ricardo's iron law of wages was never fully observed. Human consciences would not allow forever some of the conditions that survival of the fittest saw develop. Accordingly, there were laws to raise wages, both in England and on the continent. On logical grounds, Jeremy Bentham objected to this interference with pure economic laws. Quite correctly, he held that raising wages in English factories did no good whatsoever since it allowed foreign producers to capture the market.

Step by step, the syllogism took form. Unless laborers and farmers were allowed to earn enough to consume their own production, goods would have to be exported. Exports required imports, because payment could not be made secure in any other way.

As the industrial east rose to prominence in the United States, the several states sent to Washington representation that believed it had found an answer to these problems: tariffs. This was troublesome, of course, but free trade stood on still another pillar, one that has never been seriously challenged: free export of capital. Free export of capital could always bring back into play the first two conditions of free trade simply by starving local markets in the same way that low wages and low farm prices starve local markets.

The very forces of international trade could pull down any economy that outraced the others on the global scene because there was a last, unalterable condition under which world trade functioned. Currencies of the several nations were exchangeable in terms of gold, and gold made it possible for money to be the only real citizen of the world. Manipulated world raw material prices made it impossible for underdeveloped countries to avoid exploitation. Foreigners bought their copper and rubber cheap, then sold a few baubles at high prices. Wars became inevitable. Thus low world raw material prices became more deadly than a plague, and those who looked to the first cause of world poverty saw only the seeds of revolt, because envy and greed walked hand in hand without knowing it.

The Church had reason for concern. Its function was to deal with racial strife, ever-growing poverty, disruption of national morals, and the certainty that these problems had an economic as well as a religious foundation. As God is the First Cause, then surely there had to be a proximate first cause for the distress being visited on rural America. It was no longer satisfactory to deal in effects—like politicians—when the fountainhead of the problem was in sight. It made no sense to hold Saturday cleanup sessions in slum blocks when the cause was cheap food, a wave of "Having decided to quit farming" notices, and low raw material prices from Zambia to Chile, with the corn belt thrown in for good measure.

Most of the raw materials sector of the American economy was unorganized. Its prices were thus easily manipulated into line with world prices. Futures markets could do that. Free imports—wheat or cheese—could help. The trouble was American farm commodities were being produced under the American cost-of-production schedule, and it was twice as high as the schedule in most of the world. For the farmer—first of all—the ultimate consequence of low world prices was to subject American farmers to having to accept the same wages as those accepted in the lowest paid nation in world trade. Indeed, unrestricted imports from low cost-of-production areas was not unlike opening the gates to free immigration. This could not be accomplished without a depression, and the policies of driving world commodity prices lower were fairly tuned in on creating such a world depression.

In responsible Church circles, there was slowly developing a realization that the internal market of the United States was being limited because too much of the earned income had gone to the far corners of the world, either as foreign investments, or to wetnurse the graft of the greedy, or to fight the wars of the world, and keep it on relief. The natural decline in purchasing power was being stalled by underpaying farmers and by floating more debt.

No churchman objected to world relief, not always realizing that world relief was merely a stopgap thing, another attempt to deal with effects, not causes. Yet this was not really helping the poor of the world, although it was helping destroy the solvency of America.

Bulgarian cheese, Japanese electronic equipment, European manufactured goods—all produced under an income structure hardly $500 per capita a year—vied with American production created under a per capita income structure of $2,400 a year.

The shock waves had become intensified because American farm production rode along at world prices, whereas manufactured goods commanded a price closer to American cost-of-production parity. But the shock waves had to be absorbed as best possible. This had come to mean that American farmers must be processed into bankruptcy, business has to operate with a declining rate of profit, and corporations have to protect themselves with wave after wave of mergers, elimination of competition through market domination, and also through removal of bargained wages with automation.

The poverty created by all these miscalculations was being nursed by "programs." Social consciousness had come a full circle. Man, once thought of as only a producer, was being thought of now as only a consumer.

Yet the plan of God was for man to be both.

2. one international leader

Man, the fellow creator, could help the underdeveloped nations not by charity, or by requiring them to destroy their helper, but by understanding the laws of economics. Among the most literate, the idea that all this "didn't concern the Church" was standing on shaky ground while farmers were dumping milk.

At least one international leader had singled out the foundation fallacy behind the world's programmed poverty. He was Pope Paul VI. His fifth encyclical, *Populorum Progressio (On the Development of Peoples)* was written with the economics of Colin Clark in tow, and contained some of the soundest economic passages ever issued by a leader of international standing.

Reviewers, in the main, made much of the world fund idea Pope Paul wanted, but they left unmentioned the fact that the Pontiff considered it only a symbol and a spot effort at relieving poverty. The real impact of the letter was contained in paragraphs 56 through 61.

In effect, the Pope argued that nations buying cheap and selling dear not only reduce those with whom they trade to abject poverty but at the same time work at their own destruction without knowing it.

"56. *Equity in Trade Relations.* The efforts which are being made to assist developing nations an a financial and technical basis, though considerable, would be illusory if their benefits were to be partially nullified as a consequence of the trade relations existing between rich and poor countries. The confidence of these latter would be severely shaken if they had the impression that what was being given them with one hand was being taken way with the other.

"57. *Increasing Disproportion.* Of course, highly industrialized nations export for the most part manufactured goods, while countries with less developed economies have only food, fibers, and other raw materials to sell. As a result of technical progress, the value of manufactured goods is rapidly increasing and they can always find an adequate market. On the other hand raw materials produced by underdeveloped countries are subject to wide and sudden fluctuations in price, a state of affairs far removed from the progressively increasing value of industrial products. As a result, nations whose industrialization is limited are faced with serious difficulties when they have to rely on their exports to balance their economy and to carry out their plans for development. The poor nations remain ever poor while the rich ones become still richer."

One has hardly to read between the lines to realize that the Pope understands the name of the international game. Powerful trading interests can manipulate raw material prices downward, pay for less wealth than they take, and sell their manufactured goods at rigged prices. African countries with great copper mines and cheap labor thus end up pouring their economic life blood into more powerful nations, while the underdeveloped populations never achieve the wherewithal to better their existence. And those economies that literally steal the copper pay an indirect price. They dry up their own copper mines, if they have any. If they buy cheap beef from New Zealand, they dry up their own beef production in the fullness of time.

If nations have the wit to erect price supports, as did the U.S. during and after WWII, or variable levies as did the Common Market, they have still a duty to mankind, namely raising the parity on things they buy in international trade. The Pontiff's next paragraph is meaningful in this regard.

"*61. International Agreements.* In this area one cannot employ two systems of weights and measures. What holds for a national economy or among developed countries is valid also in commercial relations between rich nations and poor nations. Without abolishing the competitive market, it should be kept within the limits which make it just and moral and therefore, human. In trade between developed and underdeveloped economies, conditions are too disparate and the degree of genuine freedom available too unequal. In order that international trade be human and moral, social justice requires that it restore to the participants a certain equality of opportunity. This equality is a longterm objective, but to reach it, we must begin now to create true equality in discussions and negotiations. Here again international agreements on a rather wide scale would be helpful: They would establish general norms for regulating certain types of production for supporting certain new industries. Who is there who does not see that such a common effort aimed at increased justice in business relations between peoples would bestow on developing nations positive assistance, the effects of which would be not only immediate but lasting?"

3. *defiance of the law*

The United States program on sugar comes to mind. In 1946 the Congress passed a sugar bill. This was in keeping with American tradition. The first sugar tariff had been passed in 1789. It called for a two cent tariff on a pound of sugar. In that day and age, wages were 50 cents a day, and therefore a two cent tariff represented a very high duty. But there was sound reason behind the move. The tariff induced sugar production in the United States. The program also delivered income to nations such as Cuba (where New York

and London financiers short circuited its distribution, and paved the
way for Castro.) Nevertheless, equity of trade remains mandatory,
because income cannot be distributed if it isn't achieved in the first
place.

Unfortunately, churchmen frequently study rubrics and liturgy, not
economics, and few who read the Pope's lines understood them. Here
and there a Protestant pastor or rural priest paid out the effort to
learn about the consequence of permitting marketplace thievery.
But the churchmen who saw no identity between farming and churchly
affairs could not understand why there was a heavy automatic penalty
whenever an economy exploited its laboring people or its farmers.
Indeed, there was something almost biblical about the ratio involved.
In the case of farmers, for every dollar they were shortchanged (in
terms of honest parity) the national income was shortchanged seven-
fold, or $7.

At one of the NFO economic conferences not long before the
organization voted a milk holding action, a rural banker put it this
way to Dr. John Forbes. "Is what's happening to this economy, this
country, only economic? Or is it really a demonstration of the real
government of human life?" He went on to point out that this relationship between farm income might be just a surface manifestation
of relationships at the profoundest level—"where God governs. If that
is the case, we have all been guilty of refusing to honor a plain
relationship that's just. This business of not paying people their
just due—this injustice has got to stir the deep relationship between
God and man. It's got to. It's got to because there's been a definite
defiance of The Law."

The Law? Thou shalt not steal.

holding action

mha + 10

A NEW TYPE OF NEWS was coming in on Saturday, MHA + 10. In at
least a dozen states, rural businessmen were taking up donations to
help farmers who were dumping milk. LeRoy and Del Paulson of
Dodge Center, Minnesota, were pleasantly surprised when their family
dental bill for over $100 arrived in the mail, marked "paid" by Dr.
Ellingson. It was an excellent gesture for Easter Saturday. A touch
of humanness was what the farmers needed, and incidents like this
supplied a measure of it.

There were enough of the abrasive elements in any case. WIRL
at Peoria, Illinois, was broadcasting that the holding action would be
over on the weekend. More and more of these reports were cropping
up, and it always took energy and time to spike them.

From a reporter's vantage point, there was no reason for such
reports. Dumpings were still bigger than life despite efforts to halt
the action. More important, farmers were still joining the effort.
They were signing into NFO in ever increasing numbers and promptly
dumping milk.

All phases of the action, if not actually building, were holding their
own. At headquarters and in the field, a new determination took
hold. Farmers had decided that they simply would not lose by
default because the action had run into Easter. To a man, they were
determined to hold until at least Monday, probably longer, if anything
developed.

The sheets on the tables in the Nerve Center were filling up, Dakota
creameries, Minnesota creameries, Wisconsin creameries, Michigan
creameries, all signing NFO's short term contract. Complete com-
pilations of plant signups would not hit NFO headquarters for several
days, but all available news immediately went out. In Iowa County,

Wisconsin, 15 creameries signed before noon.

Even with all the signups to report, the hot line rarely rang on MHA + 10, so firm and desperate had the battle become. Nerves rarely exploded. The cartons of milk on the floor were gone.

Periodically, the back door to the alley was flung open to admit the spring—and in the tired sincerity and tired lines on every face one could read a desire to be back in the fields again, back where each farmer would like to be had not the powers that be made this desperate battle necessary.

When calls came, the conversations were short and methodical. Mike Summers reported that West Plains, Missouri, businessmen had turned over $1,000 to NFO "to help the effort." There was plenty of activity in the Show Me state on Saturday, particularly in the Kirksville area, where Ralph Weber, Frank Reesman and Johnny Pack were on duty. But things were also stove up across the state at Savannah, according to Gary Letts. Missouri was in the hold until it couldn't go any more, and from vantage point MHA + 10 this meant until at least next Monday.

These kind of reports were coming in from Ernie Knock in Michigan, Val Akerlund in Nebraska, and Bill Sinn in Illinois. After all, Newago County, Michigan, was dumping 150,000 pounds a day, and Nebraska was having a 50,000 pound (big for Nebraska) splash near Fremont. Bill Sinn was fighting "false reports" that the holding action was over.

Such report tickets were ricked up, hour on end, but the main attention went to signup plants.

The holding action was first, last and always a human story on MHA + 10. Yuma County, Colorado, non-members were having second thoughts about NFO. With membership agreement blanks largely unavailable, the farmers took a head start toward going with NFO by donating $50 to a holding action fund. In Platte and Goshen counties, Wyoming, where dairy cows were scarce, Martin Brill reported that NFO farmers had collected hay and donated it to their Weld County, Colorado, neighbors, who were milking and dumping with tired zeal.

1. *snow fences going up*

Airplane Joe had been coming and going from Corning's hilltop airport for several days. His passengers were always NFO officers.

In groups and singly, they hit far-away ports of call, and returned to NFO headquarters late at night. A trouble spot had developed in Tennessee. There wasn't a truck rolling in Nashville. At Country Maid, only 1,800 gallons out of a normal daily production of nearly 12,000 gallons was being processed, and it was headed for the hospitals.

Unexpectedly, labor union members had taken on the farmers' battle as their own, probably because they were trying to organize several operations themselves. Meat Cutters and Teamsters had shouldered picket signs and were marching, obstensibly for the farmers. The big story had it that two Nashville plants had closed, and Nashville milk producers were planning court action to halt the picketing. The pickets were a weapon farmers were not used to. They had done it, of course, but they had never seen the impact that goes with pickets being honored. Now, suddenly, union labor was honoring NFO pickets, and the slow paced signs had dried up the plants as surely as if every cow had passed out of the picture.

At Tullahoma, where some Tennesseans make good old fashioned Geo. Dickel Tennessee whisky and others work for government complexes, the International Brotherhood of Electrical Workers and the Air Engineering Metal Trades Council voted to support NFO.

The "we're with you" gesture from Tullahoma was appreciated sight unseen, but support from Teamsters and Meat Cutters carried with it new danger. All through the 11 day old holding action, there had been attempts to close down the effort by court order. NFO members, of course, had been cautioned not to talk to union people about gaining support for the action. To solicit support was to act in collusion, and collusion would be sudden death for the farmers. Oren Lee Staley and Albin Rust were certain that no NFO people had contacted the Teamsters. Why were they helping the farmers, rather than sending the usual moral support telegrams? Part of the answer might be found in conjecture, and part would always remain unguessable. Some of it was surely a part of the Tennessee character.

Tennessee was known as NFO's volunteer state. The organization had entered the northern counties with a bang in early 1965. In county after county capacity crowds listened to Paul Faulkerson detail the aims and aspirations of NFO. "Bigness is not the answer," Faulkerson told one audience after another. "Efficiency is not the answer. We are too efficient now. We have produced ourselves out of a market. We are producing more and we are selling it for less.

We are going to have to get a price and we have to work on that instead of production."

More often than not, Hershel Ligon of Hermitage paved the way for local meetings in Tennessee areas, and more often than not farmers actually lined up to sign with NFO. And in Tennessee, as nowhere else, newspapers gave the fast growing NFO organization fair and ample coverage.

More than most, Hershel Ligon sounded the tenor of the organizational tempo. "I spent four years fighting for my country," he told one reporter. "Now I intend to spend the rest of my life fighting for the farmer."

Earlier, the idea of NFO had crossed the border from Kentucky and much of it had been translated into newspaper copy. An excellent report was printed by the *Nashville Tennessean* under the title, *Should a Man Have a License to Farm?* A lot of farmers discussed NFO. When NFO came to Tennessee, "we were ripe."

Understandably, much of Tennessee's farm character had become embodied in the state's nickname—"The Volunteer State." The nickname originated as a result of the War of 1812, during which volunteer soldiers from Tennessee serving under General Andrew Jackson displayed marked valor in the Battle of New Orleans. Tennessee has never abandoned its "Volunteer" status.

The story of any farmer in Tennessee could be told in short staccato sentences. Return from the war. Return to farming. Work, work, and more work. Low prices. Debt. And hardly the price for a bottle of Jack Daniel's whiskey!

The NFO member in Tennessee had thousands of names, but his story had the same theme. "I feel that we farmers are entitled to a little better living," is the way Henry Oldfield of Watertown would put it. In Tennessee, the gravity of the cost-price squeeze could be read all around. Barns needed repair or replacement. Equipment was burned out or old. Old people well past retirement were being pressed into service tying and hanging tobacco. "I feel," Henry Oldfield would continue, "that we deserve a better place in society. NFO is the only way. I do some custom plowing. I told the fellows last year that they either join NFO, or make those rows a mile long."

In Tennessee land comes in small packages. Usually it has been cleared out of the rolling hills the hard way, and looking around one can almost see yesteryear, with horses straining to remove stumps. There are not too many long rows in any crop, and Henry Oldfield's ultimatum was merely a southerner's way for saying, "It's NFO, or else." Now it was hold milk, or else.

NFO had picked its best leaders for the holding action posts. They were Ray Armistead, Paul Faulkerson and Raby Steelman. Normally, Armistead worked for Bill Lashmett's Meat Commodity Department, and he continued to function in that capacity throughout the hold, but there was now the double duty of providing leadership in an explosive situation. Faulkerson was headquartering at the Lockhart Motel in Camden, but he seldom managed to hit his "office" before midnight. Raby Steelman was operating out of his home at Fayetteville, a euphemism for the fact that he spent his waking hours burning up the asphalt between Tennessee's far flung counties.

As reports came in, someone with a droll sense of humor scrawled across a pink sheet—"Snow Fences Going Up." Snow fences are made of pickets, and pickets were certainly writing the ticket in Tennessee.

In a brainstorming session at Corning, someone suggested that perhaps Teamsters were honoring NFO pickets to embarrass President Johnson. After all, James Hoffa was still in jail, and his lawyers were making a desperate fight for a hearing on a technical matter. Those who had marched through the corridors of courthouses knew that messages sometimes take an ESP route between sender and receiver. No one had to carry such a message to Washington, the speculation ran, and no one had to instruct a judge either. It was axiomatic in the legal profession that a judge's independence of political influence varied directly with the time he had been on the bench. Judges were not gods, after all. They were men with all the strengths and weaknesses of men.

If Teamsters were merely embarrassing Johnson, they might want to embarrass him in several states. The chances were against it, surely, because that would be union brinkmanship hardly justified by the goal. The NFOers at headquarters may have been right, and they may have been wrong, but they at least considered the alternatives.

In the several states, rank and file members seized up the snow fence idea. Sooner or later—probably sooner—Corning would have to make a judgment as to whether pickets helped the cause.

In the meantime those handling the signs were willing to continue. Diary farmer Joe Rochelle of Centerville, Tennessee was 70, and he had milked cows ever since he could remember. On MHA + 10, for the first time in his life, he stood on a picket line, hoisting a carton of Kroger's buttermilk to his lips. "First boughten milk I've ever drank in my life," he said. "It's not as good as mine." Rochelle was one of a hundred in front of Purity Dairies on Murfreesboro Road, Nashville. He was prepared to pitch a tent and stay on duty "until we get a fair price for our milk."

Some grocery stores started rationing milk. The supply got thin. NFO members stressed they would not interfere with deliveries to hospitals. In the hours ahead, there would be no milk at all. Teamsters refusing to cross picket lines made this a certainty. And there were plenty of pickets. "I just came down to see what was going on," said Mrs. Caleb Smith of Bell Buckle. And with that she picked up a sign and started walking a line.

2.   *two cents a quart*

Two cents a quart had become a catch phrase, a very successful one. Its simplicity had caused the AFL-CIO in Kentucky to support NFO, ministers to rally behind the cause, and the nation at large to admit the inequity of farm prices. Belatedly, documented apologetics from the trade made the scene. They came in the form of an AP milk price story, replete with chart:

If you pay 50 cents for a half-gallon of milk, here is where the money goes, according to Department of Agriculture and dairy industry studies:

> Farmer—23.5 cents.
> Retailer—7.5 cents.
> Wholesaler—7.7 cents.
> Processor and packager—7.6 cents.
> Dealer-processor administrative expenses—2.1 cents.
> Assembling of milk at central plants for processing and distribution—1.4 cents.

Studies indicate the 26.5 cents going to all middlemen combined is used for these purposes:

> Labor—10.5 cents.
> Containers and supplies—3.2 cents.
> Buildings, equipment and other overhead—3.3 cents.
> Advertising and promotion—1.7 cents.
> Transportation—2.4 cents.
> Miscellaneous—3.2 cents.
> Profits before income taxes—2.2 cents

The studies also indicate that if milk worth 50 cents at retail is used for another dairy purpose such as butter, cheese, ice cream or dried milk, the farmer gets 17.7 cents.

The chart was misleading, as was the explanation that went with it. The average farmer was not receiving 23.5 cents per half gallon. He was getting less than 18 cents for Class 1 at the time of the milk holding action, especially in the Wisconsin-Minnesota milksheds. The newsman at the AP office who prepared the story was probably honest enough, but he was clearly off base in using figures from a New York milkshed. Casual investigation would have revealed that 3.5 butterfat test Class 1 milk in Minnesota was earning $4.30 per hundredweight. The same test in New York was bringing $5.40 per hundredweight based on the chart's 23.5 cents "price farmer receives." The difference of $1.10 reflected the fact that milk from Minnesota and other midwestern states was being kept out of New York markets so that local price would stay more in line with the astronomical cost of living in the big metropolitan area.

Any individual farmer could refute the newspaper eyewash.

Based on 3.5 test, farmer Harold Murray of Campbell, Minnesota received 18.7 cents per half gallon for his milk. After paying his hauling charge, he ended up with 17.9 cents per half gallon—not the 23.5 the AP sent out across the wires. Yet almost all wire service customers printed that 23.5 cent chart. The explanation that it was in error never made the wire service news.

Still the continuing pressure of the holding action, with or without print, was news. It was being recognized as such when USDA told Pure Milk Association of Chicago that there would be a hearing on proposals for a federal milk marketing order combining the Chicago, Milwaukee, Madison and Rock River Valley markets into one. It would be held within a month after the milk action had ended.

Late on Saturday night, the guessing had it that the action would end early Monday morning. Almost any reading from the field indicated as much, unless!

The "unless" was really an unknown "if," and the membership was quite prepared to hang on *if* the "if" was good enough.

"If" unions continued to honor NFO pickets . . .

"If" NFO decided to permit a spread of the picket system . . .

"If" the short term contract continued to build past the breakover point . . .

"If" some sort of secret weapon could push those short term contracts past the breakeven point . . .

"If" a combination of all the "ifs" delivered results, then NFO would surely make the breakthrough of the century.

In the Nerve Center, exhausted workers measured the minutes before midnight. Tomorrow would be Easter Sunday, a likely time for a slowing of the pace, they agreed almost to a man. They were to be completely and articulately wrong.

mha + 11

THE SUN HAD SLID across milk dumping for 11 days now, and it was making its westward trek again. Eleven days had come and gone since Curtis Lightfoot, the NFO Chairman of Warren County, Kentucky, had told farmers about the "only hope" and how the fight would be a tough one. At first the problem was to keep Kentucky farmers from holding until the time came. Now Kentucky supervisors Earl Hatcher and Weston Edwards wondered whether some would stop when action was over. They were that mad. Anger had been building for a long time. It had taken on new fuel when S. D. Lester Jr. of Nashville Milk Producers Association warned farmers who did not ship that they would have to be inspected before pickups could be made again. Lester was all dedication and high standards when he spoke these lines, and when he paraded motives that were as pure as the driven snow. Clearly, the inspection bugbear was not to be compromised for anyone seeking a fair price.

All through the action, Carroll Upton of the Warren County Milk Bargaining Committee had been cautious. In an opening meeting he had urged NFO members to hold, and he cautioned them not to talk to non-members about helping the action other than by joining. Simultaneously, Harry Roggenkamp Sr., NFO Chairman of Bullitt County, had been touring the counties, telling members what they could and could not do. There had been demonstrations at Southern Belle Dairy and Carnation in Lexington, but that was a long time ago, at least in terms of the fact that this was MHA + 11.

The scenes of the action had been replayed across Kentucky since March 15. Tot Moore of Shepherdsville fed his milk to the hogs, and it was costing him $180 a day—a big price and a small price, depending on how you looked at it. Kentucky farmers knew what it was all

261

about. George Stiles had carried the message to the Shelby County Chamber of Commerce. He told the businessmen that 90% of the FFA boys in Kentucky were leaving the farm, and he clearly illustrated how low farm prices were feeding human beings into the city slums. The spectacle of milk being dumped prompted an apathetic public to ask questions.

"Has the American dairy farmer gone mad?" asked the Kentucky edition of the *Enquirer* out of Cincinnati.

And the answer came back. *No, we haven't gone mad. But we are mad.*

Lane Purcell, Grant County, Kentucky: "I've cut my teeth in the dirt since I was born and I've been kicked in the teeth ever since —if something isn't done soon, there won't be any farmers left."

James Bailey, Pendleton County, Kentucky: "The only reason I'm still making it is because my wife is teaching school. I'd like to make it on my own."

Not many Kentucky farmers opposed the NFO, according to *Enquirer* reporter Bob Lynn. Middlemen did. Ted Osborne, executive secretary-treasurer of the Cincinnati Milk Sales Association could hardly contain his disgust. NFO is an "immature manifestation of the farmers' frustration," he said.

But the Kentucky farmer wasn't interested in fancy talk. He shouldered his picket signs, held his milk, and reflected on how hard it was to farm in marginal country. The cancer of low prices was hard enough on farmers in the Dakotas and Illinois. In Kentucky it was murder.

1. *burr rock land*

They talked of burr rock land in Kentucky, and all around there was evidence that almost all farm land had been hacked out of the wilderness a century ago. Ruth and Patsie Shobe of Smith's Grove lived in a house that was well over a hundred years old, and just about the newest thing on the farm was the NFO membership agreement. The old and the new—that was Kentucky and NFO in a nutshell.

Cartographers have roughly divided Kentucky into land regions that sometimes tell their own story and sometimes leave the real story untold. Everyone knows of the Appalachian Plateau, the poverty belt where a maze of narrow valleys between ridges make profitable farming impossible even in good times. There are open valleys, of course, and there are farms, but in the main the Appalachian Plateau is a land of poverty where agriculture is hardly at home and where the passing of the coal mines has left a legacy of despair. Appalachia has not been invaded by NFO because it does not represent the body of Kentucky's farm production, and holds no real organizational potential.

From the Ohio River in the north—where the great stream separates Kentucky from Ohio, Indiana and Illinois—to the Tennessee border in the south, remained potential territory for NFO. The north-central part of this area was called the Bluegrass Region, and the area below it the Pennyroyal Region (after the herb of the mint family that grows there). Pennyroyal marches along almost all of the Tennessee border, reaches out to encircle the western coal fields that lie under Indiana, touches the east gulf coastal plain that borders Missouri, and still manages to arm its way up to the Ohio River below Indiana.

Kentucky is a land of cypress swamps, open fertile valleys rimmed by high rocky cliffs, and treeless sinkholes. And there is very productive farmland.

Most of the better Kentucky farms lie in the Bluegrass and Pennyroyal regions, and accordingly, that is where NFO first entered the scene. Farms averaged possibly 120 acres each, but seldom could one find a farm that was completely tillable. More likely than not, grass and woodlands took up two-thirds of a Kentucky farmer's acres. NFO manages to sign farms several hundred acres in size, and through dilligent work Kentucky NFOers have made "the dark and bloody battleground" of yesteryear a formidable entry in NFO on the march for better prices.

"We need to point out," Curtis Lightfoot would say, "that 50% of our stuff goes to market in a pickup. I'm talking about tobacco, hogs, cattle. Compared to Iowa, we'd be considered marginal farmland, but I suppose every acre in America is marginal when compared to the absolute top A-1 acre, wherever it is." Curtis Lightfoot farmed several hundred acres at Drake, Kentucky, which was only a long stone's throw from Bowling Green. He joined NFO almost as fast as NFO jumped across the border into the northern counties below Indiana. NFO marched south rapidly, Lightfoot recalls "and before you knew it the organization was signing members around Frankfort and clear down to Franklin down on the Tennessee border." In all of the organized areas, farmers were holding. "One lactating mouse apprehended crossing the border," a solid-hold area reported, and before the days was gone NFOers everywhere claimed the same for their solid-hold areas.

From steamboat graveyard in the Mississippi in the west to the low hills of Appalachia in the east, the tell-tale signs that NFO has come this way are evident. Old age always stands in stark contrast with advances, just as wealth in the Kentucky countryside contrasts sharply with real rural poverty. Only casual inquiry reveals that fine Greek revival homes that dot the farm country have not been provided for by the economics of rural America.

Always there is off-farm income in evidence. Clear-cut little towns that look prosperous beyond their means have milked their prosperity out of other little towns that are dying.

James E. Thompson ran the Pruitt Implement Company in Bowling Green, and sold John Deere tractors and New Holland farm equipment. Earlier, Thompson had a Class 1 dairy business, farming some 800 acres he owned and leasing some 800 other acres as he went along. Thompson was among the first to join NFO in Kentucky, and has been one of NFO's chief proponents in Kentucky's business and farming community.

Thompson had his land, but having a big operation he decided he simply could not continue producing milk at a loss without pulling farm, implement business and personal savings under in one fell swoop. "The only solution, keep working NFO, sign on and hang on."

Carroll Upton had a Class 1 dairy operation at Alvaton, Kentucky. "I have 70 cows. And you might say I have debts. The mortgage on my farm is now more than I paid for the farm when I bought it in 1952. As far as I'm concerned that's the biography of farming for everyone I know. We've worked harder, produced more, and have a bigger debt to show for it." You can't hire help for a farm. All we can get are factory throwouts—that's what we've got left to work on the farm. That's why I'm dumping."

That's the kind of news Lawrence Thomas and Owen Isaacs reported out of Lebanon—*milk dumping and more milk dumping.*

2. phase 2

The signups were coming in slower on Easter Sunday, but they were coming in. Albin Rust hurriedly calculated the results—pounds of milk by categories safely in tow, pounds of milk still needed. Across the flat expanse of his desk nagged the same old target figure, one that somehow had to be reached.

Whether it would be reached depended on several decisions still to be made. Shortly before noon, the NFO staff assembled in Staley's office for a session. Out of that meeting would come answers to the problems of the hour.

First up for a hearing was the picket problem. Local leaders had thrown up pickets in Nashville, and the news had spread like wildfire. If pickets could dry up Nashville, local leaders reasoned, why not give the NFO effort an added assist by throwing up pickets everywhere. It didn't take long. After a half hour or so, Lloyd Fairbanks came out of Staley's office. A few minutes later Nerve Center workers were told to put out this message:

THE INSTRUCTIONS FOR PICKETING—TO BE FOLLOWED EXACTLY

It's not illegal to picket. It's illegal only when contacts have been made to solicit support.

If there has been solicitation of support then there can be no pickets.

Two and not more than three at each truck entrance and exit. Have standby crew ready in car observing pickets but not interfering. Pickets can not talk to anyone. Ask for police protection for pickets.

Pickets stay off plant property.

Do not contact unions.

Stress the holding action still to be won at the farm level. Keep holding.

PICKET SIGNS ARE TO READ:

"Farm prices are too low."

"All we are asking is two cents a quart more at the farm level."

While operators were busy setting up conference calls, Staley and the NFO staffers tackled the next item on the agenda, Phase 2. Phase 2 had been designed to keep the holding action going while allowing farmers to ship milk. Hammered by the holding action, many cheese, butter and powdered milk processors were either short of milk or closed down. Phase 2 would allow NFO members to ship for processing again under contract. NFO members would retain title to the processed production under a lockup program, thus avoiding the cost of dumping while having the same effect. Early in the game, the NFO leadership had relied on a continuing lockup program to put the finishing touches to the drive for contracts. The big question had always been the same. When would Phase 2 be most effective?

The willingness of manufactured milk plants to sign contracts had been tested for two days now. So solid had the hold become that many plants signed short term contracts within minutes, and they were still signing.

Everyone in Staley's office that morning agreed that members would run another week, even more, if they had something to run on. Phase 2 would supply the ammunition.

The exact timing of the Phase 2 release program had run the gamut of discussion for fully a week. There had been some division of opinion on the point, but among NFO's top leaders there was also general recognition that Staley's sense of timing rated with that of a successful military officer. He could sense a mood and an opportunity for striking, and he could implement the strike in most unorthodox ways. Moving people was his forte.

The instrument for a lockup and store program had been hammered out, corrected, changed, and revised until it was not only simple, but full of teeth—and fair. So far, the contract had not caused a delay. Financing had. Storage had. The monopoly power of the bigs had.

A plan as new as Phase 2 was bound to run into difficulties, but most of these had been anticipated. Some of the processing plants said they could furnish finances through normal channels. But NFO realized that should anything "happen," this money would suddenly become unavailable.

Some of the plants that would go into the Phase 2 programs did not have their own storage facilities, and therefore had to send manufactured production to a central location. Trade practices required only one warehouse receipt on volume at a central storage facility. Since Phase 2 volume would involve several NFO members, certificates of assignment would permit lending activity under these circumstances. NFO had already protected members by making it possible for them to use certificates of assignments from warehouse receipts. In this way, each individual could have his proportionate share designated for use by his own lending agency.

Later, it was believed, NFO members could turn to the Commodity Credit Corporation for financing. CCC could be used because manufactured products were selling at the support level, and the government had established a policy of not selling products back into commercial channels at less than 110% of cost.

Preliminary plans called for NFO to use all three methods: plant financing, individual members using their own credit agencies, and later on—CCC.

A pound of milk that went into Phase 2 could not go into normal market channels, and would have the same effect as a pound of milk held on the farm.

But there were other wrinkles. Borden and Kraft had a virtual monopoly on the nation's cheese barrels. They would go merrily on their way denying NFO the use of the industry's containers. Some areas of the country really had no plants subject to a Phase 2 agreement. When the chips were down, farmers in those areas would end up shipping again.

Thus Phase 2 had to be a kicker—an extra injection of fuel into the system at a critical time. Sunday afternoon, MHA + 11 was the critical time.

With the decision made, the door to Staley's office flew open, and half-sheet instructions were started through the duplicating machine. The message came out in two forms. One was intended for supervisors who could be reached. With their tape recorders spinning, they soon had both the instructions and the text of the contract itself. The second half sheet was for supervisors away from their "offices."

IF SUPERVISOR IS NOT THERE, HIS OFFICE MUST CALL HIM AND TELL HIM HE MUST RETURN TO HIS HEADQUARTERS IMMEDIATELY BECAUSE WE HAVE A PHASE 2 PLAN WE WANT TO GIVE TO HIM AND DISCUSS WITH HIM THAT WILL WIN THE MILK HOLDING ACTION. THERE MUST BE NO LET-UP IN THE MILK HOLDING ACTION! ALL SUPERVISORS ARE TO BE ON A FULL TIME BASIS UNTIL FURTHER NOTICE.

Beyond that, supervisors were told to say only one thing to their county contacts:

WE HAVE A PHASE 2 PLAN TO USE. THIS PLAN WILL WIN THE MILK HOLDING ACTION.

3. *an injunction*

By releasing Phase 2 at the supervisor level, it was sure to generate mystery, rumor, new optimism, and a new will to win. That much was planned. What happened next pushed rumor, optimism and the will to win beyond the wildest expectation.

One of Staley's contacts called from Washington. There was a report out of the Justice Department, one that could not be ignored, that NFO would be taken to court and served with an injunction. The nature of the injunction was still being determined at the highest level.

No one knew whether to take the threat seriously. There had been other threats, and threats of threats to come. Those doing the brain-storming shifted like a backfield in motion. The immediate concensus was that the Phase 2 messages should be suspended for an hour or two while the leadership considered this latest development.

There had been other court actions. The one in Nashville had been a blockbuster. The one in Cincinnati had been turned over to an attorney, James G. Headley, and had evaporated for all practical purposes. So far NFO had been doing well in court, but so far NFO had eluded a Justice Department action. While staffers discussed the pros and cons, Nerve Center workers gnashed their teeth, and calls from supervisors in the field went unanswered. There were telephone calls from liaison men in Washington, and not a few from angles so subtle they seem hardly related to the action.

The court action, if it actually came, would be an attempt by the administration in Washington to bomb out the NFO effort. There would be polite talk about legal acts, and some Judge would issue an injunction. From a legal point of view, nobody would be hurt. But the Judge, Staley and all of NFO knew full well that a holding action was fought on economic, psychological and political fronts. The harm of the Justice Department action would be realized the minute word went to the press. It was that simple. What happened in court later on wasn't even germaine.

Staley pushed the papers on his desk to one side. Someone got NFO's audio expert, Don Mach, and the taping equipment went into motion. Cut behind closed doors and manufactured in the bellicose Staley manner, the news of a possible injunction provided an added kicker to the Phase 2 message. When Staley told the field staffers that NFO leaders would fight until "hell freezes over" he was a veritable Knute Rockne of the farm front, and there was no one at Corning who doubted that the farmers would do the same.

4. it's snowballing

The big dumping spectacles had all but faded from the scene on Easter Sunday. It took a lot of organization to put hundreds of farmers in one field for a big splash. It was much simpler to let the milk spew out on the concrete floors of milkhouses and broom it down the drain. On Easter Sunday, that's what NFO farmers were doing. Many of the Nerve Center reports (Becker County, Minnesota, 310,000 pounds dumped; Huron, South Dakota, 410,000 pounds used to fill a motel swimming pool) were really information held over from Saturday, and were readily drowned out by Phase 2 news.

Even on Easter Sunday, plants were signing contracts. Some industry captains figured they'd take off for the weekend and drink their highballs, hoping both headaches would be gone Monday morning. NFO figured differently, and members were working to make secure that *difference*.

NFO members believed they were winning. It was a genuine feeling. "It's breaking now."

"It won't last too long anymore."

"Boy, it's snowballing."

"We have no intention of slacking up—it's a fight to the end."

Comments such as these sparked NFOers as they worked on picket lines, typed up drafts of the lockup and store instrument, or simply dumped their milk.

By Sunday night, the prospect of widespread union support had all but faded. Quite simply, the unions wanted to be asked before they honored picket lines. And NFO had been instructed by counsel not to ask. Finally, the Tennessee experience proved to be in a class by itself, one that eluded explanation. The paradox was inescapable.

In Detroit, trucks rolled right past the pickets at Sealtest, and in Nashville the signs on the milk coolers said, "Sorry, Out of Milk." In Washington the USDA's *Agricultural Situation* reported that milk prices were "relatively favorable to farmers this year," and in Nashville the *Tennessean* headlined, "Mothers Seek Milk in Vain."

On MHA + 11 it took a small town to understand what was happening. Turtle Lake, Wisconsin was such a town. Along Maple Street, where all the business establishments functioned, business was drying up like a prune. Turtle Lake was only a village, 700 souls—more or less—and it was easy to see what made that town tick. It was the dairy industry, and only the dairy industry. Everyone in Turtle Lake could see that when farmers held their milk they therefore held their money. Their milk was their money. They created money with each milking. "Without a good income from the farmers, we might as well not be here," said Rodney Becker, the proprietor of a grocery store. In fact the farmer's milk was money, but milk was not legal tender. By putting coin or paper or bank credit between production and exchange of production, a society made it possible for middlemen or importers or government to single out the weakest, the most unorganized, and pay them for less than they produced.

Late at night, farmers around Turtle Lake heard that NFO President Oren Lee Staley was flying to Philadelphia in the morning to tell the farmers' story on the Mike Douglas Show. Maybe a few people would listen. Maybe they'd realize that the farmer really created money, and that when society failed to pay him a fair price, his money was not created, no more than if he hadn't produced at all.

mha + 12

THE PHONE CALLS CAME in a sporadic sequence—just often enough to keep anyone in the Nerve Center from getting any sleep. The Center's cryptic log revealed little of importance, taking individual entries as such, but by 7:00 a.m. they added up to a rather remarkable fact. The holding action had survived Easter. Phase 2 was in motion at the supervisor level. All the instruments had been double checked. Crews were mapping out the milk plants. Within a few hours they would be taking Phase 2 to processors. Don Zmolek was busily developing a log sheet, by states, on which appeared the names of plants in alphabetical order.

Things were almost too orderly and dignified in the Nerve Center early Monday morning. But that didn't last long.

"The country's going to hell," Oras Kanerva quietly informed all who would listen. "When *Capper's Weekly* starts calling farmers' wives *farmerettes,* the country's surely going to hell."

Others felt the same as Kanerva, but for less humorous reasons. Missouri was the Show Me State, probably because Congressman William Duncan Vandiver made a speech in Philadelphia in 1899 in which he said, "I come from a country that raises corn, cotton, cockleburrs, and Democrats. I'm from Missouri and you've got to show me." This morning, another Missourian was going to Philadelphia, and the world had still to show him that the family farmer was through. Oren Lee Staley, *Adams County Free Press* publisher Paul Gauthier, Staley's private secretary, Doris Peterson, and the writer were flying to the cradle of liberty because Mike Douglas had invited the farmers to tell their side of the story. So far, a Mike Douglas coordinator told Staley, no one in the processing end of the business had agreed to tell the middleman's side. The same thing had happened once before—when auto critic Ralph Nader appeared to challenge the safety of Detroit's cars. "This tells me one thing," the coordinator said. "This tells me there's a story out there that isn't being told."

With everything in tow at Corning, Staley seized the opportunity to talk to several million American citizens. There was indeed a story "out there." Farmers were being paid for less than they produced. Farm production was real money, but it wasn't legal tender.

This thought was bandied back and forth in the Lear Jet as it screamed from Des Moines to Philadelphia, where the whole proposition had been considered once or twice before.

1. *stuff for stuff*

A. H. Smyth in his *Writings of Benjamin Franklin* tells about a time, in the 1760s, when the great statesman was a dinner speaker in London. During the affairs of the evening, he was asked how he accounted for the prosperity of the American colonies. Franklin said: "That is simple. It is only because in the colonies we issue our own money. It is called colonial script and we issue it in the proper proportions to accommodate trade and commerce."

Not much later, a bill was written by the Bank of England and passed by Parliament that prohibited the colonies from issuing their own money. Henceforth, they were forced to issue bonds and sell them to the Bank of England in order to get money. Ben Franklin pointed out that from that time on, the poorhouses were always full and unemployment ran rampant. Franklin also nailed down the money issue as the original cause of the American Revolution. "The colonies would gladly have borne the little tax on tea and other matters had it not been that England took away from the colonies their money, which created unemployment and dissatisfaction."

By controlling the flow of money, the old harlot of Threadneedle Street made it possible for England to buy colonial raw materials cheap, and sell English goods dear. The process eventually bankrupted Englishmen so that a steady stream of people was ever heading to the new world. In 1775, about nine out of ten people in the colonies were farmers. The intellectuals who voted the Declaration of Independence, in the main, were farmers. They understood the nature of production from the land, and how it was the basic new wealth. They also understood how old world institutions were using their control of legal tender to pay raw material producers the world over for less wealth than the produced. It was not by accident that the Constitution required Congress to coin the money, and regulate the value thereof, and to establish standards for weights and measures.

One of the earliest forms of money in the colonies was the warehouse receipt. So many pounds of tobacco could be exchanged for such and such an article. The document facilitated transfer of equal values, or stuff for stuff.

Real goods exchanged for real goods is barter, and money that pretends to be real goods—such as gold and silver—is really material for barter.

Each nation decides its own money value in terms of gold. When a nation is a trading nation, like England, it must be able to sell cheaply to beat out competition and to maintain a favorable balance of trade. The best way to keep a favorable balance of trade is always to buy someone else's raw materials cheap, and in turn sell manufactured goods high. This cannot be accomplished if nations use an honest measure of value.

Writing in *Economic Tribulations,* Vincent Vickers of the Bank of England argued that the "world has never possessed a true and honest measure of value." He made a good case of the proposition that this lack of an honest measure of value had been "the principal irritant and restriction standing in the way of the world's economic progress, the happiness of the peoples, and the achievement of a lasting peace among nations."

International banking has always been based on gold. Long before the Middle Ages, gold had become the common commodity everyone wanted. The literature of the 19th century tells how people of affluence kept most of their wealth in gold. Much of it never left the vault of the goldsmith. A note to pay so-and-so was sufficient, and the man who got the note usually left it on deposit. This became the checking account.

In the course of time, bankers came to feel secure in issuing more bank notes than they had gold. This led to the fractional reserve— less gold than notes outstanding. It was possible, of course, for all notes to be presented for payment at once—the run on the bank! Yet such a situation might not happen in a lifetime. When people had confidence, it didn't happen at all.

Until 1929 the idea of a fractional gold reserve was accepted by everyone as the best system. Putting into circulation, say, $10 for $1 of gold seemed conceived in genuis, but alas, when the fractional reserve was extended, prices jumped almost in exact degree. In effect, credit expanded and then later contracted. Every major depression could be pinpointed that way. The mythmakers have always come out of their corners at this stage of the game. "Gold has collapsed," they have yelled.

But the observed facts indicate something else. Gold has never collapsed in the history of the world. What collapses is the paper flood. And the paper flood has always been manufacured as a temporary palliative to sooth the indigestion caused by exploitation of the raw material producer through inequitable price levels.

Thus price is the handle by which economies are swung up and down. Indeed, Irving Fisher, writing in the *Journal of the American Statistical Association* in June, 1925, challenged the old line business cycle theorists exactly that way. ". . . the tides of the sea, wave motion, or pendulum swing, we can forecast the future on the basis of a pattern worked out from past experience . . . We certainly cannot do that in predicting the weather, or Monte Carlo luck. Can we do so as to business? Not so long as business is dominated by changes in the price level."

Nothing in the world is static. Populations grow. Nations develop. If they grow and develop too fast, they soon run up too much activity for the gold supply to handle. The logical thing, of course, would be to revalue gold, but when one nation does this, gold flows to that nation and collapses the economy it leaves. Gold thus pretends a static world.

Yet gold is only a happenstance in history. The real gold of nations is the wheat, the corn, the farm production and minerals—all the raw materials. Without them the machines though necessary are useless. Gold was the starting point for money creation because in simple economies it was an easy thing to equate gold with goods, and vice versa. The minute an economy discovered it did not have enough gold to service commerce, it went to the fractional reserve.

The trouble with the fractional reserve was that it required the banker to always play the odds that depositors would not make the legendary run. Thus it developed that in the face of a run, government had to step in and take over anyway.

In and outside of formal economics, observers always have seen a "chicken and egg" causality between real money creation and legal tender creation. Even to deep thinkers, it wasn't really clear.

To a great extent, the impasse was solved when the era of monetized raw materials (90% parity) came to an end.

When the government decided to monetize farm production *only partially*, it in effect opened the way for debt creation. Unorganized farmers could not monetize production themselves through their institutional power—and so the big farm decline went into motion. To keep the full effect from being visited on the population, wholesale monetization of collateral (debt creation) was started. Still, there remains some difference of opinion regarding the significance of this money creation function. Some see in its elimination, or sharp curtailment, a solution to the economic impasse that arrives when farmers are shorn of parity income while the rest of the economy rolls merrily on its way in a wonderland of debt.

Thus, on the one hand, the Federal Reserve and the banks are blamed for turning off the credit when it reaches dangerous proportions—knocking the economy into a depression—and the Fed is again blamed if it lets credit run until the engine explodes into a social revolution.

Another element enters the calculation, namely compound interest. The British economist, Christopher Hollis, writing in *The Breakdown of Money* best stated the argument that banks should not create money at all. His matchless argument deserves greater circulation than it has so far received.

"Indeed," wrote Hollis, "the historian has to record that in almost every age there was some superstition or other of utter unreason which strangely occupied the minds of man, otherwise of activity and vigour. He has to confess that he cannot explain how it was that men once believed in the mystical significance of numbers or in the claims of astrology. We are sometimes ready to congratulate ourselves that our age has outgrown all superstitions. But the historian of the future will, I fancy, reckon in the same class as number-worship and astrology and the study of the gizzards of birds the strange superstition that, whenever money is invented, a percentage must be pair for ever afterwards as a propitiation to a banker. It is on that superstition that the whole empire of Mammon is built."

During the century since the Civil War, the fact that money (legal tender) creation has been in the hands of private banking—particularly since the creation of the Federal Reserve System—has allowed money makers to erect powerful institutional business arrangements. The upshot of it all has been that these institutions can manipulate raw material prices downward almost at will.

Pressuring the payment to raw materials into the ground assured the money makers an opportunity to uncork the paper flood. A prosperous people does not need so much credit, as a decade under 90% parity proved. A balanced economy does not need so much credit. The interest game requires credit, lots of it. According to the Keynesian formula, $1.00 of credit will create near $4.00 of national income, and Galbraith's mature corporations buy the idea because they get the business. No one bothers to tell the so-called smart businessmen that the "system" contains no provision for liquidating debt, and that debt must therefore compound itself.

"But we owe it to ourselves," cry the Keynesians, and they are right. "We will take turns going bankrupt and starting over. That way we can repudiate the debt and get rid of it." But the rolling waves of bankruptcies never seem to visit the "mature corporations" and "mature fortunes," who simply elude the piper, jump to another country, and return on the most favorable terms. They simply have to end up owning everything. When 5 to 10% of the people own it all, the rest melt into the subterranean currents that become the mainstream of social and economic chaos.

Always, it has been a vicious circle. In bygone eras, farmers devoted great energy to fighting the monetary system, something Staley and company had refused to do. Staley realized that the legal tender makers would be rather helpless if farmers simply stuck together. Even the powerful Fed could not drive farm prices into the ground if farmers took the lead and monetized their raw materials by putting their own prices on them. Even imports could not drive farmers to the wall if processors were required by contract to buy at parity from American farmers first.

That, after all, was what the milk holding action was about.

2. *we don't want any trouble*

Staley's appearance on the Mike Douglas Show was good, but it wasn't his best. There had been too many delays, from ground fog at Des Moines to traffic at Philadelphia, and by the time the big farm leader really warmed to his subject, time had expired. On the way back to the airport there was a pause for an hour or so while the *Farm Journal* staffers listened to the farmer's side of the story. Staley was really at his best in the *Farm Journal* meeting room.

He retold the story, all of it, from start to finish, and provided the editors with a scoop they could not use. He told them about Phase 2, the lockup and hold phase that might well push the effort over the top.

Most of the *Farm Journal* staffers had never met Staley. Indeed, they had met very few NFOers. Some of their field men had, but Philadelphia was a long way from Iowa, and the rank and file in NFO lived considerably west of Philadelphia.

By evening, some of the same billingsgate was making the rounds again. At Fort Wayne, a radio station reported the holding action over. One of the wire services did the same. In both cases the message came on so subtly you couldn't drive a ten penny nail through it.

Things were a little different on the Huntley-Brinkley Report. Nashville was out of milk, and this became the focal point of the presentation, but there were lines that farmers—NFO or otherwise—could not forget.

". . . it became somewhat clear that the NFO milk-withholding campaign took on meaning and developed a bite the moment the NFO labor unions threw their weight behind the farmers' efforts. It carried a strong message for the farmer, one which he has heard before, and one which he undoubtedly will choose to ignore. There is more discipline in a labor union than there is in a farmer's organization. A local of a union can achieve something pretty close to a hundred percent discipline. A group of farmers can only watch and envy."

They could envy indeed. In Poverty Valley, near Deming, Washington, a dairy farmer picked up the phone to call Corning. He wanted to know how he could help the holding action. He and his fellow farmers would volunteer money, he said, and out of the 600 producers in Poverty Valley he expected plenty of cooperation. Poverty Valley had tried holding years ago, but milk had been tanked in to break the effort.

A lettuce farmer at Blythe, California told Corning he was losing his shirt on the green stuff. He was also losing his shirt on feeding 10,000 cattle. "When will you move out here to organize?" was the question from California.

The queries were welcome, but premature. NFO had its hands full. Snow fences were going up across a wide front—all with mixed results. On the end of the hand lettered signs, farmers were uncertain. At Kansas City, one picket told a reporter: "We don't want any trouble. If there is any trouble, we're going to call the police." It sounded pretty much like a country boy lost in the ways of the city.

Pickets went up almost everywhere, but were being honored only sporadically, if at all.

Instead of dumping, pounds dumped, and non-members signed, most news items from the field had to go with pickets going up.

The hours wore on, methodical now—the first flourish of adrenalin having burned down. Blood pressures were hitting normal again, if the tempo of spirits and movements could be read correctly. The long hours had become a way of life for many NFO members. Like politicos on the hustings, NFO regulars had long lived on four hours of sleep a night when necessary. The younger among them could drop in their tracks for refreshing sleep on the spur of a moment, dead to the world almost before they hit the rack. The older men were restless.

There were no bulletins going out during the last hours of MHA + 12, only methodical lines connected with Phase 2. In the Nerve Center shortly before midnight, Staley told the workers that there had been nothing more on the injunction. Butch Swaim doubted that it would come, or at best that it wouldn't come for a couple of days. "We've done too good a job."

Still NFO had to be ready. Counsel had to be obtained. Strategy had to be planned. Yes, the organization had to be ready.

mha + 13

ON MONDAY EVENING Phase 2 was still a whispered threat. As soon as it got the green light from Corning, the shock waves would hit Washington.

The lockup program had "endurance" written all over it. It was economically sound, and avoided the harsher technique of open dumping. There was a sudden death risk in launching Phase 2, especially in the face of an injunction threat. But threats had been a common commodity ever since NFO started fighting the farmer's battle. The plain fact was that NFO needed an extra push to go over the top. Victory was so close, and yet so far.

Government is an art and a science. The seasoned government official seldom meets an issue head-on. Usually there is a third party who has the ability to establish rapport with the first and second party. A message is usually delivered this way—either to effect negotiations, or to "lay down the law."

There was a phone call from Washington to Staley's uncarpeted office at Corning shortly after Phase 2 had been unwrapped. "There's blood on the moon," a voice in Washington said. The speaker was well known to NFO and to the USDA, and the neutrality of the intermediary was recognized all around. Translated into language anyone could understand, this meant that Washington was not pleased with the progress NFO was making. An injunction would be filed in Federal Court at Des Moines, the NFO was told.

There were other messages. NFO attorney Lee Sinclair had been given 45 minutes to get over to the Justice Department. Government attorneys presented him with a rough draft. It called for a temporary restraining order and a permanent restraining order, both to be handed his honor the Judge in Des Moines.

Of a sudden, all uncertainty vanished. There would be a court order, no doubt about it. Half a hundred years from now, if anyone was still interested, a dedicated student might tunnel through the muck and paper to get at what really happened. What processor held a Gary dinner or whispered what to whom? To what extent did the hardening issue of cheap milk bounce around the circular office in Washington? *Who made the decision that raw material producers must not be allowed to monetize their production at parity?*

How cheap raw materials the world over created poverty and wars, and how those dedicated to maintaining the game called exploitation —both at home and abroad—won their battles could only surface at long intervals in history. People went to sleep quickly, and when they woke it was frequently too late.

Foundation economics had lost a round because exploitation was more attractive than sound development. Fuzzy minds reveled, drugged by the lotus of the times. Debt pretended to be earnings, and "one world" became a siren's song. Utopia was always something devoutly to be wished, but even wishing contained the seeds of destruction. All the armies that ever marched, all the navies that ever sailed, all the parliaments that ever sat, all the rulers that ever held office—all put together have not damaged the rise of man half as much as cheap raw materials.

The American Federation of Teachers endorsed the NFO hold on MHA + 13, as did several ministers and churches, but endorsement wasn't enough. NFO needed understanding. The problem facing the farmer was in the final analysis a schoolmaster's problem. An entire nation had grown up ignorant of the nature of coin and money, and how an exchange economy worked, and few could see how they were the Greek Chorus in this play about farmers.

The pickets were still walking on MHA + 13, and Richard Osterholm wasted his time by telling *Omaha World-Herald* readers that "Staley Can't Sell Neighbor," when in fact the plant at Corning had been sold and the reporter simply hadn't bothered to check out his story. Someone bothered to straighten that one out, but it didn't matter. All the headlines on MHA + 13 had been headlines before. All the men reporting into the Nerve Center had reported before.

Even Governor Romney's message to Ray Nielson had been handed out by other voices before. "Michigan dairymen have a vehicle for seeking a fair and equitable price for their dairy products and for resolving any disputes," Romney said, rejecting a bid to mediate the action.

Republican apologists were yammering on the side of NFO even though, inconsistently, they had yammered on the side of Charles Shuman's insurance company a few days earlier. Democrats behaved in the same way. Most politicans define everything in terms of apologetics for their party. The percentage of those who knew what they were talking about approached near zero.

From a technical vantage point, it was still a very tight hold, but somehow things weren't right. Even the sometimes excellent Huntley-Brinkley Report was deteriorating. When Al Rust, Phil Allen, Hugh Crane and Don Mach gathered in Erhard Pfingsten's office to look at the only TV set in NFO's Corning office complex, they saw a fairly competent actor-farmer go through a set up story. He was Marshall Thompson of Ravenna, Ohio. He had received threats, he said on the film clip. His trucks were filmed leaving the drive. The camera caught a milking machine in action, a closeup of Thompson, and a rather maudlin scene in which one of his sons mounted a tractor with a rifle across his lap. There was some commentary that one of Thompson's tanks had become contaminated.

Unfortunately, Huntley-Brinkley hadn't contacted the Nerve Center. As a matter of fact, Thompson was both a dairyman and a hauler. He had four trucks grounded because of the milk holding action. He had been reported attending NFO meetings every night, usually with a deputy in tow, and his efforts at stirring up trouble hadn't made many friends or influenced many people. The tank that had been poisoned with cynanide, fortunately, contained only a token amount of milk—a circumstance so rare it rated as a miracle. The men in Pfingsten's office watched the report, then left without a word. The performance, in their view, hardly rated a comment.

The details were still coming in. Leroy Kannas, Oliver Ross, Dale Boege, Clarence Ewert, Paul Thomsen, all reporting out of Iowa. There hadn't been a single incident in Iowa, not one. Iowa had hardly grabbed the spotlight through two weeks of milk holding, not because Iowa wasn't holding, but because men like Lance Johnson and George Jones worked Villisca and Red Oak with reckless abandon as to what inhuman hours would do to cells and protoplasm. Jim Steward and Don Trust were doing the same. Ed Shima, Willis Rowell and Bill Talbert on the Iowa staff worked to the limit of their endurance to fulfill a vow. They were not about to hand *The Des Moines Register* something lurid to write about.

Now, it looked like the focus of the holding action would come home to Iowa—this time into a Des Moines Courtroom—and as irony would have it, none of the field supervisors would be there.

No one in NFO could be blamed because the news out of Iowa was dull. Farmers couldn't be blamed if newsmen failed to find the biggest story of the century. In its proper perspective, the farm story was that big.

1. *consequence of the consequences*

".. . . exploitation of the weak by the powerful . . . has been a permanent feature in the life of most communities the world has yet seen . . ." All the theories of pure economics since Plato have not been able to over-ride this simple fact as expressed by Tawny. Boom and bust, boom and bust, one canceling out the forces unleashed by the other, so that the consequence of the consequences changes pace, but never quite ranges beyond the foundation philosophy. True, the processes of civilization have made refinement of the process necessary. Only in Hitler's Germany or Stalin's Russia did economic mandates result in wholesale slaughter of people because they no longer fit the patterns envisoned, and one could be pardoned for seeing the horrible consistency of that logic.

In the American economic system, the fruit was ever apparent, in Iowa, as elsewhere.

Exploitation of the weak colonies by the powerful King's mercantile companies, exploitation *of* the weak human *by* the strong, exploitation of the farmer by the industrialist, the threads run the length of history. It has no beginning or end. Arbitrarily, one must choose the moment in history from which to proceed forward or look back.

History records that a Dutch ship dropped anchor at Jamestown, Virginia on an August day in 1619. Its captain, a fellow named Jope, went ashore. He told tobacco man John Rolfe that he had a cargo of "20 Negars" he wanted to trade for food. The Negros probably had been captured as pirate booty from some Spanish vessel for they had names such as Pedro and Antonio, although they spoke no Spanish. Their origin mattered little to the colonists, who, after all, were indentured servants themselves. In fact, a few months earlier some 90 maidens had arrived from Europe to become wives of the first 90 bachelors who could pay the price of 20 pounds of tobacco per maiden. It has been recorded that the original 20 blended nicely with the settlers, but the same was seldom to be said of the slave trade during the next few centuries.

The slave trade was probably the most profitable economic activity ever to thrive on the face of the globe. Indeed, it has been said that the great fortunes from slave trading capitalized great "mature fortunes" still in existence. So thorough were the moguls behind slaving in destroying the evidence that to this day historians have a hard time tunneling back to get at the truth.

In 1792 a Yale-trained tutor named Eli Whitney spent a few days at the home of a widow Green in Savannah. He could hardly help noticing how tedious was the task of extracting seeds from the tenacious fibers in a boll of short staple upland cotton. His invention changed slave owning from a luxury to an economic necessity. Small farms became plantations.

Most of the slaves came from the New Guinea coast, from the Gold Coast, Gambia and Senegal. A few were kidnapped by whites, but most were captured by corrupt African chieftains and traded for rum and guns. Tough sea captains backed by English and continental money packed their human cargos in fetid holds and in two-foot spaces 'tween decks and headed for markets in the New World. After Congress declared the trade illegal in 1808, an estimated 250,000 more slaves were smuggled in. By the time the trade petered out, more than 15 million Africans had been shipped; twice as many more may have died on the way.

Yet, when the Civil War came, fewer than 5% of the south's eight million people were slave owners. But King Cotton had been established.

King Cotton was more than idea. It was a fact. Through the years there had been a transfer of the British and continental cotton industries from the Indian to American cotton because of cheap labor. Pre-war Board of Trade reports, census statistics, and cotton association data were read throughout the south with a consciousness of the role slave exploitation was playing in the industrial growth of England. Nor was England unaware of the situation. Even when England saw the gathering storms over slavery, the manufacturing interests found it impossible to turn back the tide. The Board of Trade reports of 1859 were satisfying to the southern people. In spite of 20 years of effort, the Great Britain islands could obtain 60 million pounds of cotton from India, or only 10 million pounds more than the 50 million pounds drawn from that source 59 years earlier.

In 1855 a man from Ohio named David Christy published a tome entitled, *Cotton is King, or Slavery in the Light of Political Economy.* His book in effect argued that the Union had to make peace with the south or permit peaceful secession. Stump orators, Congressmen, governors, economists, all sized on King Cotton and made it current coin. During the debates over Kansas, Senator Hammond carried the battle flag. Hammond said the north dare not drive the south to secession because no sane nation would make war on cotton. "Without firing a gun, without drawing a sword, should they make war on us we could bring the whole world to our feet. The South is perfectly competent to go on, one, two, or even three years without planting a seed of cotton. I believe that if she were to plant but half her cotton for three years to come it would be an immense advantage to her. I am not sure but that after three years total abstinence she would come out stronger than ever she was before and better prepared to enter afresh upon her great career of enterprise. What should happen if no cotton was furnished for three years? I will not stop to depict what every one can imagine, but this is certain. England would topple headlong and carry the whole civilized world with her, save the south. No, you dare not make war on cotton. No power on earth dares to make war upon it. Cotton is King."

Through all the great debates on tariffs, the south always opposed the north and the farm country west, which did not want prices subjected to attack from low income areas of the world. The south, with slave labor, believed it could compete in world markets—and by exploiting the labor of black men, perhaps it could. Now, however, the south can no more compete in world markets after paying parity wages than Kansas can sell wheat at world prices, despite pronouncements to the effect by those in high places.

Intelligence demanded that the farm sector of the American economy organize for institutional power, but wisdom requires it to understand that it is still only a single sector, not the whole, and could enjoy the fruits of progress only when all the other sectors of the economy enjoyed the fruits of progress.

None of this heady stuff bothered those with a *"get in there and get yours"* mentality. They not only didn't understand the system, they didn't even understand their own long range self-interest.

This simple fact separated the vague entity known as "the powers that be" from the farmer by a chasm intellectually a mile wide. Yet from a mile away you could still see a man dump milk. On MHA + 13, farmers were dumping milk.

mha + 14

THE YOU-PITCH-AND-I-CATCH confusion that boiled through the dairy industry on MHA + 14 was something for which no corporation could gear itself. The little plants reacted as somnambulants when NFO field personnel arrived with still another legal instrument in tow. Warren Stofferahn in South Dakota reported that one of his plants signed "without question." Many of the cheese plants were dry as a bone. For two weeks running, the days had exploded like pea-sized atom bombs. Each explosion made plant equipment radioactive, useless, less than junk.

Lauren Soth of the *Des Moines Register* hammered out an editorial that stripped down to stark nakedness all the apologetics that had nourished the milk situation to the brink of disaster in the name of free trade. The NFO was behind the times, he said.

"The milk 'strike' or withholding action of the National Farmers Organization suggests that the dairy farmer's economic situation has been growing worse. But the facts are just the opposite," editorialized Soth. It was his opening line, and it was really enough.

NFO leaders who picked up their papers at Canteri's Kitchen next door to the Corning office read all this in the back room, and their determination tightened. Those on the phones tightened their presentation in the field and drove even harder to annihilate any deficits that had sprung up in the past 24 hours. They didn't like the editorial, not so much because it was nonsense, but because they had no vehicle for talking back.

No vehicle? Not exactly. The PI Department caught the ball. An associate in Des Moines busily checked *Standard Rate and Data*. The *Des Moines Register's* rates had not been static for a decade and a half, even quick reading revealed. They had been adjusted upward on logical grounds. The cost of doing business had moved upward, and the paper didn't want to go broke, obviously.

Phil Allen was driving into St. Joseph, Missouri. He arrived at KFEQ approximately 30 minutes before air time. He had a little trouble ringing into Corning, and by the time he posed his traditional "What's New," only a few minutes remained before "ON THE AIR."

The ball went to Allen. The few facts that had been policed from the archives were all that could be given. As the neon ON THE AIR sign lit up, Allen dug deep into his knowledge of farm economics and years in broadcasting. All knowledgeable newsmen knew that the *Des Moines Register* was a "run with the hare and hunt with the hounds" operation conducted by long distance phone from New York.

The NFO membership had been singled out by "long distance" papers more interested in serving the front office than handing out straight news. At times NFO struck back. "The honesty of an article reflects no less than the honesty of the establishment," editorialized the *NFO Reporter* in one of these rare answers. "A great many people think they are thinking when they are merely rearranging their prejudices," wrote Will James, and *NFO Reporter* reminded the *Des Moines Register* of the quote. The farm organization paper scolded the big city daily with a paragraph many NFO members almost memorized:

"Not too many years ago Father Keller of the Christophers caused to be published the details of an incident that took place in a Korean prison camp. In this camp the Communists subjected prisoners to endless lectures on germ warfare as practiced by the Americans. During the lecture, the Communist officer produced a small insect on a white piece of paper. He told the prisoners that this was a germ carrier being used by the Americans, and that this single insect could wipe out the whole camp. A few soldiers looked at the insect, then passed it on. Finally a lanky farm boy picked up the deadly insect, and to the horror and amazement of many plunked it into his mouth and swallowed. Nothing happened. There were no more lectures in that camp.

"Father Keller's report comes to mind as we digest the *Des Moines Register's* NFO report. It hasn't killed us. There is only one way to deal with a big lie, and that is to pour truth on it . . ."

The truth was that on Wednesday, MHA + 14, the holding action was still very much alive, even though NFO farmers were saying,

"FOR TWO CENTS WE'D ALL GO HOME."

But there were also somber truths. The effectiveness of pickets had not spread much beyond Tennessee. There were exceptions, of course. In Louisville drivers for Sealtest refused to take milk from their plant to Kroger. Kroger in turn sent chain store drivers to pick up the milk. Next the Kroger driver refused to cross the picket line, and Kroger got no milk. But these cases were rare. Almost everywhere, drivers came and went with milk, even though much of it was powdered, watered, and Class 2 turned Class 1, according to NFO report, all of which was categorically denied by processors and chain stores. In New Jersey, health officials were "keeping our eyes on this situation." Pressed for details, Health Department official Howard Abbott acknowledged that substandard milk could be shipped from processing plants not approved by the state, or could result from the reduction of butterfat content or addition of water.

There was still another truth. Phase 2 was a reality, with instruments out, and information on successes coming in, all of it guarded and all of it privileged information, because any leak could bring fantastic pressures down on those cooperating with NFO.

1. *an anti-trust suit*

Ever since it had been installed in the Meat Commodity Department, there had been efforts to muffle the noise from the teletype. Fred Deardorff and Gene Potter had done a pretty good job simply by encasing the apparatus with walls of beaverboard. But nothing could muffle the explosion that came with this message:

BULLETIN

WASH-MAR 29—/UPI/—THE FEDERAL GOVERNMENT HAS FILED AN ANTI-TRUST SUIT AGAINST THE NATIONAL FARMERS ORGANIZATION IN AN EFFORT TO BREAK THE MILK WITHHOLDING ACTION. THE SUIT WAS FILED IN FEDERAL COURT AT DES MOINES, IOWA.

END

2:56$$$PM

It had—and it-hadn't—been expected. Within minutes every tele-type machine in the country handed the same message to broad-casters,, newspapers, stock exchanges and dairy processors who were considering the Phase 2 instruments.

Staley had on his desk the estimates that enough processors had signed contracts to equal one-third of the necessary volume. "It looked as though we had enough other processors ready to sign," he later recalled.

At this point, Staley said, NFO was ready to really hit Phase 2. The government's action was timed and delivered in order to deal a maximum of damage to the farmers' efforts. Many of the large companies had been contacted when Phase 2 went into effect. The minute the government action became front page news, bargaining stopped dead in its tracks for at least 48 hours. During this period, the big companies regrouped and organized terrific pressures.

Later, Staley explained. "We felt that by moving into Phase 2 we would get enough more processors to assure the two cents a quart increase. This is the reason the government action hit us at such a crucial time—because complete success was within our grasp."

As with all contemporary history, claims were disputed by both sides. Processors pooh-poohed the idea that NFO was even on the way. NFO, in turn, would issue this explanation:

"The lapse in bargaining brought on by the government's action unloaded several new problems on the continuing Phase 2 lockup. Some areas had only a limited number of plants subject to Phase 2 contracts. When the government action became known, many of those plants retreated and followed the lead of the bigs in putting a hard wait-and-see policy into effect. Many of the plants in the heavy producing areas that had been willing to process suddenly found reasons why they couldn't after the government filed its action."

It has been noted that at the time the Justice Department was charging NFO with trying to create a monopoly, two major processors had a monopoly on the nation's cheese barrels and they went merrily on their way denying the use of the industry's containers for an NFO purpose.

2. *an answer*

For a long moment—30 minutes perhaps—the phones quit ringing, and then, as if on signal, they started in again. An NFO staffer quickly drafted an "answer."

JOHNSON'S DEVIOUS ATTACK ON NFO

The government seeks to enjoin farmers from exercising their con-stitutional rights in a most devious way, one that strikes at the very heart of the right of American citizens to bargain collectively for economic justice at the market place.

The issue in this holding action has been clear cut. Farm milk prices have hardly changed in 15 years—the cost of producing that milk has gone up several times.

For many months, NFO has led the fight for higher income at the dairy farm. It would have taken the Johnson administration only a stroke of the pen to adjust the minimum milk price. All the dumping of milk could have been avoided if the Johnson administration would have yielded only slightly. But all fair warnings were spurned.

NFO is well aware of the fact that farmers are quitting the dairy business in droves. In Wisconsin alone, some 84 herds are closed out each week. During the past year, the slaughter of dairy animals reached fantastic proportions.

It was thus as a matter of high public duty that NFO called a holding action. All we wanted was two cents a quart more at the farm. But the hostility to fair prices for farmers proved to be durable. Its durability was attained—in some measure—by the administration's backing.

The Johnson administration has not met the problem head on. Instead, it has elected to serve the farmers with an injunction to stop alleged violence and coercion. This approach is not only devious— it violates common sense.

Public order is adequately protected by laws in every state. No injunction is necessary to tell people not to commit acts of violence. It is already against the law. As everyone knows, the NFO leadership has acted in good faith. It has instructed its local officials to assist law enforcement agencies in every case of law violation. So far there have been no such incidents that have come to the attention of the national headquarters. Scattered reports have been traced out and found to be without substance.

This puts the issuance of an injunction into a new light. Mere foundationless accusations are sufficient for an injunction. This enables industry to break any holding action or even the efforts of farmers to organize simply by putting into circulation some baseless rumor and cementing it into place with an injunction.

Since this injunction comes at a time when the holding action effort is reaching its maximum effect, since it comes exactly when the industry can no longer stand the pressure, we can only lay the burden of blame for this abuse of authority exactly where it belongs. No legalistic doubletalk can absolve the Johnson administration. No farmer can overlook this action—directed from on high—which contains the subtle seeds of destruction for the NFO effort.

This high-handed method would never be attempted against labor. Indeed, there have been more incidents in one square block during industrial srikes than there have been in 27 states during the NFO holding action.

This dictatorial method has never been used on business and industrial organization.

But for farmers—the rules go out the window. Farmers have held milk while obeying the law, and now they feel the heavy hand of the law. But processors have violated every regulation on the books during this holding action. They have watered and diluted the milk —they have used reconstituted milk, Class 2 milk and called it Class 1. Anything that was white has served as milk, and the law winked at it.

If this injunction suit is not beaten back, a terrible precedent is automatically established.

Labor unions can take fair warning that this arbitrary and devious attack is but a stepping stone toward annihilation of the working man's right to collective bargaining.

Business can take fair warning that its days of organizing and defending its interest are numbered.

But the greatest tragedy of all is still to come. Individually, farmers were slaughtering their animals because of low income before NFO led the holding action. Individually, they will again take up this method. A slaughtered dairy cow makes a holding action look pale.

President Johnson should think long and hard about this day's work. He is more upset by two cents for farmers than about farm families fed into city slums.

This injunction suit goes beyond mere denunciation. It cries out for battle—and battle it we will.

The draft was never used. For one thing it was too long. Later, some of the material was chopped up and sent through the verbal sausage machine. When it all came out shortly after 5:00 p.m. Staley issued this message:

March 29, 1967

This action that the federal government is taking against farmers to break the NFO milk holding action involves the right of farmers. The NFO has never condoned or advocated any illegal acts and it never will. Our records will prove this. The real heart of the federal action is to stop farmers from bargaining and thereby gaining fair prices for their products. This comes at a time when we were winning

*and were getting close to achieving gains that farmers so badly need
and for which they have made sacrifices. The reason that the holding
action had to be called was because the Johnson administration had
turned its back on the American farmers and left them as the forgotten
part of our nation's economy.*

*I feel this action is really in line with the Johnson administrations
policy to keep farm prices low. This action is not just against NFO,
it's against farmers, and it is going to be the test of whether or
not farmers are going to be deprived of fair prices through the
action of the Johnson administration. It come at a time when we
are close to winning. I know that all farmers will be shocked by
this type of action. The public should realize that this does not just
affect NFO members but every farmer in this nation. Of course we
will comply with any court order but we will fight with all the
strength that we can muster to protect the rights of the American
farmer, and we have no intention of quitting our fight for the farmers.*

A fiercely crew-cut marshall left Des Moines. He arrived at Corning in the early evening. He spoke briefly with a Corning policeman
before entering what NFO Public Information regular Hugh Crane
called "the den of lions." The marshall waited while Staley finished
a phone call, and uncharacteristically showed the service document
to Detroit-based newsman Jim Anderson, who just happend to be
in Corning.

The document was served on Oren Lee Staley at 7:20 p.m.

The ceremony was cordial and formal. Staley remained seated
behind a cluttered desk, shirt collar open. "I understand you have
something for me," the NFO chief said. The marshall presented his
credentials. He opened the document and pointed out its chief con-
tents. "You have until 1:00 p.m. to answer," he pointed out, "but I
guess you know more about that than I do."

Staley smiled. He probably did. He had been on long phone calls
arranging for counsel in Des Moines. NFO had engaged former Iowa
Attorney General Larry Scalise and had talked with him shortly
before the marshall arrived. He had been told about the allegations,
that NFO was in violation of the Sherman Anti-Trust Act, that as
early as 1964, NFO members had used coercion and intimidation to
monopolize the trade. The charge gave great credit to NFO for
disrupting distribution in the milk channels.

As soon as the marshall left, NFO leaders who had manned
stations throughout the long holding action filled Staley's office.

The implications were clear. They had been stated concisely in the first UPI wire service release.

There was a lull, and suddenly everything was in motion again. Herb Goodman handed a note to Staley, and Staley handed it to a typist.

"We think there is some central warehouse storage available in Wichita, Kansas, perhaps some in Colorado and some in Kansas City. Willis Rowell is checking out this possibility and will be calling back. Probably storage rates include 22 cents in and out charge and 14 cents per month per cwt. for cheese and powder. Storage rates for butter and evaporated milk will likely be 20 cents in and out and 10 cents per month per hundredweight."

Everyone was working on Phase 2. Questioned, Staley told a newsman that the next phase—Phase 3 would be victory.

But first, there was "the law."

BACKGROUND

---

the law

THE QUESTION POSED by the Justice Department when it charged NFO with being in violation of the anti-trust statutes of the United States was more enigmatic than the charges themselves. How could an organization such as NFO be in violation of the anti-trust laws when the Capper-Volstead Act specifically exempted farm organizations from the provision of anti-trust?

There is a big difference between newspaper headline and legal detail. Yet legal detail ultimately rules, even though headlines cloud the issue. A review of the quite clouded situation suggested that NFO was on sound ground.

The Capper-Volstead Act became law on February 18, 1922. It was called "An act to authorize association of producers of agricultural products." The Act came into being because of the over-abundant confusion that revolved around the Clayton Act, just as the Clayton Act had been passed to clear up problems growing out of the Sherman Anti-Trust Act.

To understand the growth of anti-monopoly law, one must look back to the fountainhead of capital economics. The foundation premise of a capital economy requires freedom from restraint of trade. In plain language, to restrain trade meant to reduce competition. The old English common law provided the base for the legal attitude in America. Yet it is a matter of record that the law always allowed bona fide partnerships, despite the fact that such arrangement obviously reduced the number of traders. The erosion of "freedom from restraint of trade" has gone on ever since. There was a time when English law prohibited *forestallings, engrossing and regrating,* quaint terms for middlemen activities in commodities. The general idea was to keep the bridge between primary producers and consumers as short as possible. Yet the last remnants of the law against middlemen went down the drain in 1844 because Parliament considered repeal "favorable to development of trade."

There was an Iowa case in 1913 which involved a cooperative. The association had included in its bylaws a five cent penalty clause, one to be invoked against farmers who broke ranks and sold to any competitor of the association. The Iowa Supreme Court held against the farmers, and the concept that prevailed was the same one that caused Parliament to elevate the middleman above the farmer as early as 1772 and as late as 1844. The same thing happened to a grain cooperative in Colorado. After that, cases piled up, all to the same effect.

Law is an abstraction. But those who write laws are men, and men respond to political pressure. The old Granger movement knew this and bargained mightily in a day and age when farmers still had the power to bargain for their votes. Suddenly, in the second and third decade of the present century, state legislatures started writing co-op laws, and courts started rewriting decisions. In Iowa, the Supreme Court upheld the right of an association formed under the cooperative act passed in 1921 to liquidated damages because the cooperative act "is as much a declaration of public policy as the earlier statute referring to pools and trusts."

Not all decisions at law have been clear cut. Judges are human, and they frequently read into a law more than they read out of it. Thus there have been cases in Illinois, New York and Alabama in which the possibility of farmers operating in restraint of trade was viewed as an absurdity, even though the cooperatives contained penalty clauses.

When ideas clash, there finally emerges a consensus. Over a period of time, state lawmaking bodies across the country wrote laws against restraint of trade, and farmers—or primary producers—were exempt. Among those grassroots legislators, there was an appreciation of the fact that the primary producer was indeed that—a primary producer. He added wealth. Unlike the insurance man or the trader, he did not profit by buying cheap and selling dear, but by creating. Thus the language of the Illinois law of 1893 declared that "the provisions of this act shall not apply to agricultural products while in the hand of the producer or raiser."

Anti-trust as it affects famers presents a clouded picture when viewed in terms of history. Courts have frequently dealt with the general idea on a brush fire basis. As a consequence, the growth of anti-trust on a common law basis turned into a hopeless mess. (Common law is essentially "case law," or law based on a previous ruling.)

In 1890 Congress passed the Sherman Anti-Trust Act, the first section of which reads as follows:

"Every contract, combination in the form of trust or otherwise, conspiracy, in restraint of trade or commerce in any Territory of the United States or of the District of Columbia, or in restraint of trade between any such Territory and another, or between any such Territory or Territories and any State, or States or the District of Columbia, or with foreign nations, or between the District of Columbia and any State or States or foreign nations, is hereby declared to be illegal . . ."

At the time the Sherman Act was under consideration, an amendment was offered:

"Provided, That this act shall not be construed to apply to any arrangements, agreements or combinations between laborers made with a view of lessening the number of hours of their labor, or of increasing their wages; nor to any arrangements, agreements, associations, or combinations among person engaged in horticulture or agriculture made with the view of enhancing the price of their own agricultural or horticultural products."

This amendment was defeated.

The Sherman Act gave rise to some curious rulings.

1. *the rule of reason*

This had been anticipated, as writers of the Upton Sinclair, Ida Tarbell and Frank Norris school less than vaguely hinted. Thurman Arnold didn't even hint. Writing in *The Folklore of Capitalism*, he noted that "The anti-trust laws were the greatest encouragement to the forming of the great corporations." Only the big operators could survive the legal entanglements foisted on business by such legislation. Not even a century later, John Kenneth Galbraith was forced to observe that "mature corporations" were secure. The laws made it so. Written for the oligarchy by the oligarchy to prevent aspiring corporations from breaking into the circle, both the Sherman and Clayton laws did exactly what they were supposed to do, even though Theodore Roosevelt could take false pride in being a trust-buster. Politically, the anti-trust laws were perfect for Theodore Roosevelt. The people thought one thing. The trusts thought another, Both were happy. Colonel Ely Garrison had every right to remark in his memoirs that "Wall Street had no cause for hysteria at the election of Theodore Roosevelt, for any serious student of history knows that the Department of Justice's investigations of Northern Securities and Standard Oil (Kuhn-Loeb interests) were initiated before Roosevelt's election and carried on without his approval."

It may be other than accident that the term "muck-raker" for people like Upton Sinclair was coined by William Loeb Jr., Roosevelt's private secretary.

It is axiomatic that "the Supreme Court follows the election returns," and it is eqaully axiomatic to add, "of ten or twelve years ago." The curious rulings in anti-trust law merely reaffirmed the character of the men, and those who appointed them, even though giants have appeared from time to time.

In a viable democracy, a refusal to rule or to rule improperly does not diminish the necessity for right reason. As Mr. Felix Frankfurther, speaking about denial of a *writ of certiorari,* correctly noted, no case vanishes because the Court has refused it. Thus big cases are rarely refused, even though the historical moment for an appropriate ruling is not to be had.

By 1967 the breakdown of anti-trust law was complete. Indeed, Anti-Trust was considered the deadest division in the Justice Department. Earlier, the Federal Trade Commission had tried to block giants like Procter and Gamble, General Foods and National Tea from expanding. The Justice Department flatly refused to do anything. Attorney General Katzenbach and Anti-Trust Chief Donald Turner were politely pointing out that the sheer size wasn't illegal.

So size went on its way, and the Federal Trade Commission could testify before the Food Commission in all frankness that within ten years 200 companies would control two-thirds of America's manufacturing.

The "rule of reason" has brought on the developments.

There was the "rule of reason" in which United States Steel was not found to be in violation of the law even though the corporation controlled 50% of the steel industry, and even though size "is an earmark of monopoly power."

Later, in the Chicago Board of Trade *v.* United States case, the Court decided that "The true test of legality is whether the restraint imposed is such as merely regulates and perhaps thereby promotes competition of whether it is such as may suppress or even destroy competition."

Through the years, the "rule of reason" was invoked time and time again. There was the glass manufacturers' case in which unions and management worked out arrangements for stabilizing the industry. The Court held that "The fact that the parties to an agreement eliminate competition between themselves is not enough to condemn it." In effect, this gave the green light to exchange of information among those engaged in the same line of business through their trade associations. At the same time, the Court has frequently refused to permit the "rule of reason" to allow price fixing among manufacturers.

Sherman Anti-Trust is a broad Act. But it takes Court rulings to really define the working mechanism of an Act. Thus the Sherman Act allows treble damages to private persons who are injured by violation of Sherman Anti-Trust, but the Courts have concluded that treble damages are not available to co-ops because an illegal practice has ruined a number of members.

Following the passage of the Sherman Act, as larger and larger marketing and bargaining associations were formed, the question of application of the Sherman Act to such associations claimed the attention of agricultural leaders. To clarify the situation, the Clayton Act of 1914 included its now famous Section 6:

"That the labor of a human being is not a commodity or article of commerce. Nothing contained in the anti-trust laws shall be construed to forbid the existence and operation of labor, agricultural, or horticultural organizations, instituted for the purposes of mutual help, and not having capital stock or conducted for profit, or to forbid or restrain individual members of such organzations from lawfully carrying out the legitimate objects thereof; nor shall such organizations, or the members thereof, be held or construed to be illegal combinations or conspiracies in restraint of trade, under the anti-trust laws."

2. capper-volstead

As the Courts read the Act, Clayton's Section 6 merely allowed farmers to join for mutual help without capital stock, but it did not allow them to adopt methods of doing business denied other lawful business organizations. Landmark cases included United States v. Dairy Co-op Association and United States v. King (the famous Aroostook Potato Case).

Since the Clayton Act did not really clear up the status of farm organizations, the Capper-Volstead Act came into being. The Capper-Volstead law in effect is an amendment of the anti-trust statutes.

It authorizes the elimination of competition among farmers by their acting through a cooperative. In more fundamental terms, Capper-Volstead authorizes farmers to unite in organizations that may act with the same force and effect as though all the agricultural products in question were being handled by one farmer.

The Committees of Congress that reported out the measure and the debates in Congress indicate that it was the intention of Congress that Capper-Volstead should exempt associations of farmers, when they operate along normal business lines, from the federal anti-trust statutes. In the Cape Cod Food Products *v.* National Cranberry Association case, the Court held that "it is not unlawful under the anti-trust acts for a Capper-Volstead cooperative, such as the National Cranberry Association admittedly is, to try to acquire even 100 per cent of the market if it does it exclusively through marketing agreement approved under the Capper-Volstead Act."

Careful inspection of the bounds imposed by law suggests that only "abnormal conduct" might subject an organization to the jurisdiction of the Department of Justice for violation of the anti-trust laws.

This explained why the government had gone the "violence" route in trying to nail down NFO. Only by making a case to the effect that NFO leadership organized and acted in collusion to create violence, and that the leadership relied on violence, could the Justice Department bring NFO under anti-trust as commonly construed. In short the government had to construct an "abnormal conduct'" case out of a few sporadic incidents that may or may not have involved individual NFO members.

The logic of law and the facts were all on NFO's side in the legal battle, but the battle had to be fought just the same. It would take a great deal of money and the best resources of talent that NFO could muster to win this fight, should the government fail to strike its colors once the holding action was over.

Thus the political use of the law and the law's abstraction figured equally in the minds of those who were heading for a Des Moines Courtroom appearance on MHA + 15.

NARRATIVE

---

holding action

mha + 15

A COURT APPEARANCE has a measure of drama about it. In front of the bench, the human process becomes abstract in the extreme. To one who had recently walked across milk-soaked acres, there was something fantastic and unreal about it all.

A case had to be heard on strictly legal lines, but all the newsmen and lawyers knew that a holding action came in several measures. Former Iowa Attorney General, Larry Scalise, now NFO's Iowa-based counsel, could only argue the legal points, and in the complaint styled United States of America, Plantiff, *v.* The National Farmers' Organization, Incorporated, Defendant, these seemed simple enough.

One of the government's several helpers, Edward R. Kenney, got to his feet. "The United States of America, plaintiff, by its attorneys acting under the direction of the Attorney General of the United States, brings this civil action to obtain equitable relief against the above-named defendant and complains and alleges . . ." The government attorney droned on, but the allegations were pretty thin. They took a long time getting to the point. Newsmen sat in the spectator's sections taking notes. NFO President Oren Lee Staley, flanked by Attorneys Lee Sinclair and Larry Scalise, listened intently.

"A substantial portion of the production and sale of milk in the United States occurs in the states of Colorado, Illinois, Iowa, Indiana, Kansas, Kentucky, Michigan, Minnesota, Missouri, Nebraska, New Jersey, New York, North Dakota, Ohio, Oklahoma, South Dakota, (hereinafter referred to as 'the marketing area states')," the government attorney said, still reading from the legal petition. He went on to detail how in 1965 the marketing area states produced over 82.9 billion pounds of milk, or approximately 66% of the nation's supply. Much of it moved across state lines on the way to market.

There were a few nods in the courtroom, but so far very little had been revealed. Every junior clerk knew these details, and most NFO farmers had them on the tips of their fingers. So far the government buildup had been less than syllogistic. The logical deficit came in for fuller treatment in point No. 8.

NFO, the allegation charged, "in efforts to increase the price for agricultural products received by its members" had held production from the market. "The success of a withholding action is dependent on the withholding from the market of a substantial percentage of the agricultural product involved," the document said.

From this allegation flowed other charges.

According to the legal document, NFO had pressed its 1964 effort forward by threatening, intimidating, harassing and committing acts of personal injury and property damage to non-members in order to restrain non-members from selling livestock during the holding operation. The same *modus operendi* was used on truckers, the government said. Further, the government charged, there were agreements and understandings with non-member farmers.

At counsel's table, attorneys were taking notes. Obviously the government was proceeding on the basis of at least two errors. It was assuming that it took great shifts in supply to affect a market, and it was assuming that NFO members were dumping in order to short the supply, rather than gain contracts and adjustments in the institutional arrangements for marketing.

Those who knew the score smiled. A few observers were of the opinion that the production of less than a majority could hardly matter, and it had been openly stated that double the NFO membership would still leave the farmers a space-age distance away from equaling the monopoly status enjoyed by the Big 9 dairy companies. However, NFO leaders and counsel knew differently. They knew that it took only 1 or 2% of the production to affect the price structure as such dramatically. Government planners who had been busily knocking farm prices downward to offset inflation also knew this.

In March 1966 all milk at wholesale reached $4.54 as compared to $4.17 during the same month a year earlier. "You should take immediate action to increase the cheddar cheese [import] quota for the current quota year ending June 30, 1966, by 926,700 pounds without awaiting the formal review and recommendations of the Tariff Commission . . ." wrote Secretary Freeman to President Johnson in a letter dated March 31, 1966. A total of 926,700 pounds of cheddar may not have sounded like much, but the planners knew that it would not take much to keep farm prices from attaining parity.

Indeed, farmers had to been blind and forgetful in order to escape knowing what was being done to farm prices, all by manipulating that 1%.

Indeed, when John F. Kennedy was a Senator he stated before a group of textile manufacturers: "Often you will find that while the import item may represent only 1% of a given commodity in proportion to the domestic production, the fact is that this 1% quoted at lower prices can seriously disrupt an entire industry."

When hogs started reaching for parity a half year earlier, it didn't take the planners long to knock prices back again. Economic Advisor Gardner Ackley told how in an interview on the *Today Show*, March 10, 1966. ". . . I mentioned the fact that increase in supplies of pork depend on the difference between the prices of hogs and the price of corn, and we're trying to hold down the price of corn. The government acquired large stocks of corn in the past price support operation. Now we're releasing them into the market."

In 1966, imports of dairy products as a percent of U. S. production reached 2.33%. A year earlier, in 1965, imports as a percent of domestic production stood at .72%. Thus a jump from 900 million pounds of milk equivalent in 1965 to 2,800 million pounds milk equivalent in 1966 was enough to offset the 3,943 million pounds drop in production that farmers going out of business had accounted for.

If the 1961 testimony of Robert G. Lewis of the USDA was to be taken seriously, then a great deal of weight had to be given to his statement: "One pound of imported cheese can materially interfere with the price support program."

If one pound of imports could drive domestic production to the shelter of the support level, then a few pounds of spilled milk had to have an immediate effect on the domestic supply, ergo price, even without NFO contracts. No one can argue the point.

Disrupting the farm price level downward, unfortunately, was the name of the game, and farmers were on deck for a last inning. The government was still pitching.

A second great error came to the fore. Any sociologist worth his salt knew that violence wrote no ticket other than oppression for a minority. In Algeria, where less than 10% of the white population was on top, and 90% natives were below, there was perhaps some anatomical justification for violence on strategic grounds, (the so-called heroic violence). But in America, where 10% Negroes were on the bottom with 90% whites on top, different sociological ground rules prevailed. Bayard Rustin and Martin Luther King were aware of this, and thus wisely counseled against violence. A minority could only bring oppression down on itself, because no majority would endure for long disruption of the social order by a minority, whatever the cause. NFO officials had discussed the point many times. If the Negro could not drive his case forward with violence, then neither could the farmer, who was even more of a minority. That the government hinged its case on this flimsy pin spoke of breath-taking ignorance, ignorance excusable in an uneducated militant, but not in a Justice Department lawyer or a literate farm leader.

The Justice Department lawyer was reading nervously:

"Beginning on or about March 15, 1967 and continuing thereafter up to and including the date of the filing of this complaint, defendant has attempted to monopolize the hereinbefore described trade and commerce in milk in violation of Section 2 of the Sherman Act. Said unlawful attempt to monopolize is continuing and will continue unless the relief hereinafter prayed for is granted."

In support of the government's case, an affidavit was read into the record. An attorney, Hugh P. Morrison Jr., had gone into the dairy country. He had investigated conditions, talked to farmers, and concluded that the NFO effort was designed to achieve monopoly status through means other than legal organization. In a word, there had been incidents and violence, and now the safety of the Amercian people required a temporary restraining order against violence.

Larry Scalise was on his feet. He asked the court to withhold its ruling until NFO could file briefs. He charged that the affidavit lacked "clarity" and "specifics." NFO had, after all, instructed its members to avoid violence. That was a matter of record. So far no evidence had been introduced to even suggest that orders for systematic violence came from NFO headquarters. "If there is any violence," Scalise argued, "then the individual, not the organization, should be restrained."

Judge Stephenson had been on the bench a long time. In legal parlance, he was not subservient to political pressure, because a judge's independence varies directly with the length of time he has been on the bench. Yet there was little he could do about this case. Law and custom more or less required a temporary restraining order simply because the government had asked for it. The burden of justice thus rested with the government's abuse of power, not with the Judge's refusal to rule out the request.

"This is only a temporary restraining order. I see no harm in enjoining the NFO both as individuals and as an organization from committing acts of violence," the Judge said.

The order was for ten days. In ten days it would be extended by mutual consent of the parties involved.

1. *the lip-service politician*

That was all.

The group around counsel's table marched out of the court, down the marble steps and was picked up by the lens of waiting cameras. There was calm anger in Staley's voice. He reiterated some parts of the statement he had given the press the day before. "LBJ has just given lip service to farmers and has promised them parity of income but has taken few steps to recognize their problem." He accused Johnson of having adopted a cheap food policy which meant low farm prices. Referring to the government's law suit, Staley said: "No decision by a Cabinet officer of this nature would be made, in our opinion, without the stamp of approval from LBJ. This was an old LBJ tactic —to confuse the issue and cause members to scatter and break our efforts."

While TV cameras spun film past the lens, Staley shot barbs into the administration. He never said "President Johnson," or "the President." The references were all to LBJ, the lip-service politician who had bombed out the NFO effort at a time when it was going over the top. He nailed down the credibility gap—the very suggestion that the Justice Department would bring such a flimsy lawsuit without the blessing of the White House. Staley was about as angry as anyone had ever recalled seeing him. He could point out that the holding action would continue, but he, more than anyone else, knew that the holding action had been bombed, and the bomb had been lobbed right out of the round office in the White House.

More important, he pointed out that Judge Stephenson was speaking in a legalistic sense, whereas the holding action was being fought out on economic, psychological and political fronts. Observers were quick to see that the "harm" of the restraining order and the lawsuit was accomplished the minute news hit the wire services.

From any logical vantage point, one could be allowed to doubt that the government had enough of a case to go to trial. *The Wall Street Journal* promptly reported that one Justice Department official said that there wasn't any precise precedent for the NFO case "because the NFO situation is novel."

The NFO situation, indeed, was novel.

2.　*this abuse of authority*

The NFO was organized under the Capper-Volstead Act, and the organization was thus exempt from the Sherman Act. That is why the Justice Department had to hang its hat on a worm-eaten peg—that of "violence." But there had been little violence. In 20 of the 25 states there had been no incidents. Not only that, public order was adequately protected by laws in every state. No injunction was necessary to tell people not to commit acts of violence. It was already against the law. The NFO leadership had acted in good faith. It had instructed its local officials to assist law enforcement agencies in every case of law violation. The scattered reports that materialized in the press were in the main traced out and found to be without substance.

This puts the issuance of an injunction into a new light. Mere foundationless accusations were seemingly sufficient for a political injunction. This enabled government and its big money cronies to attempt to break any holding action simply by asking for an injunction. On the courthouse steps, Staley hit his points with sledgehammer blows.

Within a few hours, the headlines were friendly and harsh across the nation, depending on the type of newspaper. Few ignored Staley's claim that the injunction carried "LBJ's stamp of approval."

3.　*i have just come from the courtroom*

In a few hours, NFO's own news service went into motion. NFO audio coordinator Don Mach had accompanied Staley to Des Moines. With the hearing hardly an hour old, Staley was busy in the attorney's office cutting a master tape under Mach's direction. It was a quiet, sincere report to the membership on exactly what had happened in the Des Moines Courtroom. Staley spoke off the cuff, and a little nervously. "I have just come from the courtroom . . ."

It took hardly a quarter of an hour to cut the message. After Don Mach's cutoff signal came down, Staley stepped outside, to walk down the hall, to stand under a portrait of Governor Harold Hughes and to read with amusement the Jack Bender cartoon of Scalise and Wilson reaching for the Democratic nomination for Attorney General (with the state's Central Committee kicking the ladder out from under Wilson). The framed Constitution on the wall spoke grand and pure ideals but on the firing line of life you dealt with men, not abstract sentences on parchment. Staley took one last look at a framed portrait of President and Mrs. John F. Kennedy before he entered the "studio" again.

From a legal point of view, the tape was "go." By evening, fast electronic duplicators had copied the master tape. Labels were quickly attached, and, shortly, audio reports were on their way to all the NFO supervisors in holding action offices across the country.

Across the country, NFO members were in motion. "It's a sad day for the American farmer when the United States government will take this kind of action against him when he is trying to win a fair price for his product," Minnesota State Chairman George Matson told the *Minneapolis Star*.

Also, from across the country, details were invading the Nerve Center. "Grafton Milk Company, Grafton, North Dakota, forced to ration its milk. The milk supply has been reduced by 25 to 30%, according to Luther Williamson, the owner of the firm . . ." Someone took down the details, stacks of them, and someone even bothered to note the change in tempo of headlines.

PROCESSOR SIGNS NEW NFO CONTRACT,

reported the Jordan, Minnesota *Independent*, and the *Daily Sentinel Tribune* at Bowling Green, Ohio wrapped up the day with

NFO PHASE 2 NOW IN ACTION.

Processors signing and Phase 2—they were the sum and substance of workaday MHA + 15 in all the holding action states, but hardly anyone mentioned either signups or Phase 2. All eyes were on the Des Moines courtroom. And even while the government was killing the NFO effort, the perceptive observers could visualize what the holding action had accomplished. Sometimes the accomplishment came on as an idea.

NFO HAS SOLUTION BURLEY COULD DUPLICATE

said a headline in the Russell Springs, Kentucky *Times-Journal*. Here and there results were being racked up now.

KYANA UPS PRICE TO FARMERS 12 CENTS

was the big headline in Kentucky on MHA + 15, and it would certainly have rated top priority in any newscast except for one thing. More money at the farm in Kentucky indicated to all who wished to see that NFO was going over the top, but the news died a-borning because of the government's injunction.

4. *now farmers have their choice*

When NFO President Oren Lee Staley arrived at the organization's headquarters in Corning that evening, he quietly informed the NFO regulars that the government had failed to stop the holding action, but that a temporary restraining order had been issued "to prevent violence." Later *NFO Reporter*, the organization's house magazine, correctly observed that the "restraining order merely reaffirmed existing laws against violence, intimidation and harassment." But everyone realized that such an action by the government has great "eyewash effect".

Vice President Erhard Pfingsten coined a term that other NFO members quickly adopted: "Well," Pfingsten said, "now farmers have their choice. They can join NFO or LBJ."

The slogan had a harsh ring to it, one that inside sources in Washington said "Johnson didn't like."

THE ENDINGS

---

revolution gone silent

revolution gone silent

IN THE NERVE CENTER, the phones quit ringing.

They didn't stop all at once.

First, farmers in New York, New Jersey, Pennsylvania and Illinois started shipping milk. In other states, farmers stopped dumping milk and continued building the Phase 2 program. But there was the cold fact that in many areas farmers could not store processed production.

Stung by the restraining order, NFO announced it would urge members to sell dairy cows for slaughter. At Corning, Meat Commodity Department Director Bill Lashmett and his staffers were busily setting up some 60 collection points at which farmers could unload dairy cows. It was a token effort, a protest effort. Most members would sell one or two cows, not an entire herd.

The calls were no longer coming, not from Georgia, Florida, Oklahoma, Colorado, and a few other states. But from South Dakota came word that Staley's tapes had been picked up under false pretenses.

Across the country, the weather warmed. Farmers went to the fields and found in the anodyne of hard work some relief from the tension of living with the unlivable. As they greeted each other, they said, "Now you have your choice, Join NFO or LBJ."

1. *confrontation*

LBJ had to get off the hook fast. It had been generally conceded that there would be marketing order hearings as soon as the action was over, that there would be curbs on imports, but the USDA and the government seemed committed to the proposition that "the NFO must receive no credit."

313

A realistic view of events clearly indicated that this would be impossible. NFO was going to get credit where it counted—among farmers. The Kansas City area threw in the towel early and canceled out seasonal price declines. Starting April 11, marketing order hearings were held in Denver, St. Louis, Cleveland, and Washington, D. C., with prices of milk in some 70 order areas to be affected.

The market order increases helped a little.

Suddenly, a new phenonemon appeared on the farm scene. Bureau people came from Washington for shirtsleeve conferences to determine whether farmers were unhappy. Secretary Freeman ran into this unhappiness at Hutchinson, Kansas where NFO members more than carried the ball, and where Fred Killian spoke for the lot of them when he reminded the Secretary that "at least we have the gumption to dump our milk," and was cheered when he added that the processors "beat us down and we don't have a price." Whether Freeman hoped to emerge unscratched may have been open to question in Washington, but not in the corn belt. NFOers knew that there would be a real confrontation long before the three-day trip to Kansas, Iowa, Illinois and Indiana was over.

It came at Ames, Iowa. NFO Vice President Erhard Pfingsten had taken command of the NFO group and assigned differerent points that various farmers were to bring out. From the start it became apparent that the meeting and all the floor mikes had been thoroughly rigged. The *modus operendi* called for each floor mike to be cut off the minute a question was asked. That way Freeman could respond with impunity.

Other roadblocks had materialized. Certain objections were being voiced against Pfingsten even posing questions to the Secretary. Freeman's staffers argued that Pfingsten was a national officer and that this was a meeting for state people, and that therefore he could not be extended the use of a mike during the shirtsleeve affair. Pfingsten, however, was a member of NFO's Iowa Board. The various organizations had all been assured a hearing. Pfingsten put it pretty plain. He had, he said, been designated as spokesman for the Iowa State Board, and therefore if anyone would speak for Iowa he would do so. If the Secretary wanted to go on record as denying the Iowa NFO an opportunity to speak, Pfingsten said, "I will accept that, otherwise I will expect to speak." Pfink got nodding approval, but efforts to block his appearance continued. Through the long session Pfink was kept a safe holler away from the mike. Finally Freeman said he would take two more questions. That's when Pfink "grabbed the mike and simply took it away from them," Iowa Board member Ken Johnson later recalled.

"This is the second one of these leg-pulling farces that I've attended," Pfingsten came on. "I'm glad to see that the farmers here are more inclined to speak out than their leaders are."

Pfingsten had a little speaking out of his own to do. He was quick to point out the fact that USDA was rigging figures when it compared August, a low marketing period, with the high marketing period then in progress. "So again we're being led to believe that we're producing too much and for that reason can't have any prices."

Pfingsten was used to applause, and he got plenty of it that day. After one big round, he touched on another bit of doublethink. "We've been told about the legislation we need, and yet we're not using the legislation we have. Every commodity that we do have a program on authorizes 90% supports, and yet no commodity is supported at that level. For those of you who believe that supply and demand will do your job, I would like to point out that under the LBJ administration it isn't even allowed to work. We did get into a balance of supply last fall, and our prices started moving up. LBJ and his puppets immediately went to work driving those farm prices down." Applause came on strong as Pfingsten ended that sentence. Here is a transcript of what happened next:

FREEMAN: In all fairness now, when you make those kind of charges —will you please say how this was done? I was not a party to it, and I really don't know how it happened.

PFINGSTEN: I'm about to do that . . . The farmers were blamed for the inflation at the time. I think this has been brought up before. I think you yourself made a statement—though you've tried to explain it—that you were delighted that farm prices were heading downward. Or maybe it was a slip of the tongue. I don't know. But subsequent actions lead me to believe that that's exactly what you were looking for. So [the government] dumped 250 million bushels of corn on the market last spring . . . I'd like to have explained how dumping that amount on the market raised the price any.

The Department of Agriculture raised the quotas on cheese imports. Now while you've constantly said that you couldn't cut them without changes in legislation, I'd like to know what part of the law demands that we raise the imports. This happened at a time when the price of milk was moving upward.

The Department of Commerce . . . put [an] embargo on hide exports. We've been told it couldn't have an effect of more than 25 cents a hundred on cattle, yet at that time the price of cattle did move downward $2.

You claim that there was no pork—or foreign beef—fed to our armed services. I'll accept that if you want to make a liar out of the press, because I read daily in the papers that it had been done.

Then, last fall, we were told that we needed to increase our wheat allotment by 32% . . . Yet the increase is being supported at 50% of parity. If we need the production, then why don't we get the price? [Applause.] The same thing happened to the feed grain program. We were asked to put 30% of our base acres into corn, yet we are denied the 30 cents a bushel direct payment on the increase. If we need it, then why can't we get paid for it? [Applause.]

The Department very successfully has used figures in driving prices down. The farmers' intentions to plant . . . the increased acres . . . were announced in December for the first time ever. Why? This announcement had a depressing effect.

Then, as has been pointed out, we found several million head of cattle [to report] at about the time it looked like the prices were going up, and this information sent them down again.

We're doing a lot of talking here about cooperatives doing the job, getting farmers together, and yet when they do get together we have the injunction against the NFO. Now I do not accept your explanation that it was for violence, because violence was practically non-existent, and the only two incidents named in the [government's petition] were actually committed against our farmers. The injunction did include that in 19 states we had sufficient control of the milk to cause unlawful interstate hauling, so LBJ had an injunction issued against us. He apparently wasn't interested in going after the people who were doing the unlawful hauling. So I'd say, boys, if you want to really help the situation, get LBJ off the farmer's back, [applause] I'd suggest to you, sell your milk and dump LBJ [laughter, applause].

After that, Secretary Freeman returned to Washington and assured the powers that be that farmers were certainly unhappy. And NFO was blamed for focusing national attention on the plight of farmers.

In short order, some 63 more shirtsleeve meetings were set up throughout the farm country. Singly and in waves the shock troops of USDA came out of Washington to keep the natives from getting too restless.

2. *secondary objectives*

Perhaps most important, and certainly most overlooked, was the fact that countless thousands of people turned 180 degrees in their attitude toward the farmer. Uninformed citizens frequently turned in horror from "food being spoiled," but the answers from clergymen, editors, and intellectual advisors were damning in their finality. Dale Francis, writing in *Our Sunday Visitor,* a national Catholic weekly, made an observation Dr. E. W. Mueller of the Lutheran Council had made earlier. Wrote Francis:

"Like the rest of you I've heard protests that it is a sin to dump milk when there are starving people all over the world. The milk should be given to the poor, the critics say.

"Yet labor is labor. I don't recall hearing the suggestion that striking carpenters and construction workers should be using their time during a strike building homes for people who have inadequate housing. I don't remember that anyone has suggested that workers on strike should be placing plumbing or electricity into homes that are inadequately supplied with modern facilities.

"When the day comes that all men on strike use their idle time working for others without pay then I'll take seriously the suggestion that there is something sinful about dairy farmers dumping milk."

The public understood. And, belatedly the government said it wanted to understand.

At the end of the holding action several secondary objectives had been achieved.

• *Imports of dairy products would be curtailed. Secretary Freeman, who had been reported unwilling to ask for a clamp on imports while the NFO holding action was on, broke silence and made the formal request.*

• *Informed spokesmen in agriculture were all agreed that there would be a price hike for milk producers. Marketing orders had been jarred sufficiently to force hearings.*

• *The law of supply and demand had been repealed. The fraud of rigging prices for farmers while shouting "surplus" had been effectively exposed. The federal marketing orders require farmers to be paid for Class 1 if their production went into Class 1. During the holding action Class 2 became Class 1. Therefore, farmers who got the blend price based on some of their milk going into manufactured products were entitled to collect for the full amount that ended up*

HOW MILK HOLDING ACTION INFLUENCED BUYERS

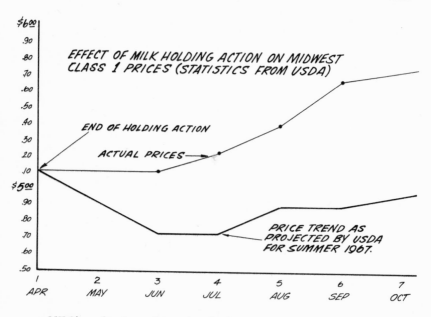

EFFECT OF MILK HOLDING ACTION ON MIDWEST
CLASS 1 PRICES (STATISTICS FROM USDA)

END OF HOLDING ACTION

ACTUAL PRICES——

PRICE TREND AS
PROJECTED BY USDA
FOR SUMMER 1967.

NFO's relentless drive for higher milk prices continued to score during the months since the holding action on milk was first called. In a sense, this graph is a scoresheet. It depicts Class 1 milk prices as projected by the USDA for the summer and fall of 1967. NFO's milk holding action changed the program. The graph takes up the price situation at the end of the holding action, and charts the actual course of price movements.

as Class 1. So said the law. "Who will enforce the law?" Only the people can enforce the law.

3. *no price, no production*

In the meantime the fight had to go on. NFO President Oren Lee Staley said as much when he issued a leader's letter:

". . . There is no turning back . . . we must not and will not turn back because this is the effort to fight the battle on all fronts for all commodities . . ."

It was NFO's determination not to turn back that spilled 35,400 farmers into the Des Moines Auditorium the afternoon of August 16, 1967, "to pick up the battle where we left off with the milk holding action," and 35,400 strong the NFOers voted to build for an all commodities holding action big enough to shut down the nation's agricultural plant. Staley drew a standing ovation as he outlined the "definite recommendations of the NFO Board of Directors," which included a "no price, no production" policy, and a resolution to "carry it out step by step."

Some of these steps were clearly visible, some were not. There was, for instance, the matter of the anti-trust suit, and the government was sending men into the field to gather evidence. They would find nothing of significance. At headquarters, NFO had a bundle of affidavits from sheriffs in 85% of NFO's counties, and these sworn statements proved that nothing had happened. No one believed that the Justice people could make a case out of nothing happening in almost all of the counties. Still, there was the lawsuit, and—face it—it took money to fight it out. NFO was not forgetting that the old I. W. W. had been "killed dead" in Court on similar charges.

Thus the big meeting for action in Des Moines telegraphed a message to Washington. Farmers would fight. They had not become disillusioned as a result of the milk holding action. The Des Moines Auditorium superintendent estimated the crowd at 35,400, and while a few newsmen might argue a few thousand one way or another, it was pretty impressive. The most discerning could visualize county-by-county meetings with NFOers and friends dropping dollar bills into barrels to fight the lawsuit, and by late fall 1967 no one doubted that NFO would come up with the money and drag all the linen through the courts.

They were unhappy enough to do that. At the meeting for action, they dovetailed this unhappiness with the similar outlook being voiced by Ed Wimmer of the National Federation of Independent Businesses, Inc. A few of the foundation terms may have been mixed up, but the fact remained that the small businessmen were talking the same language as the farmers. "If the farmer is sick," said Wimmer, "the man on Main Street is sick. If the man on Main Street is sick, Wall Street will be sick, and so will the man on Constitution Avenue."

No one doubted that the man on Constitution Avenue was watching the proceedings and when farmers departed Des Moines almost as quickly as they came their very movement wrote well defined script on the political landscape. The NFOers were a new breed of men. They did not feel ill at ease with "big" people. They did not cower under pressure. They were standing on their own hind legs. They would hold and hold and hold until the finally won.

4. *pending holding action*

NFO's 1967 convention was scheduled for December 5 and 6 in Louisville, Kentucky.

On December 4, the U. S. District Court in Des Moines dismissed the government's anti-trust suit against the NFO organization. The case was concluded on the basis of a stipulation entered into jointly by the government and NFO. There was no admission by NFO, and no finding by the Court, that any of the members had been in violation of the law.

As part of the stipulation, NFO leaders agreed the organization would provide the Anti-Trust Division of the Justice Department with "notification" of any pending holding action. No time limit was set as part of this stipulation. The NFO remained free to give this notification at any time up to the calling of the action itself.

It was also agreed that in any future government civil anti-trust suit based on the same contentions, the government would be required to file supporting affidavits of alleged facts, and that if supporting evidence satisfied the presiding judge, a preliminary injunction would be issued without opposition by the NFO. The government would not be able to ask for a temporary restraining order in future holding actions.

As part of the agreement, the government would be required to make part of any bid for a preliminary injunction a statement to the

effect that the government does not contest the legality of the holding action and peaceful picketing by at least four NFO members
at any one location. The government must notify NFO 24 hours in
advance when it contemplates court action.

5. *clearing of the air*

With this "clearing of the air," NFO members in convention, December 1967, received Vice President Hubert H. Humphrey with courtesy
and applause. Humphrey said, "I want to salute your national president." He said, "Farmers must increase their economic power in
the marketplace." He said, "Further progress toward economic equity—
economic justice—for farm people is going to depend primarily on
what they are able to do for themselves."

The Vice President of the United States thus recognized NFO.

6. *the tent of darius*

Oscar Ogg writes in *The 26 Letters* that in B.C. 512 Darius invaded
territory occupied by the Scythians. As the great warrior marched
deep into the enemy lands, a messenger arrived with "word from the
Scythians." The message came scrolled on parchment. A bird, a mouse,
a frog and three arrows had been arranged into a picture monogram,
so to speak. Darius, of course, couldn't admit he was unable to read
the idea picture, certainly not in the face of the enemy. He spent
the night in a torturous bout of ratiocination, and when he emerged
from his tent in the morning he told his generals: "Thus the enemy
writes: 'O Persians we surrender our land and our water [the frog
and the mouse]. We fly [the bird] from the might of your legions.
We are ready to turn over to you all of our arms [the arrows].' Behold,
O Persian generals, the cowardly Scythians want to surrender to us
even before they have felt the might of our swords." Darius pulled
in his guards and made ready to receive surrender on the morrow.

This miscalculation by Darius permitted one of history's first sneak
attacks. After the battle, Darius learned from a Scythian commander
what the message really meant: "O Persians, unless you can turn
yourselves into birds and fly through the air, or become as field mice
and burrow under the ground, or be as frogs and take refuge in the
swamps, you shall never escape to return to your native land but
will die by our arrows."

The Vice President of the United States was no Darius when it came to reading a crowd. The very pulse of the place told Humphrey what NFO farmers wanted to hear, but there was a great deal more to reading the message than that. The membership wanted Vice President Humphrey to read the *proof* of what NFO was all about, and this was a much tougher job than reading the tone of an audience. The *proof* meant reading the multiplier, and very few in the command tent knew how to read the multiplier these days. There was the Keynesian multiplier, and there was the farm (and raw materials) multiplier. One delivered debt that pretended to be earnings, and *one delivered income that was earned,* but hardly anyone in a top public policy position could tell the difference. By the last month of 1967, the nation could not afford a night-long session in the tent of Darius again.

the multiplier

IF THE VICE PRESIDENT of the United States read the economic record half as well as he read his Louisville NFO audience, he knew that at year-end 1967 private enterprise was earning only 55.2% of the income necessary to keep the economy in operation. He knew that loan to deposit ratios in banks were shrinking, and that the legacy of liquidity left after the Truman years had been dissipated. He knew that when cash got scarce, it tumbled faster, and that this new velocity put into motion the high cost of borrowing.

1. economic rain

The harbingers of economic rain were everywhere. The national income pie was now being sliced even worse than it had been sliced during 1929. The record was clear. During the most recent balanced period, 1949-1950, wages and interest received 64.7% of the national income, whereas the four private enterprise sectors received 35.3%.

By year-end 1967 the new trend must have alarmed even H.H.H. Wages and interest were receiving 75.7% of the national income, and the four private enterprise sectors were getting 24.3%.

Then as now the price system failed to distribute the income of the nation so that consumption could make meaningful the economy's fantastic productive power. Indeed, there was a measure of truth in what the *Energy Survey of North America* researchers had to say. Machines displaced human metabolic power, and produced more goods with less people on the payroll. And debt increased faster than either population or production. Without a concept as to the source of new earned income, industrial experts submitted to the

323

pressure to modify and expand and modernize. The economy ran out of liquidity in 1929 because it forgot that the highest multiplier stood between raw material production and national income, and that debt could only *pretend* to be earnings. Still it was the efficiacy debt creation, not new earned income, that won its spurs in the 1930s.

2. *cup of hemlock*

Even while agriculture was still drinking its cup of hemlock, John Maynard Keynes proclaimed the new creed. Pour investment into the economy, he told F.D.R., and the multiplier will repair the national income deficit.

And so, during the 1930s and 1940s, the most literate of the professors handed out a formula:

Consumer Expenditures + Investment = National Income.

There was a certain poker game causality in all this. The school-man's example might have $4,000,000 invested. This would distribute a like amount to national income under the rubrics of rent, wages, interest, profit, etc. Those who received the income, of course, would spend it, all according to a psychological "propensity" to consume. *The lower the savings, the higher the multiplier.*

The shock troops of the *new economics* picked up their training during the post WWII years. One at a time they copied into their notebooks the mechanism being recited to this day.

Take the same $4,000,000, and a propensity to consume of, say, 65%,

INCOME	EXPENDITURE
$4,000,000	$2,600,000
2,600,000	1,690,000
1,690,000	1,098,500
1,098,500	714,025
714,025	etc.

A few minutes on a Student Union calculator taught a whole generation that $4,000,000 investment in a society with a propensity to consume of 65% would account for income of $11,428,571. The multiplier became the ratio between the income increase and the amount of the new capital injection.

$$\frac{11,428,571}{4,000,000} = 2.857$$

With such a new magic in tow, why not borrow to create new capital formation? Here, after all, was a discovery as important as the wheel, was it not? By abstracting away the future, one could see great possibilities in a wonderland of debt. Writing in *A Primer on Government Spending*, Robert L. Heilbroner and Peter L. Bernstein went so far as to equate booming business with debt, lots of it. Debentures should proliferate, they said, and local and federal bonds should increase and multiply. The alternative, they said, was stagnation.

And those who saved too much simply had to go. Farmers were first in line. Indeed, Lawrence R. Klein, the American Keynesian, applauded out-migration from the farms on grounds that farmers save too much, and that they quit this tawdry practice once they become urbanized. By the late 1940s, the new economics had become Keynes turned upside down. Expansion of social programs became an end in itself. (Why would anyone save at all, argued Klein, if health and old age needs were made secure through government sponsored social programs?) A low propensity to save meant a high propensity to consume, and debt could pick up the chips in the economic poker game after that. It all added up to generating motion without motion, but such subtleties were lost in the early stages of the charade.

Blinded by the Darius syndrome, the new economists quickly forgot that without new wealth to liquidate debt, debt could only compound itself, multiply, stagger the system, and finally collapse it.

3. *excessive debt*

Centuries of banking have revealed that arithmetic is a stern master. The arithmetic of compound interest imposes certain limitations on debt expansion, limitations those in charge of public policy *circa* 1967 chose to ignore.

A 37% expansion of credit in terms of profits and savings has been considered safe in responsible banking circles. In other words, debt becomes excessive if it exceeds 37% of the value of profits and savings. The profits and savings of about \$116.5 billion in 1967 (times 37%) permitted a safe debt expansion of \$42 billion. The rest of the debt creation was excessive debt. In other words there was \$66 billion excessive debt expansion in 1967.

The propensity to consume, of course, is a psychological measurement. Psychological measurements have no absolute zero or equal intervals. Therefore, considering the loose-goose Keynesian approach, on the presumed-rigged national record propensity to consume, this excessive debt injection developed a multiplier as follows in 1967:

$$\frac{303.1}{66.0} = 4.66$$

For every dollar of excessive debt injected into the economy, approximately $4.7 dollars of income was created, if full credit were to be extended this device, and if the national income figures were honest. In terms of national income for the year, it required $5.77 income to pay $1 debt, yet each $1 debt was creating only $4.66 of national income.

Raw material figures are not available. But calculated on the rather consistent agriculture ratio of 7,

$48.9 billion gross farm income

$\times$ 7.0 ratio farm income to earned national income

342.3 total earned national income

The kited national income in 1967 was $649.6 billion.

Thus it can be seen that almost half of the national income in 1967 was being generated by excessive debt expansion. Debt compounds itself. It has to be retired out of profits and savings. Debt is a claim against future earnings.

If the debt multiplier is taking on the aura of perpetual motion, it must be remembered that the national records have been rigged once a year for six years running, first to show corporations earning more than they earn, farmers getting more than they get, the nation doing better than it is doing, and the interest mill taking *less* than it takes.

Even while the government was casting aside its lawsuit against NFO, federal records were being rigged again, this time to show a more healthy savings schedule, one up to 7.1% of after tax income, the highest since 1953. How? Starting in 1967, personal savings were figured to include payments on debt. The equity in that worn out automobile, for instance, became a *saving*. In terms of honest accountancy, the excessive debt mentioned above would have been much higher, and probably it would have hit hard the debt multiplier that looms so large.

Excessive debt feeds inflation and poverty, whether modern record readers are content to glory in debt creation and the multiplier on its way to national income or not.

As the nation continued to rush toward chaos, NFO farmers questioned politely, pleaded, begged—and finally hit the mule that was public policy squarely across the nose by voting another holding action, an all-commodity holding action.

Obviously, earned income had to be increased in terms of given debt, or debt had to be keelhauled in terms of given cash, because the alternative was a liquidity crisis dead ahead—a depression. No national leader, no monetary authority could think in terms of reducing debt, not when debt was the only thing that kept the liquidity hungry situation from falling apart.

The debt fueled multiplier was doing its multiplying alright, and farmers were continuing to consume their capital, exploit their own labor, and substitute debt for earnings. The smart set in and out of government was busily moving dollars around to cash in on the coming rise in the price of gold. That, after all, was the key.

How much would it cost the economy if the price of gold was doubled? Answer: *nothing*. The mere act of monetizing gold at a higher level would create cash without creating an increase in debt.

But the same was also true when raw materials were monetized at parity. They, in effect, cost the economy nothing, and yet at parity they supplied the economy with its balance. (When Bernard Baruch had cornered 5/16ths of the world's silver supply during the 1930s, the powers that be experienced no pangs in handing out profits by monetizing the metal at double the price, because they felt the general welfare might be served along with a rather fortunate individual. But with farms still in the hands of a couple of million people, the very idea of farmers profiting along with the nation is pooh-poohed as unrealistic.)

An economic income equation has to have balance. It cannot afford less than parity or more than parity for any of its sectors. When Leon Keyserling, as Truman's economic chief, blundered OPS into establishing price ceilings on the basis of 85% of normal operating margins, he ignored the quite simple fact that the whole is the sum of the component parts. Without full parity, business cannot pay the wages, and without parity wages, labor cannot buy the production. But last, and most important, without full parity for agriculture and other raw materials, primary producers cannot deliver the new wealth necessary to maintain a solvent economy.

The proof is contained in a series of simple equations.

Production $\times$ Price = Income.

No Production $\times$ Price = No Income.

Full Production $\times$ No Price = No Income

Full Production $\times$ Partial Price = Partial Income.

Full Production × Full Price = Full Income, or enough income to consume the production with a profit left over. The profit has to arrive in the monetization of the basic raw materials.

It is the requirement of profit that makes mandatory equitable pricing at the raw material level of the economy. Capital debt has to be paid out of profit. It cannot be paid out of more debt.

That is why the earned income multiplier that proceeds from the foundation level of raw materials holds the key to solvency, growth, prosperity and stability. It is the only answer to the poverty that has been programmed for America.

4. *the multiplier*

By definition, the income earned at the raw material level of the economy is earned. It does not have to be paid back. And it obeys a propensity to multiply as do other forms of income injected into the economy. It is spent and re-spent, and when a single dollar earned at the raw materials level finally completes its multiplier effect, it accounts for $5.00 of national income. Since there is a consistency between all raw material price levels, due to institutional arrangements the world over, arithmetic inspection reveals that $1 paid at the farm level moves on a ratio of $7 of national income.

Here the multiplier is the ratio between the national income and the price paid at the raw material level. Unless buttressed by excessive debt creation, the present state of the arts delivers a raw materials multiplier of approximately 5. During the period from 1929 to 1953, before excessive debt creation took over, the average gross savings of the national economy came to approximately 95% of the value placed on raw materials production (farm and mineral) at the beginning of the cycle. (See table on facing page.)

After 1953, record keeping in the United States government was changed so that no one could continue to draw attention to this startling fact. Salvage, for instance, was no longer treated as a raw material, and minerals were no longer accounted for separately from finished products in integrated enterprises. But the raw material multiplier cannot be embezzled out of existence so easily. There has remained a record of agricultural income, and its consistent ratio to national income on an earned basis.

COMPARISON OF TOTAL VALUE OF
RAW MATERIAL PRODUCTION AND GROSS SAVINGS*

YEAR	RAW MATERIAL PRODUCTION (BILLIONS)	GROSS SAVINGS (BILLIONS)
1929	19.7	15.5
1930	16.2	11.2
1931	11.5	8.4
1932	8.8	2.8
1933	9.5	2.7
1934	11.8	5.6
1935	13.2	7.9
1936	15.2	11.1
1937	16.6	10.8
1938	14.4	8.9
1939	15.3	12.7
1940	16.5	16.0
1941	20.6	23.0
1942	27.2	41.8
1943	30.9	47.4
1944	32.5	57.0
1945	33.5	48.5
1946	37.8	28.7
1947	46.5	25.3
1948	50.3	36.4
1949	45.4	37.0
1950	47.5	42.0
1951	54.8	51.8
1952	54.1	54.7
1953	54.0	55.8
TOTAL	703.8	663.0

Note: Average Gross Savings for 25 years approximately 95% of total
value of all raw materials.

*Compiled by Carl H. Wilken, and reprinted here from "All New Wealth Comes
From the Soil," with permission of the author.

5. *the nfo member's bid*

Thus the NFO member's bid for higher prices becomes more than a single sector's wish to preserve its way of life the way a few oldsters might want to preserve the cobbler's way of life. Indeed, on how well this bid succeeds depends the level of prosperity the entire nation can enjoy.

Unfortunately, the road back from imbalance is traumatic. It requires surgery.

It requires consumer wage and price freezes *without* freezes for commodities in their present imbalanced position. Indeed, were farm prices to be frozen at the present level, the disaster that lies ahead would most certainly be made secure.

In a word, the American economy out of whack requires restoration of farm prices to balance with the rest of the economy, with balance being calculated in terms of the last honest *Economic Report of the President,* the one for 1962. Such an adjustment, obviously, cannot be made while goods the world over can seek the high market with impunity.

Seated precariously on the edge of disaster, NFO members were prepared to battle again and again, to hold again and again, but through it all they looked at Washington and wondered: would statesmanship prevail? Even the return of parity prices could not save many rural communities, so fantastic had the "adjustment" become. Only a graduated land tax could possibly make certain the return of the optimum economic unit—the family farm—to much of the country-side, where it might repair the social safety valve that had been shut off. Looking chaos squarely in the eye, many NFO members wondered indeed: *would statesmanship prevail.*

6. *tragedy of the hour*

In the meantime, the tragedy of the hour was rapidly turning into the tragedy of the century.

By year-end 1967, the 84 dairy herds being slaughtered in Wisconsin each week had moved up to become 88 dairy herds being slaughtered in Wisconsin each week.

APPENDIX

---

the anti-trust suit

ANALYSIS

THE FARMER HAS THE FOOD, and he has it first. No one can process the raw product until the farmer sells it. It is all that simple—and that complicated. In a holding action, the hold itself bristles with deadly parallels. Other business men price their products. They make the price tag comply with the cost of producing that product. But for some reason, any attempt by farmers to do the same comes as harsh and potent mental tonic to the powers that be.

The business world is a "going concern." It must have liquidity of funds to continue exchanging goods, but it must also have liquidity of raw materials to function at all. Thus drying up the life-blood of a processor is equally as shocking to the system as drying up customers.

In all its holding actions, NFO has tried to show that without production for the plant, the customer at the other end is not even a reality. Always, NFO has argued that the customer will be at the other end of the production line equally as well when both the farmer and the processor get paid fair prices. Some processors have come to recognize that fact, and would have gladly adjusted the institutional arrangements for doing busines. They would have accepted contracts, and then recovered a fair price from the market for both the primary and the secondary producer.

Yet in a sense, farmers can win only if they are allowed to win. When the government and the money lenders decree that a processor will suffer a money liquidity crisis within a few days if he does not fight NFO and endure a raw material liquidity crisis imposed by farmers, then it is the money power that is not permitting farmers to win.

A money-credit pinch held over a red meat packer's head is enough to make him endure a hold beyond his ability, because a cut-off in credit means instant bankruptcy, whereas a hold on animals means only slow business starvation. But the milk trade is a cow of a different color. The gap between pressure from the money-credit circuit and pressure from the once-a-day milk supply is narrow. The milk hold narrowed it further still. As farmers inched ever closer to the upper hand, the government took up the cudgel with the instrument appended on page 333 this is the text of the anti-trust suit.

THE ANTI-TRUST SUIT

IN THE UNITED STATES DISTRICT COURT
FOR THE SOUTHERN DISTRICT OF IOWA
SOUTHERN DIVISION

UNITED STATES OF AMERICA,)	
)	
Plaintiff,)	
)	CIVIL ACTION
v.)	
)	No.
THE NATIONAL FARMERS' ORGANIZATION,)	
INCORPORATED,)	Filed:
)	
Defendant.)	

COMPLAINT

The United States of America, plantiff, by its attorneys acting under the direction of the Attorney General of the United States, brings this civil action to obtain equitable relief against the above-named defendant and complains and alleges as follows:

I. *Jurisdiction and Venue*

1. This complaint is filed and this action is instituted under Section 4 of the Act of Congress of July 2, 1890, as amended, commonly known as the Sherman Act (15 U.S.C. Sec. 4), in order to prevent and restrain the continuing violation by the defendant, as hereinafter alleged, of Section 2 of that Act (15 U.S.C. Sec. 2).

2. The defendant maintains offices, transacts business and is found within the Southern District of Iowa.

II. *Definitions*

3. As used in this complaint:

(a) "agricultural products" means those products produced and sold by farmers including, but not limited to, livestock and milk;

(b) "nonmember farmer" means a person engaged in the production and sale of agricultural products who is not an officer, agent, employee or member of The National Farmers' Organization, Incorporated;

(c) "processor" means a person engaged in the processing and distribution of agricultural products;

(d) "carrier" means a person engaged in the business of transporting agricultural products.

III. *The Defendant*

4. The National Farmers' Organization, Incorporated, hereinafter referred to as "NFO", is hereby made the defendant herein. NFO is a nonprofit membership corporation organized and existing under the laws of the State of Iowa with its principal place of business at Corning, Iowa. NFO's membership is composed largely of farmers.

5. NFO seeks to bargain on behalf of its membership with processors of agricultural products and to obtain "master contracts" with said processors. Said "master contracts" provide for the sale of particular agricultural products by NFO members to processors at fixed prices substantially in excess of current market prices.

IV. *Nature of Trade and Commerce*

6. A substantial portion of the production and sale of milk in the United States occurs in the States of Colorado, Illinois, Iowa, Indiana, Kansas, Kentucky, Michigan, Minnesota, Missouri, Nebraska, New Jersey, New York, North Dakota, Ohio, Oklahoma, South Dakota, Tennessee, West Virginia and Wisconsin (hereinafter referred to as "the marketing area States"). In 1965 the marketing area States produced over 82.9 billion lbs., or approximately 66%, of the nation's milk.

7. A substantial portion of the milk which is produced and sold in the marketing area States is delivered and sold by or on behalf of the producer, or processed, distributed or consumed, in a state or states other than the state in which this milk is produced. The production, sale and distribution of milk in the marketing area States constitutes interstate trade and commerce.

8. One method used by NFO in its efforts to increase the price for agricultural products received by its members has been the withholding of a product from the market. The success of a withholding action is dependent on the withholding from the market of a substantial percentage of the agricultural product involved. In 1964 defendant conducted a withholding action on livestock. During this withholding action defendant threatened, intimidated, harassed and committed acts of personal injury and property damage to non-member farmers in order to restrain non-member farmers from selling livestock and from delivering livestock to processors. Defendant further threatened, harassed and committed acts of violence to carriers and to processors, in order to restrain carriers from transporting livestock and to restrain processors from receiving livestock.

9. During the livestock withholding action referred to above, defendant entered into agreements and understandings with non-member farmers. The substantial terms of these agreements and understandings

were that non-member farmers would withhold livestock from processors when NFO members were withholding livestock. During this period defendant also entered into agreements and understandings with carriers. The substantial terms of these agreements and understandings were that carriers would refuse to transport livestock to processors when NFO members were withholding livestock.

V. *Offense*

10. Beginning on or about March 15, 1967 and continuing thereafter up to and including the date of the filing of this complaint, defendant has attempted to monopolize the hereinbefore described trade and commerce in milk in violation of Section 2 of the Sherman Act. Said unlawful attempt to monopolize is continuing and will continue unless the relief hereinafter prayed for is granted.

11. In effectuating the offense above, defendant has, among other things:

(a) through threats, intimidation, harassment and acts of violence, attempted to induce and induced non-member farmers not to sell milk and not to deliver milk to processors;

(b) through threats, intimidation, harassment and acts of violence, attempted to induce and induced carriers not to transport milk;

(c) through threats, intimidation, harassment and acts of violence, attempted to induce and induced processors to cease operations and not to receive milk.

VI. *Effects*

12. The aforesaid attempt to monopolize has had the following effects, among others:

(a) competition in the sale of milk between members of NFO and non-member farmers has been substantially restrained; and

(b) the flow of milk in interstate trade and commerce has been curtailed.

VII. *Prayer*

WHEREFORE, plaintiff prays:

(1) That the Court adjudge and decree that defendant has attempted to monopolize interstate trade and commerce, as herein alleged, in violation of Section 2 of the Sherman Act.

(2) That defendant, its officers, directors, agents, employees, and members, its successors and assigns, and all persons acting on its behalf, be enjoined during the pendency of this action and permanently from:

(a) threatening, intimidating, harassing and committing acts of violence against non-member farmers;

(b) threatening, intimidating, harassing and committing

acts of violence against non-member farmers;

(c) threatening, intimidating, harassing, and committing acts of violence against processors;

(d) engaging and participating in all other activities, agreements and understandings having the purpose or effect of continuing or renewing the violation alleged in this complaint.

(3) That plaintiff have such other, further and different relief as the nature of the case may require and the Court may deem necessary and appropriate; and

(4) That plaintiff recover the costs of this action.

RAMSEY CLARK
Attorney General

EDWARD R. KENNEY

DONALD F. TURNER
Assistant Attorney General

HUGH P. MORRISON, JR.
Attorneys, Department of Justice

GORDON B. SPIVACK
Attorney, Department of Justice

CHARLES D. MAHAFFIE, JR.
Attorney, Department of Justice

United States Attorney

About the author

Clarence Day (1874–1935) was raised at 480 Madison Avenue, the son of a successful Wall Street broker. He attended Yale and after graduating joined the navy. He retired from the navy for health reasons and took up a career as a journalist, cartoonist and writer. His biggest success came in the early 1930s when he sent tales of his childhood to Harold Ross at the *New Yorker* magazine. When serialised by Ross their popularity virtually single-handedly saved the fledgling *New Yorker* from collapse. After continuing ill health, Day died in 1935, before he could witness the far-reaching success of his creation. The book was a huge bestseller and two sequels were produced from Day's existing writings: *Life with Mother* and *God and My Father*. *Life with Father* went on to be adapted for the stage in 1939. Hugely successful, it is still one of the five longest-ever running musicals on Broadway. There was a film in 1947 directed by Michael Curtiz and it became a much-loved American TV series in the 50s.

LIFE WITH FATHER

LIFE WITH
FATHER

Clarence Day

EBURY
PRESS

Ebury Press
Random House, 20 Vauxhall Bridge Road, London SW1V 2SA

Random House Australia (Pty) Limited
20 Alfred Street, Milsons Point, Sydney, New South Wales 2061, Australia

Random House New Zealand Limited
18 Poland Road, Glenfield, Auckland 10, New Zealand

Random House South africa (Pty) Limited
Endulini, 5A Jubilee Road, Parktown 2193, South Africa

Random House UK Limited Reg. No. 954009

A CIP catalogue record for this book is available from the British Library

ISBN 0 09 188300 8

Jacket design by Jon Gray
Cover image courtesy of Popperfoto

Typeset by SX Composing DTP, Rayleigh, Essex
Printed and bound in Great Britain by
Bookmarque Ltd, Croydon, Surrey

Papers used by Ebury Press are natural, recyclable products
made from wood grown in sustainable forests.

With acknowledgments to the Editors of
The New Yorker, Harper's Magazine and
The New Republic, in which periodicals
these chapters first appeared.

Contents

Contents

A HOLIDAY WITH FATHER

❧

ONCE in a long while, as a great treat, Father took me down to his office. This could happen only on a Saturday morning, when there was no school. I felt very important and grown-up on the days I went to "The Office"—not after I got there, to be sure, but as I was leaving the house, with Mother and my three little brothers respectfully seeing me off.

If it was a rainy day, Father would prepare for rough weather by wearing a derby hat and a black rubber mackintosh over his usual tailed coat. (He seldom was informal enough to wear a sack suit in town except on warm days, or when he left New York to go to the country, in summer.) If the sun was out, he wore a silk hat and carried a cane, like his friends. When he and they passed each other on the street, they raised their canes and touched the brims of their hats with them, in formal salute.

I admired this rich and splendid gesture, and wished I could imitate it, but I was too young for a cane. I was soberly dressed in a pepper-and-salt sack suit with short pants and the usual broad flat white Eton collar that boys wore in the eighties—a collar that started out very stiff and immaculate every morning and was done for by dinner-time. Black laced or buttoned shoes and black stockings. We only wore brown in the country in summer.

On one of these Saturdays, although it was sunny, Father put on his derby. I didn't know why until later. I hopped along by his side as he walked through the long rows of comfortable-looking brownstone houses from Madison Avenue over to Sixth, climbed the stairs of the Elevated, and stood on the platform, chatting with one of his friends, while we waited for the next train.

Soon a stubby little steam-engine, with its open coal-car piled full of anthracite, and its three or four passenger-cars swinging along behind, appeared round the curve. White smoke poured from the smoke-stack. The engineer leaned out from his window. "Too-oot, too-too-toot!" whistled the engine as it came puffing in. We got on board and walked leisurely through the cars till Father found a seat that he liked.

During the journey down town, except when the smoke from the engine was too thick for me to see out, I stared fascinatedly into the windows of cheap red-brick tenements, or at the even more interesting interiors of lodging-houses for tramps. The second-floor rooms of the lodging-houses were crowded, but I envied the tramps in them. They looked so easy-going. Not a thing to do; just tilt their chairs back against the wall, in comfortable old clothes, and smoke. If I were a tramp, I wouldn't have to scrub every last bit of grime out of my knuckles each Friday, and put on tight white kid gloves, and pull some unwieldy little girl around a waxed floor at dancing school. It wouldn't cost so very much, either. The lodging-house sign said in big letters, "Ten Cents a Night."

I never had a chance to see such sights except when I went down town with Father, for Mother kept away from the Elevated. It was comparatively new, and she felt that the horse-cars were better. Besides, Sixth Avenue was so cindery and sooty that ladies disliked it. They did go that far west sometimes, to shop, and they went as far east as Lexington, but in general they lived and walked in the long narrow strip between those two boundaries.

When Father and I left the train at the end of our journey, I found myself in a tangle of little streets full of men and boys but no women. If some lonely bonnet chanced to be bobbing along in the crowd, we all stared at it. Most of the business buildings were old and many of them were dirty, with steep, well-worn wooden stairways, and dark, busy basements. Exchange Place and Broad Street were full of these warrens, and there were some even on Wall Street. The southern corner of Wall Street and Broadway was one of the dingiest. Father raised his cane and said as we passed, "That's where Great-Aunt Lavinia was born."

A few doors beyond the Assay Office we came to a neat but narrow five-story building and walked up the front stoop. This was No. 38 Wall Street. Father's office occupied the ground floor, at the top of the stoop, and on the back part of the second floor he had a small storeroom.

The office was busy in what seemed to me a mysterious way. The cashier, who never would let me go inside his cage, sat in there on a stool, with a cash drawer, a safe full of books, another safe for securities, and a tin box full of postage-stamps, which he doled out as needed. One or two book-keepers were making beautifully written entries in enormous leather-bound ledgers. They had taken the stiff white detachable cuffs off their shirt-sleeves and stacked them in a corner, and they had exchanged their regular jackets for black alpaca coats. Future book-keepers or brokers who now were little office-boys ran in and out. Western Union messengers rushed in with telegrams. In the front room there was a long table full of the printed reports issued by railroads about their earnings and traffic. Only twenty or thirty industrial stocks were traded in on the Exchange in those days, and Father's office ignored them. On or around the table were the *Commercial & Financial Chronicle*, the *Journal of Commerce*, a black-board, a ticker, and four or five whiskery men. Two were arguing heatedly about Henry Ward Beecher, and the others were shaking their heads over some crazy proposal by the "Knights of Labour" to have an eight-hour day.

Father went into his private office, where a little coal fire was burning, hung his hat on a rack, and unlocked and sat down at his desk. While he opened his mail, I proudly brought in two stone jugs of ink, one of greenish black made in England, and one to use when he wrote letters of which he wished to keep copies, because with this ink impressions could be taken to put in his files. I cleaned and filled all Father's inkwells, and put fresh steel pens in his penholders. He had quill pens at home, but he used only steel pens at the office, and as he had no stenographer he wrote a good share of the firm's letters in longhand, himself.

5

There were lots of things to do in the office besides filling inkwells. It was fun to scamper around the streets carrying all the messages (which are telephoned nowadays), or to roll coloured pencils down the clerks' slanting desk, or try to ring the bell on the typewriter. The latter was a new contraption which seldom was used except on important occasions, when the book-keeper or one of the office-boys had to stop work and pick at it.

All of a sudden it was noon. The customers left. The ticker came to a stop. At half-past twelve Father called to me and we went out for lunch.

"Will you be back, Mr. Day?" the cashier asked respectfully, but eagerly too. On days when Father said yes, all the clerks looked disappointed. They bent over their desks, saying nothing, till Father went out of the door, but if I lingered behind for a moment I heard them slamming their ledgers about. Not only did they and the office-boys all have to stay, but the rule was that they couldn't even smoke until Father had gone home for the day.

To-day he said no, however. I saw them getting out their sulphur matches as he was crossing the threshold, and the instant he stepped into the hall they struck them on the seats of their pants.

6

I trotted along at Father's side down to Beaver Street, where there stood a mellow old building. It had the look of a friendly, hospitable country hotel. There were green blinds and little outside balconies on its upper floors, and windows with looped lacy curtains; and white pillars stood at the entrance, at the top of a low flight of steps.

This was Delmonico's, and the food was so good there that even I had heard it talked of, up town. It was one of the places that just suited people like Father.

Delmonico's stood upon a triangular-shaped plot of ground, with the front doors at the apex, and when we arrived we met a bottle-necked jam at the entrance. Silk-hatted men, who had been lunching in a lingering way, had suddenly remembered apparently that they were due back in Wall Street, and they were shoving each other, politely but urgently, to force their way out.

As Father and I went in the long crowded room, the head waiter led us with a flourish to a table for two. The air was fragrant with cigar smoke and the appetizing smell of rich, greasy cooking. A stately looking foreigner who was standing at the side of the room caught Father's eye and bowed to him in a dignified way.

"Lorenzo," Father said to him, as he approached us, "this is my son."

I bobbed my head at him, rather embarrassed, and Mr. Lorenzo Crist Delmonico bowed and said he was happy to meet me.

As he left us, old François, Father's regular waiter, hurried up to our table, and he and Father had a talk, in French, about the best dish to order. They spoke so rapidly that I couldn't understand a word of it, except that François kept assuring Father that we could rely on the sauce. *"Parfaitement."* It seemed that the last time that Father had relied on this sauce, an admittedly difficult kind, he had had a severe disappointment.

When anything of this sort occurred, I had noted, François had a healing way of dealing with such a catastrophe. He seemed even more shocked and perturbed at a failure than Father, and he would snatch the offending dish away and come racing back with a substitute. Usually he was accompanied at such moments by one of the Delmonico family—Lorenzo or Charles— who bent over the table to examine the new dish as it was placed before Father, murmuring most sympathetically about the unhappy misfortune.

To-day the sauce and everything else was not only successful but perfect, and Father and François smiled and nodded in a congratulatory way to each other. I used to wonder why Father never got into rages at Delmonico's as he did at

home, but I see now that he may have felt lonely
at home, where there were no brother experts.

Father was fond of French cooking and of
being served by French waiters. At home he had
to put up with an Irish waitress who was
changed every few months, and with cooking
which, though excellent of its kind, after all
wasn't French. He ate it with relish and gusto,
when it came up to his standards, but he did so
like a city man in the country, enjoying good,
simple fare.

I didn't always appreciate French cooking
myself. It tasted all right, but it was dainty
and there wasn't much of it. It seemed to me
that Father got along with a very light lunch.
When he was having his demi-tasse, however,
and saw a hungry look on my face, he smiled
understandingly and beckoned to François, who
smiled too and presently came running back
with a large chocolate éclair. The richness of its
soft, thick yellow interior and the meltingness of
its chocolate outside were so delicious that time
stood still as I happily ate it, and I almost forgot
where I was.

After lunch, instead of taking me back up
town, Father walked down to the Battery, and to
my surprise we got on the boat at South Ferry.
We had never done this before. I now saw why
he was wearing his derby. We were going out to

the country. Off we steamed across the sweet-smelling bay filled with sail-boats and four-masted schooners and tug-boats and barges, and when we landed on Staten Island Father told me that we were going to see Buffalo Bill.

We got seats in a flimsy wooden stand full of splintery benches, and there was the Wild West spread out before us—dust, horses, and all. The wonderful marksmanship of riders who hit glass balls with their rifles—balls tossed into the air and shot at with careless ease as the horsemen dashed by; the herds of cattle, the lariats, the brass band, the old Deadwood Stage Coach, the thrilling attack on it by Indians, the last-minute rescue. Father dragged me out just before the rescue so that we could get seats on the ferrryboat, but I caught a glimpse of it anyway as I was being hauled through the exit.

I wanted to be a cowboy, I told Father on the way home. He chuckled and said no I didn't. He said I might as well be a tramp.

I wondered if I'd better tell him that this idea, too, had occurred to me, no further back than that very morning. I decided that upon the whole it mightn't be a good day to mention it, just after Father had taken me to lunch at Delmonico's. I did venture to ask him, however, what was the matter with cowboys.

Father briefly explained that their lives, their

food, and their sleeping accommodations were outlandish and "slummy." They lived in the wilds, he informed me, and they had practically gone wild themselves. "Put your cap on straight," he added. "I am trying to bring you up to be a civilized man."

I adjusted my cap and walked on, thinking over this future. The more I thought about it, the less I wanted to be a civilized man. After all, I had had a very light lunch, and I was tired and hungry. What with fingernails and improving books and dancing school, and sermons on Sundays, the few chocolate éclairs that a civilized man got to eat were not worth it.

FATHER ON HORSEBACK

❖

FATHER had been putting on weight and he didn't like it. He was a solidly-built man, but trim and erect, with a light easy step, and his extra pounds made him uncomfortable. He disapproved of them too. When the fat of fat men seemed to come natural to them, Father took it as a good joke; but he felt that it was slovenly to be careless about getting stout.

He talked about this at his club. What the saloon was to poor men and what coffee-houses had once been to Londoners, his club was to Father. It was the font and centre of his social life. He stopped there for half an hour or so on his way home from the office, or he walked down there at nine in the evening when Mother had gone up to bed. He played a game or two of billiards—not cards—or he had a whisky and soda with Commodore Brown, or he met and sized up distinguished foreigners, whom he usually didn't think much of. Or he sought for advice about fat.

Some members recommended long walks, but Father had always done a good deal of walking. The opinion of the club was that in that case he had better take up riding horseback.

The only proper way to ride horseback, Father felt, was to join one more club. He joined the Riding Club, in East Fifty-eighth Street, which provided stabling and other conveniences, and after practising in there in the tanbark ring, he rode out in the Park.

The Park itself was only a ring on a larger scale, nothing wild or adventurous; but it suited Father. He disliked wildness—he preferred things like landscapes to be orderly, and suitably arranged for his use. From this time on, he was as critical of the Park as he was of his home. He felt personally affronted for instance when the bridle-path wasn't raked properly, or when papers were left lying about.

His first horse was a powerful bay by the name of Rob Roy. This horse didn't like Father, and Father had still less affection for him. This was supposed to be of no importance—it was not even considered. Father bought him because he was spirited and sound, and able to stand work; handsome too. He paid three hundred dollars for him, and expected him to do what he was told.

Rob Roy never looked upon the transaction in this way, however. He had an independent and self-absorbed nature; he was always thinking of his own point of view. Even if he had been devoted to Father, which he never was, this would have made trouble.

One typical scene between them, I remember, occurred near the Park entrance. It was a warm autumn morning. Rob Roy and Father had trotted out of the club and into the Park, each thoroughly healthy and strong, and each intent on his thoughts. They made a fine sight as they went up the bridle-path. All their plans coincided. But then a difference between them arose. Father wished to keep on. Rob Roy didn't. I don't know why Rob Roy wanted to stop; perhaps he didn't like the way Father rode him. Anyhow he came to a halt. Rob Roy whirled around. Father reined him up sharply and struck him again. Rob Roy reared.

As they fought, Father in his anger kept hitting Rob Roy; and Rob Roy violently pawed the ground, and stamped on it, and tore it all up. They both perspired so freely that between them they must have lost gallons, and they both blindly stuck to their respective plans and would not give in.

But Rob Roy had the whole day before him, and Father did not—he had to get through his ride some time and go to his office. He decided that Rob Roy was crazy, and they returned to the club. Rob Roy was led off to his stall and rubbed down by a groom, and Father went to the dressing-room for members and rubbed dry by Jim, the attendant.

Jim was a friendly old soul. "Have a nice ride, Mr. Day?" he asked.

"Nice hell," Father shortly replied, and took his cane and went out.

These fierce morning combats gave our family a feeling of awe. We had never dreamed that anyone, man or beast, would resist Father's will. This rashness of Rob Roy's was like Satan's rebelling against God—it had a dark splendour about it, but it somehow filled me with horror.

In that fight between Satan and God, we had been told that God won. There were stray bits of evidence to the contrary lying around, but naturally we had accepted the official announcement. In the long war between Father and Rob Roy, we always assumed Father won, but there too I now see that Rob Roy may have looked at it differently. For the way that Father defeated Rob Roy was by deciding to sell him.

To us boys this seemed like a banishment. It made Rob Roy an outcast. Perhaps it only meant to him meeting a rider less uncongenial; but to us it seemed like obliterating him from the world, in the prime of his life. For years afterward he was spoken of as a strange being, a queer, insane creature, who had unaccount-ably and vainly attempted to disobey Father.

Rob Roy was a thoroughbred. His successor, a lanky brown horse named Brownie, was plain middle class. Rob Roy was an adventurer. Brownie was a sad-eyed philosopher. Some philosophers are as great-hearted as adven-turers, but they are mostly more docile. Brownie trotted wherever Father told him to, in any direction. He never once reared, never stamped on the ground, never snorted. There were sometimes little differences of opinion between him and Father, because Brownie got tired sooner than Father did, and wanted to rest. But he never made a direct issue of it, never fought for his rights; he tried to get them either by malingering or by passive resistance. For instance, Father would set out with the plan in his mind of having a glorious gallop, up hill and down dale. Well, Brownie, who had to do the galloping, would keep it up for a while—would keep it up far longer at times than he had ever intended; for he found that a whip kept landing on his flank whenever he started to slacken. But, as he lost heart in the expedition, he also lost spring; and finally he would thump along so heavily that Father let up.

In general, however, the two got along very well. Father became enthusiastic about the pleasure of riding. Being a hearty, expansive man, he talked of this often, at home. He talked of it so much, in fact, that Mother began to feel he was selfish, in that he was keeping a pleasure for himself which should be shared with his family. If riding around the Park was so exhilarating, she said we all ought to do it.

Father said he wished that we could, but there was only one horse.

This silenced the family for a while; but soon Mother spoke up: she didn't see why the rest of us couldn't ride the horse when Father was through.

The unreasonableness and impracticability of this idea made Father hot. It showed how little Mother knew about anything, especially horses, he said. He explained that Brownie was already inclined to be sluggish, and that he wouldn't be fresh enough for a man to ride if he did extra work.

Mother said firmly, then Father should get some more horses.

This took him aback. He always meant to do the right thing by us; and he began to fear that his own goodness of heart might now get him in trouble. His feeling was that when he innocently had gone in for riding, himself, he had never contemplated having to spend enough to mount the whole family. He said that if he had foreseen that we all would be wanting to ride through the Park, just because he, a hard-working man, got a little relief in that way, he would have gone without the relief, damn it. He would now. He'd sell out.

Of course he had no intention of doing this. Instead he bought one more horse, a younger and happier one, and then gave us boys poor old Brownie.

FATHER IS FIRM WITH HIS AILMENTS

❖

FATHER got annoyed at us when we didn't stay well. He usually stayed well himself and he expected us to be like him, and not faint and slump on his hands and thus add to his burdens.

He was fearless about disease. He despised it. All this talk about germs, he said, was merely new-fangled nonsense. He said that when he was a boy there had been no germs that he knew of. Perhaps invisible insects existed, but what of it? He was as healthy as they were. "If any damned germs want to have a try at me," he said, "bring 'em on."

From Father's point of view, Mother didn't know how to handle an ailment. He admired her most of the time and thought there was nobody like her; he often said to us boys, "Your mother is a wonderful woman"; but he always seemed to disapprove of her when she was ill.

Mother went to bed, for instance, at such times. Yet she didn't make noises. Father heard a little gasping moan sometimes, but she didn't want him to hear even that. Consequently he was sure she wasn't suffering. There was nothing to indicate it, he said.

The worse she felt, the less she ever said about it, and the harder it was for him to believe that there was anything really wrong with her. "He says he can't see why I stay in bed so long," she once wrote to me, when I was away, "but this colitis is a mean affair which keeps one perfectly flat. The doctor told him yesterday the meaning of colitis, but he said he 'had never heard of the damned thing, thank God.' He feels very abused that he should be 'so upset by people with queer things the matter with them and doctors all over the place.'" (Mother underlined the word "people.").

Even Mother's colds made him fretful. Whenever she had one, she kept going as long as she could, pottering about her room looking white and tired, with a shawl round her shoulders. But sometimes she had to give up and crawl into her bed.

Father pished and poohed to himself about this, and muttered that it was silly. He said Mother was perfectly healthy. When people thought they were ill, he declared, it didn't mean that there was anything the matter with them, it was merely a sign of weak character. He often told Mother how weak it was to give in to an ailment, but every time he tried to strengthen her character in this respect, he said she seemed to resent it. He never remembered to try except when she could hardly hold her head up. From his point of view, though, that was the very time that she needed his help.

He needed hers, too, or not exactly her help but her company, and he never hesitated to say so. When she was ill, he felt lost.

He usually came up from his office at about five or six. The first thing he did was to look around the house to find Mother. It made his home feel queer and empty to him when she wasn't there.

One night about six o'clock he opened the door of her bedroom. There was no light except for a struggling little fire which flickered and sank in the grate. A smell of witch-hazel was in the air, mixed with spirits of camphor. On the bed, huddled up under an afghan, Mother lay still, in the dark.

"Are you there, Vinnie?" Father said, in a voice even louder than usual because of his not being sure.

Mother moaned, "Go away."

"What?" he asked, in astonishment.

"Go away. Oh, go 'way."

'Damnation!" he said, marching out.

"Clare!"

"What is it?"

21

"Won't you *ple-e-ease* shut my door again!"

Father ground his teeth and shut it with such a bang that it made Mother jump.

He told himself she had nothing the matter with her. She'd be all right in the morning. He ate a good dinner. Being lonely, he added an extra glass of claret and some toasted crackers and cheese. He had such a long and dull evening that he smoked two extra cigars.

After breakfast the next morning, he went to her bedroom again. The fire was out. Two worn old slippers lay on a chair. The grey daylight was cheerless. Father stood at the foot of Mother's bed, looking disconsolately at her because she wasn't well yet. He had no one to laugh at or quarrel with; his features were lumpy with gloom.

"What is it?" Mother asked in a whisper, opening her weary eyes.

"Nothing," he said loudly. "Nothing."

"Well, for mercy's sake, don't come in here looking like that, Clare," Mother begged.

"What do you mean? Looking like what?"

"Oh, go away!" Mother shrieked. "When people are sick, they like to see a smile or something. I never will get well if you stand there and stare at me that way! And shut my door quietly this time. And let me alone."

Outside her door, when I asked him how

Mother was, he said with a chuckle: "She's all right again. She isn't out of bed yet, but she sounds much better this morning."

Father's own experience in a sick-room had been very few. When he was in his early thirties, he had an attack of gout which lasted three weeks. From that time until he was seventy-four and had pneumonia, he had no other serious illnesses. He said illnesses were mostly imaginary and he didn't believe in them.

He even declared that his pneumonia was imaginary. "It's only some idea of that doctor's," he said. "Nothing the matter with me but a cold." Our regular physician had died, and this new man and two trained nurses had all they could do, at first, to keep Father in bed.

The new doctor had pale-blue eyes, a slight build, and a way of inwardly smiling at the persons he talked to. He had a strong will in crises, and he was one of the ablest physicians in town. Mother had chosen him, however, chiefly because she liked one of his female cousins.

When Father got worse, the doctor kept warning him that it really *was* pneumonia, and that if he wouldn't be tractable, he might not get over it—especially at seventy-four.

Father lay in bed glowering at him and said: "I didn't send for you, sir. You needn't stand there and tell me what you want me to do. I know all about doctors. They think they know a damned lot. But they don't. Give your pills and things to Mrs. Day—she believes in them. That's all I have to say. There's no need to continue this discussion. There's the door, sir. Good-bye."

But somehow the discussion kept on, and much to his surprise Father at last became convinced he was ill. The doctor, leaving him alone in the bedroom to digest the bad news, came out in the hall, anxious and tired, to have a few words with Mother. As they stood outside Father's door whispering quietly, they heard his voice from within. Apparently, now that he knew he was in trouble, his thoughts had turned to his God. "Have mercy!" they heard him shouting indignantly. "I say have mercy, damn it!"

Any sufferings that Father ever had he attributed solely to God. Naturally, he never thought for a moment that God could mean him to suffer. He couldn't imagine God's wishing to punish him either, for his conscience was clear. His explanation seemed to be that God was clumsy, not to say muddle-headed.

However, in spite of God and the doctor, Father got over pneumonia, just as, some forty years before, he had got over his gout. Only, in conquering his gout, he had had the help of a cane and a masseur called Old Lowndes.

While the gout was besieging him, Father sat in a big chair by the fire with his bad foot on a stool, armed with a cane which he kept constantly ready. Not that he used the cane to walk with. When he walked, he hopped around on his other foot, uttering strong howls of fury. But he valued his cane highly, and needed it, too, as a war club. He threatened the whole family with it. When visitors entered the room he brandished it fiercely at them, to keep them away from his toe.

Old Lowndes was allowed to approach nearer than others, but he was warned that if he made any mistakes that cane would come down on his head. Father felt there was no knowing what harm Lowndes might have done if he hadn't shaken his cane at him and made him take care. As it was, owing largely to this useful stick, Father got well.

This experience convinced him that any disease could be conquered by firmness.

When he had a cold, his method of dealing with it was to try to clear it out by main force, either by violently blowing his nose or, still better, by sneezing. Mother didn't like him to sneeze, he did it with such a roar. She said she could feel it half across the room, and she was sure it was catching. Father said this was nonsense. He said his sneezes were healthy. And presently we'd hear a hearty, triumphant blast as he sneezed again.

Aside from colds, which he had very seldom, his only foes were sick headaches. He said headaches only came from eating, however. Hence a man who knew enough to stop eating could always get rid of one that way. It took time to starve it out thoroughly. It might take several hours. But as soon as it was gone, he could eat again and enjoy his cigar.

When one of these headaches started, Father lay down and shut his eyes tight and yelled. The severity of a headache could be judged by the volume of sound he put forth. His idea seemed to be to show the headache that he was just as strong as it was, and stronger. When a headache and he went to bed together, they were a noisy pair.

Father's code required him to be game, I suppose. He never spoke or thought of having a code; he wasn't that sort of person; but he denounced men whose standards were low, as to gameness or anything else. It didn't occur to him to conceal his sufferings, however; when he had any pains, he expressed them as fully as he knew how. His way of being brave was not to keep still but to keep on fighting the headache.

Mother used to beg him to be quiet at night, even if he did have a headache, and not wake up the whole house. He never paid the slightest attention to such a request. When she said, "Please don't groan so much, Clare," he'd look at her in disgust, as though he were a warrior being asked to stifle his battle-cries.

One evening he found Mother worrying because Aunt Emma was ill with some disease that was then epidemic.

"Oh, pooh!" Father said. "Nothing the matter with Emma. You can trust people to get any ailment whatever that's fashionable. They hear of a lot of other people having it, and the first thing you know they get scared and think they have it themselves. Then they go to bed, and send for the doctor. The doctor! All poppycock."

"Well, but Clare dear, if you were in charge of them, what would you do instead?"

"Cheer 'em up, that's the way to cure 'em."

"How would you cheer them up, darling?" Mother asked doubtfully.

"I? I'd tell 'em, '*Bah!*'"

FATHER WAKES UP THE VILLAGE

ONE of the most disgraceful features of life in the country, Father often declared, was the general inefficiency and slackness of small village tradesmen. He said he had originally supposed that such men were interested in business, and that that was why they had opened their shops and sunk capital in them, but no, they never used them for anything but gossip and sleep. They took no interest in civilized ways. Hadn't heard of them, probably. He said that of course if he were camping out on the veldt or the tundra, he would expect few conveniences in the neighbourhood and would do his best to forgo them, but why should he be confronted with the wilds twenty miles from New York?

Usually, when Father talked this way, he was thinking of ice. He strongly objected to spending even one day of his life without a glass of cold water beside his plate at every meal. There was never any difficulty about this in our home in the city. A great silver ice-water pitcher

28

stood on the sideboard all day, and when Father was home its outer surface was frosted with cold. When he had gone to the office, the ice was allowed to melt sometimes, and the water got warmish, but never in the evening, or on Sundays, when Father might want some. He said he liked water, he told us it was one of Nature's best gifts, but he said that like all her gifts it was unfit for human consumption unless served in a suitable manner. And the only right way to serve water was icy cold.

It was still more important that each kind of wine should be served at whatever the right temperature was for it. And kept at it, too. No civilized man would take dinner without wine, Father said, and no man who knew the first thing about it would keep his wine in hot cellars. Mother thought this was a mere whim of Father's. She said he was fussy. How about people who lived in apartments, she asked him, who didn't have cellars? Father replied that civilized persons didn't live in apartments.

One of the first summers that Father ever spent in the country, he rented a furnished house in Irvington on the Hudson, not far from New York. It had a garden, a stable, and one or two acres of woods, and Father arranged to camp out there with many misgivings. He took a train for New York every morning at eight-ten, after breakfast, and he got back between five and six, bringing anything special we might need along with him, such as a basket of peaches from the city, or a fresh package of his own private coffee.

Things went well until one day in August the ice-man didn't come. It was hot, he and his horses were tired, and he hated to come to us anyhow because the house we had rented was perched up on top of a hill. He said afterward that on this particular day he had not liked the idea of making his horses drag the big ice-wagon up that sharp and steep road to sell us fifty cents' worth of ice. Besides, all his ice was gone anyhow—the heat had melted it on him. He had four or five other good reasons. So he didn't come.

Father was in town. The rest of us waited in astonishment, wondering what could be the matter. We were so used to the regularity and punctilio of life in the city that it seemed unbelievable to us that the ice-man would fail to appear. We discussed it at lunch. Mother said that the minute he arrived she would have to give him a talking to. After lunch had been over an hour and he still hadn't come, she got so worried about what Father would say that she decided to send to the village.

There was no telephone, of course. There

were no motors. She would have liked to spare
the horse if she could, for he had been worked
hard that week. But as this was a crisis, she sent
for Morgan, the coachman, and told him to
bring up the dog-cart.

The big English dog-cart arrived. Two of us
boys and the coachman drove off. The sun beat
down on our heads. Where the heavy harness
was rubbing on Brownie's coat, he broke out
into a thick, whitish lather. Morgan was sullen.
When we boys were along he couldn't take off
his stiff black high hat or unbutton his thick,
padded coat. Worse still, from his point of view,
he couldn't stop at a bar for a drink. That was
why Mother had sent us along with him, of
course, and he knew it.

We arrived at the little town after a while and
I went into the Coal & Ice Office. A wiry-
looking old clerk was dozing in a corner, his
chair tilted back and his chin resting on his
dingy shirt-front. I woke this clerk up. I told him
about the crisis at our house.

He listened unwillingly, and when I had
finished he said it was a very hot day.

I waited. He spat. He said he didn't see what
he could do, because the ice-house was locked.

I explained earnestly that this was the Day
family and that something must be done right
away.

31

He hunted around his desk a few minutes, found his chewing tobacco, and said, "Well, sonny, I'll see what I can do about it."

I thanked him very much, as that seemed to me to settle the matter. I went back to the dog-cart. Brownie's check-rein had been unhooked, and he stood with his head hanging down. He looked sloppy. It wouldn't have been so bad with a buggy, but a slumpy horse in a dog-cart can look pretty awful. Also, Morgan was gone. He re-appeared soon, coming out of a side door down the street, buttoning up his coat, but with his hat tilted back. He looked worse than the horse.

We checked up the weary animal's head again and drove slowly home. A hot little breeze in our rear moved our dust along with us. At the foot of the hill, we boys got out, to spare Brownie our extra weight. We unhooked his check-rein again. He dragged the heavy cart up.

Mother was sitting out on the piazza. I said the ice would come soon now. We waited.

It was a long afternoon.

At five o'clock, Brownie was hitched up again. The coachman and I drove back to the village. We had to meet Father's train. We also had to break the bad news to him that he would have no ice-water for dinner, and that there didn't seem to be any way to chill his Rhine wine.

The village was as sleepy as ever, but when Father arrived and learned what the situation was, he said it would have to wake up. He told me that he had had a long, trying day at the office, the city was hotter than the Desert of Sahara, and he was completely worn out, but that if any ice-man imagined for a moment he could behave in that manner, he, Father, would take his damned head off. He strode into the Coal & Ice Office.

When he came out, he had the clerk with him, and the clerk had put on his hat and was vainly trying to calm Father down. He was promising that he himself would come with the ice-wagon if the driver had left, and deliver all the ice we could use, and he'd be there inside an hour.

Father said, "Inside of an hour be hanged, you'll have to come quicker than that."

The clerk got rebellious. He pointed out that he'd have to go to the stables and hitch up the horses himself, and then get someone to help him hoist a block of ice out of the ice-house. He said it was 'most time for his supper and he wasn't used to such work. He was only doing it as a favour to Father. He was just being neighbourly.

Father said he'd have to be neighbourly in a hurry, because he wouldn't stand it, and he didn't know what the devil the ice company meant by such actions.

The clerk said it wasn't his fault, was it? It was the driver's.

This was poor tactics, of course, because it wound Father up again. He wasn't interested in whose fault it was, he said. It was everybody's. What he wanted was ice and plenty of it, and he wanted it in time for his dinner. A small crowd which had collected by this time listened admiringly as Father shook his finger at the clerk and said he dined at six-thirty.

The clerk went loping off toward the stables to hitch up the big horses. Father waited till he'd turned the corner.

Followed by the crowd, Father marched to the butcher's.

After nearly a quarter of an hour, the butcher and his assistant came out, unwillingly carrying what seemed to be a coffin, wrapped in a black mackintosh. It was a huge cake of ice.

Father got in, in front, sat on the box seat beside me, and took up the reins. We drove off. The coachman was on the rear seat, sitting back-to-back to us, keeping the ice from sliding out with the calves of his legs. Father went a few doors up the street to a little house-furnishings shop and got out again.

I went in the shop with him this time. I didn't

want to miss any further scenes of this performance. Father began proceedings by demanding to see all the man's ice-boxes. There were only a few. Father selected the largest he had. Then, when the sale seemed arranged, and when the proprietor was smiling broadly with pleasure at this sudden windfall, Father said he was buying that refrigerator only on two conditions.

The first was that it had to be delivered at his home before dinner. Yes, now. Right away. The shopkeeper explained over and over that this was impossible, but that he'd have it up the next morning, sure. Father said no, he didn't want it the next morning, he had to have it at once. He added that he dined at six-thirty, and that there was no time to waste.

The shopkeeper gave in.

The second condition, which was then put to him firmly, was staggering. Father announced that that ice-box must be delivered to him full of ice.

The man said he was not in the ice business.

Father said, "Very well then. I don't want it."

The man said obstinately that it was an excellent ice-box.

Father made a short speech. It was the one that we had heard so often at home about the slackness of village tradesmen, and he put such strong emotion and scorn in it that his voice rang through the shop. He closed it by saying, "An ice-box is of no use to a man without ice, and if you haven't the enterprise, the gumption, to sell your damned goods to a customer who wants them delivered in condition to use, you had better shut up your shop and be done with it. Not in the ice business, hey? You aren't in business at all!" He strode out.

The dealer came to the door just as Father was getting into the dog-cart, and called out anxiously, "All right, Mr. Day. I'll get that refrigerator filled for you and send it up right away."

Father drove quickly home. A thunderstorm seemed to be brewing and this had waked Brownie up, or else Father was putting some of his own supply of energy into him. The poor old boy probably needed it as again he climbed the steep hill. I got out at the foot, and as I walked along behind I saw that Morgan was looking kind of desperate, trying to sit in the correct position with his arms folded while he held in the ice with his legs. The big cake was continually slipping and sliding around under the seat and doing its best to plunge out. It had bumped against his calves all the way home. They must have got good and cold.

When the dog-cart drew up at our door,

Father remained seated a moment while Morgan, the waitress, and I pulled and pushed at the ice. The mackintosh had come off it by this time. We dumped it out on the grass. A little later, after Morgan had unharnessed and hurriedly rubbed down the horse, he ran back to help us boys break the cake up, push the chunks around to the back door, and cram them into the ice-box while Father was dressing for dinner.

Mother had calmed down by this time. The Rhine wine was cooling. "Don't get it too cold," Father called.

Then the ice-man arrived.

The old clerk was with him, like a warden in charge of a prisoner. Mother stepped out to meet them, and at once gave the ice-man the scolding that had been waiting for him all day.

The clerk asked how much ice we wanted. Mother said we didn't want any now. Mr. Day had brought home some, and we had no room for more in the ice-box.

The ice-man looked at the clerk. The clerk tried to speak, but no words came.

Father put his head out of the window. "Take a hundred pounds, Vinnie," he said. "There's another box coming."

A hundred-pound block was brought into the house and heaved into the washtub. The waitress put the mackintosh over it. The ice-wagon left.

Just as we all sat down to dinner, the new ice-box arrived, full.

Mother was provoked. She said, "Really, Clare!" crossly. "Now what am I to do with that piece that's waiting out in the washtub?"

Father chuckled.

She told him he didn't know the first thing about keeping house, and went out to the laundry with the waitress to tackle the problem. The thunderstorm broke and crashed. We boys ran around shutting the windows upstairs.

Father's soul was at peace. He dined well, and he had his coffee and cognac served to him on the piazza. The storm was over by then. Father snuffed a deep breath of the sweet-smelling air and smoked his evening cigar.

"Clarence," he said, "King Solomon had the right idea about these things. 'Whatsoever thy hand findeth to do,' Solomon said, 'do thy damnedest.'"

Mother called me inside. "Whose mackintosh is that?" she asked anxiously. "Katie's torn a hole in the back."

I heard Father saying contentedly on the piazza, "I like plenty of ice."

FATHER DECLINES TO
BE KILLED

❖

I DON'T know why Father and Mother chose Irvington to go to, that summer. There were lots of other places where we boys could have enjoyed ourselves better, but we weren't consulted of course, and we'd have been surprised if we had been. The family assumed that we could have a good time anywhere. We had supposed so ourselves. But everything was wrong about Irvington.

I used to sit up on our hill and stare down at the Hudson. It had a dirty yellow-brown colour, it didn't make any noises, and I felt I never had seen such a tiresome river. Compared to the blue salt-water we were used to, it seemed too dull and lifeless to swim in. There was no bathing beach anyhow.

Down the road was the old Washington Irving house in Sleepy Hollow, which Mother insisted was lovely, but it was still as death, and two thin little old ladies who mustn't be disturbed sat and rocked on the porch.

About an hour's walk in the other direction

there was a fat boy who had rabbits, but we didn't think much of either those rabbits or the fellow who owned them.

On our hill we were surrounded by great, silent, park-like estates, belonging to great, silent, rich men who didn't want boys around. We occasionally explored these parks uninvited, but they weren't any good. And the hill that we lived on was as limited a hill as we'd ever seen.

Our garden seemed to be owned by the gardener. He wouldn't let us go in it. He doled out flowers from it to Mother and he scowled when he brought in the vegetables. When Mother asked him when he'd have more tomatoes or peas, he used to think deeply and say, "She be up in two day." He complained of the large amounts of vegetables the cook said we needed. At the end of the season we found he'd been selling the best of the produce all summer.

On one side of the garden was a small grove of trees, called "the woods." We spent most of our time in a swampy hollow in there, building a house in the underbrush. I was the Pharaoh of this sweaty enterprise and my brothers served as my subject Egyptians, at first. But as time went on and as it began to dawn upon them that this house would be mine when they finished it, they lost interest in it, and I had to do more and more of the work myself. It was a good little house, though. Its chief defect was that it was damp. It had no drainage and the trees kept dripping on it. It almost never felt dry. Also, as there was very little room in it, only one person—not counting the mosquitoes—could get inside at a time. That one person was nearly always me, until I came down with malaria.

When I got out of bed again, wandering around in the old greystone house during my long convalescence, I found thirty or forty yellow paper-bound books in the garret. The only books that Father and Mother didn't like me to read were cheap sensational novels with yellow-paper covers, such as were sold at rail-road news-stands. I had always obeyed them till now, but here were a lot of those very books right in the house, and here was I feeling for the first time in my life bored and idle. I took two of the novels downstairs with me and hid them in my bedroom closet.

After that I went to bed early every night and eagerly read those two books, hungry for adventures of any kind, even of love. I was thirteen, and love affairs were beginning to seem faintly interesting. The tedious thing about such affairs to my mind was their sickening flavour of sweetness, but in yellow-backed paper novels I hopefully assumed that they'd be less true-hearted than in other books, and more illicit, more lurid.

To my astonishment I found that this wasn't so. There was nothing sensational in those novels. I read them all the way through to make sure, but I seemed to have drawn two blanks. I took them back up to the garret and brought down some more.

I kept doggedly on through the whole collection, and when I had finished I made up my mind never to read a yellow-backed novel again. Instead of being sinful and gay they were full of moral reflections. They even had clergymen in them. They were all by one man, a writer named Anthony Trollope, whom I never had heard of, and who didn't seem much of a success at sensational fiction. I put them back up in the garret.

I didn't tell my parents about Trollope. He became one of my guilty secrets.

There had been a great deal of talk before we went to the country about what kind of carriage we'd need, for Father to drive to the station in and for Mother to use making calls. We had never owned a carriage before.

There didn't seem to be any such thing as a general-utility vehicle. A two-seated surrey would have been the nearest thing to it, but Father said that a liveried coachman wouldn't look right in a surrey, unless he were driving it, and Father wished to do the driving himself. That ruled out victorias, too. Mother said that next to a victoria she'd choose a nice buggy, but Father said that a buggy would be no use to us when we went back to town. Nobody but a countryman would drive in New York in a buggy. He said he had always loathed buggies, and that he would as lief go around in a wheel-barrow. In the end he had gone to Brewster's to get their advice, and they had fitted him out with that big English dog-cart I spoke of. When Mother remonstrated, he said that Brewster's were the best carriage-builders he knew, and the upshot of it was that Mother was driven around in that dog-cart for years.

It seemed very pleasant to us boys to drive in that dog-cart. It was high, and it had no bothersome doors, sides, or windows, like cabs. On rainy days, the coachman put rubber covers on the cushions and we wore rubber coats. It was a strong heavy vehicle that would stand a lot of knocking about. But it had only two wheels, of course, and it didn't suit Mother. She said it jiggled too much. No matter how tightly she pinned on her hat, Sunday mornings, she arrived at the church door shaken loose on top and bunched up below. And the combination of rain and a dog-cart didn't suit her at all.

The very first drive that we took in it, there was a shower. The dog-cart was stopped. Father and Mother and I and Morgan, the coachman, stood up and put on our rubber coats, and Morgan got out the large rubber apron. Mother then raised her umbrella to protect her big ribbony hat.

Father, sitting on the box seat beside her, stared at this in horror. "You can't put up that thing," he said.

"I can so," Mother answered indignantly.

"I can't drive if you do," Father said. "How the devil can a man see to drive with you bobbing that big thing in front of us?"

"I'm *not* bobbing it," Mother cried. "It's the wind. Do please hurry, Clare. This is awful!"

"Awful?" said Father, trying to hold his whip crosswise, with the umbrella jerking and beating against it. "It's damnable."

"Well then, why didn't you get a buggy, as I told you?" said Mother.

"Will you kindly hold that thing out of my way?" Father shouted. "Upon my soul, this is positively disgraceful. Stop, Vinnie! Stop! You're poking it right in my eye! You can't carry an umbrella in a dog-cart."

When we arrived at the house, half an hour later, with the rain pouring down, they were still hotly debating this question. I don't remember that it ever was settled, though it was debated for years.

One windy night, a week later, there was another and heavier storm, which began just as Father and Cousin Julie were going out to a dinner-party. Neither of them wanted to go, and Julie hadn't even been invited, but Mother declared that they had to. She had written and accepted the invitation for Father and herself ten days ago, she explained, and it was only because she really felt too ill to stir that she was sending Julie instead. Father said he felt sick himself, a lot sicker than Mother, but Mother said he couldn't back out at the last moment and there was no time to send word. So she hurried them off in their evening finery in that cold wind and rain, up high in the air on that shelterless dog-cart, along the unlighted roads.

In general, the roads around Irvington were dusty but good. The great trouble was they were hilly. So far as we boys were concerned, we liked them, but Brownie did not. Brownie was not made for hills, and neither, of course, was the dog-cart. Father said it would have been better to have had a short, stocky cob for such work. Brownie was of an opposite type, he was lanky and limp—so limp that Mother said he was becoming unnaturally elongated, pulling that cart up those hills.

On the other hand, it was because of those hills that our horseback rides were such fun. Father rode every morning before he took the train to the city, and we boys took turns going with him. Little by little we explored every inch of that beautiful countryside.

I was riding with Father one day in September when he found a new road. I galloped ahead, up a hill. Just over the crest of it, hidden from sight till it was too late to stop, was a washout—a deep, ditchlike chasm across the road—which my horse luckily jumped, almost before I had seen it. A little farther on I reined him in and looked back, to see if Father had cleared it.

Father was lying face downward in the road. His horse, which had fallen beside him, was thrashing around with its feet. It scrambled up just as I turned, and I saw it step over Father.

I galloped back, dismounted, and managed to roll and push Father over. He was senseless. I sat down in the road with his head on my lap and wiped the blood off his face. I had never seen him helpless before. It gave me a strange feeling.

I had slung the reins of the two horses over my arm. They kept pulling and tugging to get at the grass on the bank.

As Father didn't come to, or stir, I began shouting for help. It was a still Sunday morning.

The road ran through cornfields and pastures, and there were no passers-by.

Presently, as I sat there, making all the noise I could, I saw Father frown. His eyes were shut; gravel and mud were ground into his face and he looked done for; but I now felt more hope. I threw back my head, and yelled louder than ever. "Hi! Hi! Hi there, help!"

'Way off in a hollow was a yellow farm-house. At last I saw a man coming out of it. He shut the door and walked down a grassy path and up the hill toward us.

He got Father to his feet, after a while. We went slowly along to the house with Father stumbling between us. We put him in a chair, on the grass, and washed his face. He held his head up better after this, but he didn't seem to understand questions.

The farmer and I anxiously discussed different plans. We decided I'd better unsaddle my horse and hitch him up to the farmer's buggy, put Father in, and drive him home just as quick as I could.

Father paid no attention to what we were doing. When the buggy was ready, however, and we tried to pick him up and dump him in, he objected. He was so groggy and his muscles were so slumpy he could hardly sit up, but he clung to the idea that he was out for a nice morning ride. He absolutely refused to have anything to do with a buggy. "Take that damn thing away," he said, and added that he wanted his horse.

The farmer and I were taken aback by this. We had naturally supposed that we were in charge of things, and that Father's ideas didn't count. I still thought so. I told the farmer that all Father needed was a little persuasion. We tried a great deal of it. We got nowhere at all. Shaken up though he was, Father's firm belief in his impregnability remained unimpaired, and he was still somehow the master of the whole situation.

He kept on demanding his horse so imperiously that I gave in. I unharnessed my own horse and resaddled him, put the buggy back in the barn, and with the greatest misgivings the farmer and I hoisted Father up on his mount. He looked as though he'd fall off every minute, but to our amazement he didn't. I said good-bye to the farmer, and Father and I rode up the hill.

It was a long, silent ride. Father came out of his stupor at moments better than I had hoped. At other times he sank back and wobbled about in the saddle. But his knees held on, even when he shut his eyes and seemed not to know what was happening.

We got back to the main road at last. Farther on we came to Dr. Coudert's place. I got off and rang the front doorbell.

Dr. Coudert was upstairs, dressing for church. He looked out of his bedroom window.

"Why, good morning, Day," he called down to Father. "What's the matter?"

"Marrer is," Father said thickly, "some accident. Want you come my house. Fix it."

He turned and trotted away, lurching in the saddle. I hurried off after him.

At our doorway, when he saw Mother come running out, exclaiming at our being late, he tried to dismount by himself. "Vinnie, dear Vinnie," he muttered, and toppled into our arms.

We got him to bed. Dr. Coudert found a great, dull, dark-red place at the nape of his neck, and said that it was pretty serious, but that there was nothing to do but apply ice-bags and wait.

Mother immediately telegraphed to Uncle Hal. He was Father's elder brother; he had retired from business and he was taking his ease at some summer resort, which he did not wish to leave, but he took a train and got up to Irvington that same afternoon. Mother explained to him that Father had to have somebody run the office for him, and that Uncle Hal was the only one whom he would trust. Uncle Hal knew Father too well to take this as a compliment. Father trusted him more than others, yes; but, as Uncle Hal knew from long experience, Father didn't like to trust anyone.

However, Uncle Hal began spending his days down in Wall Street, and faithfully coming up to Irvington to make his reports. He was a large, stout, phlegmatic man, with a face that seemed to be carved from old wood, he could make it so completely expressionless. In behind this, if you watched his eye closely, you could sometimes see a twinkle.

One afternoon when I was in Father's room, changing his icebags, Uncle Hal tiptoed heavily in, and sat down at the side of the bed. He told Father about a few routine matters, in his deliberate way, and then put his fingers together and waited to be cross-examined.

Father feverishly began firing questions at him. "What did you do about those Rome Watertown bonds?" he demanded. "Did you straighten out those legal matters with Choate & Larocque?" The answers to these and other questions were only half-satisfactory. Uncle Hal was a thoroughly sound, careful man; he had made no mistakes, and there was nothing that Father could reasonably object to, exactly, but it exasperated him to discover that his office was not being conducted in quite his own regular manner. "I won't have my office run that way!" he finally roared.

Uncle Hal looked at him stolidly.

Mother rushed in. "Oh, Hall, what *are* you doing!" she shrieked. "I begged you not to excite him!"

Uncle Hal turned his large frame half-around in his chair and regarded Mother stolidly too.

"Never knew such a damned way of doing things in my life," Father groaned.

"Come Hal!" Mother cried. "Come out here in the hall with me, and let me explain *again* to you! Don't sit there, Hal, making things worse like this."

They went out together.

Later on, looking out of the window, I saw Uncle Hal slowly heave himself up into the dog-cart, which always shook him up like a jelly, and which he hated like poison. The coachman drove him off, jiggetty-jig, jiggetty-jog, to the station.

It was weeks before Father got up again. I suppose he had had a concussion of the brain, but we boys weren't told any details. All we knew was that Father had to stay in bed and that he was strangely quiet at first, although later he became his old self again and made a great deal of noise about it. Meanwhile I had a fine time riding his horse, which had more spirit than ours.

After Father got well, he seemed to want to forget the whole incident. He never went back to see that farmer who had tried to lend him his buggy. He didn't seem appreciative of what Mother had done either, she felt, until one day, as a surprise, he gratefully bought her a beautiful ring with three rubies. When Dr. Coudert heard about this, he strongly approved. He told Father that he owed his life to Mother, she had been such a good nurse; and when Mother heard him say it, she nodded her head violently and said that was true.

FATHER HIRES A COOK

❦

ONE late afternoon when Father came up from down town, he found his home much upset. Our cook had walked out and left us. I was a child of four, George was two, and there was a new baby besides. Mother was ill. She hadn't been able to leave us to go to an agency. And she was no hand at cooking herself, the outlook for dinner was poor.

This state of affairs was unprecedented in all Father's experience. In his father's home, they never changed their servants suddenly; they seldom changed them at all; and as his mother was a past mistress of cooking, he had always been doubly protected. Since his marriage, he had had to live a much bumpier life. But this was the worst yet.

He asked Mother, who was lying in bed, what she was going to do about it. There were no telephones then, and she couldn't do anything at all, at the moment; but she said she would try to go to an agency in the morning and see what she could find. "In the morning? Good God!" Father said. "Where is the place, anyhow?" And

53

he clapped on his hat and strode out again, over toward Sixth Avenue.

As I heard the story years afterward, it was late when he got there, and he bounded up the front stoop two or three steps at a time, and went quickly into the little office, where the gaslights were burning. He had never been in such a place before, and to his surprise it was empty, except for a severe-looking woman who sat at a desk at one side. "Where do you keep 'em?" he urgently demanded, his mind on the question of dinner.

She looked at him, got out her pen, and opened a large book deliberately. "I will take your name and address," she informed him, "and then, if you please, you may give me the details as to what kind of person you require and when you would wish her to call."

But Father had no time, he told her, for any damned fol-de-rol. "Where do you keep 'em?" he said again. She was standing in the way of his dinner. I can imagine how his face must have reddened and how his eyes must have blazed at her. "I am asking you where you keep them!" he roared.

"Why, the girls are in there," the lady explained, to calm him, "but clients are not allowed in that room. If you will tell me the kind of position you wish me to fill for you, I will have one come out."

Before she'd half-finished, Father had thrown open the door and gone in. There sat a crowd of the girls, young and old, sickly and brawny, of all shapes and sizes; some ugly, some pretty and trim and stylish, some awkward; nurses, ladies' maids, waitresses, washerwomen, and cooks.

The manager was by now at Father's elbow, trying to make him get out, and insisting that he tell her the position he wished her to fill. But Father was swiftly glancing around at the crowd, and he paid no attention. He noticed a little woman in the corner, with honest grey eyes, who sat there, shrewd-looking and quiet. He pointed his cane over at her and said, "I'll take that one."

The manager was flustered, but still she kept trying to enforce her authority. She protested she didn't yet knew the position. . . .

"Cook," Father said, "cook."

"But Margaret doesn't wish to be a cook, she wants—"

"You can cook, can't you?" Father demanded.

Margaret's plain little face was still pink with excitement and pleasure at being chosen above all that roomful by such a masterful gentleman.

Father had probably smiled at her, too, for they liked each other at once. Well, she said, she had cooked for one family.

"Of course she can cook," Father said.

He said, afterward, when describing the incident, "I knew at once she could cook."

The manager didn't like this at all. The discipline of the office was spoiled. "If you are going to take her anyhow," she said acidly, "what day would you wish her to come, and will you please give me your name?"

"Yes, yes," Father said, without giving it. "Come on, Margaret." And he planked down the fee and walked out.

Margaret followed him through the door and trotted over to our home at his heels. He sent her down to the kitchen immediately, while he went upstairs to dress.

"I don't know why you make such a fuss about engaging new servants. It's simple enough," he said comfortably to Mother that evening, after Margaret's first dinner.

It was the first of a long series, for she stayed with us twenty-six years.

FATHER FEELS STARVED

❧

IN the summers, when we went to the country, our usual plan was to hire a temporary cook to go with us, so that Margaret could stay in town. We hated to leave her, but the idea was that somebody must stay to take care of the house. There were no electric burglar alarms in those days, and few special watchmen. Little Margaret made a pretty small watchman, for she was no size at all, but she had an indomitable spirit. So we'd leave her on guard while we went up to our summer home in Harrison with a substitute cook.

But this didn't work well. No matter how few the substitute's faults were, Father had no patience with them. One summer, I remember, there was a nice woman, Delia, who got on well with Mother because she was so obliging and pleasant, but who didn't suit Father at all. "I don't give a damn how obliging she is," he kept saying. "If she won't oblige me by cooking something fit to eat, she can go."

This didn't sound unreasonable, but Delia cooked well enough for the rest of us, and

57

Mother hated to risk getting someone else who'd be temperamental. Our dining-room consequently became a battleground morning and night. At breakfast, Father would put down his coffee-cup in disgust and roar: "Slops! Damn it, slops! Does she call this confounded mess coffee? Isn't there a damned soul in Westchester County who knows how to make coffee but me? I swear to God I can't even imagine how she concocts such atrocities. I come down to this room hungry every morning, and she tries to fill me with slops. Take it away, I tell you!" he would bellow to the waitress. "Take this accursed mess away!" And while she and Delia were frantically hurrying to make a fresh pot, he would savagely devour his omelet and bacon, and declare that his breakfast was ruined.

The longer Delia stayed with us, the more alarmed Father became. He ate heartily, as Mother kept pointing out to him, but he said he didn't feel nourished. He said it was no use to argue about it; he felt all gone inside. One night after he had had a four-course dinner, he fretfully got up from the table, went into the library with his cigar, and moaned that he was starved. His moans were, as always, full-throated, and they came from the heart. Every now and then, when his miserable condition seemed to strike him afresh, he laid down his book and shouted "Starved! Starved!" in a grief-stricken roar.

When Mother went in the library to quiet him, he told her he'd be damned if he'd stand it. "I refuse to be sent to my grave, do you hear me, by that infernal bog-trotting imbecile you keep in my kitchen."

"Now, Clare, a Japanese is coming tomorrow, I told you. This is Delia's last night. I do hope you'll like Tobo. He won't know our ways right at the start, of course, but he is a very good cook."

Father was appeased for the moment by the dismissal of Delia. But the next night, when he found that the first dish was too Oriental, he said in an annoyed tone to Mother, "Will you kindly explain to your man Tobo that I am not a coolie?" And after eating the rest of his dinner, he pushed his plate away and went up to his bedroom, declaring vehemently that he was poisoned. He undressed, lay down on his sofa, and filled the air with deep groans.

From time to time he stopped and dozed a little, or listened to what he could hear of our talk. His feeling was that we shouldn't be talking at all. We ought to be sitting with bowed heads in silence until he recovered. "Poisoned!" he suddenly boomed, to remind us. "Oh, God! I am poisoned!"

At this point, Mother, who was down in the library, laughed. Father heard her. He jumped up from his sofa and marched from his bedroom indignantly into the hall. "I'm a sick man!" he thundered robustly. "And nobody in this house gives a damn!"

Mother hurried upstairs to see what he wanted. He insisted on her rubbing his back. Sick or well, that always soothed him, and he would have liked her to do it for hours. He loved to close his eyes, with someone's hand moving quietly on him, while a feeling of comfort flowed into his thoughts and his nerves.

Mother didn't think much of rubbing, however. She didn't like it herself. When anyone rubbed her, she stiffened and resisted at once. Consequently she had no idea of the right way to do it. When she had to rub Father, she always got tired of it in a very few minutes.

She gave him some hasty little rubs and digs as well as she could, but just as he was beginning to relax, she said, "There now, Clare, that's enough." Father was so disappointed by this that it reminded him that he was poisoned, and the only cure he could think of was the dismissal of Tobo.

The next day old Margaret was sent for to come at once to the country, and the house in town was locked up and left to take care of itself.

She came in a hack from the Harrison station. She was an odd sight. Her face looked familiar in her little black bonnet, tied under her chin, but she seemed strangely swollen and bulky; she stuck out in queer places; and as she crowded through the back door, she bruised me with her hard, bony hip. Only it wasn't her hip, it turned out; it was her favourite saucepan, which was tied to her waist under her skirt. Several large spoons, a dipper, a skillet, and two pair of shoes were made fast under it elsewhere. In her arms she had some bundles wrapped in newspapers, which Mother thought at first held her clothes, but when Margaret opened them we found they contained cheeses, melons, fresh coffee, a leg of lamb, some sweet potatoes, and other provisions. Margaret had no faith at all in being able to buy any supplies in the country. She had brought as complete a larder to Harrison as though we were at the North Pole.

"But didn't you bring any clothes with you, Margaret? Not even an apron?" asked Mother.

Little Margaret pursed her lips closely together and didn't answer at first. Then, as Mother stood waiting, she said unwillingly, "I have me other clothes on me."

She had wanted to have her hands free, it seemed, to bring us something good to eat. So under her street dress she was wearing two other dresses on that hot summer day, a collection of stiffly starched petticoats, three aprons, two nightgowns, and pretty much all the rest of her wardrobe.

As she was climbing upstairs to unpeel and unpack herself, Father saw her. "Is that you, Margaret?" he called, suddenly feeling much better. "Thank God!"

FATHER THUMPS ON THE FLOOR

OLD MARGARET was just the kind of cook that we wanted. Lots of cooks can do rich dishes well. Margaret couldn't. But she cooked simple, everyday dishes in a way that made our mouths water. Her apple-pies were the most satisfying pies I've ever tasted. Her warmed-up potatoes were so delicious I could have made my whole dinner of them.

Yet even Margaret sometimes miscalculated. A large, royal-looking steak would be set before Father, which, upon being cut into, would turn out to be too underdone. Father's face would darken with disappointment. If the earth had begun to wobble and reel in its orbit he could scarcely have been more disapproving. He would raise his foot, under the table, and stamp slowly and heavily three times on the rug. Thud; thud; thud.

At this solemn signal, we would hear Margaret leave the kitchen below us and come clumping step by step up the stairs to the dining-room door.

"Margaret, look at that steak."

Margaret would step nearer and peer with a shocked look at the platter. "The Lord bless us and save us," she would say to herself in a low voice. She would then seize the platter and make off with it, to better it the best way she could, and Father would gloomily wait and eat a few vegetables and pour out a fresh glass of claret.

Father and Margaret were united by the intense interest they both took in cooking. Each understood the other instinctively. They had a complete fellow-feeling. Mother's great interest was in babies—she had never been taught how to cook. All she wanted was to keep Father pleased somehow; and if it was too difficult she didn't always care about even that.

At table it was Father who carved the fowl, or sliced the roast lamb or beef. I liked to watch him whet the knife and go at it. He had such a fine, easy hand. To a hungry boy, he seemed over-deliberate and exact in his strokes, yet in a moment or two he had done. And usually the cooking had been as superb as the carving. Sometimes it was so perfect that Father's face would crinkle with pleasure and with a wink at us he'd summon Margaret with his usual three measured thumps. She would appear, clutching her skirts with both hands, and looking worried.

"What's wanting?" she'd ask.

"Margaret," Father would tell her affectionately, "that fricasseed chicken is *good*."

Margaret would turn her wrinkled face aside, and look down, and push the flat of her hand out toward Father. It was the same gesture she used when she said "Get along with you" to flatterers. She couldn't say that to Father, but she would beam at him, and turn and go out, and stump back down the dark little stairs without ever a word.

Every once in a while, when the household bills were getting too high, a platter with three tiny French chops on it would be placed before Father, and a larger dish full of cold corned beef or Irish stew before Mother. At this sight we boys would stop talking and become round-eyed and still.

Father would look over at Mother's dish to see if it seemed appetizing, for he often said there was nothing better than one of Margaret's stews. The stew usually seemed possible enough to him, yet not quite what he wanted. He would then ask Mother if she'd have a chop.

Mother always said, "No."

"They look nice and juicy," Father would urge her, but she would say again she didn't want any, and turn her eyes away from the platter.

Father would then look around at the rest of us, doubtfully. He had four sons, all with appetites. He would clear his throat as though getting ready to offer a chop to each boy in turn; but he usually compromised by saying, "Will anyone else have a chop?"

"No, Clare," Mother would quickly and impatiently reply, "they're for you. The rest of us are going to have stew to-night." And she'd smile brightly but a little watchfully around at us boys, to be sure that we were making no fuss about it, while she hurried to get the thing settled.

We boys would then earnestly watch Father while he ate the three chops.

Not that we didn't like Margaret's stew, which was the best in the world, but we regarded dinner as a special occasion, and we often had stew for lunch.

If some of us had taken up Father's offer, and left him with only one chop or none, I suppose that he would have asked Mother, "Where are the rest of the chops?" and been very cross about it when she told him there weren't any more. But his offer of them to us was sincere, though it cost him a struggle. He wanted plenty of food bought for everyone. His instincts were generous. Only, it made him cross if he suffered for those generous instincts.

66

Long after Margaret died, Father was speaking one night of how good her things always had tasted.

"I wish she could hear you," said Mother. She smiled tenderly at the thought of that gallant and dear little figure. "If anybody ever was sure of going to Heaven," she added, "I know it was Margaret."

This struck Father as a recommendation of the place. He took a sip of cognac and said casually, "I'll look her up when I get there. I'll have her take care of me."

Mother started to say something but checked herself.

"What's the matter?" he asked.

"Well, Clare dear," said Mother, "Margaret must be in some special part of Heaven, she was so good. You'd be very fortunate, Clare, to get to the same part as Margaret."

"Hah!" Father said, suddenly scowling. "I'll make a devil of a row if I don't."

THE GIFT OF SONG

ONE day when I was about ten years old, and George eight, Father suddenly remembered an intention of his to have us taught music. There were numerous other things that he felt every boy ought to learn, such as swimming, blacking his own shoes, and book-keeping; to say nothing of school work, in which he expected a boy to excel. He now recalled that music, too, should be included in our education. He held that all children should be taught to play on something, and sing.

He was right, perhaps. At any rate, there is a great deal to be said for his programme. On the other hand, there are children and children. I had no ear for music.

Father was the last man to take this into consideration, however: he looked upon children as raw material that a father should mould. When I said I couldn't sing, he said nonsense. He went to the piano. He played a scale, cleared his throat, and sang *Do, re, mi*, and the rest. He did this with relish. He sang it again, high and low. He then turned to me and told me to sing it, too, while he accompanied me.

I was bashful. I again told him earnestly that I couldn't sing. He laughed. "What do *you* know about what you can or can't do?" And he added in a firm, kindly voice, "Do whatever I tell you." He was always so sure of himself that I couldn't help having faith in him. For all I knew, he could detect the existence of organs in a boy of which that boy had no evidence. It was astonishing, certainly, but if he said I could sing, I could sing.

I planted myself respectfully before him. He played the first note. He never wasted time in explanations; that was not his way; and I had only the dimmest understanding of what he wished me to do. But I struck out, haphazard, and chanted the extraordinary syllables loudly.

"No, no, no!" said Father, disgustedly. We tried it again.

"No, no, no!" He struck the notes louder.

We tried it repeatedly. . . .

I gradually saw that I was supposed to match the piano, in some way, with my voice. But how such a thing could be done I had no notion whatever. The kind of sound a piano made was different from the sound of a voice. And the various notes—I could hear that each one had its own sound, but that didn't help me out any: they were all total strangers. One end of the piano made deep noises, the other end shrill; I could make my voice deep, shrill, or medium; but that was the best I could do.

At the end of what seemed to me an hour, I still stood at attention, while Father still tried energetically to force me to sing. It was an absolute deadlock. He wouldn't give in, and I couldn't. Two or three times I had felt for a moment I was getting the hang of it, but my voice wouldn't do what I wanted; I don't think it could. Anyhow, my momentary grasp of the problem soon faded. It felt so queer to be trying to do anything exact with my voice. And Father was so urgent about it, and the words so outlandish. *Do, re, mi, fa, sol, la, si, do*!" What a nightmare! Though by this time he had abandoned his insistence on my learning the scale; he had reduced his demands to my singing one single note: *Do*. I continually opened my mouth wide, as he had instructed me, and shouted the word *Do* at random, hoping it might be the pitch. He snorted, and again struck the piano. I again shouted *Do*.

George sat on the sofa by the parlour door, watching me with great sympathy. He always had the easy end of it. George was a good brother; he looked up to me, loved me, and I couldn't help loving him; but I used to get tired of being his path-breaker in encounters with

Father. All Father's experience as a parent was obtained at my hands. He was a man who had many impossible hopes for his children, and it was only as he tried these on me that he slowly became disillusioned. He clung to each hope tenaciously: he surrendered none without a long struggle; after which he felt baffled and indignant, and I felt done up, too. At such times if only he had repeated the attack on my brothers, it might have been hard on them, but at least it would have given me a slight rest. But no, when he had had a disappointment, he turned to new projects. And as I was the eldest, the new were always tried out on me. George and the others tried along happily, in comparative peace, while I perpetually confronted Father in a wrestling match upon some new ground. . . .

Mother came into the room in her long swishing skirts. Father was obstinately striking the piano for the nine thousandth time, and I was steadily though hopelessly calling out *Do*.

"Why, Clare! What *are* you doing?" Mother cried.

Father jumped up. I suppose that at heart he was relieved at her interruption—it allowed him to stop without facing the fact of defeat. But he strongly wished to execute any such manoeuvre without loss of dignity, and Mother never showed enough regard for this, from his point of view. Besides, he was full of a natural irritation at the way things resisted him. He had visited only a part of this on me. The rest he now hurled at her. He said would she kindly go away and leave him alone with his sons. He declared he would not be interfered with. He banged the piano lid shut. He said he was "sick and tired of being systematically thwarted and hindered," and he swore he would be damned if he'd stand it. Off he went to his room.

"You'll only have to come right back down again," Mother called after him. "The soup's being put on the table."

"I don't want any dinner."

"Oh, Clare! Please! It's oyster soup!"

"Don't want any." He slammed his room door.

We sat down, frightened, at table. I was exhausted. But the soup was a life-saver. It was more like a stew, really. Rich milk, oyster juice, and big oysters. I put lots of small hard crackers in mine, and one slice of French toast. That hot toast soaked in soup was delicious, only there wasn't much of it, and as Father particularly liked it, we had to leave it for him. But there was plenty of soup: a great tureen full. Each boy had two helpings.

Father came down in the middle of it, still

offended, but he ate his full share. I guess he was somewhat in need of a life-saver himself. The chops and peas and potatoes came on. He gradually forgot how we'd wronged him.

There were too many things always happening at our family dinners, too many new vexations, or funny things, for him to dwell on the past.

But though he was willing enough, usually, to drop small resentments, nevertheless there were certain recollections that remained in his mind—such as the feeling that Mother sometimes failed to understand his plans for our welfare, and made his duty needlessly hard for him by her interference; and the impression that I was an awkward little boy, and great trouble to train.

Not that these thoughts disturbed him, or lessened at all his self-confidence. He lit his cigar after dinner and leaned back philosophically, taking deep vigorous puffs with enjoyment and drinking black coffee. When I said, "Good night, Father," he smiled at me like a humorous potter, pausing to consider—for the moment— an odd bit of clay. Then he patted me affectionately on the shoulder and I went up to bed.

THE NOBLEST
INSTRUMENT

◇

FATHER had been away, reorganizing some old upstate railroad. He returned in an executive mood and proceeded to shake up our home. In spite of my failure as a singer, he was still bound to have us taught music. We boys were summoned before him and informed that we must at once learn to play on something. We might not appreciate it now, he said, but we should later on. "You, Clarence, will learn the violin. George, you the piano. Julian—well, Julian is too young yet. But you older boys must have lessons."

I was appalled at this order. At the age of ten it seemed a disaster to lose any more of my freedom. The days were already too short for our games after school; and now here was a chunk to come out of playtime three days every week. A chunk every day, we found afterward, because we had to practise.

George sat at the piano in the parlour, and faithfully learned to pound out his exercises. He had all the luck. He was not an inspired player, but at least he had some ear for music. He also had the advantage of playing on a good robust instrument, which he didn't have to be careful not to drop, and was in no danger of breaking. A piano had some good points.

But I had to go through a blacker and more gruesome experience. It was bad enough to have to come in from the street and the sunlight and go down into our dark little basement where I took my lessons. But that was only the opening chill of the struggle that followed.

The whole thing was uncanny. The violin itself was a queer, fragile, cigar-boxy thing, that had to be handled most gingerly. Nothing sturdy about it. Why, a fellow was liable to crack it putting it into its case. And then my teacher, he was queer too. He had a queer pickled smell.

I dare say he wasn't queer at all really, but he seemed so to me, because he was different from the people I generally met. He was probably worth a dozen of some of them, but I didn't know it. He was one of the violins in the Philharmonic, and an excellent player; a grave, middle-aged little man—who was obliged to give lessons.

He wore a black, wrinkled frock-coat, and a discoloured gold watch-chain. He had small, black-rimmed glasses; not tortoiseshell, but thin rims of metal. His violin was dark, rich, and polished, and would do anything for him.

Mine was bulky and awkward, brand new, and of a light, common colour.

The violin is intended for persons with a passion for music. I wasn't that kind of person. I liked to hear a band play a tune that we could march up and down to, but try as I would, I could seldom whistle such a tune afterward. My teacher didn't know this. He greeted me as a possible genius.

He taught me how to hold the contraption, tucked under my chin. I learned how to move my fingers here and there on its handle or stem. I learned how to draw the bow across the strings, and thus produce sounds. . . .

Does a mother recall the first cry of her baby, I wonder? I still remember the strange cry at birth of that new violin.

My teacher, Herr M., looked as though he had suddenly taken a large glass of vinegar. He sucked in his breath. His lips were drawn back from his teeth, and his eyes tightly shut. Of course, he hadn't expected my notes to be sweet at the start; but still, there was something unearthly about that first cry. He snatched the violin from me, examined it, readjusted its pegs, and comforted it gently, by drawing his own bow across it. It was only a new and not especially fine violin, but the sounds it made for him were more natural—they were classifiable sounds. They were not richly musical, but at least they had been heard before on this earth.

He handed the instrument back to me with careful directions. I tucked it up under my chin again and grasped the end tight. I held my bow exactly as ordered. I looked up at him, waiting.

"Now," he said, nervously.

I slowly raised the bow, drew it downward . . .

This time there were *two* dreadful cries in our little front basement. One came from my new violin and one from the heart of Herr M.

Herr M. presently came to, and smiled bravely at me, and said if I wanted to rest a moment he would permit it. He seemed to think I might wish to lie down a while and recover. I didn't feel any need of lying down. All I wanted was to get through the lesson. But Herr M. was shaken. He was by no means ready to let me proceed. He looked around desperately, saw the music-book, and said he would now show me that. We sat down side by side on the window-seat, with the book in his lap, while he pointed out the notes to me with his finger, and told me their names.

After a bit, when he felt better, he took up his own violin, and instructed me to watch him and note how he handled the strings. And then at last, he nerved himself to let me take my violin up again. "Softly, my child, softly," he begged me, and stood facing the wall. . . .

We got through the afternoon somehow, but it was a ghastly experience. Part of the time he was maddened by the mistakes I kept making, and part of the time he was plain wretched. He covered his eyes. He seemed ill. He looked often at his watch, even shook it as though it had stopped; but he stayed the full hour.

That was Wednesday. What struggles he had with himself before Friday, when my second lesson was due, I can only dimly imagine, and of course I never even gave them a thought at the time. He came back to recommence teaching me, but he had changed—he had hardened. Instead of being cross, he was stern; and instead of sad, bitter. He wasn't unkind to me, but we were no longer companions. He talked to himself, under his breath; and sometimes he took bits of paper, and did little sums on them, gloomily, and then tore them up.

During my third lesson I saw the tears come to his eyes. He went up to Father and said he was sorry but he honestly felt sure I'd never be able to play.

Father didn't like this at all. He said he felt sure I would. He dismissed Herr M. briefly— the poor man came stumbling back down in two minutes. In that short space of time he had gallantly gone upstairs in a glow, resolved upon sacrificing his earnings for the sake of telling the truth. He returned with his earnings still running, but with the look of a lost soul about him, as though he felt that his nerves and his sanity were doomed to destruction. He was low in his mind, and he talked to himself more than ever. Sometimes he spoke harshly of America, sometimes of fate.

But he no longer struggled. He accepted this thing as his destiny. He regarded me as an unfortunate something, outside the human species, whom he must simply try to labour with as well as he could. It was grotesque, indeed a hellish experience, but he felt he must bear it.

He wasn't the only one—he was at least not alone in his sufferings. Mother, though expecting the worst, had tried to be hopeful about it, but at the end of a week or two I heard her and Margaret talking it over. I was slaughtering a scale in the front basement, when Mother came down and stood outside the door in the kitchen hall and whispered, "Oh, Margaret!"

I watched them. Margaret was baking a cake. She screwed up her face, raised her arms, and brought them down with hands clenched.

"I don't know what we shall do, Margaret."

"The poor little feller," Margaret whispered. "He can't make the thing go."

79

This made me indignant. They were making me look like a lubber. I wished to feel always that I could make anything go. . . .

I now began to feel a determination to master this thing. History shows us many examples of the misplaced determinations of men—they are one of the darkest aspects of human life, they spread so much needless pain: but I knew little history. And I viewed what little I did know romantically—I should have seen in such episodes their heroism, not their futility. Any rôle that seemed heroic attracted me, no matter how senseless.

Not that I saw any chance for heroism in our front basement, of course. You had to have a battlefield or something. I saw only that I was appearing ridiculous. But that stung my pride. I hadn't wanted to learn anything whatever about fiddles or music, but since I was in for it, I'd do it, and show them I could. A boy will often put in enormous amounts of his time trying to prove he isn't as ridiculous as he thinks people think him.

Meanwhile Herr M. and I had discovered that I was nearsighted. On account of the violin's being an instrument that sticks out in front of one, I couldn't stand close enough to the music-book to see the notes clearly. He didn't at first realize that I often made mistakes from that cause. When he and I finally comprehended that I had this defect, he had a sudden new hope that this might have been the whole trouble, and that when it was corrected I might play like a human being at last.

Neither of us ventured to take up this matter with Father. We knew that it would have been hard to convince him that my eyes were not perfect, I being a son of his and presumably made in his image; and we knew that he immediately would have felt we were trying to make trouble for him, and would have shown an amount of resentment which it was best to avoid. So Herr M. instead lent me his glasses. These did fairly well. They turned the dim greyness of the notes into a queer bright distortion, but the main thing was they did make them brighter, so that I now saw more of them. How well I remember those little glasses. Poor, dingy old things. Herr M. was nervous about lending them to me; he feared that I'd drop them. It would have been safer if they had been spectacles: but no, they were pince-nez; and I had to learn to balance them across my nose as well as I could. I couldn't wear them up near my eyes because my nose was too thin there; I had to put them about half-way down where there was enough flesh to hold them. I also had to tilt my head back, for the music-stand was a little too tall for me. Herr M. sometimes mounted me on a stool, warning me not to step off. Then when I was all set, and when he without his glasses was blind, I would smash my way into the scales again.

All during the long winter months I worked away at this job. I gave no thought, of course, to the family. But they did to me. Our house was heated by a furnace, which had big warm air-pipes; these ran up through the walls with wide outlets into each room, and sound travelled easily and ringingly through their roomy, tin passages. My violin could be heard in every part of the house. No one could settle down to anything while I was practising. If visitors came they soon left. Mother couldn't even sing to the baby. She would wait, watching the clock, until my long hour of scale-work was over, and then come downstairs and shriek at me that my time was up. She would find me sawing away with my forehead wet, and my hair wet and stringy, and even my clothes slowly getting damp from my exertions. She would feel my collar, which was done for, and say I must change it. "Oh, Mother! Please!"—for I was in a hurry now to run out and play. But she wasn't being fussy about my collar, I can see, looking back; she was using it merely as a barometer or gauge of my pores. She thought I had better dry myself before going out in the snow.

It was a hard winter for Mother. I believe she also had fears for the baby. She sometimes pleaded with Father; but no one could ever tell Father anything. He continued to stand like a rock against stopping my lessons.

Schopenhauer, in his rules for debating, shows how to win a weak case by insidiously transferring an argument from its right field, and discussing it instead from some irrelevant but impregnable angle. Father knew nothing of Schopenhauer, and was never insidious, but, nevertheless, he had certain natural gifts for debate. In the first place his voice was powerful and stormy, and he let it out at full strength, and kept on letting it out with a vigour that stunned his opponents. As a second gift, he was convinced at all times that his opponents were wrong. Hence, even if they did win a point or two, it did them no good, for he dragged the issue to some other ground then, where he and Truth could prevail. When Mother said it surely was plain enough that I had no ear, what was his reply? Why, he said that the violin was the noblest instrument invented by man. Having silenced her with this solid premise he declared that it followed that any boy was lucky to be given the privilege of learning to play it. No boy should expect to learn it immediately. It required persistence. Everything, he had found, required persistence. The motto was, Never give up.

All his life, he declared, he had persevered in spite of discouragement, and he meant to keep on persevering, and he meant me to, too. He said that none of us realized what he had had to go through. If he had been the kind that gave up at the very first obstacle, where would he have been now—where would any of the family have been? The answer was, apparently, that we'd either have been in a very bad way, poking round for crusts in the gutter, or else non-existent. We might have never even been born if Father had not persevered.

Placed beside this record of Father's vast trials overcome, the little difficulty of my learning to play the violin seemed a trifle. I faithfully spurred myself on again, to work at the puzzle. Even my teacher seemed impressed with these views on persistence. Though older than Father, he had certainly not made as much money, and he bowed to the experience of a practical man who was a success. If he, Herr M., had been a success he would not have had to teach boys; and sitting in this black pit in which his need of money had placed him, he saw more than ever that he must learn the ways of this world. He listened with all his heart, as to a god, when Father shook his forefinger, and told him how to climb to the heights where financial rewards were achieved. The idea he got was that perseverance was sure to lead to great wealth.

Consequently our front basement continued to be the home of lose causes.

Of course, I kept begging Herr M. to let me learn just one tune. Even though I seldom could whistle them, still I liked tunes; and I knew that, in my hours of practising, a tune would be a comfort. That is, for myself. Here again I never gave a thought to the effect upon others.

Herr M., after many misgivings, to which I respectfully listened—though they were not spoken to me, they were muttered to himself pessimistically—hunted through a worn old book of selections, and after much doubtful fumbling chose as simple a thing as he could find for me—for me and the neighbours.

It was spring now, and windows were open. That tune became famous.

What would the musician who had tenderly composed this air, years before, have felt if he had foreseen what an end it would have, on Madison Avenue; and how, before death, it would be execrated by that once peaceful neighbourhood. I engraved it on their hearts; not in its true form but in my own eerie versions.

It was the only tune I knew. Consequently I played and replayed it.

Even horrors when repeated grow old and lose part of their sting. But those I produced were, unluckily, never the same. To be sure, this tune kept its general structure the same, even in my sweating hands. There was always the place where I climbed unsteadily up to its peak, and that difficult spot where it wavered, or staggered, and stuck; and then a sudden jerk of resumption—I came out strong on that. Every afternoon when I got to that difficult spot, the neighbours dropped whatever they were doing to wait for that jerk, shrinking from the moment, and yet feverishly impatient for it to come.

But what made the tune and their anguish so different each day? I'll explain. The strings of a violin are wound at the end around pegs, and each peg must be screwed in and tightened till the string sounds just right. Herr M. left my violin properly tuned when he went. But suppose a string broke, or that somehow I jarred a peg loose? Its string then became slack and soundless. I had to retighten it. Not having an ear, I was highly uncertain about this.

Our neighbours never knew at what degree of tautness I'd put such a string. I didn't myself. I just screwed her up tight enough to make a strong reliable sound. Neither they nor I could tell which string would thus appear in a new rôle each day, nor foresee the profound transformations this would produce in that tune.

All that spring this unhappy and ill-destined melody floated out through my window, and writhed in the air for one hour daily, in sunshine or storm. All that spring our neighbours and I daily toiled to its peak, and staggered over its hump, so to speak, and fell wailing through space.

Things now began to be said to Mother which drove her to act. She explained to Father that the end had come at last. Absolutely. "This awful nightmare cannot go on," she said.

Father pooh-poohed her.

She cried. She told him what it was doing to her. He said that she was excited, and that her descriptions of the sounds I made were exaggerated and hysterical—must be. She was always too vehement, he shouted. She must learn to be calm.

"But you're down town, *you* don't have to hear it!"

Father remained wholly sceptical.

She endeavoured to shame him. She told him what awful things the neighbours were saying about him, because of the noise I was making, for which he was responsible.

He couldn't be made to look at it that way. If there really were any unpleasantness then I was responsible. He had provided me with a good teacher and a good violin—so he reasoned. In short, he had done his best, and no father could have done more. If I made hideous sounds after all that, the fault must be mine. He said that Mother should be stricter with me, if necessary, and make me try harder.

This was the last straw. I couldn't try harder. When Mother told me his verdict I said nothing, but my body rebelled. Self-discipline had its limits—and I wanted to be out: it was spring. I skimped my hours of practice when I heard the fellows playing outside. I came home late for lessons—even forgot them. Little by little they stopped.

Father was outraged. His final argument, I remember, was that my violin had cost twenty-five dollars; if I didn't learn it the money would be wasted, and he couldn't afford it. But it was put to him that my younger brother, Julian, could learn it instead, later on. Then summer came, anyhow, and we went for three months to the seashore; and in the confusion of this Father was defeated and I was set free.

In the autumn little Julian was led away one afternoon, and imprisoned in the front basement in my place. I don't remember how long they kept him down there, but it was several years. He had an ear, however, and I believe he learned to play fairly well. This would have made a happy ending for Herr M. after all; but it was some other teacher, a younger man, who was engaged to teach Julian. Father said Herr M. was a failure.

FATHER TRIES TO MAKE MOTHER LIKE FIGURES

❧

FATHER was always trying to make Mother keep track of the household expenses. He was systematic by nature and he had had a sound business training. He had a full set of account books at home in addition to those in his office—a personal cash-book, journal, and ledger—in which he carefully made double entries. His home ledger showed at a glance exactly how much a month or a year his clothes or his clubs or his cigar bills amounted to. Every item was listed. He knew just how every one of his expenses compared with those of former years, and when he allowed the figures to mount up in one place, he could bring them down in another.

Before he got married, these books had apparently given him great satisfaction, but he said they were never the same after that. They had suddenly stopped telling him anything. He still knew what his personal expenses were, but they were microscopic compared to his household expenses, and of those he knew nothing, no details, only the horrible total. His money was flowing away in all directions and he had no record of it.

Every once in so often he tried to explain his system to Mother. But his stout, leather-bound ledgers, and his methodical ruling of lines in red ink, and the whole business of putting down every little expense every day, were too much for her. She didn't feel that women should have anything to do with accounts, any more than men should have to see that the parlour was dusted. She had been only a débutante when she married, not long out of school, and though she had been head of her class, and wrote well and spelled well, and spoke beautiful French, she had never laid eyes on a ledger. Every time Father showed her his, she was unsympathetic.

Figures were so absorbing to Father that for a long time he couldn't believe Mother really disliked them. He hoped for years that her lack of interest was due only to her youth and that she would outgrow it. He said confidently that she would soon learn to keep books. It was simple. Meanwhile, if she would just make a memorandum for him of whatever she spent, he would enter it himself in the accounts until he could trust her to do it.

That day never arrived.

Father knew where some of the money went,

for part of the expenses were charged. But this was a poor consolation. Although the household bills gave him plenty of data which he could sit and stare at, in horror, he said that many of the details were not clear to him, and most of the rest were incredible.

He tried to go over the bills regularly with Mother, as well as he could, demanding information about items which he did not understand. But every now and then there were items which she didn't understand, either. She said she wasn't sure they were mistakes, but she couldn't remember about them. Her mind was a blank. She behaved as though the bill were a total stranger to her.

This was one of the features that annoyed Father most.

Mother didn't like these sessions a bit. She told us she hated bills, anyhow. When they were larger than she expected, she felt guilty and hardly dared to let Father see them. When some of them seemed small to her, she felt happy, but not for long, because they never seemed small to Father. And when she spotted an error—when she found, for instance, that Tyson, the butcher, had charged too much for a broiler—she had to fly around to the shop to have it corrected, and argue it out, and go through a disagreeable experience, and then when she told Father how hard she had worked he took it as a matter of course, and she indignantly found that she never got any credit for it.

Sometimes I had to do this kind of thing, too. There was a man named Flannagan over on Sixth Avenue who supplied us with newspapers, and I used to be sent to rebuke him when he overcharged. Father said Flannagan had no head for figures. After checking up the addition and recomputing the individual items, he would generally discover that the bill was anywhere from three to fourteen cents out. He then sent for me, handed me the correct amount of change and the bill, and told me to go over to see Flannagan the next day, after school, and warn him that we wouldn't stand it.

I got used to this after a while, but the first time I went I was frightened. Flannagan was a large man who looked like a barkeeper and whose face was tough and belligerent. When I marched into his dark little shop and shakily attempted to warn him that we wouldn't stand it, he leaned over the counter, stared down at me, and said loudly, "Har?"

"Excuse me, Mr. Flannagan," I repeated, "here is your bill but it's wrong."

"*Har?*"

"It seems to be just a little wrong, sir. Eight cents too much for the *Sun*."

Flannagan snatched the bill from me and the money, and went to his desk. After working over it with a thick pencil, and smudging the bill all up, front and back, he snarled to himself, and receipted it the way Father wished. Then he chucked it disdainfully on the counter. I picked it up and got out.

"Confound it all," Father said when he got it, "don't muss my bills up so."

"It was Mr. Flannagan, Father."

"Well, tell him he must learn to be tidy."

"Yes, sir," I said hopelessly.

I liked figures myself, just as Father did, and I thought it was queer Mother didn't. She was as quick at them as anybody, yet she didn't get any fun out of writing them down and adding them up. I liked the problems in my school arithmetic, and I deeply admired Father's account books. I didn't dare tell him this, somehow. He never offered to let me examine those big, handsome books. He kept them locked up in a desk he had, down in the front basement.

If I showed Father one of my arithmetic lessons, he was interested—he got up from his chair and put down his newspaper and sat at the dining-room table with a pencil and paper, to see how well I had done. But Mother didn't want to go into such matters.

Every month when the bills came in, there

was trouble. Mother seemed to have no great extravagances. But she loved pretty things. She had a passion for china, for instance. She saw hundreds of beautiful cups and saucers that it was hard to walk away from and leave. She knew she couldn't buy them, and mustn't, but every so often she did. No one purchase seemed large by itself, but they kept mounting up, and Father declared that she bought more china than the Windsor Hotel.

Father couldn't see why charge accounts should be a temptation to Mother. They were no temptation to him. He knew that the bill would arrive on the first of the month and that in a few days he would pay it. He said he had supposed that Mother would have the same feelings that he had about this.

But Mother was one of those persons for whom charge accounts were invented. When she bought something and charged it, the first of the next month seemed far away, and she hoped that perhaps Father wouldn't mind—he might be nice about it for once. Her desire for the thing was strong at that moment, the penalty was remote, and she fell.

She was a different woman entirely when she had to pay cash. It was hard to get cash out of Father, she never got much at one time, and as she looked in her pocket-book she could see her precious little hoard dwindling. She fingered a purchase and thought twice about it before she could bear to part with the money. But shopping on a charge account was fun. She tried not to let herself be tempted, but of course she was, all the time, and after she had conscientiously resisted nine lovely temptations, it didn't seem really wicked to yield to the tenth.

Father did his level best to take all the fun out of it for her. Once every month regularly he held court and sat as a judge, and required her to explain her crimes and misdemeanours. When she cried, or showed that she was hurt, it appeared that Father, too, felt hurt and worried. He said again and again at the top of his voice that he wished to be reasonable but that he couldn't afford to spend money that way, and that they would have to do better.

Once in a while when Father got low in his mind and said that he was discouraged, Mother felt so sorry that she tried hard to keep count of the cash for him. She put down all sorts of little expenses, on backs of envelopes or on half-sheets of letter paper of different sizes, and she gave these to Father with many interlineations and much scratching out of other memoranda, and with mystifying omissions. He would pore over them, calling out to her to tell him what this was, or that, in a vain attempt to bring order out of this feminine chaos.

Mother could sometimes, though not very often, be managed by praise, but criticism made her rebellious, and after a dose of it she wouldn't put down any figures at all for a while. She had to do the mending and marketing and take care of the children, and she told Father she had no time to learn to be a book-keeper too. What was the use of keeping track of anything that was over and done with? She said that wasn't her way of doing things.

"Well," Father said patiently, "let's get at the bottom of this, now, and work out some solution. What *is* your way of doing things? Tell me."

Mother said firmly that her way was to do the very best she could to keep down expenses, and that all her friends thought she did wonderfully, and the Wards spent twice as much.

Father said, "Damn the Wards! They don't have to work for it. I don't wish to be told what they spend, or how they throw money around."

Mother said, "Oh, Clare, how can you! They don't. They just like to have things go nicely, and live in a comfortable way, and I thought you were so fond of Cousin Mary. You know very well she is lovely, and she gave the baby a cup."

Father declared that he might be fond of Cousin Mary without wanting to hear so damned much about her. He said she cropped up every minute.

"You talk of your own family enough," Mother answered.

Father felt this was very unjust. When he talked of his own family he criticized them, and as severely as he knew how. He held tightly on to himself in an effort to keep to the subject. He said that the point he was trying to make was that Cousin Mary's ways were not his ways, and that consequently there was no use whatever discussing them with him.

Mother said, "Goodness knows *I* don't want to discuss things, it's always you who are doing it, and if I can't even *speak* of Cousin Mary—"

"You can, you can speak of her all you want to," Father hotly protested. "But I won't have Cousin Mary or anyone else dictating to me how to run things."

"I didn't say a word about her dictating, Clare. She isn't that kind."

"I don't know what you said, now," Father replied. "You never stick to the point. But you implied in some way that Cousin Mary—"

"Oh, Clare, please! I didn't! And I can't bear to have you talk so harshly of her when she admires you so."

Something like this happened to every financial conversation they had. Father did his best to confine the discussion to the question at issue, but somehow, no matter how calmly he started, he soon got exasperated and went galloping fiercely off in any direction Mother's mind happened to take; and in the middle of it one of the babies would cry and Mother would have to go off to see what was wrong, or she would have to run down to leave word for Mrs. Tobin, the washerwoman, to do Father's shirts differently, and when Father complained Mother reminded him reproachfully that she had to keep house.

Father was baffled by these tactics. But every time he went back down to the basement and ruled neat lines in his ledgers, he made up his mind all over again that he wouldn't give up.

FATHER AND HIS
HARD-ROCKING SHIP

FATHER said that one great mystery about the monthly household expenses was what made them jump up and down so. "Anyone would suppose that there would be some regularity after a while which would let a man try to make plans, but I never know from one month to another what to expect.

Mother said she didn't, either. Things just seemed to go that way.

"But they have no business to go that way, Vinnie," Father declared. "And what's more I won't allow it."

Mother said she didn't see what she could do about it. All she knew was that when the bills mounted up, it didn't mean that she had been extravagant.

"Well, it certainly means that you've spent a devil of a lot of money," said Father.

Mother looked at him obstinately. She couldn't exactly deny this, but she said that it wasn't fair.

Appearances were often hopelessly against

Mother, but that never daunted her. She wasn't afraid of Father or anybody. She was a woman of great spirit who would have flown at and pecked any tyrant. It was only when she had a bad conscience that she had no heart to fight. Father had the best of her there because he never had a bad conscience. And he didn't know that he was a tyrant. He regarded himself as a long-suffering man who asked little of anybody, and who showed only the greatest moderation in his encounters with unreasonable beings like Mother. Mother's one advantage over him was that she was quicker. She was particularly elusive when Father was trying to hammer her into shape.

When the household expenses shot up very high, Father got frightened. He would then, as Mother put it, yell his head off. He always did some yelling anyhow, merely on general principles, but when his alarm was genuine he roared in real anguish.

Usually this brought the total down again, at least for a while. But there were times when no amount of noise seemed to do any good, and when every month for one reason or another the total went on up and up. And then, just as Father had almost resigned himself to this awful outgo, and just as he had eased up on his yelling and had begun to feel grim, the expenses, to his utter amazement, would take a sharp drop.

Mother didn't keep track of these totals, she was too busy watching small details, and Father never knew whether to tell her the good news or not. He always did tell her, because he couldn't keep things to himself. But he always had cause to regret it.

When he told her, he did it in as disciplinary a manner as possible. He didn't congratulate her on the expenses having come down. He appeared at her door, waving the bills at her with a threatening scowl, and said, "I've told you again and again that you could keep the expenses down if you tried, and this shows I was right."

Mother was always startled at such attacks, but she didn't lose her presence of mind. She asked how much less the amount was and said it was all due to her good management, of course, and Father ought to give her the difference.

At this point Father suddenly found himself on the defensive and the entire moral lecture that he had intended to deliver was wrecked. The more they talked, the clearer it seemed to Mother that he owed her that money. Only when he was lucky could he get out of her room without paying it.

He said that this was one of the things about her that was enough to drive a man mad.

The other thing was her lack of system, which was always cropping up in new ways. He sometimes looked at Mother as though he had never seen her before. "Upon my soul," he said, "I almost believe you don't know what system is. You don't even want to know, either."

He had at last invented what seemed a perfect method of recording expenses. Whenever he gave any money to Mother, he asked her what it was for and made a note of it in his pocket notebook. His idea was that these items, added to those in the itemized bills, would show him exactly where every dollar had gone.

But they didn't.

He consulted his notebook. "I gave you six dollars in cash on the twenty-fifth of last month," he said, "to buy a new coffee-pot."

"Yes," Mother said, "because you broke your old one. You threw it right on the floor."

Father frowned. "I'm not talking about that," he answered. "I am simply endeavouring to find out from you, if I can—"

"But it's so silly to break a nice coffee-pot, Clare, and that was the last of those French ones, and there was nothing the matter with the coffee that morning; it was made just the same as it always is."

"It wasn't," said Father. "It was made in a damned barbaric manner."

"And I couldn't get another French one," Mother continued, "because that little shop the Auffmordts told us about has stopped selling them. They said the tariff wouldn't let them any more, and I told Monsieur Duval he ought to be ashamed of himself to stand there and say so. I said that if I had a shop, I'd like to see the tariff keep me from selling things."

"But I gave you six dollars to buy a new pot," Father firmly repeated, "and now I find that you apparently got one at Lewis & Conger's and charged it. Here's their bill: 'one brown earthenware drip coffee-pot, five dollars.'"

"So I saved you a dollar," Mother triumphantly said, "and you can hand it right over to me."

"Bah! What nonsense you talk!" Father cried. "Is there no way to get this thing straightened out? What did you do with the six dollars?"

"Why, Clare! I can't tell you now, dear. Why didn't you ask at the time?"

"Oh, my God!" Father groaned.

"Wait a moment," said Mother. "I spent four dollars and a half for that new umbrella I told you I wanted, and you said I didn't need a new one, but I did, very much."

Father got out his pencil and wrote, "New Umbrella for V." in his notebook.

"And that must have been the week," Mother

went on, "that I paid Mrs. Tobin for two extra days' washing, so that was two dollars more out of it, which makes it six-fifty. There's another fifty cents that you owe me."

"I don't owe you anything," Father said. "You have managed to turn a coffee-pot for me into a new umbrella for you. No matter what I give you money for, you buy something else with it, and if this is to keep on, I might as well not keep account books at all."

"I'd like to see you run this house without having any money on hand for things," Mother said.

"I am not made of money," Father replied. "You seem to think I only have to put my hand in my pocket to get some."

Mother not only thought this, she knew it. His wallet always was full. That was the provoking part of it—she knew he had the money right there, but he tried to keep from giving it to her. She had to argue it out of him.

"Well, you can put your hand in your pocket and give me that dollar-fifty this minute," she said. "You owe me that, anyhow."

Father said he didn't have a dollar-fifty to spare and tried to get back to his desk, but Mother wouldn't let him go till he paid her. She said she wouldn't put up with injustice.

Mother said it hampered her dreadfully

never to have any cash. She was always having to pay out small amounts for demands that she had forgot to provide for, and in such emergencies the only way to do was to juggle things around. One result, however, of all these more or less innocent shifts was that in this way she usually took care of all her follies herself. All the small ones, at any rate. They never got entered on Father's books, except when they were monstrous.

She came home one late afternoon in a terrible state. "Has it come yet?" she asked the waitress.

The waitress said nothing had come that she knew of.

Mother ran upstairs with a hunted expression and flung herself down on her bed. When we looked in, she was sobbing.

It turned out that she had gone to an auction, and she had become so excited that she had bought but not paid for a grandfather's clock.

Mother knew in her heart that she had no business going to auctions. She was too suggestible, and if an hypnotic auctioneer once got her eye, she was lost. Besides, an auction aroused all her worst instincts—her combativeness, her recklessness, and her avaricious love of a bargain. And the worst of it was that this time it wasn't a bargain at all. At least she didn't think

it was now. The awful old thing was about eight
feet tall, and it wasn't the one she had wanted.
It wasn't half as nice as the clock that old Miss
Van Derwent had bought. And inside the hood
over the dial, she said, there was a little ship
which at first she hadn't noticed, a horrid ship
that rocked up and down every time the clock
ticked. It made her ill just to look at it. And she
didn't have the money, and the man said he'd
have to send it this evening, and what would
Father say?

She came down to dinner, and left half-way
through. Couldn't stand it. But an hour or two
later, when the doorbell rang, she bravely went
to tell Father.

She could hardly believe it, but she found that
luck was with her, for once. If the clock had
come earlier, there might have been a major
catastrophe, but Father was in a good mood and
he had had a good dinner. And though he never
admitted it or spoke of it, he had a weakness for
clocks. There were clocks all over the house,
which he would allow no one to wind but
himself. Every Sunday between breakfast and
church he made the rounds, setting them at the
right time by his infallible watch, regulating
their speed, and telling us about every clock's
little idiosyncrasies. When he happened to be
coming downstairs on the hour, he cocked his

ear, watch in hand, to listen to as many of them as he could, in the hope that they would all strike at once. He would reprove the impulsive pink clock in the spare room for striking too soon, and the big solemn clock in the dining-room for being a minute too late.

So when Mother led him out in the hall to confess to him and show him what she had bought, and he saw it was a clock, he fell in love with it, and made almost no fuss at all.

The let-down was too much for Mother. She tottered off to her room without another word and went straight to bed, leaving Father and the auctioneer's man setting up the new clock alongside the hat-rack. Father was especially fascinated by the hard-rocking ship.

FATHER HAS TROUBLE
WITH THE LAND OF
EGYPT

❧

ONE winter when most of us boys were away,
Mother was invited to go to Egypt with Mrs.
Tytus and two or three others. Mrs. Tytus's son,
Bob, was in charge of the party. They were
going to sail up the Nile in a houseboat, they
would see Luxor and Memphis, and altogether
it seemed to be an ideal opportunity. Mother
loved travel. She was eager to see any place that
was new to her, even a place that was
comparatively near-by like the Whitneys' camp
up in Maine, and as Egypt was ten times as far
away it seemed ten times as attractive.

She explained to Father what a wonderful
chance it was. He was not impressed. He said
she wanted to go anywhere, always, and he had
never seen such a woman. Most women were
glad to have a home, he said, and knew enough
to appreciate it, but the only thing Mother
seemed to want was to be on the go.

He went on to say that he himself had some

sense, however, and that he would no more think of going to Egypt than to the North Pole. In a year or two, if he could get away from business, they might go to London and Paris once more, but not one of the Day family had ever even set foot in Egypt, and nobody else he knew had, either, except Charlie Bond, who was one of those restless fellows anyhow and was always doing queer things. He said it was a wild and entirely unsuitable country, and that never in any circumstances whatever would he take Mother to Egypt.

"But that's just why I want to go, Clare, dear. You don't understand."

Father stared at her, and said, "What! What's why you want to go? Of course I don't understand."

"Why, because you don't like it. I thought it would please you."

The veins in Father's forehead began to swell. "You thought it would *please* me?"

"Oh, Clare, dear, don't be stupid. I knew you wouldn't want to take me over to Egypt yourself, but don't you see, if Mrs. Tytus takes me, you won't ever have to."

This theory that Mother was only trying to save him trouble by getting on a ship and going to Egypt completely dumbfounded Father. But Mother clung firmly to it. She said of course she hated to have him miss seeing the Pyramids, but still she wouldn't enjoy dragging him off there if he was so unwilling, so he could just stay home and be comfortable in his own way while she went quietly over with Mrs. Tytus and hurried straight back.

To help clinch the matter, she brought Mrs. Tytus to see him. She brought young Bob Tytus, too. She told Father how much her letter of credit should be, and when he protested, she said she was saving him money, because it would be nearly twice as much if he took her himself.

When Father said violently that he wished her to remain at his side, she said everybody had to go away sometimes, and Dr. Markoe had warned her she must.

Dr. Markoe was a man Father liked. Mrs. Tytus was tactful and beautiful. Mother was pertinacious. Between them all, they actually bore Father down, and on the appointed day Mother got aboard the ship, letter of credit and all, with Father swearing that now he would have to worry about her all winter, and he wouldn't be happy for a minute until she got back.

"Good-bye, darling," she said. "Do be quiet and nice while I'm gone."

"I won't!" he shouted, kissing her, and he marched stiffly off, saying, "I hope you are satisfied," and then turned back at the foot of the gang-plank, calling loudly, "Dear Vinnie!" Mother waved her hand, the whistles blew hoarsely, and the crowds swirled and jostled, hiding these two from each other as the ship slid away.

Father began looking for letters the very next morning, and when none came he cursed the pilot and the postman, and said that he had a bad headache. But a letter did arrive in a few days, when the pilot had had time to mail it, and after the first three or four weeks we heard from Mother often.

Some of the letters told us how she was constantly meeting people she knew, not only on the ship but at every port where Mrs. Tytus and she went ashore. "Your mother has the damnedest number of friends I ever heard of," said Father. "She's everlastingly meeting some old friend or other wherever she goes. I never see people I know when I'm travelling. But there isn't a city in Europe where your mother wouldn't spot a friend in five minutes." And when a letter came saying she had just climbed Mt. Vesuvius and had found old Mr. and Mrs. Quintard of Rye at the top, peering down into the crater, Father said that upon his soul he never knew anyone like her.

Other letters were full of household advice

and instructions about menus, or warnings to Father to keep an eye on the rubber tree and to speak about washing the curtains. Others abused the bad habits of foreigners and the inconveniences and troubles she met. "Well, why doesn't she stay home, then?" Father demanded triumphantly. Though he swore at every foreigner who dared to inconvenience her, he relished the complaints in these letters.

But when Mother left civilization behind her, even a far outpost like Cairo, and went off up the Nile in a thing called a dahabeah, manned by native boatmen, and when letters came from queer-sounding ancient cities in the interior, Father got nervous. He said it was a wild, harum-scarum thing to do. Moreover, it was entirely needless. He said he could see all of Egypt he wanted to without leaving New York—there were enough musty old mummies in the Museum to satisfy anybody. "But your mother wouldn't look at them; no, they weren't dead enough for her; she had to go traipsing off to see a mummy on its native heath. Why, somebody even brought an obelisk over here at great expense," he went on, "and left it to crumble away in the Park, where people can see it for nothing, but for some reason or other it isn't crumbly enough for your mother."

There were letters about the strange range of

hills back of Thebes, and the great colonnades at Karnak, and the statues and tombs, which Father pished at impatiently; and there were letters about fleas, and moonlight and Nubian songs, and finally letters with snapshots. Father said he hated these photographs. He spent a great deal of time staring at them in deep disapproval. There was one in particular of Mother looking very roguish and chic in her voluminous dress, sitting way up on top of a tall and insolent camel, with two big black men in white turbans standing off at one side. No other member of the party around. Not a soul in sight but the black men and Mother. Father looked at that photograph often and groaned about it at night and kept shouting things to himself about "the ends of the earth."

Soon after that, Mother turned around and headed for home. Father grew more and more eager to have her back, every day. Up to this time he had been comparatively quiet, for him, but the nearer the day of her return came the more noisy and impatient he got. Even at the pier, he made indignant remarks about how slow the ship was, getting in.

He forgot this mood, however, the minute he hugged her, and he instantly took charge of her things—all except her black bag, which she would never let anyone touch—and he ordered all the customs inspectors around and got Mother through in a jiffy, and he found a man to shoulder her trunk and he picked out the best hackman, and as the carriage rattled off over the cobblestones, Mother said she was glad to be back.

Father had taken particular pains to have everything in the house in its place, so that when Mother came in the door, she would say that home was just the way she had left it. Instead, what she actually said was "Oh, this poor room! Why, I never!" and she put down the black bag and began setting the chairs at different angles and moving her favourite ornaments affectionately as she straightened them out. "Poor things," she said, as she patted them, "didn't anybody know enough to turn you around the way you belong?" Father followed her, looking puzzled at these minute changes, and calling her attention to the rubber tree, which had grown half a foot. "Well," Mother said, "of all the forlorn objects, with those dead leaves left hanging there!" But when Father's face fell and she saw how disappointed he looked, she smiled at him to console him and said, "You did the best you could, darling." And she climbed upstairs to unpack.

The letter of credit had been very much on

Father's mind. He had never before given Mother the management of any such sum. He was so happy to have her back that he said nothing about this at first. He was waiting for Mother to speak of it. But she said nothing either.

He had two expectations about it, and he didn't know which to trust. One was hopeful but slightly unreal. The other, based on long experience, was pessimistic.

It had been a large letter of credit, not as much as Mrs. Tytus had recommended but still, he felt, generous. He felt he had a right to expect that Mother hadn't spent all of it, but had left a substantial balance undrawn which he could now restore to his bank account. His other and realer expectation was that she had spent every cent and had possibly even had to borrow from Mrs. Tytus besides. The fact that she was avoiding the subject pointed to this latter outcome.

One night, after she had gone up to bed, she came back down for a moment to hand him some papers. "You might be going over these, Clare," she said. "I couldn't keep track of everything for you; I tried my best but I couldn't. But I saved all the bills." And she went off to bed again.

Father checked them over, one by one,

carefully. They were full of strange-looking details:

CAIRO, *Feb. 24, 1900.*

MRS. DAY,
   Room 195,
      Shepheard's Hotel.

To 1 Passage to Second Cataract	£23	0	0
To 60 days on Dahabeah Tih	85	16	0
	£108	16	0

"Second Cataract!" Father muttered to himself vehemently. What would such a woman do next?

These bills supplied Father with more details than he had hoped to keep track of, and there was none of them that he felt much inclined to dispute. But as there were still several hundred dollars unaccounted for he waited for Mother to confess what she had done with the balance.

Day after day went by without her saying one word. He began to fear that things must be serious. He became so alarmed that it would have been a relief to him to know the worst and be done with it. But do what he could—without direct questioning—he could get nothing out of her.

Mother had noticed his fumbling hints of course, and she did have a confession to make. But first she went and had a long talk with a young girl she was fond of—a girl whose name was Wilhelmine Johnson, whom George afterward married. Mother confided to Wilhelmine in secret that the situation was this: she hadn't spent all her letter of credit but she hated to give up the balance. It was wicked of her to feel that way, she supposed, but she meant to keep it herself.

Wilhelmine instantly took a strong stand about this. She said that on no account should Mother hand over that money to Father. Mother had always wanted to have some money of her own, Wilhelmine reminded her, and now here was her chance.

As Mother listened to this advice she felt happy, but she also felt frightened. It seemed to her far more daring to hang on to that money than it had been to ride on a camel. But while she was away all those months she had had a taste of what independence was like, and she was reluctant to drop back into her Victorian rôle.

When at last she nerved herself to tell Father, he felt better at once, but he smilingly reproved her for not having come to him sooner; and as to her keeping the money he said that that was all nonsense. He said that she was home now, thank God, and as he always paid all her bills at home she had no use for this money.

"Yes I have too," Mother said.

"Well, what will you use it for, then?" Father asked.

Mother didn't wish to explain. As a matter of fact she had no very definite ideas as to what she wanted some cash of her own for—she only knew that she wanted it. She said: "Oh, there are lots of little things I could use it for, Clare. Things I'd like to get when I need them, without so much talk."

This seemed unconvincing to Father. He demanded the balance. He felt that he was the natural custodian of any such fund and the only safe place for it was in his bank account, as Mother, of course, didn't have one. But Mother insisted on hiding it away in her own bureau drawer. Father pointed out how reckless this was, but he could do nothing with her. That voyage to Egypt had changed her; she was always much harder to manage after that sail up the Nile.

As a gracious concession, however, she presented Father with a large pale-blue scarab, mounted to use as a scarf-pin, which she said she hadn't really meant to let him have until Christmas. Father looked at this object without enthusiasm and asked what it was. When he was told that it was the image of a sacred beetle, he immediately pushed it away. He didn't want any dead beetles in his scarf, he declared. He told Mother she could send it right back to the tomb it had come from. He said that he begged to inform her that he was not a mummy.

FATHER TEACHES ME TO BE PROMPT

FATHER made a great point of our getting down to breakfast on time. I meant to be prompt, but it never occurred to me that I had better try to be early. My idea was to slide into the room at the last moment. Consequently, I often was late.

My brothers were often late, too, with the exception of George. He was the only thoroughly reliable son Father had. George got down so early, Father pointed out to me, that he even had time to practise a few minutes on the piano.

The reason George was so prompt was that he was in a hurry to see the sporting page before Father got hold of the newspaper, and the reason he then played the piano was to signal to the rest of us, as we dressed, which team had won yesterday's ball game. He had made up a code for this purpose, and we leaned over the banisters, pulling on our stockings and shoes, to hear him announce the results. I don't remember now what the titles were of the airs he selected, but the general idea was that if he played a gay, lively air it meant that the Giants had won, and when the strains of a dirge or lament floated up to us, it meant that Pop Anson had beaten them.

As Father didn't approve of professional baseball, we said nothing to him about this arrangement. He led his life and we led ours, under his nose. He took the newspaper away from George the moment he entered the room, and George said good morning to him and stepped innocently into the parlour. Then, while Father watched him through the broad doorway and looked over the political head-lines, George banged out the baseball news for us on the piano. Father used to admonish him with a chuckle not to thump it so hard, but George felt that he had to. We were at the top of the house, and he wanted to be sure that we'd hear him even if we were brushing our teeth. George always was thorough about things. He not only thumped the piano as hard as he could but he hammered out the tune over and over besides, while Father impatiently muttered to himself, "*Trop de zèle.*"

Upstairs, there was usually some discussion as to what kind of news George was sending. He had not been allowed to learn popular tunes, which it would have been easy for us to recognize, and the few classic selections which were available in his little music-book sounded pretty much alike at a distance. George rendered these with plenty of goodwill and muscle but not a great deal of sympathy. He regarded some of the rules of piano-playing as needlessly complicated.

The fact remained that he was the one boy who was always on time, and Father was so pleased by this that he bought a watch for him with "George Parmly Day, Always on Time" engraved on the back. He told me that as I was the eldest he had meant to give me a watch first, and he showed me the one he had bought for me. It was just like George's except that nothing had been engraved on it yet. Father explained that to his regret he would have to put it away for a while, until I had earned it by getting down early to breakfast.

Time went on, without much improvement on my part. Dawdling had got to be a habit with me. Sometimes my lateness was serious. One morning, when breakfast was half over and I had nothing on but a pair of long woollen drawers, Father called up from the front hall, napkin in hand, that he wouldn't stand it and that I was to come down that instant. When I shouted indignantly that I wasn't dressed yet, he said he didn't care. "Come down just as you are, confound it!" he roared. I was tempted to take him at his word, but thought there might be some catch in it and wouldn't, though I hurried, of course, all I could. Father ate his usual hearty breakfast in a stormy mood, and I ate my usual hearty breakfast in a guilty and nervous one. Come what might, we always ate heartily. I sometimes wished afterward that I hadn't, but it never seemed to hurt Father.

Mother told Father that if he would give me the watch, she was sure I'd do better. He said that he didn't believe it, and that that was a poor way to bring a boy up. To prove to him that he was wrong, Mother at last unlocked her jewel-box and gave me a watch which had belonged to one of her elderly cousins. It was really too valuable a watch for a boy to wear, she said, and I must be very careful of it. I promised I would.

This watch, however, turned out to be painfully delicate. It was old, I was young. We were not exactly made for each other. It had a back and front of thin gold, and as Mother had had the former owner's monogram shaved off the front cover, that cover used to sink in the middle when pressed. Also, the lid fitted so closely that there was barely room for the glass crystal over the face. Such a very thin crystal had to be used that any pressure on the lid broke it.

I didn't press on the lid, naturally, after the first time this happened. I was careful, and everything would have gone well enough if other boys had been careful, too. It was not practicable, however, for me to make them be careful enough. When I had a fight, friendly or otherwise, I used to ask my opponent if he would be so kind as not to punch me on the left side of my stomach. He might or might not listen. If he and I were too excited and kept on long enough, the watch crystal broke anyway. There was never time to take off my watch first, and anyhow there was no place to put it. A watch that goes around the streets in a boy's pocket has to take life as it comes. This watch had never been designed for any such fate.

The first two crystals I broke Mother paid for, as Father disapproved of the whole business and would have nothing to do with it. Mother was always short of small change, however, and I hated to trouble her—and she hated to be troubled, too. "Oh, Clarence, dear! You haven't broken your watch again?" she cried when I opened the cover the second time to show her the shattered fragments. She was so upset that I felt too guilty to tell her the next time it happened, and from then on I was reduced to the necessity of paying for the damage myself.

My pocket-money never exceeded a dollar a

month. Every new crystal cost twenty-five cents. It was a serious drain.

Wrestling and rolling around on the floor with Sam Willets, my watch quite forgotten, I would suddenly hear a faint tinkle and know that I was once more insolvent. I would pick out the broken glass and leave the watch with no crystal till I had twenty-five cents on hand, but these delays made me nervous. I knew that Mother wanted to feel sure I was taking good care of the watch, and that she might look at it any evening. As soon as I had the money, I hurried over to Sixth Avenue, where two old Germans kept a tiny watch shop, and left it there to be fixed. One of my most dismal memories is of that stuffy little shop's smell of sauerkraut, and how tall the glass counter then seemed, and the slowness of those two old Germans. When I got there late and they made me leave the watch overnight, I didn't have one easy moment until I got it back the next day. Again and again I argued with them that twenty-five cents was too much, especially for a regular customer, but they said it didn't pay them to do the work even for that, because those thin old-fashioned crystals were hard to get.

I gave up at last. I told Mother I didn't want to wear the watch any more.

Then I found, to my amazement, that this

way out of my troubles was barred. The watch was an heirloom. And an heirloom was a thing that its recipient must value and cherish. No good Chinese, I read later on in life, fails to honour his ancestors; and no good boy, I was told in my youth, fails to appreciate heirlooms.

I left Mother's room in low spirits. That night, as I wound up my watch with its slender key, I envied George. Father had selected the right kind for George; he knew what a boy needed. It had a thick nickel case, it had an almost unbreakable crystal, and it endured daily life imperturbably, even when dropped in the bathtub.

It seemed to me that I was facing a pretty dark future. The curse of great possessions became a living thought to me, instead of a mere phrase. The demands that such possessions made on their owners for upkeep were merciless. For months I had had no money for marbles. I couldn't even afford a new top. In some way that I didn't fully understand I was yoked to a watch I now hated—a delicate thing that would always make trouble unless I learned to live gingerly.

Then I saw a way out. All this time I had kept on being late for breakfast at least once a week, out of habit, but it now occurred to me that if I could reform, perhaps Father might relent and give me that reliable nickel watch he had bought. I reformed. I occasionally weakened in my new resolution at first, but every time that crystal got broken I was spurred on to fresh efforts. When I had at length established a record for promptness that satisfied Father, he had my name engraved on the watch he had bought, and presented it to me. He was a little surprised at the intense pleasure I showed on this occasion, and as he watched me hopping around the room in delight he said "There, there" several times. "Don't be so excited, confound it," he added. "You'll knock over that vase."

Mother said she couldn't see why Father should give me a nickel watch when I had a gold one already, but he laughed and told her that "that old thing" was no kind of a watch for a boy. She reluctantly laid it away again to rest in her jewel-box.

Her parting shot at Father was that anyhow she had been right; she had said all along that a watch was what I needed to teach me how to be prompt.

FATHER INTERFERES WITH THE TWENTY-THIRD PSALM

✧

WHEN we boys were little, we used to go to Mother's room Sunday evenings, on our way upstairs to bed, and sit in a circle around her, while she told us a story from the Bible or talked to us about how good we ought to be and how much we ought to love God. She loved God herself as much as she dared to, and she deeply loved us, and she was especially tender and dear on those Sunday evenings. One of my brothers told me years afterward how much they had meant to him in those days, and how he had cherished the memory of them all his life.

I was a little older than my brothers, though, and my feelings were mixed. I loved Mother and hated to disappoint her, but I couldn't respond as easily as the other boys to her gentle appeals. I never seemed to have the emotions that she waited for me to show. I wish now that I could have listened uncritically and have thought only of the look in her eyes. What difference need it have made to me whether we had the same ideas about God, or whether the stories Mother thought lovely seemed less so to me? But there I sat, staring uncomfortably at the carpet and trying to avoid answering questions.

One night she repeated the Twenty-third Psalm to us and asked us to learn it by heart. "The Lord is my shepherd," she whispered, softly. "He maketh me to lie down in green pastures: he leadeth me beside the still waters." She raised her eyes and went on bravely, although with a quiver of fear: "Thy rod and thy staff they comfort me." She had often felt the Lord's rod.

I heard Father going by in the hall. He looked in at the doorway and smiled affectionately at us and at Mother. Then he went off, and I heard his firm step as he walked on toward his room.

He hadn't meant to interfere with Mother's teachings. He hadn't spoken one word. But I found myself speculating, all of a sudden, on what his opinion would be of the Twenty-third Psalm.

I couldn't imagine Father being comforted by the Lord's rod and staff, or allowing anybody whatever to lead him to a pasture and get him to lie down somewhere in it. I could see him in my mind's eye, in his tailed coat and top hat, refusing point-blank even to enter a pasture. He would as soon have thought of wearing overalls. In spite of my admiring him for this attitude, it seemed wicked of him. I felt resentful about it. It would have been so much easier for me to be properly reverent if he had not been around. My idea was that if Mother was too religious, Father wasn't religious enough.

"Good night, Clarence," I heard Mother saying. "You won't forget, darling?"

I kissed her and went out, wondering what I was not to forget. Oh, yes—she had asked us to learn that psalm by heart.

Up in my bedroom, I got out my Bible. It was full of paper book-marks, to help me find texts that I'd had to memorize, and these book-marks in turn were full of pictures I had drawn of Biblical scenes. A picture of Adam looking doubtfully at the Tree of Knowledge in Eden, with a complete set of school books dangling heavily down from its boughs. A picture of Sarah "dealing hardly with Hagar," driving her out with a broomstick. A picture of the sun, moon, and stars bowing politely to Joseph.

I sat down and added to the collection a picture of Job in pyjamas, weeping copiously as he endeavoured, on top of all his other trials, to learn the Twenty-third Psalm. I also drew his three unsatisfactory friends, sitting in a row staring at Job. Each friend wore a sardonic expression and had a large moustache and imperial like Napoleon the Third.

I got out another Bible that Mother had lent me. This one was in French, and it sometimes shocked me deeply to read it. As my belief was that when God had created the world He had said, "Let there be light," it seemed to me highly irreverent to put French words in His mouth and have Him exclaim, "*Que la lumière soit!*" Imagine the Lord talking French! Aside from a few odd words in Hebrew, I took it completely for granted that God had never spoken anything but the most dignified English.

The French were notoriously godless, however. It made me laugh, though it frightened me, too, to see what liberties they had taken. In my English Bible, David was a fine Anglo-Saxon type, "a youth, ruddy and of a fair countenance." In the French, he was a revolting little snip from the boulevards, "*un enfant, blond, et d'une belle figure.*" Where my Bible spoke of "leviathan," the French said, "*le crocodile*," which ruined the grandeur and mystery of that famous beast. And where mine said, "Behold now behemoth," they said, "*Voici l'hippopotame!*"

Instead of the children of Israel fearing lest the Lord should be wroth, the French said, "*les enfants d'Israël*" were afraid lest "*le Seigneur*" should be "*irrité.*" This word "*irrité*" appeared everywhere in the French version. It wasn't only the Lord. Cain was "*très irrité.*" Moïse (which seemed to me a very jaunty way of referring to Moses) was "*irrité*" again and again. Everybody was "*irrité.*" When my regular Bible, the real one, impressively described men as "wroth," their anger seemed to have something stately and solemn about it. If they were full of mere irritation all the time, they were more like the Day family.

I turned at last to the Twenty-third Psalm. They had spoiled that, too. They had twisted it around until it read as though the scene were in Paris. "Green pastures" were changed into "*parcs herbeux,*" and "thy rod and thy staff" had become "*ton bâton,*" as though the Lord were leading David up and down the Bois de Boulogne like a drum-major.

I decided to go to bed and let that psalm wait for a day or two. But before putting the books back on my shelf, I hunted up the one place in the French Bible that I really liked. "Blessed are the meek," my English Bible said, "for they shall inherit the earth." I had always hated that verse. It made all religion so difficult. Uriah Heep typified the meek, to my mind. The meek were a snivelling, despicable, and uncomfortable lot. But in poring over the French Bible one evening, I had found to my delight that some daring Frenchman had altered this passage and had changed the Sermon on the Mount into something that a fellow could stand. "*Heureux les débonnaires*," he had represented Jesus as saying, "*car ils hériteront de la terre.*"

The debonair! That was more like it! I cheerfully jumped into bed.

MOTHER AND THE ARMENIAN

MOTHER used to take us boys to a summer resort in our vacations. In all such places there was usually an Armenian, prowling around the hotel piazza. Blue-black hair, dark skin, gleaming eyes, a hooked nose, perfect teeth. Mother said that there wasn't a lady on the piazza who didn't envy those teeth. The Armenian was always trying to catch the eye of one of them to see if he couldn't persuade her to look at his rugs or his silks. "Not buy, Madam! Just look!" She would say no; but he would tell her they were "Oh so beautiful," and offer to give her some perfume, till perhaps if it were a dull afternoon she would roll up her knitting, and saunter down to the end of the hall where his dark little room was.

Since Mother had both a kind heart and a weakness for rugs, she was occasionally snared in this fashion and shown some bargain, some rug that was intrinsically priceless and could never be duplicated, but which could be had for a few hundred dollars, as it happened, that morning. The crisis that made such a price possible would to-morrow be gone, but to-day it was here, and a wise and clever woman would seize it. Whoever did would be helping a most grateful young man get through college. He was no dealer; he was just a poor student with a few priceless rugs, and if the lady would only make him an offer she could buy at her own figure. She could make him an offer, surely, *some* offer; let it be what it might.

It began to seem unreasonable to Mother not to make him some offer, especially as he was trying to get through college, and it might be a bargain. So she silently tried to figure how much she'd have had to pay at places like Sloane's; and then she took a lot off; and then she felt a little ashamed at taking so much off—she didn't wish to cheat the young man. He seemed to mean well, poor creature. So she worked her price up a little, in her mind, and then got a bit frightened because, after all, it was a good deal of money—though it did seem perfectly safe to pay that much, since Lord & Taylor's or Arnold Constable's would have charged more. Still, you never could tell about a rug, because it might not be genuine, and she wished the young man had let her alone and could get through college without her, though he didn't much look as though he would manage it; he could hardly speak English—and how could the poor thing talk to the professors, or the professors to him, when even on the subject of rugs he had to use a sort of sign language which consisted of hunching his shoulders till she feared he would dislocate them, and picking out sums on his fingers in the most confusing manner. However, she had better make him an offer, she felt, and then perhaps he'd stop smiling, which no doubt he intended as pleasant, but his breath was so bad.

So she finally said, fingering the rug in a dissatisfied way, that she supposed she could give him a hundred for it. The Armenian's smile instantly disappeared. He walked off in gloom. Then he rushed back, excited and jerky, and began a long rapid expostulation that threatened to deafen us. Mother reluctantly raised her bid to a hundred and twenty to stop him, whereupon it suddenly appeared that he had misunderstood her first offer. He had supposed it to be two hundred, not one. She meant *two* hundred and twenty? Mother said, No, one hundred and twenty was all she had offered. The Armenian then tottered around, sank into a chair, and sort of hissed through his teeth, with such a ghastly look that it made Mother fear he might be having a fit. It began to seem advisable to her to do anything she could to get out of it, and then never buy anything again for the rest of her life. So she miserably and angrily said she would make it one-fifty. She had to say it several times, however, before he seemed to hear her, and even then he received it only with low shrieks and groans in Armenian. He said that now he would have to give up college, because he could not bear such losses. All he had ever hoped of America, he said, was that he wouldn't lose too much money here, but he had found that no one cared how badly he ruined himself, nor did they understand rugs. Poor Mother, half dismayed, half indignant, said she did not want the rug; she had only made him an offer because he had asked her to, and she would now like to go. This brought on a frightful collapse, so full of despair it seemed mortal. He was heard, however, to murmur what she took to be a dying request that she would take the rug with her and split the difference and leave him alone in his agony. On the way out, she had to tell the hotel-clerk to pay him and have it charged on the bill.

At the end of the week, when Father came to visit us and stay over Sunday, Mother had to explain to him that he was now the owner of a rare Eastern rug. Her attempts to announce this to him as a triumph somehow fell very flat. He began by not believing his ears, no matter how many times she repeated it. "Rug? Rug? You say you've bought a *rug*? Nonsense! Pooh! Don't be ridiculous!" And when he found that the story seemed true, and that he couldn't thrust it away, his face turned a dark unhealthy red and he burst into roars of resentment. He shouted that he had only just arrived from hard toil in the city, in search of "a little damned peace," that was all that he asked, instead of which, before he had had time to smoke one cigar, he was harried and tortured and victimized by a pack of low swindlers, with whom his own family had leagued themselves, to render him penniless. He urgently demanded to see the rug so that he could throw it straight out of the window, and the Armenian after it. He swore he'd break every bone in his body. All reports as to the rarity and value of the rug he discredited, declaring he could buy better for fifty cents a barrel on Front Street. He then marched to the Armenian's parlour, with vague but violent intentions, only to find that that astute sufferer had closed his place up. The door was shut and locked and a sign was on it:

BAK
NEKS
WEK

"What's this gibberish?" Father demanded.

"You said his name was Dourbabian."

Poor old fawning Dourbabian! His things were not good value at the time; but they at least have become so. That rug and the sofa-cushion covers and great squares of silk which Mother picked up in the eighties would cost a lot more to-day. She had to keep them out of Father's sight though, until he had forgotten their origin.

Years afterwards, one day, when the newspapers printed some clergyman's denunciations of Turkey for its cruel Armenian massacres, I thought of how Father had longed to massacre Dourbabian, and reminded him of it. Though older and calmer on some subjects he was still resentful on this. "That's just like a parson," he said, "to sympathize with those fellows, without even asking first what they have done to the Turks."

FATHER OPENS MY MAIL

THERE was a time in my boyhood when I felt that Father had handicapped me severely in life by naming me after him. "Clarence." All literature, so far as I could see, was thronged with objectionable persons named Clarence. Percy was bad enough, but there had been some good fighters named Percy. The only Clarence in history was a duke who did something dirty at Tewkesbury, and who died a ridiculous death afterwards in a barrel of malmsey.

As for the Clarences in the fiction I read, they were horrible. In one story, for instance, there were two brothers, Clarence and Frank. Clarence was a "vain, disagreeable little fellow," who was proud of his curly hair and fine clothes, while Frank was a "rollicking boy who was ready to play games with anybody." Clarence didn't like to play games, of course. He just minced around looking on.

One day when the mother of these boys had gone out, this story went on, Clarence "tempted" Frank to disobey her and fly their kite on the roof. Frank didn't want to, but

141

Clarence kept taunting him and daring him until Frank was stung into doing it. After the two boys went up to the roof, Frank got good and dirty, running up and down and stumbling over scuttles, while Clarence sat there, giving him orders, and kept his natty clothes tidy. To my horror, he even spread out his handkerchief on the trapdoor to sit on. And to crown all, this sneak told on Frank as soon as their mother came in.

This wasn't an exceptionally mean Clarence, either. He was just run-of-the-mill. Some were worse.

So far as I could ever learn, however, Father had never heard of these stories, and had never dreamed of there being anything objectionable in his name. Quite the contrary. And yet as a boy he had lived a good rough-and-tumble boy's life. He had played and fought on the city streets, and kept a dog in Grandpa's stable, and stolen rides to Greenpoint Ferry on the high, lurching bus. In the summer he had gone to West Springfield and had run down Shad Lane through the trees to the house where Grandpa was born, and had gone barefoot and driven the cows home just as though he had been named Tom or Bill.

He had the same character as a boy, I suppose, that he had as a man, and he was too

independent to care if people thought his name
fancy. He paid no attention to the prejudices of
others, except to disapprove of them. He had
plenty of prejudices himself, of course, but they
were his own. He was humorous and confident
and level-headed, and I imagine that if any boy
had tried to make fun of him for being named
Clarence, Father would simply have laughed
and told him he didn't know what he was
talking about.

I asked Mother how this name had ever
happened to spring up in our family. She
explained that my great-great-grandfather was
Benjamin Day, and my great-grandfather was
Henry, and consequently my grandfather had
been named Benjamin Henry. He in turn had
named his eldest son Henry and his second
son Benjamin. The result was that when Father
was born there was no family name left.
The privilege of choosing a name for Father
had thereupon been given to Grandma, and
unluckily for the Day family she had been
reading a novel, the hero of which was named
Clarence.

I knew that Grandma, though very like
Grandpa in some respects, had a dreamy side
which he hadn't, a side that she usually kept to
herself, in her serene, quiet way. Her romantic
choice of this name probably made Grandpa

smile, but he was a detached sort of man who didn't take small matters seriously, and who drew a good deal of private amusement from the happenings of everyday life. Besides, he was partly to blame in this case, because that novel was one he had published himself in his magazine.

I asked Mother, when she had finished, why I had been named Clarence too.

It hadn't been her choice, Mother said. She had suggested all sorts of names to Father, but there seemed to be something wrong with each one. When she had at last spoken of naming me after him, however, he had said at once that that was the best suggestion yet—he said it sounded just right.

Father and I would have had plenty of friction in any case. This identity of names made things worse. Every time that I had been more of a fool than he liked, Father would try to impress on me my responsibilities as his eldest son, and above all as the son to whom he had given his name, as he put it. A great deal was expected, it seemed to me, of a boy who was named after his father. I used to envy my brothers, who didn't have anything expected of them on this score at all.

I envied them still more after I was old enough to begin getting letters. I then discovered that when Father "gave" me his name he had also, not unnaturally I had to admit, retained it himself, and when anything came for Clarence S. Day he opened it, though it was sometimes for me.

He also opened everything that came addressed to Clarence S. Day, Jr. He didn't do this intentionally, but unless the "Jr." was clearly written, it looked like "Esq.," and anyhow Father was too accustomed to open all Clarence Day letters to remember about looking carefully every time for a "Jr." So far as mail and express went, I had no name at all of my own.

For the most part nobody wrote to me when I was a small boy except firms whose advertisements I had read in the *Youth's Companion* and to whom I had written requesting them to send me their circulars. These circulars described remarkable bargains in magicians' card outfits, stamps and coins, pocket-knives, trick spiders, and imitation fried eggs, and they seemed interesting and valuable to me when I got them. The trouble was that Father usually got them and at once tore them up. I then had to write for such circulars again, and if Father got the second one, too, he would sometimes explode with annoyance. He became particularly indignant one year, I remember, when he was repeatedly urged to take advantage of a special bargain sale of false whiskers. He said that he couldn't understand why these offerings kept pouring in. I knew why, in this case, but at other times I was often surprised myself at the number he got, not realizing that as a result of my postcard request my or our name had been automatically put on several large general mailing lists.

During this period I got more of my mail out of Father's waste-basket than I did from the postman.

At the age of twelve or thirteen, I stopped writing for these childish things and turned to a new field. Father and I, whichever of us got at the mail first, then began to receive not merely circulars but personal letters beginning:

DEAR FRIEND DAY:

In reply to your valued request for one of our Mammoth Agents' Outfits, kindly forward post-office order for $1.49 to cover cost of postage and packing, and we will put you in a position to earn a large income in your spare time with absolutely no labour on your part, by taking subscriptions for *The Secret Handbook of Mesmerism*, and our *Tales of Blood* series.

And one spring, I remember, as the result of what I had intended to be a secret application on my part, Father was assigned "the exclusive rights for Staten Island and Hoboken of selling the Gem Home Popper for Pop Corn. Housewives buy it at sight."

After Father had stormily endured these afflictions for a while, he and I began to get letters from girls. Fortunately for our feelings, these were rare, but they were ordeals for both of us. Father had forgotten, if he ever knew, how silly young girls can sound, and I got my first lesson in how unsystematic they were. No matter how private and playful they meant their letters to be, they forgot to put "Jr." on the envelope every once in so often. When Father opened these letters, he read them all the way through, sometimes twice, muttering to himself over and over: "This is very peculiar. I don't understand this at all. Here's a letter to me from some person I never heard of. I can't see what it's about." By the time it had occurred to him that possibly the letter might be for me, I was red and embarrassed and even angrier at the girl than at Father. And on days when he had read some of the phrases aloud to the family, it nearly killed me to claim it.

Lots of fellows whom I knew had been named after their fathers without having such troubles. But although Father couldn't have been kinder-hearted or had any better intentions, when he saw his name on a package or envelope it never dawned on him that it might not be for him. He was too active in his habits to wait until I had a chance to get at it. And as he was also single-minded and prompt to attend to unfinished business, he opened everything automatically and then did his best to dispose of it.

This went on even after I grew up, until I had a home of my own. Father was always perfectly decent about it, but he never changed. When he saw I felt sulky, he was genuinely sorry and said so, but he couldn't see why all this should annoy me, and he was surprised and amused that it did. I used to get angry once in a while when something came for me which I particularly hadn't wished him to see and which I would find lying, opened, on the hall table marked "For Jr.?" when I came in; but nobody could stay angry with Father—he was too utterly guiltless of having meant to offend.

He often got angry himself, but it was mostly at things, not at persons, and he didn't mind a bit (as a rule) when persons got angry at him. He even declared, when I got back from college, feeling dignified, and told him that I wished he'd be more careful, that he suffered from these mistakes more than I did. It wasn't *his* fault, he pointed out, if my stupid correspondents couldn't remember my name, and it wasn't any

pleasure to him to be upset at his breakfast by
finding that a damned lunatic company in
Battle Creek had sent him a box of dry bread-
crumbs, with a letter asserting that this rubbish
would be good for his stomach. "I admit I threw
it into the fireplace, Clarence, but what else
could I do? If you valued this preposterous
concoction my dear boy, I'm sorry. I'll buy
another box for you to-day if you'll tell me
where I can get it. Don't feel badly! I'll buy you
a barrel. Only I hope you won't eat it."

In the days when Mrs. Pankhurst and her
friends were chaining themselves to lamp-posts
in London, in their campaign for the vote, a
letter came from Frances Hand trustfully asking
"Dear Clarence" to do something to help
Woman Suffrage—speak at a meeting, I think.
Father got red in the face. "Speak at one of their
meetings!" he roared at Mother. "I'd like
nothing better! You can tell Mrs. Hand that it
would give me great pleasure to inform all those
crackpots in petticoats exactly what I think of
their antics."

"Now, Clare," Mother said, "you mustn't talk
that way. I like that nice Mrs. Hand, and
anyhow this letter must be for Clarence."

One time I asked Father for his opinion of a
low-priced stock I'd been watching. His opinion
was that it was not worth a damn. I thought this

over, but I still wished to buy it, so I placed a scale order with another firm instead of with Father's office, and said nothing about it. At the end of the month this other firm sent me a statement, setting forth each of my little trans-actions in full, and of course they forgot to put the "Jr." at the end of my name. When Father opened the envelope, he thought at first in his excitement that this firm had actually opened an account for him without being asked. I found him telling Mother that he'd like to wring their damned necks.

"That must be for me, Father," I said, when I took in what had happened.

We looked at each other.

"You bought this stuff?" he said incredu-lously. "After all I said about it?"

"Yes, Father."

He handed over the statement and walked out of the room.

Both he and I felt offended and angry. We stayed so for several days, too, but we then made it up.

Once in a while when I got a letter that I had no time to answer I used to address an envelope to the sender and then put anything in it that happened to be lying around on my desk—a circular about books, a piece of newspaper, an old laundry bill—anything at all, just to be amiable, and yet at the same time to save myself the trouble of writing. I happened to tell several people about this private habit of mine at a dinner one night—a dinner at which Alice Duer Miller and one or two other writers were present. A little later she wrote me a criticism of Henry James and ended by saying that I needn't send her any of my old laundry bills because she wouldn't stand it. And she forgot to put on the "Jr."

"In the name of God," Father said bleakly, "this is the worst yet. Here's a woman who says I'd better not read *The Golden Bowl*, which I have no intention whatever of doing, and she also warns me for some unknown reason not to send her my laundry bills."

The good part of all these experiences, as I realize now, was that in the end they drew Father and me closer together. My brothers had only chance battles with him. I had a war. Neither he nor I relished its clashes, but they made us surprisingly intimate.

FATHER SENDS ME TO THE WORLD'S FAIR

❧

FATHER and Mother and my brothers went out to the World's Fair in Chicago in 1893. I was finishing my freshman year at Yale, and by the time I got home they had gone. Father had written me that I had better follow on and join them, but I couldn't. I had spent all my allowance. There would be no more money coming to me until college opened again in September. In the meantime I didn't even have car fare or money enough for tobacco. It wasn't this that bothered me, however, or not going out to Chicago. It was the fact that for the first time in my life I had got deep in debt.

I owed Warner Hall forty-two dollars for seven weeks' board, I owed Dole for a heavy turtle-neck sweater, and De Bussy, Manwaring & Co. for ascot ties and shirts and a pair of pointed-toed shoes. I owed Heublein's for the rounds of drinks I had signed for, on what had once seemed jolly nights. I was in debt to Stoddard the tobacconist for sixty or seventy dollars for all sorts of fancy pipes—one of them was a meerschaum head of a bull with large amber horns. The total due to these and other tradesmen was nearly three hundred dollars, and I didn't see how I could have been so reckless, or when I could ever pay up. Worst of all, my creditors too had become pessimistic.

I borrowed a nickel for car fare from old Margaret, after she had cooked me my breakfast, put a sandwich and a banana in my pocket, and went down town at once to Father's office to ask for a job. They didn't have any work for me down there and didn't want me around, but it was lucky I went, because while I was eating my sandwich one of my creditors entered. He had come down to New York with a bundle of overdue bills to see whether he could collect any of them by calling upon his customers' parents.

I was appalled. It had never occurred to me that anyone would come to Father's office like this. It seemed to me most underhanded. If Father had been there and I hadn't, I'd have been in serious trouble, for Father had warned me repeatedly to keep out of debt. I was thoroughly frightened, and I attempted to frighten that creditor. I said in a loud, shaky voice that if he was going to behave in this manner, I would never buy anything more from him as long as I lived.

He said he was sorry to hear it. But he didn't

sound very sorry. Times were bad, he explained, and he had to have money. I didn't believe him. Looking back, I realize that the long depression of the nineties had started and banks were beginning to close, but I knew nothing about this at that time. I was preoccupied with my own troubles. These looked blacker than ever to me when my creditor said, as he left, that since my father was out, he would have to call on him again the next time he came to New York.

I didn't know what to do. But one thing was clear. I saw I must stick around Father's office for the rest of that summer. So as soon as he got back from the Fair, I begged him to give me a job. I didn't need any vacation, I told him, and I would be getting a lot of valuable experience if he would let me go to work.

After thinking it over, he said that perhaps I could make myself useful as an office-boy while his clerks were taking turns going on their vacations. I started the very next day at four dollars a week.

I might have got slightly better wages elsewhere, but I couldn't have made enough anyway to pay much on my bills, and the most important thing was not to make a few dollars extra but to stand on guard at the door of Father's office to keep my creditors out. When I was sent out on an errand, I ran all the way there and back. When I was in the office, turning the big iron wheel on the letter-press, I always kept one eye on the grated window where the cashier sat at his counter, to make sure that no buzzards from New Haven were coming in to see Father.

But late in the summer I got into trouble. The cashier told Father that I had taken hold better than he had expected, and that although I was not very accurate I was punctual and quick and seemed to be especially interested in getting down early. Father was so pleased that he sent for me to come into his inner office and told me that he had decided I had earned a vacation.

I said that honestly and truly a vacation was the last thing I wanted.

He smiled at the immense pleasure I seemed to be taking in sealing envelopes and filling inkwells, but he explained that he wanted me to have some rest and recreation before college opened, and he added that he would advise me to go to Chicago and see the World's Fair.

I said I didn't care about seeing the Fair.

Father didn't quite like this. "I have just told you, Clarence," he said, "that I would advise you to go." I saw that he would regard it as disrespectful of me if I refused.

I uncomfortably made a partial confession. I

said I couldn't afford to go to Chicago. I didn't have any money.

Father was surprised. "What about your allowance?" he asked.

"I'm sorry to say I've spent it all, Father."

"That was very imprudent of you," he observed.

I said in a low voice that I knew it.

Father said that he hoped this would be a lesson to me to be more careful in future. By failing to exercise even the most ordinary prudence, he explained in his firm, friendly way, I had deprived myself of seeing a sight that might never come again in my lifetime. He said he felt badly about it.

I didn't, however. I went back to working the letter-press. I liked to turn the big, painted iron wheel and tighten the plates. We didn't use carbons. Instead, after writing letters by hand in copying ink or else on the typewriter, we pressed them down hard on damp tissue-paper to make copies to file. It took a good deal of practice to do this correctly. If the tissue was too dry, the copy was so faint it could hardly be read, and if I got it too wet, it made the ink run and smudged the whole letter.

The next day, Father interrupted me at this interesting occupation again. He had had a long talk with Mother, it seemed, and, as all the rest of the family had seen the Fair, they wanted me to go, too. He said that he would therefore help me out this once and give me some money, and he asked how much I had saved from my wages.

I had saved nearly all of them, as a matter of fact. I had spent less than a dollar a week. Margaret had wrapped up little lunches for me, and my only other needs had been a hair-cut and car fares and a new pair of cuffs. But as I had been using all I saved to pay small instalments to those men in New Haven, I had only forty-eight cents on hand.

"Well, the devil!" Father laughed disappointedly. "You have attended to your duties here faithfully enough, I suppose, but I see you have a damn lot to learn."

I thought to myself that he little knew how much I was learning.

He lit a cigar and looked at me reflectively. "Clarence," he said, "I think I should reproach myself afterward if I allowed you to miss seeing this Fair. It is a great educational opportunity that may never recur. So I will make you a present of one hundred dollars to enable you to go to Chicago."

"Thank you very much, Father," I said, as he shook hands with me, "but if you wouldn't mind, I'd rather have the money, sir."

Father frowned.

I stood beside his desk, waiting. A hundred dollars would be a magnificent windfall for me and my creditors.

His reply killed my hopes. "I see no point in giving you a hundred dollars to fritter away as you have done with your other funds," he said. "If you don't choose to avail yourself of this educational—"

"Oh, I do, sir," I said. If the only way to get that hundred dollars was to go to Chicago and back, I saw that of course I'd better go. I felt sure I could save at least some of it to use in paying my bills.

I went to the cashier and begged him to keep an eye out for my creditors and not let any of them in, in my absence. He said he would do all he could, but he wouldn't like to be caught surreptitiously keeping out callers. I argued that these people would annoy Father if they saw him, and that they ought to be treated like book-agents; but he said Father might regard their disclosures as important, however unwelcome, and that he couldn't keep anyone out who came on legitimate business.

I almost gave up going, at this. But Father and Mother were so eager to give me a treat that I couldn't. I had to pretend to be eager myself, with my heart in my boots.

I wrote to my creditors that I would begin

paying my bills very soon and that I hoped they would wait.

Father asked me what road I was getting a ticket on. He said the Lake Shore was the best. I made some vague answer to that. I didn't like to tell him, after he had been so generous to me, that I had bought a cut-rate ticket to Chicago and back, for eleven dollars, on an Erie Special Excursion. The Erie was so awful in those days that it was a joke. It didn't go nearly as far as Chicago, of course, but it had arranged for trackage rights over a number of other one-horse railroads for its Special Excursions.

It took that train three days and two nights, if I remember correctly, to get to Chicago. We stopped at every small station. We waited for hours on sidings. Most of the time I had very little idea where we were. The Excursion wandered around here and there, in various parts of this country and Canada, trying to pick up extra passengers. Of course, the train had no sleeping-cars or diner—only day coaches. There was quite a crowd of us in them—men, women and children. In the seat back of mine was a woman with two babies. I had my seat pretty much to myself, however, because the old man who sat with me spent most of his time in the smoker. I didn't go to the smoker myself. I had nothing to smoke.

All the windows were open, it was so hot. We were coated with coal-dust. The washroom got out of order and had to be locked. The little drinking-tank was soon emptied. Most of us had nothing to eat, and we slept sitting up. But it was fun. Nearly everybody but the overworked train-men was good-natured and friendly. At every stop we'd all pile out of the cars and bolt for the wash-room in the station, or try to buy pie and sandwiches and stand in line at the water-cooler, and those of us who went dry at one stop would try again at the next. At one little place where the station was locked and there was no other building in sight, we had the best luck of all, because there was a pond near the tracks, rather yellow, but with plenty of water for everybody. I was rinsing my undershirt in it when the whistle blew, and I only just managed to scramble aboard the train as it started. The day before that, at a little place where the eating was good, several passengers who didn't run fast enough had been left behind.

At Chicago, I hunted up a boarding-house. As those near the Fair Grounds were expensive, I went to the outskirts, where I found an old boarding-house near the railroad which was clean and decent. I sent off a postcard to Mother saying that the Fair was simply fine, and got a good bath and sleep.

I went to the Fair the next day. My boarding-house was so far out that I had to go by train, but the fare was low and the station was handy. And when I walked into the Fair Grounds, I was deeply impressed. They were a wonderful sight. The vast buildings weren't solid stone, of course, and they wouldn't be there a hundred years hence, but in the meanwhile they provided a vision of grandeur, at least for innocent eyes. The eyes, for example, of persons who had come on the Erie.

I sat in the Court of Honour, I walked admiringly around the artificial lagoon, I sauntered through one or two of the exhibition halls, and went back to my boarding-house.

On my next visit, I explored the grounds more thoroughly and I was upset to find that all the places which I wanted to see most cost money. This was particularly true of the Midway Plaisance, a broad promenade lined with side-shows. There were Bedouins, a Ferris Wheel, a fearsome (canvas) Hawaiian volcano, a wonderful captive balloon, and a "Congress of Beauty." And there was also a real Dahomey village of genuine savages. I could reach out and touch them as they stalked about scowling; and whenever I did I could hear them muttering things to themselves. They occasionally danced in a threatening manner uttering genuine war-cries; and the guide-book said, "They also sell products of their mechanical skill." And, in what had excited the most talk of all in the newspapers, there were dancing girls with bare stomachs, who wriggled in what clergymen said was a most abandoned way, right before everybody.

I had heard so much about these girls that I forgot all my vows to economize and went into their tent. They didn't come up to my hopes. I had already noticed in New Haven that such things never did.

That night in my boarding-house, I counted my money, and I saw that if I had good times on the Midway, I'd have a bad time with creditors. My creditors won and I didn't go to the Midway again.

There was a great deal else to see, however, and I saw nearly all of it, because it was free. But as Father had said, it was educational. I spent hours and hours roaming through the principal exhibits which were supposed to be good for the mind. They were interesting but monotonous. It was like visiting a hundred museums at once. A few of these palaces fascinated me when I came to them fresh; the Krupp guns were better than anything on the Midway. But the showmanship wasn't. Herr Krupp had announced, by the way, that he was presenting the biggest gun of all to America, "for the defence of the great port of Chicago."

These free exhibits increased my expenses, some days; they made me so hungry. I had a hard time trying to be economical at the White Horse Inn, I remember. This was a reproduction of an old English inn, swollen to an extraordinary size, and the big chops at the next table looked juicy and the steaks smelled delicious. And every time I went to the Transportation Building and got in a coma, I had to revive myself on beer and cheese afterward in a place called Old Vienna.

Father had especially enjoined upon me the duty of studying the Transportation Exhibits, because he was an officer or director of several small railroads, and he hoped that by and by I might be too. It was quite an assignment. That building had eighteen acres of floor-space. It was built in the form of several large train-sheds. The guide-book explained that "in style it is somewhat Romanesque," and it added that "ornamental colour designs, in thirty different shades, of its exterior, produce an effect almost as fine as embroidery."

On rainy days I didn't go to the Fair Grounds. I sat in my boarding-house and saved money. But this was dull and I felt lonely, so I bought a chameleon for company. He wasn't much company. On the other hand, as the end of his tail had been broken off, he only cost twenty cents. He wore a chain with a little brass collar at one end and a pin at the other, and I stuck the pin in the window curtain to tether him, and fed him live flies.

I wanted to go home after a week of this, but I figured that I'd better not. Father might think I had been too lavish with his money if it only lasted a week. So I stayed on for over a fortnight to inspire him with confidence in me, and make him see that I wasn't always a spendthrift in spite of my bad freshman record.

When I wasn't at the Fair, I wandered around Chicago. There was something about Chicago I liked. It seemed bigger and busier to me than New York, and much fatter, much more spread out and roomy.

At last, when I thought Father must surely be feeling that I had used up that hundred dollars, I packed my suitcase, pinned the chameleon to the lapel of my coat, and embarked again on the Erie. The chameleon had a miserable time on the train and the rest of his tail got joggled off, but even so he was luckier than he knew, for we made much better time going east than we had made going west.

I had gone away worried and alarmed, but I came home in triumph. No creditors had gone to the office, I learned, and I had saved fifty-two dollars to send to New Haven. I hadn't brought home any presents for the family, but I presented the chameleon to Mother.

Father and I had a little talk about what I had liked. "Did you see the Midway?" he asked.

"I saw a little of it," I said cautiously. "Did you see it, Father?"

"Yes," he said, "I was interested in those filthy Hottentots. How people can live in that disgusting manner I don't understand. I didn't know it was allowed."

He was pleased when he found I had gone only once to the Midway and had apparently spent all the rest of my time in the right places.

"Well," he finally said in approval, "I gather, then, that you found it was an educational experience for you."

"Yes, Father," I told him, "I did."

FATHER'S OLD TROUSERS

❖

FATHER didn't care much for jewellery. He disliked the heavy watch-chains which were worn by the men of his time, chains with charms dangling down from the middle. His had none of these things on it; it was strong and handsome but simple. His studs and cuff-links were on the same order, not ornate like those then in fashion. His ring was a solid plain band of gold, set with a rectangular sapphire. All these objects we regarded with a reverence which we felt was their due. There was a special sort of rightness about Father's things, in our eyes, and we had a special respect for them because they were Father's.

Father had had a lighter ring once, with a smaller sapphire, which he had worn as a young man. He had discarded it as less suitable for him, however, as he got on in life, and it had been put away long ago in the safe in our pantry.

Mother didn't like to have it lying idle there, year after year. After I left college, she decided that I had better wear it, so that the family

would get some good out of it once more. One
afternoon she and I went into the crowded
pantry, with its smell of damp washcloths, and
she took it out of the safe.

I did not want a ring, but Mother presented
this one to me with such affection that I saw no
way to get out of accepting it. She put it on my
finger and kissed me. I looked at the thing. The
sapphire was a beautiful little stone. I thought
that after a while I might learn to like it,
perhaps. At any rate, there was nothing to get
out of order or break.

I soon discovered, however, that this ring was
a nuisance—it was such hard work not to lose it.
If I had bought and paid for it myself, I suppose
I'd have cherished it, but as it had been wished
on me, it was only a responsibility. It preyed on
my mind. After a little while, I stopped wearing
it and put it away.

When Mother noticed that it wasn't on my
finger, she spoke out at once. She said there
wasn't much point in my having a ring if I
merely kept it in my bureau drawer. She
reminded me that it was a very handsome ring
and I ought to be proud to wear it.

I explained that I couldn't get used to
remembering that I was wearing a ring, and had
several times left it on public washstands and
got it back only by sheer luck. Mother was

frightened. She instantly agreed that it would be a terrible thing to lose Father's ring. It went back into the safe in the pantry.

Several years later, it was taken out again, and after another little ceremony it was entrusted to George. He had even more trouble with it than I'd had. He, too, decided that he didn't wish to wear it himself, so, as he had married, he gave it to his wife, who adored it. Everyone was happy for a while until Mother happened to see Father's ring nestling on Wilhelmine's finger. Mother was very fond of Wilhelmine, but this strange sight disturbed her. She felt that the only right and appropriate use for that ring was for it to be worn by one of Father's sons. She asked George to take it away from Wilhelmine and return it. He silently did so, and back it went again to the pantry.

It was a curious fact that everything that Father had ever owned seemed to be permanently a part of him. No matter what happened to it, it remained impressed with his personality. This isn't unusual in the case of a ring, I suppose, but the same thing was true even of Father's old neckties, especially from his point of view. I don't think he cared what became of that ring, the way Mother did, but when he gave me an old necktie or a discarded pair of trousers, they still seemed to him to be his. Not only did he feel that way about it but he made me feel that way, too. He explained to me that he gave things which he didn't care about to the coachman or the Salvation Army, but that when he had a particularly handsome tie which had plenty of wear in it yet, or a pair of trousers which he had been fond of, he saved anything of that sort for me.

A pair of striped trousers which he had worn to church on Sundays for years went up to New Haven with me one Christmas, when I was a junior, and as I was short of clothes at the time they came in very handy. I had to be careful not to take off my coat while I was wearing them, though. They looked oddly baggy in the seat when exposed to full view—on nights when I was playing billiards in a poolroom, for instance. They also made it harder for me to climb Osborn Hall's iron gate. This gate was ten feet high, with a row of long, sharp spikes at the top, and to get quickly over it in Father's trousers was quite a feat.

There was no point in getting over it quickly. In fact, there was no point in getting over it at all. Osborn Hall was used solely for lectures, and we saw quite enough of it in the daytime without trying to get in there at night. Besides, we couldn't get in anyhow, even after climbing the gate, because the big inside doors were locked fast. After standing in the vestibule a minute, between the doors and the gate, there was nothing to do but climb back again and go home to bed. This seemed like a useful or stimulating performance, though, when we had been drinking.

On nights like these, as I was undressing in my bedroom, I sometimes had moral qualms over the way that I was making Father's trousers lead this new kind of life. Once in a while such misgivings would even come over me elsewhere. They were not clear-cut or acute, but they floated around in the back of my mind. Usually I paid little attention to what clothes I had on, but when I did happen to notice that I was wearing those trousers into places which were not respectable, I didn't feel right about it.

Then one week I lent them to a classmate of mine, Jerry Ives, to wear in his rôle of a fat man in some Psi U play. Father wasn't fat, but he was much more full-bodied than Jerry, and there was plenty of room in his trousers for a pillow and Jerry besides. I thought no more of the matter until the night of the play, but when the curtain went up and I saw Father's Sunday trousers running across the stage pursued by a comic bartender who was yelling "Stop thief!" I felt distinctly uncomfortable.

After that, nothing seemed to go right with

them. The fact was, they simply didn't fit into undergraduate life. The night that I most fully realized this, I remember, was when a girl whom Father would have by no means approved of sat on what was my lap but his trousers. Father was a good eighty miles away and safely in bed, but I became so preoccupied and ill at ease that I got up and left.

FATHER LETS IN THE TELEPHONE

❧

Up to the late eighteen-nineties, when Father walked in the front door of his home and closed it behind him, he shut out the world. Telephones had been invented but, like most people, he hadn't installed one. There was no way for anybody to get at us except by climbing up the front stoop and ringing the bell; and if the bell rang late at night, Father looked out of the window to see who it was. He thought nothing of this—homes had always been shut off since men began building them, and it seemed only natural.

Once in a long while a messenger boy would bring him or Mother a telegram—maybe two or three times a year. As this generally meant bad news, we were nervous about getting telegrams.

No telegraph poles were allowed on Fifth Avenue, but they stood in long rows on other thoroughfares. Old Margaret was mystified by all those wires, up in the air. We had wires in our house, to be sure; they had been strung inside the walls to ring bells with; but they were good, honest, old-fashioned wires and to make them work we had to pull them. There was none of this dangerous stuff called electricity in them. Electricity was much too risky a thing to put in a home, and neither we boys nor Margaret could make out what it was. All we knew about it was that there were electric batteries in the Eden Musée which could and did give anyone who paid twenty-five cents a shock. You were supposed to give yourself as big a shock as you could stand. We had been cautious in trying them, except George, who had had a startling experience. He had taken hold of one end of the thing in his right hand and moved it way up, till the indicator pointed to far more "current" than the rest of us had been able to stand, and yet he stood there at ease for a while as though he were completely immune. Then the lady in charge noticed that George hadn't taken the other end in his left hand at all. He hadn't understood that he ought to. When she told him that the way to feel the current was to hold one end in each hand, he immediately seized the left hand one without lowering the right from its height. It was grandly exciting to the rest of us to see how violently this shook him up, and how the lady screamed until attendants rushed over and managed to shut off the current.

After a while the telegraph company persuaded Father to let them install a brand-new invention, just inside of one of our back bedroom windows, where it couldn't do any harm. This was a small metal box with a handle. A wire led from it which was connected with a telegraph pole, but although there was some electricity in it there was only a little, and the company guaranteed it was safe. The handle was made to look just like those on the pull-bells which we were used to. When we pulled it, the box began to buzz, and somehow that sent a signal to the nearest telegraph office, where a row of little messenger boys was supposed to be waiting. The office then sent a boy to our house ready to run any errand.

This "buzzer," as we called it, seemed almost as remarkable to us as that lamp of Aladdin's. By giving some extra pulls on it and making it buzz enough times, the directions said, a policeman could be summoned, or even a fire engine.

How long it would have taken for a police-man to come we never had occasion to learn. It took a messenger boy from twenty to forty-five minutes—that is, if we were lucky. The branch office was nearly a mile away and it had only one little benchful of boys. If the boys were all out when we buzzed for one, the manager had no way to tell us. We might be impatient. He wasn't. He peacefully waited till some boy got through other errands.

On stormy days sometimes, when a friend wished to send us a message or break an engagement, a messenger would surprise us by coming without being buzzed for. He stood outside the front door, with a black rubber hood dripping with rain hanging down from his cap, blowing on his cold fingers and stamping, and ringing away at the bell. And when one of us opened the door, the boy would thrust in a wet letter and hoarsely ask us to sign the name and the hour on a small smudgy slip.

All these delays were more or less put up with, however. There was no other service to turn to. And anyway people seldom used messengers— they were not only slow but expensive. We ran our own errands.

When the telephone was invented and was ready to use, hardly anybody cared to install one. We all stuck to our buzzers. Messenger boys were quite enough of a nuisance, suddenly appearing at the door with a letter and expecting an answer. But they came only a few times a year, and a telephone might ring every week. People admitted that telephones were ingenious contraptions and wondered just how they worked, but they no more thought of getting one than of buying a balloon or a diving-suit.

As a matter of fact, for a long time they were of little use in a home. Since almost nobody had them but brokers, there was no one to talk to. The telephone company sent us circulars in which they made large claims: they said that an important department store now had a telephone, and three banks had ordered one apiece, and some enterprising doctors were getting them. But though people saw vaguely that a telephone might be a convenience if every household installed one, they decided to wait in a body until everyone did.

Father had to have one down town, but he wouldn't use it himself; he had it put in the back office, where the book-keeper dealt with it, bringing Father the message if necessary. The typewriter and a gelatine hektograph were in the back office, too. But the idea of putting these business conveniences in a home seemed absurd.

Mother agreed with Father—she didn't like telephones either. She distrusted machines of all kinds; they weren't human, they popped or exploded and made her nervous. She never knew what they might do to her. And the telephone seemed to her, and many other people, especially dangerous. They were afraid that if they stood near one in a thunderstorm they might get hit by lightning. Even if there wasn't any storm, the electric wiring might give them a shock. When they saw a telephone in some hotel or office, they stood away from it or picked it up gingerly. It was a freak way to use electricity, and Mother wouldn't even touch the queer toy. Besides, she said, she had to see the face of any person she talked to. She didn't want to be answered by a voice coming out of a box on the wall.

Little by little, however, and year by year, telephones came into use. Some of the large markets and groceries installed them. The livery stable. Some druggists. And once in a while, when Father had a bad cold and couldn't go to the office, he saw it would be a business convenience to have one at home.

After ten or fifteen years, in spite of his still having misgivings, he got one. It was put on a wall on the second floor, where everybody could hear its loud bell. We didn't give it much of a welcome. It seemed to us rude and intrusive, and from the first it made trouble. It rang seldom but it always chose a bad moment, when there was nobody on that floor to answer. Mother would pick up her skirts and run upstairs, calling to it loudly "I'm coming! I'm coming!" but the fretful thing kept right on ringing. Father couldn't regard it as inanimate either. He refused to be hurried like Mother, but he scolded and cursed it.

The outer world now began intruding upon us at will. This was hard to get used to. Even Mother felt there was too much of it. As for Father, he met these invasions with ferocious resentment. When somebody telephoned him and he couldn't make out at once who it was, and when there was nothing he could shake his fist at but a little black receiver which was squeaking at him, he said it was horrible. "Speak up, speak up, damn it!" he would shout at the telephone, getting red in the face. "What is it, who are you? I can't hear a word you are saying. I can't hear a damned word, I tell you."

"Clare, give me that telephone!" Mother would cry, rushing in.

"I will not give you this telephone!" Father would roar in reply, without taking his lips from the transmitter. "Will you let me alone? I am trying to find out who the devil this person is. Halloa! I say halloa there, do you hear me? Who are you? Halloa! . . . What's that? . . . Oh, it's you, Mrs. Nichols." Here his voice would grow a little less forbidding, and sometimes even friendly. "Yes, Mrs. Day's here. How are you? . . . Oh, do you wish to speak to Mrs. Day? . . . Eh? . . . Very well then. Wait a moment." And he would at last allow Mother to get at the box on the wall.

When Father called a number himself, he usually got angry at "Central." He said she was deaf, she was stupid, he told her she wasn't attending to her duties in a suitable manner. If she said a number was busy, he'd protest: "I can't sit here waiting all day. Busy? Busy be damned!"

He always assumed when the bell rang that it was a message for him. The idea that it might be a call for Mother or one of the rest of us seemed wholly improbable. If he let anyone but himself answer, he would keep calling out and asking who it was and what it was all about anyhow, while we tried, in the midst of his shouts, to hear some of the message. When we said it was something that didn't concern him, he was incredulous, and had to have it explained to make sure.

One day a new friend of mine, a girl who had moved down to live in a settlement house in the slums, telephoned to invite me to lunch with some visiting Russians. Father answered the telephone. "Yes, this is Mr. Day. Speak up, hang it! Don't mumble at me. Who are you? . . . *What?* Come to lunch? I've had lunch. . . . Next Friday? Why, I don't want to lunch with you next Friday. . . . No. . . . Where? Where do you say? . . . In

Rivington Street? The devil! . . . Yes, my name is Clarence Day and I told you that before. Don't repeat. . . . Lunch with you in Rivington Street? Good God! I never heard of such a thing in my life! . . . Russians? I don't know any Russians. . . . No, I don't want to, either. . . . No, I haven't changed. I never change. . . . What? . . . Good-bye, Madam. Damn!"

"I think that was a friend of mine, Father," I said.

"A friend of yours!" he exclaimed. "Why, it sounded to me like some impudent peddler's wife this time, arguing with me about lunching with her somewhere down in the slums. I can't stand it, that's all I have to say. I'll have the confounded thing taken out."

FATHER ISN'T MUCH HELP

❖

In Father's childhood it was unusual for boys to take music lessons, and his father hadn't had him taught music. Men didn't play the piano. Young ladies learned to play pretty things on it as an accomplishment, but few of them went further, and any desire to play classical music was rare.

After Father grew up, however, and began to do well in his business, he decided that music was one of the good things of life. He bought himself a piano and paid a musician to teach him. He took no interest in the languishing love songs which were popular then, he didn't admire patriotic things such as "Marching Through Georgia," and he had a hearty distaste for songs of pathos—he always swore if he heard them. He enjoyed music as he did a fine wine or a good ride on horseback.

The people he associated with didn't care much for this kind of thing, and Father didn't wish to associate with the long-haired musicians who did. He got no encouragement from anyone and his progress was lonely. But Father was not the kind of man who depends on encouragement. He had long muscular fingers, he practised faithfully, and he learned to the best of his ability to play Beethoven and Bach.

His feeling for music was limited, but it was deeply rooted, and he cared enough for it to keep on practising even after he married and in the busy years when he was providing for a house full of boys. He didn't go to symphonic concerts and he never liked Wagner, but he'd hum something of Brahms while posting his ledger, or play Mozart or Chopin after dinner. It gave him a sense of well-being.

Mother liked music too. We often heard her sweet voice gently singing old songs of an evening. If she forgot parts here or there, she swiftly improvised something that would let the air flow along without breaking the spell.

Father didn't play that way. He was erecting much statelier structures, and when he got a chord wrong, he stopped. He took that chord apart and went over the notes one by one, and he kept on going over them methodically. This sometimes drove Mother mad. She would desperately cry "Oh-oh-oh!" and run out of the room.

Her whole attitude toward music was different. She didn't get a solid and purely personal enjoyment from it like Father. It was more of a social function to her. It went with dancing and singing. She played and sang for fun, or to keep from being sad, or to give others pleasure.

On Thursday afternoons in the winter, Mother was always "at home." She served tea and cakes, and quite a few people dropped in to see her. She liked entertaining. And whenever she saw a way to make her Thursdays more attractive, she tried it.

About this time, Mother's favourite niece, Cousin Julie, was duly "finished" at boarding school and came to live with us, bringing her trunks and hat-boxes and a great gilded harp. Mother at once made room for this beautiful object in our crowded parlour, and the first thing Julie knew she had to play it for the Thursday-afternoon visitors. Julie loved her harp dearly but she didn't like performing at all—performances frightened her, and if she fumbled a bit, she felt badly. But Mother said she must get over all that. She tried to give Julie self-confidence. She talked to her like a determined though kind impresario.

These afternoon sessions were pleasant, but they made Mother want to do more. While she was thinking one evening about what a lot of social debts she must pay, she suddenly said to

Father, who was reading Gibbon, half-asleep by the fire, "Why not give a musicale, Clare, instead of a series of dinners?"

When Father was able to understand what she was talking about, he said he was glad if she had come to her senses sufficiently to give up any wild idea of having a series of dinners, and that she had better by all means give up musicales, too. He informed her he was not made of money, and all good string quartets were expensive; and when Mother interrupted him, he raised his voice and said, to close the discussion: "I will not have my peaceful home turned into a Roman arena, with a lot of hairy fiddlers prancing about and disturbing my comfort."

"You needn't get so excited, Clare," Mother said. "I didn't say a word about hairy fiddlers. I don't know where you get such ideas. But I do know a lovely young girl whom Mrs. Spiller has had, and she'll come for very little, I'm sure."

"What instrument does this inexpensive paragon play?" Father inquired sardonically.

"She doesn't play, Clare. She whistles."

"Whistles!" said Father. "Good God!"

"Very well, then," Mother said after an argument. "I'll have to have Julie instead, and Miss Kregman can help her, and I'll try to get Sally Brown or somebody to play the piano."

"Miss Kregman!" Father snorted. "I wash my hands of the whole business."

Mother asked nothing better. She could have made a grander affair of it if he had provided the money, but even with only a little to spend, getting up a party was fun. Before her marriage, she had loved her brother Alden's musicales. She would model hers upon those. Hers would be different in one way, for Uncle Alden had had famous artists, and at hers the famous artists would be impersonated by Cousin Julie. But the question as to how expert the music would be didn't bother her, and she didn't think it would bother the guests whom she planned to invite. The flowers would be pretty; she knew just what she would put in each vase (the parlour was full of large vases); she had a special kind of little cakes in mind, and everybody would enjoy it all thoroughly.

But no matter what kind of artists she has, a hostess is bound to have trouble managing them, and Mother knew that even her home-made material would need a firm hand. Julie was devoted to her, and so was the other victim, Sally Brown, Julie's schoolmate. But devoted or not, they were uneasy about this experiment. Sally would rather have done almost anything than perform at a musicale, and the idea of playing in public sent cold chills down Julie's back.

The only one Mother worried about, however, was Julie's teacher, Miss Kregman. She could bring a harp of her own, so she would be quite an addition, but Mother didn't feel she was decorative. She was an angular plain-looking woman, and she certainly was a very unromantic sight at a harp.

Father didn't feel she was decorative either, and said, "I'll be hanged if I come." He said musicales were all poppycock anyway. "Nothing but tinkle and twitter."

"Nobody's invited you, Clare," Mother said defiantly. As a matter of fact, she felt relieved by his announcement. This wasn't like a dinner, where she wanted Father and where he would be of some use. She didn't want him at all at her musicale.

"All I ask is," she went on, "that you will please dine out for once. It won't be over until six at the earliest, and it would make things much easier for me if you would dine at the club."

Father said that was ridiculous. "I never dine at the club. I won't do it. Any time I can't have my dinner in my own home, this house is for sale. I disapprove entirely of these parties and uproar!" he shouted. "I'm ready to sell the place this very minute if I can't live here in peace, and we can all go and sit under a palm tree and live on breadfruit and pickles!"

On the day of the musicale, it began to snow while we were at breakfast. Father had forgotten what day it was, of course, and he didn't care anyhow—his mind was on a waistcoat which he wished Mother to take to his tailor's. To his astonishment, he found her standing on a stepladder, arranging some ivy, and when he said "Here's my waistcoat," she gave a loud wail of self-pity at this new infliction. Father said in a bothered way: "What is the matter with you, Vinnie? What are you doing up on that ladder? Here's my waistcoat, I tell you, and it's got to go to the tailor at once." He insisted on handing it up to her, and he banged the front door going out.

Early in the afternoon, the snow changed to rain. The streets were deep in slush. We boys gave up sliding downhill on the railroad bridge in East Forty-eighth Street and came tramping in with our sleds. Before going up to the play-room, we looked in the parlour. It was full of small folding chairs. The big teakwood arm-chairs with their embroidered backs were crowded off into corners, and the blue velvety ottoman with its flowered top could hardly be seen. The rubber tree had been moved from the window and strategically placed by Miss Kregman's harp, in such a way that the harp would be in full view but Miss Kregman would not.

Going upstairs, we met Julie coming down. Her lips were blue. She was pale. She passed us with fixed, unseeing eyes, and when I touched her hand it felt cold.

Looking over the banisters, we saw Miss Kregman arrive in her galoshes. Sally Brown, who was usually gay, entered silently later. Miss Kregman clambered in behind the rubber tree and tuned the majestic gold harps. Mother was arranging trayfuls of little cakes and sand-wiches, and giving a last touch to the flowers. Her excited voice floated up to us. There was not a sound from the others.

At the hour appointed for this human sacrifice, ladies began arriving in long, swishy dresses which swept bits of mud over the carpet. Soon the parlour was packed. I thought of Sally, so anxious and numb she could hardly feel the piano keys, and of Julie's icy fingers plucking valiantly away at the strings. Then Mother clapped her hands as a signal for the chatter to halt, the first hesitating strains of music began, and someone slid the doors shut.

When we boys went down to dinner that evening, we heard the news, good and bad. In a way it had been a success. Julie and Sally had played beautifully the whole afternoon, and the ladies had admired the harps, and applauded, and eaten up all the cakes. But there had been two catastrophes. One was that although Miss Kregman herself had been invisible, everybody had kept looking fascinatedly at her feet, which had stuck out from the rubber tree, working away by themselves, as it were, at the pedals, and the awful part was she had forgotten to take off her galoshes. The other was that Father had come home during a sweet little lullaby and the ladies had distinctly heard him say "Damn" as he went up to his room.

FATHER SEWS ON A BUTTON

◈

It must have been hard work to keep up with the mending in our house. Four boys had to be kept in repair besides Father, and there was no special person to do it. The baby's nurse did some sewing, and Cousin Julie turned to and did a lot when she was around, but the rest of it kept Mother busy and her work-basket was always piled high.

Looking back, I wonder now how she managed it. I remember her regularly going off to her room and sewing on something, right after dinner or at other idle moments, when she might have sat around with the rest of us. My impression as a boy was that this was like going off to do puzzles—it was a form of amusement, or a woman's way of passing the time.

There was more talk about Father's socks and shirts than anything else. Most of this talk was by Father, who didn't like things to disappear for long periods, and who wanted them brought promptly back and put in his bureau drawer where they belonged. This was particularly true of his favourite socks. Not the plain white ones which he wore in the evening, because they were all alike, but the coloured socks that were supplied to him by an English haberdasher in Paris.

These coloured socks were the one outlet of something in Father which ran contrary to that religion of propriety to which he adhered. In that day of sombre hues for men's suits and quiet tones for men's neckties, most socks were as dark and severe as the rest of one's garments; but Father's, hidden from the public eye by his trousers and his high buttoned shoes, had a really astonishing range both of colour and fancy. They were mostly in excellent taste, but in a distinctly French way, and Wilhelmine used to tease him about them. She called them his "secret joys."

Father got holes in his socks even oftener than we boys did in our stockings. He had long athletic toes, and when he lay stretched out on his sofa reading and smoking, or absorbed in talking to anyone, these toes would begin stretching and wiggling in a curious way by themselves, as though they were seizing on this chance to live a life of their own. I often stared in fascination at their leisurely twistings and turnings, when I should have been listening to Father's instructions about far different matters.

Soon one and then the other slipper would fall off, always to Father's surprise, but without interrupting his talk, and a little later his busy great toe would peer out at me through a new hole in his sock.

Mother felt that it was a woman's duty to mend things and sew, but she hated it. She rather liked to embroider silk lambrequins, as a feat of womanly prowess, but her darning of Father's socks was an impatient and not-too-skilful performance. She said there were so many of them that they made the back of her neck ache.

Father's heavily starched shirts, too, were a problem. When he put one on, he pulled it down over his head, and thrust his arms blindly out right and left in a hunt for the sleeves. A new shirt was strong enough to survive these strains without splitting, but life with Father rapidly weakened it, and the first thing he knew he would hear it beginning to tear. That disgusted him. He hated any evidence of weakness, either in people or things. In his wrath he would strike out harder than ever as he felt around for the sleeve. Then would come a sharp crackling noise as the shirt ripped open, and a loud wail from Mother.

Buttons were Father's worst trial, however, from his point of view. Ripped shirts and socks

with holes in them could still be worn, but
drawers with their buttons off couldn't. The
speed with which he dressed seemed to
discourage his buttons and make them desert
Father's service. Furthermore, they always gave
out suddenly and at the wrong moment.

He wanted help and he wanted it promptly at
such times, of course. He would appear at
Mother's door with a waistcoat in one hand and
a disloyal button in the other, demanding that it
be sewn on at once. If she said she couldn't just
then, Father would get as indignant as though
he had been drowning and a life-guard had
informed him he would save him to-morrow.

When his indignation mounted high enough
to sweep aside his good judgment, he would say
in a stern voice, "Very well, I'll sew it on myself,"
and demand a needle and thread. This
announcement always caused consternation.
Mother knew only too well what it meant. She
would beg him to leave his waistcoat in her
work-basket and let her do it next day. Father
was inflexible. Moreover, his decision would be
strengthened if he happened to glance at her
basket and see how many of his socks were
dismally waiting there in crowded exile.

"I've been looking for those blue polka-dotted
socks for a month," he said angrily one night
before dinner. "Not a thing is done for a man in

this house. I even have to sew on my own buttons. Where is your needle and thread?"

Mother reluctantly gave these implements to him. He marched off, sat on the edge of his sofa in the middle of his bedroom, and got ready to work. The gaslight was better by his bureau, but he couldn't sit on a chair when he sewed. It had no extra room on it. He laid his scissors, the spool of thread, and his waistcoat down on the sofa beside him, wet his fingers, held the needle high up and well out in front, and began poking the thread at the eye.

Like every commander, Father expected instant obedience, and he wished to deal with trained troops. The contrariness of the needle and the limp obstinacy of the thread made him swear. He stuck the needle in the sofa while he wet his fingers and stiffened the thread again. When he came to take up his needle, it had disappeared. He felt around everywhere for it. He got up, holding fast to his thread, and turned around, facing the sofa to see where it was hiding. This jerked the spool off on to the floor, where it rolled away and unwound.

The husbands of two of Mother's friends had had fits of apoplexy and died. It frightened her horribly when this seemed about to happen to Father. At the sound of his roars, she rushed in. There he was on the floor, as she had feared. He was trying to get his head under the sofa and he was yelling at something, and his face was such a dark red and his eyes so bloodshot that Mother was terrified. Pleading with him to stop only made him more apoplectic. He said he'd be damned if he'd stop. He stood up presently, tousled but triumphant, the spool in his hand. Mother ran to get a new needle. She threaded it for him and he at last started sewing.

Father sewed on the button in a violent manner, with vicious haulings and jabs. Mother said she couldn't bear to see him—but she couldn't bear to leave the room, either. She stood watching him, hypnotized and appalled, itching to sew it herself, and they talked at each other with vehemence. Then the inevitable accident happened: the needle came forcibly up through the waistcoat, it struck on the button, Father pushed at it harder, and it burst through the hole and stuck Father's finger.

He sprang up with a howl. To be impaled in this way was not only exasperating, it was an affront. He turned to me, as he strode about on the rug, holding on to his finger, and said wrathfully, "It was your mother."

"Why, Clare!" Mother cried.

"Talking every minute," Father shouted at her, "and distracting a man! How the devil can I sew on a button with this gibbering and buzz in my ears? Now see what you made me do!" he added suddenly. "Blood on my good waistcoat! Here! Take the damned thing. Give me a handkerchief to tie up my finger with. Where's the witch-hazel?"

FATHER AND THE
CRUSADER'S THIRD WIFE

◈

ONE of the ways in which Father and Mother were as alike as two peas was in their love of having good times. When they went to a dance or a dinner where they enjoyed themselves, they were full of high spirits. They had a lot of gusto about it, and they came home refreshed.

But there was this great difference: Mother always wanted to go; Father never. Mother was eager, and she was sure in advance they would like it. She had a romantic idea, Father said, that all parties were pleasant. He knew better. He said he hated them. All of them. He refused to go anywhere. When Mother asked him about accepting this or that invitation, he said she could go if she liked, but he certainly wouldn't. He would settle down in his chair and say, "Thank God, *I* know enough to stay home."

But Mother couldn't go to a dance or a dinner without him. That would have been impossible in those days. It was almost unheard of. The result was that she accepted all invitations and didn't tell him until the time came to go, so that Father went out much more than he meant to; only he always made a scene first, of course, and had to be dragged. Every time he got into the carriage and drove off to their friends, he felt imposed upon and indignant, and Mother was almost worn out.

The surprising thing was that after all this, both of them had a good time. They both had immense stores of energy and resilience to draw on. Mother would alight from the carriage half-crying, but determined to enjoy herself, too; and Father, who could never stay cross for long, would begin to cheer up as soon as he went in the big, lighted doorway. By the time they were at table or in the ballroom, they were both full of fun.

"Aren't you ashamed of yourself," she would say, "making such a fuss about coming!"

But Father had forgotten the fuss by then, and would ask what on earth she was talking about.

When he sat next to some pretty woman at table, his eye would light up and he would feel interested and gallant. He had charm. Women liked him. It never did them any good to like him if the wine wasn't good, or if the principal dishes weren't cooked well. That made him morose. But when the host knew his business, Father was gay and expansive, without ever a thought of the raps Mother would give him on the head going home.

"Clare, you were so silly with that Miss Remsen! She was laughing at you all the time."

"What are you talking about now?" he would chuckle, trying to remember which was Miss Remsen. He was not good at names, and pretty women were much the same to him anyhow. He was attentive and courtly to them by instinct, and Mother could see they felt flattered, but no one would have been as startled as Father if this had made complications. He thought of his marriage as one of those things that were settled. If any woman had really tried to capture him, she would have had a hard time. He was fully occupied with his business and his friends at the club, and he was so completely wrapped up in Mother that she was the one his eye followed. He liked to have a pretty woman next to him, as he liked a cigar or a flower, but if either a flower or a cigar had made demands on him, he would have been most disturbed.

It thrilled Mother, at parties, to meet some distinguished and proud-looking man, especially if he made himself agreeable to her, for she greatly admired fine males. She was critical too, though; they had to be human to please her. She was swift at pricking balloons. If there were no one of this high type to fascinate her, she liked men who were jolly; quick-minded men who danced well or talked well. Only they mustn't make love to her. When they did, she was disappointed in them. She said they were idiots. She not only said so to others, she said so to them. "Mercy on us, Johnny Baker," she'd say crossly, "don't be such a fool!"

Johnny Baker belonged to his wife, that was Mother's idea, and if he didn't know it, he was stupid. Mother hated stupidity. She seemed to go on the principle that every man belonged to some woman. A bachelor ought to be devoted to his mother or sister. A widower should keep on belonging to the wife he had lost.

This last belief was one that she often tried to implant in Father. He had every intention of outliving her, if he could, and she knew it. He said it was only his devotion to her that made him feel this way—he didn't see how she could get on without him, and he must stay alive to take care of her. Mother snorted at this benevolent attitude. She said she could get on perfectly well, but of course she'd die long before he did. And what worried her was how he'd behave himself when she was gone.

One day in an ancient chapel near Oxford, they were shown a tomb where a noble crusader was buried, with his effigy laid out on top. Mother was much impressed till the verger pointed to the figure beside him, of the lady who had been his third wife. Mother immediately struck at the tomb with her parasol, demanding, "Where's your first, you old thing!"

The verger was so shocked that he wouldn't show them the rest of the church; but Mother didn't want to see it anyway. She told the verger he ought to be ashamed of himself for exhibiting an old wretch like that, and she went out at once, feeling strongly that it was no place for Father.

FATHER AMONG THE POTTED PALMS

⊷

ALTHOUGH Father enjoyed himself when Mother and he went to parties, the idea of giving a party in his own home seemed monstrous. The most he would consent to was to have a few old friends in to dinner. He said that when Mother went beyond that, she turned the whole place upside down. He said he declined to have his comfort "set at naught" in that manner.

Father put comfort first in his home life: he had plenty of adventure down town. But Mother got tired of dining with nobody but his old friends all the time. She wanted to see different houses, new people. By temperament she was an explorer.

She knew that an explorer who got no invitations to explore sat at home. And the surest way to get invitations was to give them, and to all sorts of people, and turn Father's home upside down whether he liked it or not.

To forestall opposition, Mother's method was to invite one couple whom Father knew, so that when he looked around the table one or two of the faces would be familiar, but as to the others she experimented. If questioned by Father as to who'd be there, she said, "Why, the Bakers, and I hope a few others." This reassured him till the night of the dinner arrived. Then, when he came home and found potted palms in the hall, it was too late to stop her.

That dinner for "the Bakers and a few others" was a dinner of ten, and the principal guests were the Ormontons, whom Mother had been determined to invite ever since she had met them. She didn't really know what they were like yet, but they had looked most imposing.

One night just a week before the event, we heard a ring at the front door. It was about seven o'clock. We were just finishing our six-o'clock dinner. Mother had come in so late from the Horse Show that she hadn't bothered to dress; she had thrown off her frock on her bed and slipped into a wrapper. Bridget, the waitress, an awkward girl whose mouth dropped wide open in crises, went to answer the bell.

We heard her open the door. Then, in the silence, there was the sound of somebody going upstairs. We looked in surprise at one another. Only dinner guests ever went up automatically that way, expecting to take off their coats and wraps in some upper bedroom.

Mother leapt from her chair and ran out to the hall. She had guessed what was happening. Sure enough, there was Bridget, staring helplessly with her mouth gaping open, at two stately figures, the Ormontons, resplendently marching upstairs.

At the head of those stairs was Mother's bedroom, in the wildest disorder. Another moment and Mrs. Ormonton would have gone in there to take off her wraps. "Why, Mrs. Ormonton!" Mother called, in a panic. "Haven't you made a mistake?"

The march upward was halted. The two dignified figures looked solemnly over the banisters.

"It's *next* Tuesday that you're coming to dine!" Mother cried, clutching in dismay at her wrapper.

Mr. Ormonton stared disapprovingly at Mother a moment. Then, as he began to take in what had happened, he pursed his lips, his eyes popped and he turned and scowled at his wife. She looked at him in fright and slumped slowly, like a soft tallow candle.

"*Next* Tuesday," Mother faintly repeated.

The Ormontons pulled themselves together and came slowly down.

They stood helplessly in the hall by the hat-rack. As they had dismissed their carriage, they had no way to remove themselves from our home. A street-car was impossible for an Ormonton in full evening dress. They would have to wait till a cab could be sent for, which would take at least half an hour and probably more.

If we could have offered them some impromptu little meal, it might have been welcome to both of them, but we boys had eaten every last scrap, and Mother couldn't think how to manage it. She didn't feel she knew them well enough to have that awful Bridget bring up some cold meat and a glass of milk and an old piece of pie. So they waited in their sumptuous clothes, cross and wretched and hungry. They had little or no sense of fun, even in their happiest moments, and they certainly did not feel light-hearted as they sat in our parlour. Mother had to make conversation, in her wrapper, till almost eight o'clock. Mr. Ormonton said nothing whatever. He felt too much wronged, too indignant. Father strolled in and offered him a cigar. It was stiffly declined.

A week later, when they again rang the bell, they were stiffer than ever. But by that time our easy-going household was completely transformed. Instead of Bridget and her elbows, a butler suavely opened the door. Large potted palms stood in the hall. The Ormontons felt more at home.

They could not have imagined how much work Mother's preparations had cost. To begin with, she had gone to a little shop she had found on Sixth Avenue, under the Elevated, a place where they sold delicious ice-cream and French pastries and bonbons, which was run by a pleasant and enterprising young man named Louis Sherry. He had arranged to send over old John, a waiter, to be our butler *pro tem.*, and a greasy and excitable young chef to take charge of our kitchen, and they had brought with them neat-covered baskets which they wouldn't let us boys touch.

Old John and Mother had a great deal to do in the dining-room: getting out arsenals of silver to be laid at each place, putting leaves in the black-walnut table, filling vases with flowers, arranging little plates of salted almonds and chocolates, and I don't know what else. The heavy plush furniture in the parlour had to be rearranged, too, and piles of special plates taken down from the pantry top shelf, and an elaborately embroidered tablecloth and napkins got out of the linen closet. And after Mother had run around all day attending to these, and had laid out the right dress and slippers, and done things to her hair, she had ended by desperately tackling the worst job of all, which was to put her bedroom in order.

This room, in spite of Mother's random efforts, had an obstinate habit of never being as neat and pretty-looking as she wished it to be. On the contrary, it was always getting into a comfortable, higgledy-piggledy state. And every time Mother gave a dinner, she felt guiltily sure that the ladies who took off their wraps in it would have gimlet eyes. Everything, therefore, had to be put away out of sight. Her plan was to do this so neatly that any drawer which these prying creatures might open would be in beautiful order. But she never had time enough, so after the first two or three drawers had had their upper levels fixed up, things were pushed into the others any which way, and when she was through they were locked. Letters and pieces of string were hurried off the dressing-table, medicines and change off the mantel, stray bits of lace, pencils, veils, and old macaroons off the bureau. Some were jammed into cabinets that were already so full they could hardly be shut, some disappeared into hat-boxes or were poked up on dark closet shelves. Among these jumbled articles were many that would be urgently needed next week, but by that time even Mother couldn't remember where on earth she had put them, and she spent hours hunting hopelessly for a lost glove or key. When the bedroom was "picked up" at last, it had lost its old friendly air. A splendid spread lay on the bed smoothly. The bolster and pillows were covered as elaborately as if no one used them to sleep on. A big china kerosene lamp and some pink-shaded candles were lit. And Mother, all tired out, was being laced up the back in her tight-fitting gown.

Father had none of this work to do in his room. In fact he had no work at all. He dressed for dinner every night anyhow, and his room was always in order. Everything he owned had its place, and he never laid his clothes down at random. There were two drawers for his shirts, for example, another drawer for his socks, his shaving-kit was always on his English shaving-stand by the window. On his bureau were a pair of military hairbrushes, two combs, and a bottle of bay rum—nothing else. Each of his books had its own allotted place on his shelves. And on each shelf and in every drawer there was extra room. Nothing was crowded.

When he undressed to go to bed, he began by taking the things out of his pockets and putting them into a little drawer which he reserved for that purpose. He then hung his suit on its own regular hook in his closet and laid his underwear in the wash-basket. He never left anything lying around on the chairs. He did these things so swiftly that he could dress or undress in ten minutes, and when he turned out the gas and opened his big window, his room was as trim as a general's.

On the night of the dinner, he came home at his usual hour, swore at the potted palms, and took John down to the cellar to get out the right wines. Then he went to his room; and as dinner was later than usual, he had a short nap. He got up a quarter of an hour or so before it was time for the guests to arrive, screwed in his studs, shaved and dressed, gave his white tie a sharp, exact twist, and peacefully went down to the parlour. Finding Mother there, adjusting a smoky lamp, he said he'd be damned if he'd stand it, having his comfort interfered with by a lot of people he did not wish to see. He added that if they didn't come on time, they needn't expect him to wait—he was hungry.

But the guests soon began clattering up to our door over the cobblestones in their broughams, and Father smiled at the men and shook hands warmly with the best-looking women, and got all their names mixed up, imperturbably, until John opened the great sliding doors of the little dining-room, and they went in to dinner.

As for the rest of the evening, it was just another dinner for Father, except that he had sherry and champagne instead of claret, and some dishes by a good chef. But Mother, looking critically around at her social material, and watching the service every minute, had to work to the last. No matter how formal and wooden her material was, it was her business to stir them to life and make the atmosphere jolly. She usually succeeded, she was so darting and gay, but on this high occasion some of the guests couldn't be made to unbend.

Father didn't notice that they were wooden, nor did he feel disappointed. With a good dinner and sound wines inside him, he could enjoy any climate. He also enjoyed talking to people about whatever came into his head, and he seldom bothered to observe if they listened or how they responded.

Bridget's duties were to stay in the pantry and help John and keep quiet. She stayed in the pantry all right, but she flunked on the rest of it. Each time that she dropped something, she made a loud, gasping sound. John went on about his business, ignoring this in a severe and magnificent manner, but nobody else was quite able to, except, of course, Father. To Mother's relief, he unconsciously saved the day for her by being too absorbed in his own conversation to hear these weird interruptions.

The climax came at dessert. By that time,

Bridget was completely demoralized, and she so far forgot herself as to poke her face outside the screen and hiss some question hoarsely at John. An awful silence came over the table. But Father, who felt as astonished as anybody, took no pains to conceal it. He turned squarely around and demanded: "What the devil's that noise?"

Father's utter naturalness made even Mr. Ormonton smile. All formality melted away, to Mother's surprise and delight, and though Father had no idea he had caused it, a gay evening began.

FATHER HAS A BAD NIGHT

❧

ONE winter morning when Father left the Riding Club on horseback and rode through East Fifty-eighth Street, his horse fell with him. Not only did the stupid animal fall but he landed on Father's foot.

Father pulled his foot out from under, got the horse up, and went on to the Park for his ride. But he found later that one of his toes had been bent and that he couldn't straighten it out.

This was not only an inconvenience to Father, it was a surprise. He knew other men got smashed up in accidents, but he had assumed that that was because they were brittle. He wasn't. He was constructed in such a manner, he had supposed, that he couldn't be damaged. He still believed that this was the case. Yet one of his toes had got bent.

That toe never did straighten out and Father talked of it often. He felt that he had had a strange experience, one that was against Nature's laws, and he expected those who listened to his story to be deeply concerned and impressed. If they weren't, he repeated it.

We heard it at home hundreds of times, one year after another. "That's enough about your toe," Mother would cry. "Nobody cares about your toe, you know, Clare!"

But Father said that of course people did. He told all his friends at the club. "You know what happened to me? Why, one morning when the pavement was icy, that bay cob that Sam Babcock sold me fell on my toe—and he *bent* it! Never had such a thing happen to me all my life. Bent my toe! It's getting a corn on it now. Here. On top. My shoemaker says he can't fix it. There's nobody as stupid as a shoemaker, except that bay cob."

From this time on, although he still was contemptuous of diseases, Father began to dislike to hear any accounts of other men's accidents. They seemed to him portents of what might happen, even to him.

One day in the country, when he took the train at the Harrison station, he saw a pretty neighbour of ours, young Mrs. Wainwright, sitting in the car with her boy. He stopped to say how d'ye do, intending to sit and talk with her. But she said, as she greeted him, "I'm taking my little son in to the dentist—he's had such a sad accident, Mr. Day. He's broken off two front teeth."

The boy grinned, Father looked at the broken stumps, and his face got all twisted and shocked. "Oh, my God!" he said. "Oh! Oh!" And he hurriedly left her, to sit in some other car. When he got home that evening, he complained about this occurrence, and blamed Mrs. Wainwright for showing him her family horrors.

"Your husband felt so badly about my little boy," Mrs. Wainwright said next week to Mother. "How sympathetic he is, Mrs. Day."

A year or so later, Father had another of these situations to face. The doctors had to operate on one of my legs for adhesions. Worst of all, since for some reason I couldn't be moved at that time to a hospital, I was operated on at home.

They left me feeling comfortable enough, with my leg trussed up in plaster. But Mother was troubled and unhappy about it, and when Father came in and she ran to him to pour out her woes she disturbed him.

He couldn't get away from it this time. There was no next car to go to. He puckered his face up in misery. He chucked his coat and hat in the closet. He finally told Mother he was sorry for me but he wished she would let him be sorry in peace. The whole damn house was upset, he said, and he wanted his dinner.

When he had his dinner, he couldn't enjoy it. He could only half enjoy his cigar. He felt distressed but didn't wish to say so. He was cross to Mother. He swore. Mother said he was heartless and went off to bed.

He felt badly to think that I might be suffering. But he didn't at all like to feel badly. He didn't know much about suffering, and the whole situation confused him. He walked up and down and said "Damn." He said he wished to God that people would take care of themselves the way he did, and be healthy and not bother him this way. Then he lit another cigar, sat down to read, and tried to forget all about it. But as his feelings wouldn't let him do that, he helplessly frowned at his book.

Mother had told him not to go up to see me, but after a while he just had to. He came quietly up to the top floor, groped around in the dark, and looked in my door. "Well, my dear boy," he said.

His voice was troubled and tender.

I said, "Hello, Father."

That made him feel a little better, and he hopefully asked me, "How are you?"

I made an effort and replied, "I'm all right."

"Oh, damn," Father said, and went down again.

I knew it was the wrong thing to say. If I had been angry at my leg and the ether, he would have felt reassured. He liked a man to be brave in a good, honest, full-blooded way. He hated to see him merely lie still and pretend he was all right when he wasn't.

He sat up late, smoking and reading or pacing the floor, and when he went to bed himself he slept badly. That was the last straw. He got up and moved into the spare room in the rear of the house. I was in the room just above. I could hear him talking bitterly to himself about the way they had tucked in the sheets. Even after he had got them fixed properly, his mind was not at rest. He tossed impatiently about, got up and drank some water, said it was too warm, dozed a little, woke up again, hunted around for the switch, turned the light on, and felt miserable. As he never did anything in silence, his resentment burst out in groans. They grew louder and louder.

My leg was feeling easier by that time. I had no pain to speak of, and I slept all that Father would let me. Mother, on the floor below Father, with her ears stuffed with cotton, slept too. But the spare-room bed was by an open window facing the quiet back yards, and as the neighbours, it seemed, had no cotton, they hadn't much chance to rest.

The next day, Mother happened to stop in to see Mrs. Crane, who lived a few doors away from us, and started to tell her about my operation. But Mrs. Crane interrupted.

"Oh yes, Mrs. Day," she said. "My daughter and I knew something had happened. It must have been terrible. We were so sorry for him. We could hear him groaning all night. How very hard it must have been for you. My daughter and I got a little sleep toward morning, but I'm afraid you had none at all."

On her way home, Mother met another of the neighbours, Mrs. Robbins, who lived on the other side of our block in the next street, and whose rear bedrooms faced ours. Mrs. Robbins, too, knew all about it.

"My room is in the front of the house," she said, "so I didn't know what had happened until Mr. Robbins told me at breakfast. He talked of nothing else all this morning. He couldn't believe that I hadn't heard the—er—your poor son's dreadful cries."

Mother waited that evening for Father to get home from his office. The minute he came in, she pounced on him. "Oh, *Clare!*" she said. "I am so ashamed of you! You get worse and worse. I saw Mrs. Crane to-day and Mrs. Robbins, and they told me what happened last night, and I don't believe any of the neighbours got one wink of sleep."

"Well," Father answered, "neither did I."

"Yes, but Clare," Mother impatiently cried,

seizing his coat lapels and trying to shake him, "they thought it was Clarence making those noises and all the time it was you!"

"I don't give a damn what they thought," Father said wearily. "I had a bad night."

FATHER AND HIS OTHER SELVES

❖

FATHER'S attitude toward anybody who wasn't his kind used to puzzle me. It was so dictatorial. There was no live and let live about it. And to make it worse he had no compunctions about any wounds he inflicted; on the contrary, he felt that people should be grateful to him for teaching them better.

This was only one side of him, of course, as I realized better later, for I saw even more of him after I grew up than I had in my childhood. He was one of the jolliest and most companionable men I ever knew. He always seemed to have a good time when he went to the club. He liked most of the men whom he met there, and they felt that same way toward him. One or another of them walked home with him, usually, and stood talking with him by the front stoop. And when he rode with his friends in the Park or went for a sail on some yacht, or when he and his fellow-directors of some little railroad spent a week on a tour of inspection, they came back full of fun.

It was only with men of his own sort that he did this, however. They understood him and he them. They all had an air and a feeling, in those days, of enormous authority. When they disagreed, it was often quite violently, but that didn't matter. At bottom they thoroughly approved of and respected each other.

Toward people with whom he didn't get on well, though, he was imperious, and when they displeased or annoyed him, it made him snort like a bull.

I disapproved of this strongly when I was a boy. It seemed natural to me that any father should snort, more or less, about the behaviour of his wife, or his children, or his relatives generally. It seemed natural, too, for a man to make his employees live exactly as he decreed. That sort of thing was so much in the air that I, for one, didn't question it. But Father didn't stop there; he expected everyone else to conform, even people he read about in the newspapers. Even historical characters. He never failed to denounce them indignantly when he found that they hadn't.

He felt the same way about persons he passed in the street. And sometimes in a horse-car he looked around at his fellow-passengers like a colonel distastefully reviewing a slatternly regiment. They didn't all have to be bankers or lawyers or clubmen—though if they were, all the better—but they did have to be neat and decent. And self-respecting. Like him. He would glare at men whose vests were unbuttoned, or whose neckties were loose, or whose general appearance was sloppy, as though they deserved hanging. He said he hated slovenly people. He said that they were "offensive."

"What difference does it make to you, Father?" I'd ask him. He didn't explain. I could have understood his quietly disliking them, for a sense of the fitness of things was strong in him; but why did he feel so much heat?

One day I came upon a magazine article which discussed this very matter. No ego ought to feel entirely separate, the writer explained. It should think of others as its own alter egos—differing forms of itself. This wasn't at all the way I looked at others. I expected nearly all of them to be different and I was surprised when they weren't. This magazine writer said that only unsocial persons felt that way. Well, at least this idea made Father's attitude understandable to me. If he was simply thinking of others as his own other selves, that might be why, when they didn't behave as such, he got in a passion about it.

Every morning Father sat in the big armchair in the dining-room window to look over his newspaper and see just what his alter egos had been up to since yesterday. If they hadn't been up to anything, he turned to the financial pages or read one or two editorials—one or two being all he could stand, because he said they were wishy-washy. If, however, the Mayor had been faithless again to Father's ideals, or if Tammany Hall had done anything at all, good or bad, Father ringingly denounced these atrocities to us little boys and to Mother.

For a long time none of the rest of us joined in these political talks. This suited Father exactly. He didn't wish to be hindered, or even helped, when he was letting off steam. After a while, though, Mother began attending a class in current events, which an enterprising young woman, a Miss Edna Gulick, conducted on Tuesdays. Social, musical, and literary matters took up most of Miss Gulick's mind. But though she didn't go deeply into politics or industrial problems, merely darting about on the surface in a bright, sprightly way, she did this so skilfully, and made everything seem so clear to Mother, that the most baffling and intricate issues became childishly simple.

The day after one of these classes, just when Father was whole-heartedly bombarding President Benjamin Harrison and somebody named William McKinley for putting through a new tariff and trying their best to ruin the country, Mother boldly chimed in. She said she was sure that the President's idea was all right; he had only been a little unfortunate in the way he had put it.

Father laid down his paper in high displeasure. "What do *you* know about it?" he demanded.

"Miss Gulick says she has it on the best authority," Mother firmly declared. "She says the President prays to God for guidance, and that he is a very good-hearted man."

"The President," said Father, "is a nincompoop, and I strongly suspect he's a scallawag, and I wish to God you wouldn't talk on matters you don't know a damned thing about."

"I do too know about them," Mother exclaimed. "Miss Gulick says every intelligent woman should have some opinion—about this tariff thing, and capital and labour, and everything else."

"Well, I'll be damned," Father said in amazement. "Who, may I ask, is Miss Gulick?"

"Why, she's that current-events person I told you about, and the tickets are a dollar each Tuesday," said Mother.

"Do you mean to tell me that a pack of idle-minded females pay a dollar apiece to hear another female gabble about the events of the day?" Father asked. "Listen to *me* if you want to know anything about the events of the day."

"But you get so excited, Clare dear, and you always talk so long and so loud that I never can see what you're getting at. About tariffs. And strikes."

"It is a citizen's duty," Father began, getting angrily into his overcoat, but Mother wouldn't be interrupted.

"Another reason that we all like Miss Gulick so much," she went on, "is that she says kindness is much more important than arguments. And she says it makes her feel very sad when she reads about strikes, because capital and labour could easily learn to be nice to each other."

Father burst out of the house, banging the door, and finished buttoning his coat on the top step of our stoop. "I don't know what the world is coming to anyhow," I heard him exclaim to a few surprised passers-by on quiet Madison Avenue.

FATHER FINDS GUESTS
IN THE HOUSE

◈

FATHER was a sociable man; he liked to sit and talk with us at home, or with his friends at the club. And in summer he permitted guests to stay with us out in the country, where there was plenty of room for them, and where he sometimes used to feel lonely. But in town he regarded any prolonged hospitality as a sign of weak natures. He felt that in town he must be stern with would-be houseguests or he'd be overrun with them. He had no objection to callers who dropped in for a cup of tea and got out, but when a guest came to our door with a handbag—or, still worse, a trunk—he said it was a damned imposition.

What complicated the matter was that nobody stayed with us usually except Mother's relatives. Father's relatives were well-regulated New Yorkers who stayed in their own homes, and he often told Mother that the sooner hers learned to, the better.

He had strong feelings about this and they always seemed to come out with a bang. When he got home for dinner and when Mother was obliged to confess that some of her relatives were concealed in the spare room, up on the third floor, those relatives were likely to wonder what was the matter downstairs. If Mother hadn't slammed the door, they would have heard indignant roars about locusts that ought to be sent back to Egypt instead of settling on Father.

Most of the guests had good consciences, however, and had been led to suppose Father loved them; and as they themselves were hospitable persons who would have welcomed him at their homes, they didn't suspect that those muffled outcries were occasioned by them. They merely felt sorry that poor Father was feeling upset about something. Mother encouraged them in this attitude; she said Father was worried about things and they must pretend not to notice. When Father glared speechlessly around the table at dinner, they felt sorrier for him than ever. Aunt Emma, who was a placid soul, once asked him if he had ever tried Dicer's Headache Lozenges, which were excellent in moments of depression and had also helped her anaemia. Father nearly burst a blood-vessel telling her that he was not anaemic.

One of the things that Father especially

detested about guests was the suddenness with which they arrived. So far as he knew, they invariably came without warning. The reason Mother never told him in advance was that he'd then have had two explosions—one when he was forbidding their coming, and one when they came.

Father made repeated attempts to acquaint Mother with his views about guests. This objectionable tribe, he explained to her, had two bad characteristics. One was that they didn't seem to know enough to go to hotels. New York was full of such structures, he pointed out, designed for the one special purpose of housing these nuisances. If they got tired of hotels, he said, they should be put aboard the next train at once, and shipped to some large, empty desert. If they wanted to roam, the damn gipsies, lend 'em a hand, keep 'em roaming.

But a still more annoying habit they had, he said, was that they wanted to be entertained, and every single one of them seemed to expect him to do it. Not content with disrupting the orderly routine of his household and ringing the bell every minute and sitting too long in his bathtub, they tried to make him go gallivanting off with them to a restaurant or give up his after-dinner cigar to see some long-winded play. He said to Mother, "I wish you to understand clearly that I am not a Swiss courier. I must decline to conduct groups of strangers around town at night. You can tell Emma that it is my desire to live here in peace, and that I do not intend to hold a perpetual Mardi Gras to please gaping villagers."

We didn't have visitors often, but still we did have a spare room. In this chamber was a little round fireplace, with a grate sticking out of it, surrounded by a white marble mantel. The mantel would have looked cold and tomb-like if left to itself, but hanging from its edge there was a strip of red velvet about six inches deep, with a wavy gold border. On the mantel was a pink porcelain clock, trimmed with gilt, with a sweet-toned French bell. Two graceful though urn-like pink vases stood at the ends of the mantel, and on each side of the clock was a large Dresden figure. One was a curtsying shepherdess with a small waist, in a pink-and-green petticoat, and opposite her there danced a rosy shepherd, with one arm gone, playing away on a pipe.

The walls and carpet were dark. At each window were two sets of curtains, one lacy and white and one of thick silk brocade. The tie-backs consisted of elaborate loops with big tassels.

The principal pieces of furniture were a solid black mahogany bureau, tall and heavily carved, and a bed to match, so broad that it could have easily held several guests. Beside the bed stood a square black commode, with a white marble top.

This room, although sombre, seemed waiting to be lived in; it had an air of dignified welcome. But when a guest started to investigate, he found that this was misleading. Except for the top of the bureau, there was really no place to put things. Every drawer was filled to bursting already with the overflow of other rooms. One of the two big closets was locked. In the other were ball dresses, an umbrella-stand, piles of magazines, a small pair of steps, a job lot of discarded bonnets, and a painting of old Mr. Howe. After taking a good look at this closet, a guest generally gave up all hope of unpacking and resigned himself politely to camping out the best way he could.

His mind had little opportunity, however, to dwell on these small inconveniences, for he soon became engrossed by the drama of our family life. Our disconcerting inability to conceal any of our emotions absorbed him.

I never supposed that our daily lives were different from anyone else's until I went off on visits myself. At Jeff Barry's home, when I saw his dignified old parents being formally polite to each other, I thought they were holding themselves tightly in, and I used to wonder which of them would blow up first. I was relieved yet depressed when they didn't. They were so gentle and had such quiet ways that they seemed to me lifeless.

On a visit to the McGillians, I was shocked to discover that a married pair could be mean to each other. Even their children made sarcastic and biting remarks, as though they were trying to hurt one another in what I thought an underhand way. All our family got hurt often enough, but at least it wasn't deliberate. Our collisions were impulsive and open. We all had red hair, and got angry in a second, but in a minute or two it was over.

Another family whose customs seemed strange to me was Johnny Clark's. Professor Clark, Johnny's father, when he was annoyed wouldn't speak. Around the first of the month, when the bills came in, he would sit without saying a word all through dinner, looking down at his plate. After we boys left the room, we heard Mrs. Clark beg him to tell her what she was to do. She said she was willing to live in a tent and spend nothing if he would only be pleasant. Mr. Clark listened to her in silence and then went off to his study.

This seemed to me gruesome. In our household, things got pretty rough at times but at least we had no black gloom. Our home life was stormy but spirited. It always had tang. When Father was unhappy, he said so. He poured out his grief with such vigour that it soon cleared the air.

If he had ever had any meannesses in him, he might have tried to repress them. But he was a thoroughly good-hearted and warm-blooded man, and he saw no reason for hiding his feelings. They were too strong to hide anyway.

One day while Father was in his office down town, Auntie Gussie and Cousin Flossie arrived. Mother immediately began planning to take them to dine at the Waldorf, a much-talked-of new hotel at Fifth Avenue and Thirty-third Street, which she very much wanted to see. She knew Father mightn't like the idea, but he would enjoy himself after he got there, and she thought she could manage him.

When he came in, she went to his bedroom to break the good news to him that instead of dining at home he was to go off on a gay little party. She meant to do this diplomatically. But she wasn't an adept at coaxing or inveigling a man, and even if she had been, Father was not at all easy to coax. Whenever she was planning to manage him, the very tone of her voice put him on guard; it had an impatient note, as though really the only plan she could think of was to wish he was manageable. So on this occasion, when she tried to get him in a good mood, he promptly got in a bad one. He looked suspiciously at Mother and said, "I don't feel well."

"You need a little change," Mother said. "That'll make you feel better. Besides, Gussie's here and she wants to dine with us to-night at the Waldorf."

Father hated surprise attacks of this kind. No matter how placid he might be, he instantly got hot when one came. In less than a second he was rending the Waldorf asunder and saying what he thought of anybody who wanted to dine there.

But Mother was fully prepared to see him take it hard at the start. She paid no attention to his vehement refusals. She said brightly that the Waldorf was lovely and that it would do him good to go out. There was no dinner at home for him anyway, so what else was there to do?

When Father took in the situation, he undressed and put on his nightshirt. He shouted angrily at Mother that he had a sick headache. It made no difference to him whether there was any dinner or not. He couldn't touch a mouthful of food, he declared. Food be damned. What he needed was rest. After tottering around, putting his clothes away, he darkened his room.

He climbed into bed. He pulled up the sheets, and he let out his breath in deep groans.

These startling blasts, which came at regular intervals, alarmed Auntie Gussie. But when she hurried down to help, Mother seemed annoyed and shooed her back up.

The next thing she knew, Mother impatiently called up to her that she was waiting. She had got tired of scolding Father and trying to make him get out of bed, and had made up her mind to dine at the Waldorf without him. She and Auntie Gussie and Flossie marched off by themselves. But they had to come back almost immediately because Mother didn't have enough money, and when she rushed into Father's sick-room and lit the gas again and made him get up and give her ten dollars, his roars of pain were terrific.

After they went out, his groans lessened in volume and were presently succeeded by snores. Father had a good nap. When he woke up, he felt happier. He said his headache was gone. He came downstairs in his dressing-gown and slippers, and sent for some bread and milk. He ate several huge bowlfuls of it with gusto, peacefully smoked a cigar, and was back in his bed again, reading, when Mother came home.

FATHER AND HIS PET RUG

FATHER liked spending his summers in the country, once he had got used to it, but it introduced two major earthquakes each year into his life. One when he moved out of town in the spring, and one in the fall when he moved back. If there was one thing Father hated it was packing. It seemed a huddled, irregular affair to a man with his orderly mind. For a week or more before it was time to begin he was upset by the prospect. He had only a few drawers full of clothes to empty into a trunk, but it had to be done in a certain particular way. No one else could attend to it for him—no one else could do the thing properly. All that Mother could do was to have his trunk brought to his room. When it had been laid in a corner, gaping at him, his groaning began. He walked around, first putting his shirts in, then his clothes and his underwear, then burrowing under and taking some out again to go in the suitcase, then deciding that after all he would not take part of what he had packed. During all such perplexities he communed with himself, not in silence.

The first sounds that used to come from his room were low groans of self-pity. Later on, as the task he was struggling with became more and more complicated, he could be heard stamping about, and denouncing his garments. If we looked in his door we would see him in the middle of the room with a bathrobe, which had already been packed twice in the suitcase and once in the trunk, and which was now being put back in the trunk again because the suitcase was crowded. Later it would once more go back in the suitcase so as to be where he could get at it. His face was red and angry, and he was earnestly saying, "Damnation!"

Long before any of this began Mother had already started her end of it. Father packed only his own clothes. She packed everything else: except that she had someone to help her, of course, with the heavy things. In the fall, for instance, a man named Jerome sometimes went up to the country to do this. He was a taciturn, preoccupied coloured man, an expert at moving, who worked so well and quickly that he kept getting ahead of his schedule. It was distracting to Mother to plan out enough things to keep Jerome busy. It was also distracting to see him sit idle. He was paid by the day.

But the principal problem that Mother had to attend to was Father. He said that he didn't really mind moving but that he did object to the fuss. As to rugs, for instance, he refused to have any at all put away until after he and all his belongings had been moved from the house. This seemed unreasonable to me—I said he ought to allow them to make a beginning and put a few away, surely. He would admit, privately, that this was true, perhaps, but here was the trouble: if he once let Mother get started she would go much too far. "When your mother is closing up a house," he said, "she gets too absorbed in it. She is apt to forget my comfort entirely—and also her own. I have found by experience that if I yield an inch in this matter the place is all torn up." He added that he had to insist upon absolute order, simply because the alternative was absolute chaos. Furthermore, why shouldn't the process be orderly if it were skilfully handled? If it wasn't, it was no fault of his, and he declined to be made to suffer for it.

Mother's side of it was that it was impossible to move out imperceptibly. "Things naturally get upset a little, Clare dear, when you're making a change. If they get upset too much I can't help it; and I do wish you would stop bothering me."

One result of this difference was a war about the rugs every fall. Two or three weeks before they left, Mother always had the large rug in the hall taken up—there was no need of *two* rugs in the hall, she told Father.

"I won't have it, damn it, you're making the place a barracks," he said.

"But we're *moving*," Mother expostulated; "we must get the house closed."

"Close it properly then! Do things suitably, without this cursed helter-skelter." He retreated into the library where he could sit by a fire, while Mother went in and out of cold rooms and halls with her shawl on.

The library had two large heavy pieces of furniture in it—a grand piano, and a huge desk-like table piled with papers and books. This table filled the centre of the room and stood square on a rug. It was hard work to lift that heavy table to get the rug out from under it. Until this was done, every year, Mother kept thinking about it at night. Strictly speaking, it wasn't necessary to have that rug put away much beforehand, but she wanted to get it over and done with so that she could sleep. But Father was particularly dependent on this rug because he liked to sit in the library; he was always determined that it shouldn't be touched till he left.

He couldn't however, remain on guard continuously. He sometimes had to go out. In fact, he was manoeuvred into going out, though this he never quite learned. In the late afternoon when he supposed the day's activities over, he would come out of the library and venture to go off in the motor. Not far, just to get the evening paper, which was a very short trip. His mind was quiet: he assumed that nothing much could be done in his absence. But just as he was leaving he would be given some errand to do—some provisions to buy in the next town beyond, or a book to leave at some friends. Or if this might make him suspicious, nothing would be said as he left, but the chauffeur would be given instructions what to say when he had bought Father's paper.

"There are some flowers in the car, sir, that Mrs. Day . . ."

Father looked up from his paper, and looked threateningly over his glasses. "What's all this?" he said. "*What?*"

The chauffeur repeated mildly "—that Mrs. Day wishes left at the church."

"Damn the church," Father answered, going back to the market reports. Not that he was down on that institution, he believed in it firmly, but he expected the church to behave itself and not interfere with his drives. However, he was looking through his paper, and he didn't say no, and the chauffeur didn't give him time to anyhow, but cranked up the car, and off they went down the Post Road, all the way into Rye.

When they got home, Father hung up his overcoat in the cold hall, and grasping his evening paper he marched back to the library fire. . . .

Meantime things had been happening. Mother had had the big table lifted, and had got up the rug; and Jerome had lugged it out to the laundry yard to beat it. After that, his orders were to roll it and wrap it and put it away. While he was doing this, which was naturally expected to take him some time, Mother thankfully went up to the china-room to pack certain cups. She always felt a little more peaceful when Jerome was fully occupied. . . .

A little later, when she was in her own room and had just sat down for a minute, for the first time that day, and was sorting the linen, and humming, there was a knock at the door.

Mother sat up sharply, every bit of her alert again. "Who is that?"

She heard a deprecating little cough, then Jerome's quiet voice. "Now—er—Mrs. Day?"

"Well, what *is* it, Jerome?" Mother wailed. She had thought she had left that man enough to do for once anyhow, but here he was back on her hands again. "What is it *now*?" she said in despair. "Have you finished that work?"

"No'm," Jerome said reassuringly. "I ain't finished that yet." He paused, and coughed again, conscious that he was bringing poor news. "Mr. Day, he's hollerin' consid'able, down in the liberry."

"What about? What's the matter with him?"

Jerome knew she knew well enough. He said, "Yes'm," mechanically; and added in a worried way, as if to himself, "He's a-hollerin' for that rug."

Mother didn't like Jerome to use that word, "hollerin'." It wasn't respectful. But it was so painfully descriptive that she couldn't think what other word he could substitute. She put down the linen. I never could see why she didn't stay quietly in her room, at such moments, and let Father keep up his hollerin' till he cooled off. But I was an outsider in these wars, and Mother of course was a combatant. She charged out into the big upper hall, and at once began an attack, launching her counter-offensive vigorously, over the banisters. She called loudly upon Father to stop right away and be still; and she told him how wicked it was of him to make trouble for her when she was working so hard. Father, from his post in the library, boomed a violent reply. It was like an artillery bombardment. Neither side could see the other. But they fired great guns with great vigour, and it all seemed in earnest.

Jerome stood respectfully waiting, wondering how it would come out. He was wholly in the dark as to which side was winning, there was so much give and take. But the combatants knew. Mother presently saw she was beaten. There was some note she detected in Father's voice, deeper than bluster; or some weariness in herself that betrayed her. At any rate, she gave in.

She turned to Jerome. He saw that she was thinking how she could fix it. Jerome felt dejected. Had that big old rug got to be toted back into the library?

"Jerome, I'll have to give Mr. Day one of those rugs from the blue-room—one of the long narrow white fur pair. You know which I mean?"

"Yes'm," Jerome said with partial relief. "Put it under that desk?"

"No, between the desk and the fireplace. By Mr. Day's chair. That's all that's necessary. He just wants something under his feet."

This wasn't at all Father's idea of what he wanted, as Jerome soon discovered when he took the long white fur rug down to him. Father was so completely amazed he forgot to be angry.

He had supposed he had won that bombardment. He had made Mother cease firing. Yet now after he had lowered his temperature again back to normal, and settled down to enjoy the fruits of his victory, namely his own big square rug, here was Jerome bringing him instead a long narrow hairy monstrosity.

"What's that?" he demanded.

Jerome limply exhibited the monstrosity, feeling hopeless inside, like a pessimistic salesman with no confidence in his own goods.

"What are you bringing that thing in here for?"

"Yessir, Mr. Day. Mrs. Day says put it under your feet."

Father started to turn loose his batteries all over again. But his guns had gone cold. He felt plenty of disgust and exasperation, but not quite enough fury. He fired what he had at Jerome, who stood up to it silently; and he kicked the offending white fur rug, and said he wouldn't have it. But something in the air now seemed to tell him, in his turn, he had lost. Even Jerome felt this, and put the rug under his feet, "temporary," leaving Father trying to read his paper again, indignant and bitter. He particularly disliked this white rug. He remembered it now from last year.

Mother went back to the linen. The house

became quiet. The only sounds were thuds in the laundry yard, where Jerome was at work, beating and sweeping his booty, concealed by the hedge.

By the library fire Father was turning over the page of his paper, and glaring at the white rug, and saying to himself loudly, "I hate it!" He kicked at the intruder. "Damn woolly thing. I want my own rug."

FATHER AND THE
FRENCH COURT

✧

EXCEPT in his very last years, when he began to get shaky, Father wasn't bored in his old age, like some men. He kept up his billiards, enjoying the hard shots, until his eye grew less true; and he always found it absorbing to try to beat himself at solitaire. He enjoyed his drives until automobiles came and ruined the roads with their crowding. He enjoyed having a go at the morning paper, in a thoroughly combative spirit. Every time the President said or did anything which got on the front page, Father either commended him—in surprise—for having some backbone for once, or else said he was an infernal scoundrel and ought to be kicked out of office. "And I'd like to go down there and kick him out myself," he'd add fiercely. This was especially the case in President Wilson's two terms. There was something about Woodrow Wilson that made Father boil.

His dentist had made a bridge for him, at this time, to replace a lost tooth in front. Father soon took it back. "What's wrong, Mr. Day?" Dr.

Wyant said. "Is the occlusion imperfect?"

"Why, your thing won't stay in; that's what's wrong with it," Father replied.

Dr. Wyant was puzzled. "You mean that the denture seems to work loose when you are at table?"

"No," said Father, "it stays in when I eat, and it usually stays in when I talk, but when I read my paper in the morning, and say what I think of that man Wilson, your thing pops right out."

So life wasn't boring in his old age to Father. He read more books then, too; particularly books about past and current political clashes. In these he always took sides. When his side won, he wanted their victory to be decisive; but if the other side won, they needn't hope to inflict a decisive defeat. The harder they pressed Father, the angrier and more determined he got; the more bloodthirsty, I was about to say, but he was always that, win or lose. This made reading an active and exciting way of spending his time.

He didn't care much for detective stories. The people in them were flashy. He no more wished to read about rascals than he did about saints. When he read fiction, he went back to Dickens or Dumas or Thackeray. In his forties he often bought paper-bound books on the train—W. Clark Russell's sea tales, or novels by a new man, R. L. Stevenson, which were then coming out. Some cost fifty cents, some twenty-five. And he always liked books about horses, provided they weren't sentimental. But problem novels, especially Mrs. Humphrey Ward's, seemed to him bosh, also any books with triangles in them, or "men like that fellow Hamlet." Father preferred to read about people who knew their own minds.

He liked English history, but chiefly of the days before Cromwell. From about 1630 on, it was American Colonial times that he turned to, as though some ancestral self in him was retracing its steps.

One day Mother was persuaded, by a beautifully dressed woman book-agent, to buy on instalment a set of *Memoirs of the French Court*. She never read them—she hated the hard cynical tone of that period, and "those wicked women who robbed the poor queens of their silly old husbands." And she wailed with remorse and despair when each instalment fell due. A package of two volumes, at ten dollars apiece, was delivered each month. "Oh dear!" she would cry, as she hunted through her bureau drawers and her purse, to get twenty dollars together without using the Altar Society's money (which could never even be touched, it was so sacred, and yet was always sitting there, staring at her). "Those dreadful French creatures, they come so often I just can't stand it. I *did* hope there wouldn't be any *this* month. Why, if they are going to keep on coming like this I don't know what I shall do!"

She had been ashamed to tell Father about them. She hid the books from him. But when paying twenty a month became too harassing, as it very soon did, she burst in on him one day and said she had been buying him a present which she hoped he'd appreciate; and she dumped all she had of the French Court on his library table.

Father was startled. He put on his glasses suspiciously and said: "What the devil's all this?"

"Oh, *Clare*," Mother said, impatiently pushing him, "don't be so *stupid*. It's the French Court, I tell you. It's a present for you."

"I don't want it." said Father.

"Yes you do too!" Mother shrieked. "You haven't even looked at it. It cost me enough, I can tell you. It's a very nice present."

She hurried back upstairs before he could refuse it again, leaving him wondering what she was up to.

The following month he found out. Two more volumes arrived, and she told him there was twenty dollars to pay on them. Father promptly exploded.

"But the messenger's waiting in the hall!" Mother cried.

"He can go and wait in hell!" Father shouted. "I hope he sizzles there, too."

"Oh, Clare, he can hear you," Mother begged him. "Please, Clare. Do behave." And after the battle was over, Father was out twenty dollars.

"I thought you said those books were a present," he said to her, later.

"But not *all* of them, Clare," Mother said reproachfully, as though he was being too greedy. "The ones that I gave you were a present, but of course you must pay for the others."

Father bitterly warned her never to do such a fool thing again, and set to work to try to get his money's worth out of the French Court. He toiled through its oily intrigues as long as he could stand it, but he had to give up in disgust. He put away the kings, queens, and courtesans in an orderly row, with a yawn. They were nothing but a damned pack of foreigners. His ancestral self wasn't there.

One point I've left out is that each volume had the owner's monogram on it. This had made the set seem quite de luxe when the agent hypnotized Mother. But even then Mother had been doubtful about the French Court; she hadn't felt sure they were nice, though she had hoped for the best, and she thought it would be safer not to have her own monogram on them. So she had had the agent use Father's. This afterward seemed to prove she really had meant them to be a gift from the start. Father didn't believe it for a moment. Yet there was the evidence.

"I can't make Vinnie out," I heard him mutter, staring hard at the monogram.

They had been married for almost fifty years.

FATHER PLANS TO GET OUT

ONE evening when Father and Mother and I were in the library talking, a trained nurse came in to take Mother's blood pressure, as the doctor had ordered. This was a new thing in Mother's life. It alarmed her. She turned—as she always did when she was in any trouble—to Father.

"Clare," she said urgently to him, "you must have yours taken too."

Father scowled at the nurse. Blood pressure was something which he had been hearing more about than he liked. He had just passed his seventieth birthday, many of his old friends had died, and when he and a few other survivors met at the funerals that came often now, Father had seen some of them shaking their heads and whispering things about "blood pressure." What angered Father about it was that it seemed able to kill healthy men—men who he had felt sure would last for the next twenty years. Like himself. He'd talk at the club with one of them in the evening, after a few games of billiards, and the next week he'd pick up the paper and see that that man had died.

Father said he wouldn't mind if people died only once in a while, as they used to. He said we all had to die, he supposed. But he didn't know what the matter was nowadays. Somebody died every month. And it never was a wizened old walnut, like John Elderkin, it was always some sound, healthy man. No excuse for it. When he asked his friends at the club to explain it, he never got a clear answer. All they could talk of down there was blood pressure.

He said he was beginning to hate all these funerals. They were getting to be disturbing and unpleasant things to attend. He told General Anderson he didn't see why they kept going to them. General Anderson frowned and said they had to. "If you don't go to other men's funerals," he told Father stiffly, "they won't go to yours." But Father said he didn't intend to die at all if he could help it, so they couldn't go to his anyway.

"When somebody dies, the people who loved them want to say good-bye," Mother said. "That's what I feel when I go to a funeral. You didn't use to mind going, Clare."

"Well, Vinnie," Father replied, "that was when I was younger. But what bothers me now is those parsons. Every time I go to a funeral they get out one of their books and read the part that says that the years of a man are threescore and ten. I know that I'm seventy, but I'm as well as I ever was, hang it. I'm tired of hearing so much about this threescore and ten business."

The trained nurse stood there waiting. Father glared at her blood-pressure apparatus, and told her to take it away. "I don't know what it's all about," he said, "and I don't want to either. I won't have anything to do with this blood pressure."

"Everybody has blood pressure, Mr. Day," the nurse said.

"A lot of them have," Father replied, "but I haven't. I won't."

"If yours is all right," the nurse explained, "this little indicator will show it."

Mother said: "Please, Clare, let her take it, while the thing's right here in the house, and we don't have to pay a doctor to do it. It's costing enough for Miss Bassett—let's get our money's worth somehow."

"Oh well, pshaw," said Father, "if it will gratify your whim, go ahead."

Miss Bassett adjusted the strap on his arm. He sat there, red-faced and confident. She looked at the indicator. It recorded no special blood pressure.

Father laughed.

But Miss Bassett, examining the indicator

again, saw that it hadn't worked; and when she readjusted it, the pressure was abnormally high.

"Pooh! What of it?" said Father; "all poppycock."

"No, Mr. Day, really," she said, "that condition is dangerous."

Father's face slightly stiffened. He stopped joking, rose with unwilling concern, walked away, grew quite angry, and said in a self-controlled tone that he didn't believe a word of it.

'You ought to take aconite, Mr. Day," the nurse told him.

"Pah! Never!" said Father.

His need seemed to be to forget it, put it out of his mind. I took some of the stable accounts out of my pocket that I had been attending to for him. He usually hated to bother going over them with me. "May I ask you about these, Father?" I said.

He thankfully sat down at the desk and examined each item, and when we had finished he seemed to have sponged off his slate.

His arteries were beginning to get in poor shape, at that time. There were lots of things about his machinery that wouldn't have suited the doctors. I thought of how he hated to go to a dentist or oculist. I thought of how much food his digestion constantly had to put up with. But he seemed to make his machinery serve by expecting much of it. Perhaps that kept him hearty. He at least gave it no doubts to deal with, no doubts of itself.

Mother's habitual attitude was exactly the opposite. She read books on how to take care of herself, she tried different "health-foods," and the ominous warnings of advertisers frightened her dreadfully. But she came of a long-lived family, good hardy stock, and Father did, too, and both of them lived to a ripe and far from languid old age.

Mother used to go to the cemetery in Woodlawn with her arms full of flowers, and lay the pretty things by some headstone, as a sign of remembrance. After a while she bought a cast-iron chair and left it out there, inside the square family plot, so that when it took her a long time to arrange her flowers she could sit down and rest. This was a convenience, but unluckily it was also a worry, because absent-minded visitors to neighbouring graves began to borrow that chair. They dragged it off across the grass to sit and grieve in, and forgot to return it. Mother then had to hunt around for it and drag it back, which made her feel cross, and thus spoiled the mood she had come out in. She didn't like this a bit.

One Sunday, when she herself was past

seventy, and when Father in spite of his blood pressure and everything else was nearly eighty, she asked him if he wouldn't like to drive out with her to Woodlawn. She hadn't any flowers to take, but she had happened to think of that chair, though she didn't say so to Father. She merely said that it was a beautiful day and that it would do him good to go out.

Father refused. Positively. He winked robustly at me and said to Mother, "I'll be going there soon enough, damn it."

Mother said that he ought to come because one of the headstones had settled and she wanted him to tell her whether he didn't think it needed attention.

Father asked whose headstone it was, and when Mother told him, he said: "I don't care how much it's settled. I don't want to be buried with any of that infernal crowd anyhow."

Mother, of course, knew how he felt about some of the family, but she said that he wouldn't mind such things when it was all over.

Father said yes he would. He became so incensed, thinking of it, that he declared he was going to buy a new plot in the cemetery, a plot all for himself. "And I'll buy one on a corner," he added triumphantly, "where I can get out!"

255

Mother looked at him, startled but admiring, and whispered to me, "I almost believe he could do it."

RICHARD USBORNE

Plum Sauce

A P G Wodehouse Companion

'Wodehouse?
He exhausts superlatives'
STEPHEN FRY

Plum Sauce
A PG Wodehouse Companion

Richard Usborne

In Plum Sauce, Richard Usborne – long regarded as the leading authority on Wodehouse – finally brings together the best of his much-loved commentary on the great man's words to form the perfect companion to his work. In witty and idiosyncratic prose that miraculously keeps pace with Wodehouse's own, Usborne brings order to the vast and tangled fictional world that Wodehouse stitched together in a writing career stretching over 70 years and nearly 100 books.

This 'dip-in' entertainment introduces us to all the great creations: Jeeves and Wooster, Psmith, Ukridge, Uncle Fred, Lord Emsworth and the world of Blandings. It offers character sketches of the rest of the Wodehouse cast from Gussie Fink Nottle to the chorus of Aunts and Drones, and witty plot summaries of all Wodehouse's books. Copiously illustrated with original dust-jacket artwork and sketches from the Strand Magazine, Plum Sauce also has fun with Wodehouse's incomparable skill with language, the bizarre rules at play in his fictional world, and gathers the choicest nuggets of Wodehouse prose on themes ranging from women to drink.

The Best of

JAMES THURBER

'Superb' WOODY ALLEN

Better to Have Loafed and Lost
The Best of James Thurber

James Thurber was the most original, influential and, lest we should forget, funniest American humorist of the modern era. Writing and drawing cartoons for the *New Yorker* magazine from it's beginnings in the 1920s, he steadily shaped his very own comic universe: a world populated by the neurotic and occasionally delusional and governed by absurd and sometimes insane logic where the trival anxieties of daily life slowly grind you down. Thurber's tales, related in bewildered deadpan, are always excruciatingly funny and quietly disturbing too.

This brand new collection reassembles his finest work for a new generation. Featuring all his famous obsessions: the battle of the sexes, his family, animals, travel and, of course, everyday insanity. His short pieces, drift between surreal fiction and eccentric memoir. Spanning his whole career, *Better to Have Loafed and Lost* includes all his classics, 'The Dream Life of Walter Mitty', 'The Catbird Seat', and half-forgotten gems that might be new even to Thurber fans.